John Odonovan

Annals of Ireland

Three fragments

John Odonovan

Annals of Ireland
Three fragments

ISBN/EAN: 9783743350175

Manufactured in Europe, USA, Canada, Australia, Japa

Cover: Foto ©ninafisch / pixelio.de

Manufactured and distributed by brebook publishing software (www.brebook.com)

John Odonovan

Annals of Ireland

ANNALS OF IRELAND.

THREE FRAGMENTS,

COPIED FROM ANCIENT SOURCES

By DUBHALTACH MAC FIRBISIGH:

AND EDITED,

WITH A TRANSLATION AND NOTES,

FROM A MANUSCRIPT PRESERVED IN THE BURGUNDIAN LIBRARY AT BRUSSELS.

BY

JOHN O'DONOVAN, LL.D., M.R.I.A.,

PROFESSOR OF CELTIC LANGUAGES, QUEEN'S COLLEGE, BELFAST;
CORRESPONDING MEMBER OF THE ROYAL ACADEMY OF SCIENCES, BERLIN.

DUBLIN:
Printed at the University Press,
FOR THE IRISH ARCHÆOLOGICAL AND CELTIC SOCIETY.
1860.

DUBLIN:
PRINTED AT THE UNIVERSITY PRESS,
BY M. H. GILL.

THE

IRISH ARCHÆOLOGICAL AND CELTIC SOCIETY.

MDCCCLX.

Patron:

HIS ROYAL HIGHNESS THE PRINCE CONSORT.

President:

His Grace the Duke of Leinster.

Vice-Presidents:

The Most Noble the Marquis of Kildare, M. R. I. A.
The Right Hon. the Earl of Dunraven, M. R. I. A.
The Right Hon. Lord Talbot de Malahide, M. R. I. A.
Very Rev. Charles W. Russell, D. D., President of Maynooth College.

Council:

Eugene Curry, Esq., M.R.I.A.
Rev. Thomas Farrelly.
Rev. Charles Graves, D.D., F.T.C.D., M.R.I.A.
Rev. James Graves, A.B.
Thomas A. Larcom, Major-General R.E., M.R.I.A.

Patrick V. Fitzpatrick, Esq.
John C. O'Callaghan, Esq.
John O'Donovan, Esq., LL.D., M.R.I.A.
Geo. Petrie, Esq., LL.D., M.R.I.A.
Rev. William Reeves, D.D., M.R.I.A.
Wm. R. Wilde, Esq., F.R.C.S.I., M.R.I.A.

Secretaries:

Rev. J. H. Todd, D.D., Pres. R.I.A. | J. T. Gilbert, Esq., M.R.I.A.

INTRODUCTORY REMARKS.

HE following Three Fragments of Annals, never before published, were copied in the year 1643 for the Rev. John Lynch, author of "Cambrensis Eversus," by Dubhaltach Mac Firbisigh, or, as he anglicized his name, "Dudley Firbisse"[a], from a vellum MS., the property of Nehemias[b] Mac Egan, of Ormond, chief Professor of the old Irish or Brehon Laws; but the MS. from which the present text has been obtained, and which is now preserved in the Burgundian Library at Brussels (7, c. n. 17), is not in Mac Firbis's hand, but in that of a scribe who copied immediately from his MS., as appears from several marginal remarks.

The name of this second transcriber nowhere appears. It is quite clear,

---

[a] *Dudley Firbisse.*—For some account of Dudley Firbisse the reader is referred to "Genealogies, Tribes, and Customs of Hy-Fiachrach."—Introduction, p. vii. to xii. Mr. O'Conor, of Belanagare, informs us, in a letter published by Dr. Ledwich in his "Antiquities of Ireland" (2nd ed., Dublin, 1804), p. 303, that Duald Mac Firbis was instructed by the Mac Egans of Ormond, who were hereditary Brehons, and professors of the old Irish laws. It would also appear that he studied for some time with the O'Davorans of Thomond. For his Translations from Irish Annals for Sir James Ware, the reader is referred to the "Miscellany of the Irish Archæological Society," vol. i. p. 198 to 263.

[b] *Nehemias* is the usual Latinized form of Gilla-na-naemh, as appears from a Gloss in Lib. T. C. D., H. 2, 13.

clear, from his marginal observations, that he was a classical scholar, and a critic of considerable acumen; and that he had carefully compared these Fragments with the "Annals of the Four Masters." He also made an Index to the whole, in which he gives the dates from the "Annals of the Four Masters," which dates Lynch has adopted in his "Cambrensis Eversus" without any attempt at correcting them, although they are sometimes two and three years before the true years.

In the present edition of these Fragments the chronology of the Annals of Ulster is generally followed, with the addition of one year. The original Fragments exhibit the Anno Domini in very few instances; and even where they do, their dates are almost invariably incorrect.

Of the age or nature of the MS. from which Mac Firbis copied these Fragments of Annals, we have no clue to form any correct opinion, as he, or the later transcriber who followed him, has evidently modernized the orthography. He tells us, in several places, that the MS. was effaced, and that he could not read some important passages in consequence of the shattered condition of the old book.

The first Fragment relates chiefly to the Northern Ui Neill, and was, probably, compiled in Ulster originally; but the other two evidently belong to Ossory, or Laeighis (now Leix), and must have been compiled in some monastery in either of these territories. This is evident from the first lengthened notice in these Fragments: namely, of Feradhach, son of Duach, King of Ossory, whose death is entered in the "Annals of the Four Masters," at the year 582. It is also very evident, from the detailed accounts given of the renowned deeds of Cearbhall, King of Ossory, and of Cenneidigh, son of Gaeithin, King of Laeighis. The Comharba, or successor, of Molua of Cluainferta-Molua, is also referred to as having composed poems in praise of this Cearbhall.

It

It is a very curious fact, that while these Fragments dwell with particular emphasis upon the achievements of the princes of the territories of Ossory and Leix, and of those of their relatives, the Ui-Neill, not a single reference is made to the Dal gCais, who soon afterwards eclipsed, not only the princes of those territories, but the more powerful and royal Ui Neill themselves; and, what is still more remarkable, in the account of the Battle of Bealach Mughna, in which Cormac Mac Cullinan was killed, A. D. 908, there is not one word said about the claim of the Dal gCais to the kingdom of Munster, although the work called "Cath Bealaigh Mughna," quoted by Keating, dwells upon it with remarkable emphasis. The inference to be drawn from this fact is, either that the Dal gCais had not risen to any remarkable point of power or celebrity before 908, or that the writers of these Annals were hostile to them.

The more lengthened stories and details of battles, in these Fragments, are curious specimens of Irish composition. Some of them have evidently been abstracted from long bardic descriptions of battles, and are interspersed with the wonderful and wild, the supernatural and incredible.

In the translation of the present Fragments nothing has been changed or modified; but the originals are given with scrupulous fidelity, as specimens of the manner in which our ancestors intermingled the wildest fiction with historical facts. The reader will remark this in the legend of Donnbo, in the description of the Battle of Almhain, as well as in the account of the shout of the King's Jester at the same battle, which continued to be heard in the sky for an incredible period of time.

The account of the battles between the Aunites, or Danes, and Norwegians, in Carlingford Lough, and elsewhere in Ulster, has probably been taken from an Ulster work on the Wars of the Danes and Norwegians in Ireland, now unfortunately lost or unknown. The account of these wars, now in progress of printing by Dr. Todd, is a Munster and Dalcassian production, and dwells almost exclusively upon the achievements of the men of Munster, especially upon the renowned deeds of the Dalcassian race of Thomond, who are panegyrized in glowing bardic eloquence. The present Fragments, however, make no mention whatever of any opposition given by the Dal gCais, or other Munster tribes, to the Danes, from which it is sufficiently obvious that they were extracted from local Annals preserved by the Ui Neill, and other tribes who were adverse to the Munstermen.

The account of the Gall-Gaels of Ireland who had joined the Danes, and lapsed into Paganism, is very important, as our previous ideas about them were very confused. O'Flaherty thought that these Gall-Gadelians were confined to the western islands of Scotland ("Ogygia," Part iii., c. 75); but it is clear from these Annals that they were also in Leinster and various parts of Ireland.

The account of the attack on Chester, in the third Fragment, was, probably, taken from some English or Welsh annalist, but no narrative exactly like it has been found in Geoffrey of Monmouth, or any English chronicler.

The account of the battle between the Norwegians and Moors in Mauritania, and of the Blue-men brought by the former into Ireland, has not been found in any other writer.

As already observed, the spelling has been modernized by the later scribes, but very old words and phrases, with some idioms now obsolete, will be observed throughout; such as ꝓpuaiplɼ, acacomnaic, pop mapb, &c. The spelling of the MS. has been carefully preserved throughout, though it is evidently not as old as the language in which these Fragments are written.

J. O'D.

FRAGMENTA ANNALIUM HIBERNIÆ.

FRAGMENTA ANNALIUM HIBERNIÆ.

RAGMENTA tria Annalium Hiberniæ extractum [*sic*] ex codice membranco Nehemiæ mac Ægan senis, Hiberniæ Juris peritissimi, in Ormonia, per Ferbissium ad usum R. D. Joannis Lynch.

Ab anno Christi circiter 571 ad annum plus minus 910.

[FRAGMENTUM I.]

[A. D. 573.] Kl. Cat Ƿeiṁin in quo uictuṗ eṗt Colman beg mac Diaṗmada et iṗṗe euaṗit. bṗenann bioṗoṗ quieuit in Chṗiṗto, etxxx. anno aetatiṗ puae, uel ccc°.

K. K. K. K. K. K. K. Leiġin na ṗect Kallanda ṗin ṗeaċam.

[581.] Kal. Cat Manann in quo Aodan mac Gabṗain uictoṗ eṗat.

[582.] Kal. Maṗbaò Ƿeaṗaòaiġ Ƿinn, mic Duaċ, ṗi Oṗṗaiġe. Aṗ é ṗo imuṗṗo an tṗeaṗ ṗí ṗe ṗé Colaim cille do ċuaid do ċum niṁe,

---

ᵃ *Feimhin*,—otherwise Magh Feimhim, a large plain in the barony of Iffa and Offa, in the county of Tipperary. The dates printed within brackets are added by the Editor. F. M. signify Four Masters.

ᵇ *Brenann of Biror*.—i. e. St. Brendan of Birr, in the King's County, of whom, see Four Masters, A. D. 571, p. 206; and Adamnan's "Vita Columbæ," lib. iii. c. 2; Colgan's Acta SS., p. 193; also Lanigan's

FRAGMENTS OF ANNALS OF IRELAND.

THREE fragments of Annals of Ireland, extracted from a vellum manuscript [the property] of Gilla-na-naemh Mac Egan, senior, a man most learned in the Irish laws, in Ormond, by Mac Firbis, for the use of the Rev. Mr. John Lynch.

From about the year of Christ 571 to about the year 910.

[FRAGMENT I.]

[A. D. 573.] Kal. The battle of Feimhin[a], in which Colman Beg, son of Diarmaid [chief of the southern Ui-Neill] was defeated, but he himself escaped. Brenann of Biror[b] quievit in Christo, in the 180th year of his age, vel ccc.

K. K. K. K. K. K. K. I leave these seven years vacant.

[581.] Kal. The battle of Mannan[c], in which Aodhan MacGabrain [King of Scotland] was victorious.

[582, F. M.] The killing of Feradhach Finn[d], son of Duach, King of Osraighe. He was the third king, who, in the time of Colum Cille, went

"Ecclesiastical History of Ireland," vol. ii. p. 38, *sq*.

[c] *Manann*.—i. e. the Isle of Man. See

Annals of Tighernach, and of Ulster, A. D. 581.

[d] *Feradhach*, King of Osraighe, or Os-

nime, ⁊ ap é po an páċ aṁail po innip Colam Cille o'Aoḋ mac
Ainmipeċ.

Cpeblaıo mór oo ġabáil an Peapaḋaıġ. Clann Conla oo ċoıȝeaċc oo ġabaıl caıȝe paıp: uaıp ḋo Chopca Laoıȝoe o'Peapaoaċ mac Ouaċ, uaıp peaċc píȝ oo ȝaḃpao Oppaıȝe oo Copco
Laoıȝoe, ⁊ peaċc pıȝ oo Oppaıȝıḃ po ȝap pıȝe Chopća
Laoıȝoe.

Coccaḋ ıapaṁ ooponṁ pe Cloıno Conla, ⁊ ap ann po baoıpıum
'na ċulȝ, aȝup a peoıo uıle aıȝe ann; aṁaıl ba bép oo na pıȝaıḃ
cuılȝ umpa o'ıoḃap .ı. poıall ap ċapup a ccpıann ⁊ a ccpannoca
aıpȝıo, ⁊ a ccopáın, ⁊ a n-epȝpaḋa, oo caḃaıpc opoȝnam 'pan
oíḋċe; a mbpıanouıḃ, ⁊ a ppıċcealla, ⁊ a ccaṁáın cpéouma pa
poȝnum an laoı.

Rob ıomḋa ınuppo peoıo aȝ Pspaoaċ, papa mór a nȝpaḋ laıp, ⁊
oona ap olc ppıċ ıao, óıp ní ċualapom a bſȝ nó a mór óıp no aıpȝıo,
oȝ cpén no aȝ cpuaȝ a n-Oppaıȝıḃ, na hıpȝabċa aıȝıpıoṁ oo cappaınȝ a ınmup pın uaḋ oo ċuṁoaċ na péo paın. Canȝaccap cpa
a meıc o' ıonnpoıcċıo Pspaoaıȝ conıȝe an colcc oo bpeıċ na péo
leó. Cpéo ap áıl ouıḃ, a ṁaca, ol Pspaoach? Na peoıo oo
bpeıċ lınn, ol na mıc. Ní bspéaoı, ap Pspaoaċ, uaıp olc ppıċ ıao.
Sochaıḋe pa cpaıoıupa ȝa ccınól; aȝup ceaoaıȝım-pı mo ċpáo
péın oom naıṁoıḃ umpu. Ro ımcıȝpıoc a ṁıc uaḋ, aȝup· po ȝappoın
aȝ aıċpıȝe oíćpa; cancucap ıapam clann Conla, aȝup po ṁapbpao

---

sory. Four Masters, A. D. 582, and Note.

e *Aedh, son of Ainmire.*—He was monarch of Ireland from A. D. 628 to 642.

f *The race of Connla.*—i. e. of Connla, son of Breasal Breac, ancestor of all the chiefs of Osraighe, except the seven here mentioned.

g *Corca-Laighdhe.*—This was the name of the inhabitants of the S. W. portion of the present county of Cork. O'Driscoll was chief of this race and territory after the establishment of surnames in Ireland. It was co-extensive with the present diocese of Ross. This interchange of the Kings of

went to heaven; and this was the reason, as Colum Cille had told to Aedh, son of Ainmire^e.

Feradhach was seized with great sickness; [and] the race of Connla^f came to take a house upon him, because Feradhach, son of Duach, was of the Corca-Laighdhe^g, for seven kings of the Corca-Laighdhe assumed the kingship of Ossory, and seven kings of the Osraighi took the kingship of Corca-Laighdhe.

He afterwards waged war with the race of Connla; and he was in his couch, having all his valuables^h there, as was the custom of kings to have couches of yew around them, in which they had a collection of their bars and ingots of silver, and their cups and vesselsⁱ, to give them for service by night, and their chess-men and chess-boards, and their hurlets of bronze for day service.

Many were the valuables in the possession of Feradhach, and great was his love of them; but in an evil way did he acquire them, for he had not heard of rich or poor in Osraighe, having little or much of gold or silver, that he did not seize, to take such property from him to ornament these valuables. His sons came to Feradhach, to his bed, to carry away the valuables with them. "What is your desire, O my sons?" said Feradhach. "To carry away the valuables with us," replied the sons. "Ye shall not carry them away," said Feradhach, "for they were ill-gotten. I have oppressed many in procuring them, and I consent to be oppressed myself by my enemies on account

Corca Laighdhe and Osraighe is not noticed in the "Tribes and Territories of the Corca Laighdhe," printed for the Celtic Society, "Miscell.," p. 1, *sq*.

^h *Valuables*, ⁊c. —Property of any kind; *gaza*, but particularly jewels. See the Will of Cathair Mor, in "Leabhar na gCeart," and O'Flaherty's "Ogygia," Part iii., c. 59.

ⁱ *Vessels*, epepaða.—In the Life of St. Darerca the *escra* is described as a silver drinking vessel—"Quoddam argenteum vasculum unde potentibus personis haurire solent quod Hybernica lingua vocatur escra."—*Brussels MS*.

ꞅαꞃ Ƒeαꞃαꞃαch, ⁊ ꞃuꞅꞅꞃαꝺ nα ꞃeoꝺα ⁊ ꝺo ćuαıꝺ Ƒeαꞃαꝺαć ꝺo cum nıṁe.

Ꝁαl. ⁊ α ꞃí ꞃo αn ꞅeαṫꞃαṁαꝺ Ꝁαl. ꞃꞃ ꝺon 32 Ꝁαl. ꞇeꞃꞇα αᵹ αn ꝺeeꞃꞇ.

Ⱥuıeꞃ Coloım Cılle lꞃꞃuı αnno αeꞇαꞇıꞅ ꞃuαe, unꝺe Ƒeꝺelm ceeınıꞇ :

   Uċ ıαꞃ ꞃíꞃ αn ꞇhe ᵹαḃṙα ıꞃ ın lín
   he ḃꞃeec ḃαoı ı mḃóınn.

32 Ꝁαl. ꞃeαċom.

Ꝁαl. Ⱥ° Ⱦm. ꝺeꞃ. Ƒıonꞇαn uα Ꞓαċαċ Ⱥb Cluαnα eıꝺneċ, eꞅın moıαċ nα hꞒoꞃꞃα quıeuıꞇ ın quınꞇα ꝼeꞃıα, unꝺe Colınαn mαc Ƒeαꞃᵹuꞃα ceeınıꞇ :

   Ⱦıα Ⱦαꞃꝺαoın ꞃuꞅꞅαꝺ Ƒıonꞇαn,
   Iꞅ ꞃo ᵹıneꝺ αꞃ ꞇαlmαın,
   Ⱥꞃ ꝺıα Ⱦαꞃꝺαoın αꞇ ḃαċ
   Ⱥꞃ mo ꞃ́ıαꞃꞇαıḃ coımᵹelα.

Ꝁαl. Inıcıum ꞃeᵹımınıꞅ Ⱥoꝺα Uαıꞃıoꝺnαıᵹ.

Ꝁαl. Ⱥoꝺ Uαıꞃıoꝺnαċ ıncıꞃıꞇ ꞃeᵹnαꞃe uıı. αnn̄. .ı. Ⱥoꝺ mαc Ⱦoṁnαıll, mıc Ⱳuıꞃċeαꞃꞇαıᵹ, mıc Ⱳuıꞃċꝺαıᵹ, mıc Ꞓoᵹαın.

Ƒċꞇ nαon ꝺα ꞇꞇαımc ꞅé nα mıᵹꝺαııinα ꝺαꞃ lαꞃ Oṫnα Ⱳuꞃα, ꞃα ınꝺαıl α láṁα αꞃ αn αḃoınn αꞇá ꝺαꞃ láꞃ αn ḃαıle. Oċαm αınıı

ʲ *Valuables.*—Which were really their own; and therefore Feradhach, having voluntarily abandoned them, went to heaven.

ᵏ *The 24th.*—This correction of the observation, "I omit 32 years," is itself evidently an error; for, if the last entry relating to Feradhach, son of Duach, belongs to the year 582, the year 610 is the twenty-eighth year after it.

ˡ *Boyne.*—A marginal note opposite these lines says: "Hæc erant in margine," i. e. in the margin of the original MS. The verses here quoted are not found elsewhere.

ᵐ *Fintann Ua Enchach.*—Who this Finntan was, is not yet cleared up. See Archdall's Monast. Hib., p. 591, and Colgan's

account of them." His sons departed from him, and he took to earnest penance. The race of Connla afterwards came and slew Feradhach, and carried away the valuables^j, and Feradhach went to heaven.

[594.] Kal. And this is the 24th^k [recte 28th] Kal. of the 32 Kals. omitted at the *Deest*.

The repose [*quies*, i. e. death] of Colum Cille, in the 76th year of his age. Unde Fedelm cecinit :

> Alas! in truth he who was caught in the net ;
> The speckled salmon who was in the Boyne^l.

I omit 32 years.

Kal. A. D. 610, Fintan Ua Eachach^m, Abbot of Cluain-eidhnech, head of the monks of Europe, died on Thursday; hence Colman, son of Fergus, sung :

> On Thursday Fintan was born,
> And was conceived upon the earth.
> And on Thursday he died
> Upon my white sheets.

[605.] Kal. The beginning of the reign of Aedh Uairidhnach^n.

Kal. Aedh Uairidhnach began to reign [and reigned] 8 years; i. e. Aedh, son of Domhnall, son of Muirchertach, son of Muredach, son of Eoghan.

On one occasion he came, when a royal prince, to Othain-Mura^o; he washed his hands in the river which is in the middle of the town.

Othain

Acta SS., pp. 350, 355. The first of January, 610, was Thursday. This date is not found in any other Annals.

^n *Aedh Uairidhnach.*—Monarch of Ireland from the year 605 till 612.

^o *Othain-Mura.*—Othain, or Fothain

Mupa (Fothain of S. Mura), now Fahan, near Loughswilly, barony of Inishowen, county of Donegal. The river is now a very small stream. This singular story about Aedh Uairidhnach is not found elsewhere, so far as the Editor knows.

ainm na habann ap uaite ainmigtip an baile .i. Otain. Ra gap
don uipce da cup má aigid, pa gap pfp da muintip fpip, A pí, ap
pé, na cuip an uipge pin po tagaid. Cédon? ap an pí. Ap náp
lfm a pád, ap pé. Cá náipe ata duit ap an fipinde do pád? ap an
pig. Ap ead po, ap pé, ap paip an uipge pin ata pialtfc na
clépec. An ann, ap an pí, téid an clépec péin ap imtelgud? Ap
ann go veimin, ap an tócclac. Ni namá, ap an pí, cuippead pom
aigid, act cuippead im bél ⁊ ibad, ag ol tpí mbolgoma de, uaip
ap pacapbaicc lfm ant uipce i ttéid a imtelgun.

Ra himmpiod pain do Múpa, ⁊ po altaig buide do Dhia ap
ipip map pin do beit ag Aod, ⁊ po gaipmed cuicce iapdain Aod
Allain, ⁊ Aod Uaipiodnac ainm oile do, ⁊ a pfd po pad Mupa
pip: A mic iomtain, ap pé, log na haipmiden pin tugaip do'n
Eglaip, geallaim-pi duit i ffiadnaipe Dé pige n-'Eipenn do gabail
go gaipid, agup go mbépa buaid ⁊ copgup dod námoib, ⁊ nid
bépa bap anabaid, ⁊ caitpe copp an coimofd ap mo láim-pi, ⁊
guidpead-pa an coimdid lat, go mba cpíne bépup tu don
bioc.

Níop bud cian tpa iapdain co po gap Aod Allan pige
n'Eipenn, ⁊ do pad pfpanna putaca do Mupa Otna.

Rucc iapam Aod Allan copgaip iomda do Laignib, ⁊ da
naimdib ap ceana.

Ro buí tpa oct mbliadna i pige n-'Eiprnn, ⁊ pa gap galap
baip

ᵖ *Jakes*, Pialtcc.—i. e. veil-house, i. e. latrina, the Temple of Clausina.

ᵠ *Another name*.—This is a mistake; for Aedh Allan, monarch of Ireland, flourished from A.D. 734 to 743, whereas Aedh Uairidhnach came to the throne in the year 605, and died in 612. This mistake is continued throughout; and wherever, in this legend, our author has Aedh Allan, we must read Aedh Uairidhnach. For all that is known of the history of St. Mura Othna [or Mura of Fothain—*Othna* (for *Fothna*) is the *gen.* of Fothain], see Dr. Todd's Irish Nennius; Appendix, "Duan Eirennach." In the

Othain is the name of the river; and it is from it the town is named Othain. He took of the water to put it on his face, but one of his people checked him: "O King," said he, "do not put that water on thy face." "Why so?" said the King. "I am ashamed to tell it," replied he. "What shame is it for thee to tell the truth?" said the King. "This is it," said he: "It is upon this water the *jakes* of the clergy is situated." "Is it into it," said the King, "the [chief] cleric himself goes to stool?" "It is verily," replied the young man. "Not only then," said the King, "will I put it [the water] upon my face, but I will put it into my mouth, and I will drink it" (drinking three sups of it), "for to me the water into which his fæces drop is a communion."

This was told to Mura, and he returned thanks to God for Aedh's having a faith like this; and he afterwards called unto him Aedh Allan; and Aedh Uairidhnach was another name[q] for him. And Mura said to him: "Beloved son," said he, "I promise to thee, in the presence of God, the reward of that veneration which thou hast shown to the church: [viz.] that thou shalt obtain the sovereignty of Erin soon, and that thou shalt gain victory, and triumph over thy enemies; and thou shalt not be taken off by a sudden death, but thou shalt take the body of the Lord from my hand; and I will pray to the Lord that thou mayest depart old from this world."

It was not long after this until Aedh Allan assumed the kingdom of Erin; and he granted fertile lands to Mura-Othna.

Aedh Allan afterwards gained many victories over the Leinstermen, and his enemies in general.

He was eight years in the sovereignty of Erin, and then his death sickness

margin of the MS. is this note: "*Vide infra*, p. 15, Aoḋ Allan et Aoḋ Uaıṗıoḋ- naċ sunt *diversi*:" i. e. Aodh Allan and Aodh Uairidhnach are different persons.

baip anopm Aoḋ Allan, ⁊ pa ċuap uaḋ ap cſon Múpa. Táinig
Múpa, ⁊ po ṗáiḋ an pí pip: A cléipiġ, ap ré, pap meallaip, uaip
do paopum paill ap áp n-aiṫpiġe, uaip do paoileamap cpéḋ
ḃpéiṫipi beiṫ go mba cpín mé im ḃṫaiḋ : ⁊ an dap linn ata báp
i ppacup daṁ. Ap píp, ap an cléipeaċ, atá báp i ppoġup daic,
⁊ pa timḋiḃeaḋ do paoġal ⁊ tuccaip peipce an ċoiṁḋſḋ, ⁊ innip
ġa ní do piġnip in pa ċpáiḋip an coimḋiḋ. Inḋippḋ, ap an pí,
buḋ ḋóiġ lſm do cpáḋ an coiṁḋſḋ. Ra puabpap, ap ré, pip
'Eipenn do cinol do ċum an cpléiḃepi ċaip .i. Cappluoig da ċom-
apḋúceaḋ ṫuap, ⁊ tſaċ ḋíṁop do ḋſnaiṁ ann, ⁊ apſo pob ail go
ppaiciṫea cene an ciġi pin gaċ cpáṫnóna i mḃpſṫnaiḃ, ⁊ i n-Aipiup
Ġaoiḋiol, ⁊ pa peadap po ba diomap mop pain.
Rob olc pin, ap an cléipeaċ, ⁊ ní hſo pin po timiḋiḃſo do paoġal.
Ra puaiḃpiup dono, ap an pí, opoiċſo do ḋſnaṁ i cCluain
Ipáipo, ⁊ a ḋſnaiṁ go mopbalta piom co po maipſo m'ainṁpi paip
go bpáṫ.
Ra innip neiṫi imda aṁlaiḋ pin.
Ní ní ḋiḃ pin, ap an cleipeaċ, cimdiḃiup do paoġal.
Atá dono agum ní oile, ap an pí .i. an ṁipgaip puil agom do
Laiġniḃ ; uaip apeaḋ pob áil daṁ a ppip uile do timapgain do ċum
cata, ⁊ a mapḃaḋ uile ann, a mna ⁊ a moġaḋ do taḃaipc pin
poġnaṁ do Uiḃ Néill. Sinn tuaipceapt n-'Eipſon do taḃaipt po
Miḋe, ⁊ pip Miḋe pop Laiġniḃ. Uċ, uċ, tpa, ap an cléipeaċ
apſo

<small>
^e *Carrlaegh*.—Carrleagh, a mountain near Ailech, in the barony of Inishowen, county of Donegal.

^f *Airiur Gaeidhel.*—i. e. *regio Gadelio-rum*, now Argyle, in Scotland.

^g *That was bad.*—Did the Irish erect palaces of great altitude, or great stone bridges, in the year 612, when King Aedh Uairidhnach died? It is very much to be suspected that this romantic story was written after the introduction of Norman towers and castles into Ireland.

^h *Cluain-Iraird.*—Now Clonard, in the county of Meath.
</small>

sickness seized on Aodh Allan, and he sent for Mura. Mura came, and the King said to him: "O cleric," said he, "thou hast deceived us, for we have neglected our penance, because we thought that through thy word it would come to pass that we should be aged in life, and now, methinks, death is near me." "It is true," said the cleric, "death is near thee! and thy life has been cut short, and thou hast incurred the anger of the Lord; and tell what thou hast done by which thou hast offended the Lord." "I will declare," replied the King, "what I think has offended the Lord: I desired," said he, "to collect the men of Erin to this mountain to the east; i. e. Carrlaegh^r, to raise it, and to erect a very great house upon it; and my wish was, that the fire of that house, every evening, might be seen in Britain, and in Airiur-Gaeidhel^s; and I know that that was a great pride."

"That was bad", replied the cleric; "but that is not what has cut short thy life."

"I also desired," said the King, "to build a bridge at Cluain-Iraird^u, and to build miraculously, that my name might live upon it for ever."

He also told many things of a similar nature.

"It is not any thing of these," said the cleric, "that shortened thy life."

"I have another thing to tell," said the King: "the hatred which I have for the Leinstermen; for my wish would be, to collect all their men to battle, and to kill them all therein, and to bring their women and their slaves to serve the Ui-Neill^w; to bring our race in the north of Erin into Meath, and to settle the men of Meath in Leinster."

"Alas!

---

^w *The Ui-Neill.*—i. e. nepotes Neill, i. e. the race of Niall of the Nine Hostages, of whom Aedh Uairidhnach was at this time head and King. St. Mura was the patron of the Cinel-Eoghain, or Race of Owen, who formed a large section of this family.

αρſờ ρın ρο τımὀıbıὀ ὐο ϝαοξαlρο, uαıρ αn cıneαὐ ρın αρ mıορ-
cαıρ lατρα .ı. Lαıξın, αταατ nαοım οξ ſρnαıξτε leο ϝϝıαὀnαıρı αn
ċοımὀſὀ, ⁊ αρ mοο ατα bρıξıὐ, ⁊ αρ τρερε ὐά n-ıρnαıξτε αnὀάρ
ὐοm ıρnαıξέı ρı. Αέτ έſnα αρ τρόcαρ cαοnuρραċ αn cοımὀıu, ⁊
ὐſnα hıοὀραıρτ ρέın ὐο ὐαρ έſn hαınξıὀεαέτα ρın ρο bαοı ıo
έροıὀε ὐο Lοıξınb ξο ραὐαıρ α ϝϝlαıέıuρ αρ buαıne ınαρ αn ϝlαıέıuρ
αımρıορὀα.

Rα hοnξαὀ αn ραın αn ρıı, ⁊ ρο cαıέ cορρ αnn cοımὀſὀ, ⁊ ϝuαıρ
bάρ ρο cſnuαıρ, ⁊ ὐο ċuαıὀ ὐο ċum neıme.

Sſέτ Ƙαl ρſchοm.

Inıτıum ρεξımınıρ Mαοılέοbα.

Ƙαl. Mαοlcοbα mαc Αοὐα, mıc Αınmıρεέ ρεξnαuıτ τρıbuρ
αnnıρ. Stellα ıρα hορα τερτıα ὐıeı.

Ƙαl.

Ƙαl. Ƶuın Mαοılcοbα mıc Αοὐα lα Suıbne Menn mıc Fıαchnα.
(ſuıερ Oıαρmαὐα τερτıı αbbατıρ Cluαnα Iραıρὐ. Inıτıum ρεξımınıρ Suıbne Mınn.

Ƙαl. Suıbne mſn ρο ξαρ ρίξε n-'Eıρenn ı nὐεαξαıὀ Mαοılcοbα
ρıu. blıαὐnα ξο ττορchαıρ lα Conξαl cαέέ mαc Scαnlαın.

Lαα αen ὐ'Fıαcnα ὐ'αταıρı αn Suıbne ρın αξ ὐul ὐρıuρα
αρατάıρı, uαıρ nίορ bο ρί ρıοın ıτıρ, ὐο ραὐ ὐα mſnmαın αmαıl ρο
ξαὐ cαέ α nὐεαξαıὀ α έέlε ρıξε nα h-'Eıρenn. Tαımcc mıαὀ
meαnmαn ⁊ mὐıοccbαlα mόρα ραε, ⁊ ραınτ ρıξε nα h-'Eıρenn ὐο
ξαbάıl ὐό, ⁊ τάmıξ ρειmhε ὐα έαıξ, ⁊ ρα ınnıρ ὐά mnαί. ⁊ α ρſὀ ρο
ραıὀ α bſn ıuρ: uαıρ nαέ ρα ϝuαbρuıρ ξuρ αıοıu ρın, αρ ρί, nί
                                                        ϝαıcıın

[1] *Immolate.*—See Dr. Reeves's note on the signification of this word.—Adamnan, p. 435.

[2] *Seven years.*—In the margin: "Desunt hic 7 Kal."

[3] *Maelcobha.*—He began his reign in the year 612; "Ogygia," p. iii., c. 98, and was slain in 615.

[4] *A star.*—The appearance of this star is not mentioned in any other Annals.

"Alas! alas!" said the cleric, "this is what has shortened thy life; for this people, which is hateful to thee, i. e. the Leinstermen, have saints to pray for them before the Lord, and Brigit is greater than I, and her prayers are more powerful than my prayers. But, however, the Lord is merciful and forgiving, and do thou immolate[x] thyself to him for the cruelty which was in thy heart towards the Leinstermen, that thou mayest be in a kingdom more lasting than thy temporal kingdom.

The King was then anointed, and he took the body of the Lord, and, dying immediately, went to heaven.

I omit seven years[y].

[612.] The beginning of Maelcobha's[z] reign.

Kal. Maelcobha, son of Aedh, son of Ainmire, reigned three years. A star[a] was seen the third hour of the day.

Kal.

[615.] Kal. The killing of Maelcobha, son of Aedh, by Suibhne Menn, son of Fiachna. The repose of Diarmaid[b], third Abbot of Cluain-Iraird. The beginning of the reign of Suibhne Menn.

Kal. Suibhne Menn assumed the sovereignty of Erin after Maelcobha, for thirteen years, until he was slain[c] by Congal Caech, son of Scanlan.

One day, as Fiachna[d], the father of this Suibhne, was going to visit his ploughing—for he was not at all a king—he called to mind how persons succeeded to each other in the sovereignty of Erin; he was seized with great pride of mind and ambition, and a covetousness of

[b] *Diarmaid.*—The death of this third Abbot of Clonard is not recorded in the published Annals, nor noticed by Archdall.
[c] *Was slain.*—In the year 628.
[d] *Fiachna.*—This story of Fiachna, the father of the Irish monarch, Suibhne Menn, is not given by any of the other Annalists, nor even by Keating, who was very fond of giving stories of the same kind. It is clearly not very old.

faicim a cuilbċe ꞅe ꝼꞅi ċaoꞃa aguꞅ oo ꞅṅcaccaʙ i ꝼꝼeaċꞅꞃa coꞃnaṁ ꞃiġe, uaiꞃ ní ——— ʙí i coꞃc, aꞃ ꞅeiꞃioṁ, na caiꞃmiꞃg imum; aċc cuċċuꞃ liꞅo aguꞅ ʙiaʙ iꞅciġ, aꞃ ꞅé, aguꞅ cinolcuꞃ maiċe inaċ cuccainn, ⁊ caʙaiꞃ lóꞃ ʙóiʙ; aguꞅ gaiꞃmiʙ a ṁnaoi ċuicce anoꞃain ⁊ compaiciʙ ꝼꞃia, aguꞅ gaċ iṁꞃaʙhaʙ ꞃa ʙui ꞃeiṁe na mꞅnmain ꞃa ċṁꞃ ꞃa coimꞃeꞃc uaʙ, ⁊ aꞃ ac an ṁnaoi ꞃa ʙaoi an ciṁꞃaʙhaʙ ꞃa ʙaoi aiciꞃiuṁ iaꞃ ꞅin, ⁊ aꞃ anʙ ꞅin ꞃa coimꞃꞃeʙ an Suiʙne Mꞅnoꞃa a ṁʙꞃoinn a ṁáċaꞃ. In can cꞃa ꞃa eiꞃigꞅiṁ ó ṁnaoi, aʙ ʙꞅic an ʙꞅi: an ʙcinolꞃaiʙeaꞃ caċ iꞅceaċ aꞃ ꞃí? Acc, aꞃꞃ Fiachna, Ní oingiuṁ aꞃ ꝼꞃoċuiʙeʙ ꝼéin .i. ꞃiġe ꝼꞅꞅca ʙo ċoꞃnaṁ. Cuigċeaꞃ aꞃꞃin iaꞃam conio ʙa aigniuʙ móꞃ ꞃeṁ-ċeċcaċ na ʙcuiꞃcigċio ʙo ʙeꞃaʙ na clanna aigenca móꞃa.

Lá ʙono ʙon cSuiʙne ꞃi na gilla óg na ċaicċ ⁊ a ʙꞅi, ꞃa ꞃaiʙ ꞃa ṁnaoi; aꞃ iongnaʙ liom, aꞃ ꞅé, a laigꞅo ꞃo gaꞃ ó Cenel Eogain cigꞅꞃinuꞃ ꝼoꞃ caċ moꞃꞃa: aꞃeʙ ꞃa ꞃáiʙ an ʙꞅi cꞃe cenel ꝼoċuiʙeʙ, ciʙ ʙuiʙꞃi, aꞃ ꞅí, gan cꞃuaꞅ ʙo ʙꞅnaṁ, ⁊ ʙul ꞃompa ʙo ċoccaʙ ꝼꞃia caċ, ⁊ coꞃguꞃ ʙo ʙꞃeic go minic. Aꞃ aṁlaiʙ ꞅin ʙiaꞅ, aꞃ éiꞃioṁ.

Caimigꞃim iaꞃ ꞅin amaċ aguꞅ ꞅé aꞃṁċa ꞅa maiʙin aꞃ na ʙáꞃaċ, ⁊ ʙo ꞃála occlaoċ ʙo luċc . . . . ⁊ eiꞃiʙe aꞃṁċa, ⁊ ʙo ꞃoine coṁꞃac ꝼꞅiꞅ go ꞃo giall an cóglaċ ʙo ꞃinʙ gae ʙó, ⁊ ꞃo giall ꞅluag moꞃ ʙo aṁlaiʙ, ⁊ ꞃo gaʙ ꞃiġe n-'Eiꞃenn.

Kal. Moꞃꞃ Suiʙne Minn.

[715.]

ᵉ *The race of Eoghan.*—i. e. the descendants of Eoghan, son of Niall of the Nine Hostages (ancestor of the O'Neills and other families of Ulster), father of Muiredhach, the great-grandfather of Suibhne Menn. See next note.

ᶠ *The death of Suibhne Menn.*—He was son of Fiachna, who was the son of Feradhach, son of Muirchertach, son of Muiredhach, son of Eoghan, son of Niall of the Nine Hostages, and was monarch of Ireland for thirteen years. He was slain by Congal Claen, King of Ulidia, according to the Four Masters, in 623, but, according to the Annals of Ulster, in 627; the true year was 628. See O'Flaherty's "Ogygia," Part

of assuming the sovereignty of Erin; and he came on to his house and told his wife so; and his wife said to him: "As thou hast not desired this till this day," said she, "I do not see its meetness in a man of thy age and antiquity now to contend for a kingdom, for not ———" "Hold thy peace," said he; "do not hinder me; but let ale and food be brought into the house, and let noble chieftains be invited to us, and let them have abundance." And he then called his wife to him, and cohabited with her, and all the aspirations which he had had previously in his mind he expelled from him by coition, after which the woman possessed the imaginations which he had had previously; and it was then this Suiblme Menn was conceived in his mother's womb. When he arose from the woman, the woman said: "Shall all be collected to the house," said she. "No," replied Fiachna, "we shall not mock ourselves by contesting for a kingdom." From this it is to be understood that it is from the previous aspiring notions of the parents that ambitious children are begotten.

One day, when this Suibhne was a young man, at his house with his wife: "It is a matter of wonder to me," said he, "how few of the race of Eoghan[c] have, up to this time, taken chieftainship over all." And the woman said, in a kind of derision, "Why dost not thou," said she, "exercise hardihood, and go in their van to fight with all, and to gain frequent triumphs?" "It is so it shall be," said he.

He afterwards came forth armed on the following day, and he met a young hero of the people of . . . . who was armed, and he fought with him, and the young hero submitted to him at the point of a spear, and a great host submitted to him likewise, and he assumed the sovereignty of Erin.

[628.] Kal. The death of Suibhne Menn[f].

[715.]

iii., c. 93. There is a chasm here of nearly a whole century—from 628 to 714; but the matter is nearly supplied by the second Fragment, to be presently given.

[715.] Fogartac hua Cernaig do miḋiri na riġe, unde dicttum:
Serra Fozurtac an flait
Ain ḟoa or bit bír
An tan ar mbep ní bí ní
lap rin ar pi pia cinn mír.

[716.] Kal. Cumurce aonaiġ Taillten la Fozurtac i toreair inac Maoilruḃa 7 mac Duinnrléiḃe.

[717.] Kal. Anartariur Auzurtur pellitur. Fror meala pluit rurep forram Laginorum: pluit etiam fror airgid i n-Oeain móir, fror cruitneacta i n-Oeain mbicc. Tunc natur ert Niall Conoail, mac Feargail, unde Niall Frorac uocatur ert.

Coronuceaḋ Pfoair Arrtol do ġaḃáil do muintir Iac forro; uair coronuceaḋ Simóin Oruaḋ ro ḃaoi forro co niece rin, amail areḋ ro ḃaoi ror Colom cille féin.

[718.] Kal. Theodoriur imperat anno uno.
[719.] Kal. Leo imperat annir ix.
[720.] Kal. Inorḃ Maiġe breaġ la Catal mac Fionhġuine, rí Muṁan, 7 Murchaḋ mac mbrain ri Laiġen. Inrḃ Laiġen la Feargal mac Maoilúin. In araiḃ lerraiḃ airirfn roġaḃain comaḋ irin trfr bliaḋain reṁaino, .i. an deaċmhaḋ bliaḋain flaitiura

---

g *Fogartach Ua Cernaigh.*—See Four Masters, A. D. 712, 714, 719. The Annals of Ulster give the dates thus: 713. " Fogartach hua Cernaigh, de regno expulsus est, in Britanniam ivit." 715. Fogartach nepos Cernaigh, iterum regnat." He became undisputed monarch of Ireland in 719 [*O'Flah.*, 722], but was slain by Cinaeth, his successor, in 724.

h *Tailltin*, now Teltown, on the River Blackwater, in Meath, midway between Navan and Kells. See Four Masters, 715, and Ulster, 716.

i *Anastasius.*—i. e. Anastasius II., resigned in January, 716.

j *Othain-mor.*—Now Fahan, near Lough Swilly, in the barony of Inishowen. Othain-Beg is a subdivision of Othainmor. See p. 11, n.°, *supra*. These three showers are noticed by the Four Masters

[715.] Fogartach Ua Cernaigh[g], again in the sovereignty, unde dictum est :

Fogartach the chieftain prevails.
What is noble is above the world.
When he says there is nothing,
After that he is king before a month.

[716.] Kal. The confusion of the fair of Tailtinn[h] by Fogartach, in which fell the son of Maelrubha, and the son of Donnsleibhe.

[717.] Kal. Anastasius[i] Augustus pellitur. A shower of honey fell upon the foss of Leinster. It rained also a shower of silver at Othain Mor[j], and of wheat at Othain Beg. Then was born Niall Condail, son of Ferghal, whence he was called Niall Frosach [i. e. of the showers].

The tonsure of Peter the Apostle[k] was taken by the family of Ia, for it was the tonsure of Simon Magus they had till then, as had Colum Cille himself.

[718.] Kal. Theodosius[l] imperat anno uno.

[719.] Kal. Leo[m] imperat annis novem.

[720.] Kal. The plundering of Magh Breagh[n] by Cathal, son of Finguine, King of Munster, and Murchadh, son of Bran, King of Leinster. The plundering of Leinster by Ferghal, son of Maelduin. I find in other books that it was in the third year preceding; i. e. the tenth

at A. D. 716, and by the Annals of Ulster at 717. The true year is 715. Niall Frosach, who received his cognomen from having been born in the year in which these remarkable showers fell, was monarch of Ireland from 763 to 770.

[k] *The tonsure of Peter the Apostle.*—"A.D. 718.—Tonsura coronæ super familia Iae."

—Ann. Tighern. See Bede's Eccles. Hist., lib. v., c. 21; Reeves's Adamn., xlvii., 350.

[l] *Theodosius.*—Meaning Theodosius III., A. D. 717.

[m] *Leo.*—A. D. 718.

[n] *Magh Breagh.*—A large plain in Meath. Four Masters, 717; Annals of Ulster, 720 [721].

ꝼlaitiura Ƒeaꞃꝃail do ꝅnítea an timꞃaöꞃa Laiꝅſi, ⁊ ꝅomað na ðiꝅail táinic Mꞃꞃchað mac bꞃain ꝅo ꝼſꞃaib Muṁan d'inðꞃſð Maiꝅe bꞃeaꝃ. Ꝅibé bliaðain ðib ꞃin tꞃa do ꞃiꝅne Ƒeaꞃꝃal inðꞃaða moꞃa i Laiꝅniḃ .i. aloꞃꝅað ⁊ a nðóð, ⁊ a maꞃḃað, ⁊ ꞃa ꝅeall nać anꞃað ne ꞃin, no ꝅo ttuꝅta ðo an boꞃoṁa ꞃo ṁait Ƒinnaéta do Molinꝅ, ⁊ ꝅo ðtuꝅta bꞃaiꝅðe ðó ꞃe tiꝅeaꞃnaꞃ ⁊ ꞃeꞃ in ćuꞃ. Do ꞃaðꞃat laiꝅin bꞃaiꝅðe ðó, ⁊ ꞃa ꝅeallꞃat an cíꞃ.

Iꞃ ino aimꞃiꞃ ꞃin do ꞃiꝅne Ƒeaꞃꝃal ꞃaiꞃtini ðá ṁacaib .i. ð'Aoð Allan, aꝅuꞃ do Niall Cunðail, [ðá nꝅoiꞃei Niall Ƒꞃaꞃach] ⁊ aꞃ aꞃ ꞃo ꞃo áꞃ ðoꞃoiṁ on.

.i. Lá tancattuꞃ cuicce do h-Ailfe Ƒꞃiꝅꞃſnn, .i. Aoð an mac ba moo .i. óclać ꝅlic, aimnuꞃ, beoða, aðacomꞃaicꞃiðe, aꞃ aṁlað táiniꝅ ꝅo nibinönib móꞃa ðaꝅaꞃmita ime do cum Aliꝅ. Aꞃ aṁlað imuꞃꞃo tainiꝅ an mac ba ꞃóo, ꝅo ciuin ⁊ ꝅo mſꞃaꞃða, ꝅo ꞃſðaṁail, ⁊ co n-uaitib, ⁊ aꞃꞃeð ꞃo ꞃáð aꞃ anaꞃꞃaðe ꞃéin, ⁊ aꞃ onóiꞃ ðá ataiꞃ : aꞃ cóꞃa ðaṁꞃa, aꞃ ꞃé, ðol aꞃ aoiðheét amać iná aiꞃiꞃiṁ ða aiꝅið aꝅaðꞃa anoćt. Cia ðia ttaṁöuiꞃi, a ṁic, aꞃ an tataiꞃ, ꞃin do ꞃáð? ⁊ an mac aꞃ ꞃiniu taoi, aꝅaꞃ ataꞃaiðe tꞃí coimlíon ꞃꞃiтꞃa [eið ꞃaðeꞃa] ꝅan ðánoćt aꝅað in taiꞃiꞃin i n-Aileać inoćt amhail ataꞃuṁ aꝅ taiꞃꞃim co n-a ṁuintiꞃ? Ꞃa ꞃað mait lſmꞃa, aꞃ Niall, co nðeaꞃmaðꞃom inaile ćeðna ꞃꞃiтꞃa. Ni ꞃaꝅa ioiꞃ anoćt, a ṁic, aꞃ Ƒeaꞃꝃal, aꝅuꞃ biað i ꞃꞃaꞃꞃað tatꞃaꞃ ⁊ do ṁátaꞃ.

Ruccað

ᵒ *Whichever year.*—The Four Masters state that Leinster was five times devastated by the Ui-Neill, in the ninth year of the reign of Ferghal.

ᵖ *Boromean tribute.*—See Annals of the Four Masters, A. D. 106, p. 100.

ᵠ *A prediction.*—i. e. a surmise, conjecture, or opinion concerning their future careers. This account of Ferghal and his sons is not in any other accessible Annals, and it evidently found its way into Mac Egan's vellum Book from some romantic

tenth year of the reign of Ferghal [721] this plundering of Leinster took place, and that it was in revenge for it that Murchadh, son of Bran, came with the men of Munster to plunder Magh Breagh. But whichever year" it was, Ferghal committed great depredations against the men of Leinster; i. e. he burned, consumed, and killed them, and he vowed that he would not desist until he was paid the Boromean tribute[p] which Finnachta had remitted to Moling, and until hostages were given him for [i. e. in acknowledgment of his] lordship and the tribute. The Leinster-men gave him hostages, and promised the rent.

At this time Ferghal gave out a prediction[q] to his sons: viz., Aedh Allan and Niall Condail, and the cause of his doing so originated thus:—

On a certain day they came to him to Ailech-Frigrinn[r]: viz. Aedh the elder son, who was a cunning, fierce, lively young hero, and he came to Ailech surrounded by numerous well-armed troops; but the younger son came silently, modestly, and peaceably, with few attendants; and he said, to humble himself and to honour his father: "It is fitter for me," said he, "to go and lodge out than to remain thy guest to night." "What induces thee to say this, my son," said the father, "while my elder son, who has thrice thy number [of attendants] is staying at Ailech to-night? Why hast thou not the same confidence to remain at Ailech to-night as he has, in remaining with his people?" "I should like," replied Niall, "that he would do the very same towards thee." "Thou shalt not depart hence to-night, O son," said Ferghal, "but thou shalt remain with thy father and thy mother."

After

story, probably no longer extant.

[r] *Ailech Frigrinn.*—So called from Frigrenn, the builder of the fort; now Greenan-Ely, an ancient cyclopean fort on Greenan Hill, near Lough Swilly, in the barony of Inishowen. For the history of this place, see the Ordnance Memoir of the Parish of Templemore, published in 1835.

Ruccaḃ iap rin an mac buḋ pine, .i. Aoṅ, 'rin riġ tṡe mór cona muinntip. Ruccaḃ ono an mac óg .i. Niall i tteaċ naoiḃinn noeppiḃ. Ra ḟiṫaiġiḋ iapttain, ⁊ pa ḃ'áil ḃon aṫaip a noearḃaḋ maille, ⁊ tanaice a noeipeḃ oiḃċe ḃo cuin an taiġe i paiḃe an mac ba pine, ⁊ pa ḃaoi acc cloipteċt ḟiipin tṡe rin: ap ḃíġaip tpa palaċ pa ḃáp 'pan taiġ rin. Ra ḃattap puippeoipi, ⁊ cain- teḃa, ⁊ eaċlaċa, ⁊ oḃloipi, ⁊ baċlaiġ aġ bṡṁoiġ ⁊ acc buipeḃaiġ ann; upeam aġ ól, ⁊ upeam na ccouḃlaḃ, ⁊ upeam oġ pġeaṫpaiġ, upeam oce cupiṡnnaiġ ⁊ oc ḟṡtċuipiġ; timpanaiġ ⁊ epuitipi oġ rṡnnain; upeam oġ inapḃaġaḋ, ⁊ oc pṡpbaġaḃ. Aḃ cuala Ḟṡi- ġal aṁlaiḋ rin iaḃ, aġap táimġ iap rin ḃ'innpoiceiḃ an taiġe ḃeppiḃ i paḃa an mac ap póo, ⁊ pa ḃaoí aġ cloiptṡet pip an tṡe rin, ⁊ ní cuala naċ ní ann aċt atluċċaḃ buiḃe ḃo Ohia [pa] ġaċ ní puapattuip, ⁊ epuitipeċt ciuin biṅḃ, ⁊ ḃuana molta an coimḃeḃ ġa nġaḃail, ⁊ pa aipiġ an pí co móp uamon ⁊ ġráḋ an coimḃeḃ ipin taiġ rin.

Táimġ an pí ap a haitle rin ḃá leaḃaiḃ féin, ⁊ tucc ġo móp ḃa niḃ puḃiuċċaḃ an ḃá tṡe rin.

Táimic maḋain moċṡpaċ pan tṡe móp i paḃa an mac ba pine, ⁊ ap inbṡetain pa féḃ taḃall an taiġe pa imaḃ pġeaṫpaiġe ⁊ palċaip ⁊ bpṡntataḃ, ⁊ imaḃ con oc itṡ pġeaṫpaiġe. Saċ imuppo uile na ġpeanóṙaḃoiġ [no i ḃtoiṅchim puain] ipaiġ aṁail ḃeittíp maipḃ, ġenmota mac an pí féin; ap amlaiḋ imuppo po ḃaoipiḋe ina ċouḃlaḃ aṁail pa beit aġ ipnaiḋe caṫa ⁊ pé na piġleaḃaiḃ, pġiat móp ḃá leit clí, ⁊ ḃa lṡġa láiṁópa ḃá leit ḃep: claiḃeaḃ mop intlaipi ópouipi pop a ṗliapaiḃ, analpaḋaċ móp inaċ ⁊ ipteaċ ḃa ċup ḃó, aṁail naċaḋa ḃuini ḃa ċup ap ṫpeipi ⁊ ap ṫpiċċe.

Níop

* *Snoring*.—There is probably here some defect of transcription; the words left out are probably no in-a ḃ-toiṅchim puain: the meaning doubtless is, that some were snoring, and others were lying senseless as if dead.

After this the eldest son, Aedh, was brought into the great regal house with his people; but the younger son, Niall, was conveyed into a beautiful private apartment. They were afterwards served [with food and drink], and the father wished to test them both; and he came, towards the end of the night, to the house where the eldest son was, and he remained to listen to [what was going on in] that house. They were indeed very dirty in that house. There were jesters, and lampooners, and horseboys, and clowns, and buffoons, roaring and vociferating there,—some drinking, some sleeping, and some vomiting; some piping, some whistling; tympanists and harpers playing; some disputing, some quarrelling! Ferghal heard them [getting on] so; and he afterwards came to the private house in which the younger son was [lodged], and he remained listening to [what was going on in] that house; but he heard nothing there but thanksgiving to God for all that they had received, and gentle, melodious harp-playing, and songs of praise to the Lord being sung; and the King perceived that the fear and love of God were in that house.

After this the King returned to his own bed, and he meditated deeply in his mind the condition of these two houses.

Early in the morning he came into the great house in which the elder son was, and it was with difficulty he could remain in the house, in consequence of the vomiting, filth, and stench, and the number of hounds that were eating the vomits. And all the persons in the house were snoring [or sleeping] as if they were dead! except the King's son alone; but he was sleeping in his royal bed [in such a posture] as if he were awaiting a battle,—a large shield on his left side, and two great half darts on his right, a long polished golden-hilted sword on his thigh, and he inspiring and respiring as if another man were putting him to his strength and dexterity!

Níor fhéd ono fuiress rair irtaig ná méd rob élneigte an t-aér irin tig rin, ⁊ táinig irin tré 1 roibe an mac ba roo, ⁊ gin roill táinice, ra airig an mac óg é, uair nír bo coolað ðó, act ag guiðe an coimðeð ra ðaoi. Ra eirig fo céðóir 1 n-aigið a atair don ðérguð ríogða 1 roibe, uair ar amlaið ra ðaoí, ⁊ mar rróill ime go cciumraið óir ⁊ airgio, ⁊ fo orlaig an tré re na atair, ⁊ ó táinig an tatair irtré do rað ða láim fo bragaið a mic, ⁊ do rað róg do, ⁊ tancatur maille gur fo ruiðfour for an ðerguð ríogða; ra raig an mac comráð ar túr ar an atair, ⁊ arfó ro ráið; a atair, ar ré, an ðar linn ar imfnímhat nfinéoðoltaé rugair an aðaig aréir ar, arfó ar lfé anora coolað rin leabaið rin go trát eirge ðo ló. Do rigne an t-atair amlaið, ⁊ mar táinig trát eirge ðo ló ra ergeðor imaille, ⁊ ra ráið an mac fria a atair: A atair imnain, ar ré, arfó ar cóir ðuit fleðuccað ðúinn male fria rérúnn, uair marað ogainn lfé na ðtugað ðo biað ⁊ ðo lionn uaiori a réir ðúin, agar ní tarrnaig ðo rain muair tugrað timchirdi an mac lfðuair mór lán ðo míoð ⁊ biað láimiomða, ⁊ ra flegaiðrioc go taoi reittamail i maille anorin.

'Ó ro eirig eat, táinig an ri ainat na tré féin, ⁊ ro innir i friagnairi eaté amail ðo biað toigte na ðá mac úð, ⁊ a ðuibairt go ngeðað an mac ra rinc rige ⁊ go mað treaðair, eroða, beoða, ereara é, rartola é a rige. An mac ba luga murrro, co ngeðað rige go eraiððea é conðail, ⁊ go mað elúa é ríogða a elann, ⁊ go ngeðdair rige an ðara real. Ireð ðono rin ro comailleð co nuigi rin.

Ingín ðo Congail mic Feargura Fánað, matair an mic ba rine ⁊ ro chit rug rí an mac rin .i. Aoð Allan, agur ro bé ro aðbar

¹ *Pure-minded.*—The word conðail is glossed innraic (worthy, pure, honest), in H. 3, 18, p. 653.

ᵘ *Congal, son of Fergus of Fanaid.*—He was monarch of Ireland from the year 704 to 711. See Annals of the Fours Masters, A. D. 702, Annals of Ulster, A. D. 704, and O'Flaherty's "Ogygia," Part iii., c. 93.

He [the King] was not able to remain in the house in consequence of the great corruption of the air within it; and he came on to the house in which the younger son was, and, though he came stealthily, the young son perceived him, for he was not asleep, but praying to the Lord. He rose up at once, to meet his father, from the royal couch on which he was, for he was dressed in a satin tunic, with borders of gold and silver, and he opened the house for his father; and when the father entered the house, he folded his arms around the neck of his son, and kissed him, and they came together and sat upon the royal couch, and the son first began the conversation with the father, and said: "Father," said he, "thou hast, methinks, passed the last night pensively and sleeplessly, and thou oughtest now to sleep in this bed till the rise of day." The father did so; and as the day appeared, both arose up together, and the son said to the father: "Dear father," said he, "thou oughtest to entertain us in reason, for we have still remaining half what was given by thee last night to us of food and of drink;" and he had not finished [these words] when servants brought him a second great vessel full of mead and various viands, after which they feasted together silently and calmly!

When all had arisen, the King came forth into his own house, and told, in the presence of all, how the houses of his two sons were; and he said that the elder son would assume the sovereignty, and that he would be firm, brave, and vigorous, severe and self-willed, during his reign; also that the younger son would assume the sovereignty, and that he would be pious and pure-minded', and that his descendants would be illustrious and royal, and that they would assume the sovereignty alternately. And this was verily fulfilled so far.

Now the daughter of Congal, son of Fergus of Fanaid", was the mother of the elder son, and it was secretly she brought forth that son; i.e. Aedh Allan, and this is the reason why Ferghal had this

girl

aḃḃap beiṫe ꝑo cliṫ na hinġine oġ Ḟeapġal : a haṫaip, .i. Congal ꝺa hiṁḃaipṫ ꝺon coimṁiꝺ ⁊ a beiṫ a caillṫeaċṫ, ⁊ ꝺo paꝺ a haṫaip iomaꝺ óip ⁊ aipġiꝺ, aġuꝱ cpuiꝺ ꝺi a ċoiṁéꝺ a ġꝱuipa. Ġiꝺeaꝺ ṫpa pa ṁeall náṁa coiṫċꝱnn an ċmiuꝺa ꝺaonꝺa .i. Ꝺiaḃal, í ; ꝺo paꝺ ġpáꝺ uḞꝱipġal mac Ṁaoilꝺúin, ⁊ ꝺo paꝺ Ḟꝱipġal ġpaꝺ ꝺipi. Ro coimpaiġpeaꝺ ꝺno maille Ḟeapġal ⁊ inġꝱn Conġail Cinꝺmaġaip. Rioġꝺomna Eipꝱnn an ṫan ꝱin Ḟꝱipġal. Rí Eipꝱnn imoppo Conġal. Ra miꝱ an ꝑeap pa ḃaí ꝱṫuppa ꝱin ꝺo Conġal. ꝺa ꝺoiliḃ imuppo co móp lá Conġal an pġel ꝱin : .i. a inġꝱn ꝺo ṁeallaꝺ, ⁊ a ꝺuḃaipṫ ná maippꝱꝺ ꝑeap an pġeoil muna ꝑꝑáġbaꝺ ꝑéin ꝺeiṁin an pġeoil. Ro ḃaoi iapaṁ ꝑeap an pġeoil oġ ipnaiꝺe ġo mbeiṫċíꝱ a naoin ionaꝺ, Ḟeapġal ⁊ inġꝱn Conġail, ⁊ map pa baṫṫup i n-aoin-ionaꝺ, Ḟeapġal ⁊ inġꝱn Conġail, ṫainiġ ꝑeap an pġeoil ꝺ'ionnpoiġhiꝺ Conġail, ⁊ pa imip ꝺo a mbeiṫ i n-aoin-ionaꝺ. Ṫainiġ Conġal peiṁe ꝺ'ionꝑoiċċhiꝺ an ṫiġe i papaṫṫup, ⁊ map pa capiġ inġꝱn Conġail éipion co na ṁuinṫip ꝺo ċum an ṫiġe, uaip po ba ġlic amnup ainġiꝺ ipi, aṁail po bꝺ a h-aṫaip, pa ꝑoiliġ ꝑon évaṫ Ḟꝱipġal, ⁊ pa ꝑuiꝺ ꝑéin ꝑop an évaṫ iapṫṫaim. Ṫainiġ caṫ móp baoi ipṫaiġ ꝺ'ionꝑoiċċiꝺ Ḟꝱipġail co n-ꝺuaiꝺ a ċopa, ⁊ ġo po ꝑluiġ an caṫ ploiṫi mopa ꝺo ċopaib Ḟeapġail. Ꝺo paꝺ Ḟeapġal an laṁ ꝱċa, ⁊ pa ġaḃ 'ma ꝑlucaiṫ an caṫ, ⁊ pop mapḃ.

Ro ꝑéġ ṫpa Conġal an ṫꝱċ ime, ⁊ ní ꝑaca Ḟꝱipġal ann. Ṫainiġ poiṁe ꝺ'innpoiġhiꝺ ꝑip an pġeoil, ⁊ po báiꝺ é i n-aḃainn. Ṫainiġ iapṫṫain ꝺ'ionꝑoiġiꝺ a inġine ꝑéin, ⁊ pa ḃaoi aġ iappaiꝺ loġṫa ꝱuippe aṁail biꝺ oġ ipi ⁊ na beṫṫíp ciopṫa ꝑaippioṁ ꝑpia. San coṁpac cliṫi ꝱin ṫpá po coimppꝱꝺ Aoꝺ Allan.

Ap

¹ *Ceannmaghair.*—This place is still so called in Irish, and in the anglicised form Kinnaweer. It is situated at the head of Mulroy Lough, in the territory of Fánaid, barony of Kilmacrenan, and county of Donegal. See Four Masters, A. D. 702, note ⁹, and A. D. 1392. In the old translation of the Annals of Ulster Cenn-Magair is referred to as if it were the same as Fanaid; but it is now considered as the

girl secretly: her father, Congal, had devoted her to God, and she was in a nunnery, and her father had given much gold and silver and cattle to her for preserving her virginity. But however, the general enemy of the human race, namely, the devil, deceived her; she fell in love with Ferghal, son of Maelduin, and Ferghal loved her. Ferghal and the daughter of Congal of Ceammaghair[v] cohabited together. Ferghal, at this time, was a royal heir apparent of Erin, and Congal was King of Erin. The man who was [the messenger] between them told this to Congal, and Congal was much grieved at the news of the seduction of his daughter, and he said that the bearer of the story should not live unless he verified it to him. The bearer of the story was waiting until Ferghal and the daughter of Congal should be in one place; and when they were in one place, the bearer of the story came to Congal and told him of their being in one place. Congal came forward to the house in which they were, and as the daughter of Congal perceived him and his people approaching the house,—for she was cunning, sharp, and peevish, as was her father,—she covered Ferghal under the clothes, and afterwards sat upon the clothes herself. While Ferghal was in this position, a large cat which was in the house came to him, and biting at his legs, devoured large pieces of flesh off his legs. Ferghal put down his hand, and taking the cat by the throat, choked her.

Congal searched the house all round, but did not see Ferghal in it. He came forward to where the bearer of the story was, and drowned him in a river! He afterwards came to his daughter, and asked forgiveness of her because she was [as he supposed] a virgin! that his crime against her might not be upon him[w]. By this secret connexion Aedh Allan was begotten!

Now,

north-west part of it.

[w] *Might not be upon him.*—i. e. that his sin in accusing his daughter, who was a consecrated virgin, might be forgiven him.

Ap na bpeit ımuppo, Aoḋ Allaın, pa ṡıḃ a ṁataıp é do dıḃ mnáıḃ (pa ba taıpıpı lé) dá ḃáḋaḋ, ná pıonnaḋ a h-ataıp puıppe, ⁊ na pṡızaıḋeḋ an tataıp ppıa. Ḃṡı do Cınél Conaıll dıḃpıden dno, ⁊ ḃṡı do Cenel Eoġaın. An ḃṡı Eoġanat tpa nıap pa ġaıp 'na láıṁ an aoıdın mḃız nálaınn pa líonaḋ ó ġpáḋ ⁊ ó ṗeıpc na naoıdıne í; ıpḃ po páıḋ pa ınraoı comta, a pıup ıoṁmaın, ap pí, nota malaıpt na naoıḋınepı ap cóıp, att ap a coıṁéd zo maıt. A pḃ po paıopıöı, annpa latpa é ına pe na ṁataıp péın, ⁊ ıp ṗpıde pa ṡpaıl poıpne a ḃáduḋ, ap ıomoṁon peıpzı a hataıp. Ra zap peapz lıpıde, ⁊ pa cuıp an Leanaṁ pop láp, ⁊ po deaḃtaıġpıot maılle .ı. an dapa dé za anacal, ⁊ an ḃí oıle za ḃaduḋ. Ġıdead po popuaıpliz an ḃṡı Eoġanat an mnaoı oıle, ⁊ pa zaḃ a huḃall pluzatan zo pa paoṁ cat ní na papattuıp at deaḃaıḋ .ı. an lṡnaṁ do lṡpuzaḋ. Ra lṡpaızead leo map aon ıap pın an lṡnaṁ.

Tápla tpá péẟt aon mataıp an lṡnaıṁ ıp ın tṡé ı paḋa an lenaṁ a ceınn ceıtpe mḃlıaḋan, ⁊ zan a pıup dı a ḃeıt a ṁḃṡeaıḋ. Ap ann po ḃaoı an ınacaoıṁ zá éluıẟı. Do pála mṡnına a ṁataıp paıp, ⁊ po pıappuıḋ cıa aop an ınacaoıṁ ud ap pı? Apḃ pa páıḋ tát zuı bo mac ceıtpe nıḃlıaḋan. Ro zaıpm pí na mna taıpıpı úd ap a hamup ⁊ apḃ pa páıḋ pıu: ap móp an col do pızıupa, ap pı ap ımzaḃaıl peıpze m'ataıp .ı. mac na haoıpı ud do malaıpt. Att pa páıopıot na mná pṡıapı: na déna toıpı ıtıp, ap pıaıḋ, ap é pud an mac pın, ⁊ pıṅe pa coméd é. Do pad pı aıpẟeda ıomḋa do na mnáıḃ ıapταın, ⁊ puccaḋ uaıte an mac zo dıcelta d'ınnpoıcéıḋ a ataıp péın .ı. Pṡpıẟal.

Inġṡn

---

¹ *Cinel-Conaill and Cinel-Eoghain.*— These were two kindred races in Ulster descended from Eoghan and Conall, two sons of the monarch Niall of the Nine Hostages, who died in 406. They gave names to the territories of Tir-Eoghain [Tyrone] and Tir-Chonaill [Tyrconnell]. O'Neill was, in later ages, the chief of the one, and O'Donnell of the other; but before the English invasion, Mac Laughlin was dominant in Tyrone, and O'Muldory, or O'Canannan, in Tyrconnell.

Now, when Aedh Allan was born, his mother gave him in charge to two women (who were dear to her) to be drowned, that her father might not discover her crime, or be angry with her. One of these women was of the Cinel-Conaill, and the other of the Cinel-Eoghain`. When the woman of the Cinel-Eoghain took into her hands the beautiful little infant, she was filled with love and affection for it, and she said to her female companion: " Dear sister," said she, " it is not right to destroy this infant, but to preserve it well." The other replied: " He is dearer to thee than to his own mother, who commanded us to drown him, from fear of the anger of her father." The other became angry, and laid the child on the ground, and they fought with each other, the one for preserving, and the other for drowning him. But the Cinel-Eoghain woman prevailed over the other, and held her by the apple of the throat until she consented to her wishes; namely, to rear the child. After this both conjointly reared the child.

On one occasion, at the end of four years, the mother of the child happened to come into the house in which the child was, not knowing that he was alive. The child was at his play, and the mother's mind was fixed upon him, and she asked : " What age is yon child ?" said she. All replied that he was a child of the age of four years. She called these trusted women to her, and said to them : " I committed a great wickedness," said she, " in destroying a son [who would now be] of that age, to escape the anger of my father." But the women said to her: " Be not sad at all ;" said they, " yon child is that son, and we were they who preserved him." She afterwards gave great rewards to the women, and the boy was conveyed away^r from them privately to his own father, Ferghal.

Now,

^r *Conveyed away.*—This is a better story than the account of his descendant Ferdoragh, Baron of Dungannon, who, according to Fynes Moryson, was fourteen years old before Con O'Neill, Earl of Tyrone, knew that he was his son.

Ingen ımuppo pí Cıanacta mácaıp ın Neıll Conbaıl, ⁊ hıpıne bũ ap caoım ⁊ ap pospaıde baoí a n-Eıpınn na haımpıp; act cına bá haınbpıct í go poda, go ttáıng gup an ccaıllıg naoım, go Luacpın b'ıappaıd puıppıpde epnaıgte do dénaım puıppe ppıp an coınded ná puptact, ⁊ do pınne Luacpınn pın, ⁊ po coınpped Nıall ıapttaın ı mbpoınn ıngıne pıg Cıanacta, ⁊ pugad ıapttaın, ⁊ apí ba píogan 'Eıpenn an tan po ag Fpıgal.ᵃ

Cıd pıl ann tpa act ó po labaıp do na ınacaıb amaıl a buppa-
maıp pa a ploıg, ⁊ pa puıcal poppa ⁊ ap cac uıle léıptıonol do
oſnaın pan bliadaın bud nípa d'ınnpoıgıd Laıgen do tobac na
bopuma poppa, uaıp nip coınaıllpıc Laıgın aınaıl po geallpat.

Kal. Ab ınıtıo Munbı ın. dcccc.xxııı. ab ıncapnatıone Domını
dccxxıı.

Cat Alınaıne ıtıp Laıgnıu ⁊ huıb Neıll. In tertıo Decem-
bpıp pa cuıped an cat pa. Caıup an cata pa .ı. an bopoma po
maıt Fınnacta do Molıng a tobac dFpıgal ⁊ ıpd on na pa puıl-
ngeadoıp Laıgın, nıp tucpat Laıgın do Loıngpec mac Aongupa, ⁊
ní tucpat do Congal Cınnınagaıp, cıa po puılngettup dımnıd ó
Congal, agup ní moo dno pob áıl dóıb a tabaıpt d'Fpıgal, uaıp
po taıppıngpıot ımbpatpaıb Molıng pa geall na bepeta uata
tpé bíta an bopoma ó Laıgnıb. Ba tpom tpa la Fpıgal pın .ı.
Laıgın do mıncomall angeallta ppıp, go po puacpad pluaıgen
dıpeacpa

ᵃ *Cianachta.*—A territory in East Meath, of which Duleek was the capital, inhabited by a sept of the race of Tadhg, son of Cian, son of Oilioll Olum, King of Munster.

ᵃ *Luaithrinn.*—St. Luchrinna, a virgin, the patroness of the church of *Kill-Luaith-rinne*, in the territory of Corann, county of Sligo. Luchrinna was of the same race as this Queen of Ireland; that is, of the race of Tadhg, grandson of Oilioll Olum.—See Colgan's "Acta Sanctorum," p. 756.

ᵇ *Almhain.*—Now Allen, a celebrated hill, situated about five miles to the north of the town of Kildare. This battle is entered in the Annals of the Four Masters at the year 718, in the Annals of Ulster at 721, and in the Annals of Tighernach

Now, the daughter of the King of Cianachta[a] was the mother of Niall Condail, and she was the fairest and the mildest woman that was in Erin in her time. She was, however, barren for a long time, until she came to the holy nun Luaithrinn[a] to request of her to pray to God for her relief; and Luaithrinn did so, and Niall was afterwards conceived in the womb of the daughter of the King of Cianacta, and he was born [in due time] afterwards, and she was Queen of Erin, with Ferghal, at this time.

Howbeit when he spoke concerning his sons, as we have said, before his hosts, he commanded them and all in general to assemble all their forces in the following year to invade Leinster, to force the Borumean tribute from them, for the Leinster-men did not perform what they had promised.

[A. M. 5924.] Kal. *Ab initio Mundi* v.m. dcccc.xxiv. *ab incarnatione Domini* Dcc. xxii.

[722.] The battle of Almhain[b] [was fought] between the Leinster-men and the Ui-Neill. *In tertio Decembris* this battle was fought. The cause of this battle was this: the Borumean tribute which Finnachta had remitted to Moling[c] was demanded by Ferghal, and this the Leinstermen would not brook. The Leinstermen had not paid it to Loingsech, son of Aengus[d], nor to Congal of Cennmaghair[e], though they had suffered sore annoyances from the hands of Congal; neither were they willing to pay it to Fergal, for they insisted upon the

---

at 722, which last is the true year. It is stated in the Annals of Clonmacnoise that King Ferghal had 21,000 men in this battle, and the Leinster-men only 9000.

[c] *Moling.*—i. e. St. Moling, who was Bishop of Ferns, A. D. 691 to 697. See Lanigan, vol. iii., pp. 132-135.

[d] *Loingsech, son of Aengus.*— He was monarch of Ireland from A. D. 695 to 704.

[e] *Congal of Cennmaghair.*— He was monarch of Ireland from A. D. 704 to 711, when Fergal, son of Maelduin, succeeded. See "Ogygia," Part iii., c. 93.

ḋireaċra ḃíṁór uaḋ ror Lė́ṫ Cuinn .i. ror Eoġan ⁊ ror Conall ⁊ ror Airġiallaiḃ ⁊ Miḋe, an cėṫraṁaḋ bliaḋain a rlaiṫiura réin, no i ṫríṡr ḃliaḋain ḋéc, uṫ quiburḋam placeṫ, ḋo ṫoḃaċ na boroṁa.

Ḃa ṗaḋa ṫra ro ḃár oġ an ṫinolram, uair arreḋ aḋ beireḋ ġaċ rear ḋo Leiṫ Cuinn ġur a roiċeaḋ an ruaccraḋ .i. "ḃá ṫṡí Ḋonnḃó ar an rluaġaḋ, raġaura." Ḋonnḃó imurro mac Ḃainṫreaḃṫaiġe eiriḋe ḋreararḃ Rorr, aġar ní ḋeaċhaiḋ lá na aiḋċi a ṫaiġ a máṫar imaċ riaṁ, ⁊ ní raiḃe i n-Eirinn uile buḋ caoiṁe, no buḋ rṡir ċruṫ no ḋelḃ, no ḋṡnam iṁár. Ní raḃa i n-Eirinn uile buḋ ġnaḋḋa, no buḋ rṡġaine iṁár, ⁊ ar uaḋ buḋ rṡir riann erra ⁊ iurġela ror ḋoṁon; arė buḋ rṡir ḋo ġlėr eaċ, ⁊ ḋo inḋrma rlṡġ, ⁊ ḋ'riġe rolṫ, ⁊ buḋ rṡr riaiċni [.i. inġne inṫlecṫa] na einec; ḋc quo ḋiciṫur:—

'Aille macaiḃ Ḋonnḃo bánḋ
Ḃinne a laiḋ luaiḋiḋ beoil
Aine óġaiḃ Inniri Pail
Ra ṫóġaiḃ ṫáin ṫrillri a ṫreoir.

Niar licc ḋno a ṁáṫair Ḋonnḃo la Prṡġal, ġo ṫṫuccaḋ Maol mic

---

f *During this world's existence.*—The writers of the Ui Neill, among whom Adamnan is set down, insisted that the great St. Moling obtained a remission of this tribute by an equivocation which was altogether unworthy of a saint, and therefore many subsequent monarchs of the Ui Neill attempted to compel the Leinstermen to pay it. See "Annals of the Four Masters," A. D. 106, p. 99, and A. D. 593, p. 216, *et seq.*

g *Leth-Chuinn.*—i. e. Conn's half, i. e. the north half of Ireland.

h *Cinel Eoghain.*—i. e. the race of Eoghan, or the men of Tyrone [Tir-Eoghain] and their relatives.

i *Cinel-Conaill.*—i. e. the race of Conall, or the inhabitants of Tirconnell.

j *Airghialla.*—i. e. the inhabitants of the present counties of Louth, Armagh, and Monahan.

k *Donnbo.*—No account of this personage is to be found in any other authority; and this legend must have found its way into

the words of Moling, to whom it was promised that the Borumean tribute should never, during this world's existence[f], be demanded from the Leinster-men. Now Fergal deemed this intolerable; namely, that the Leinster-men should not keep their promise to him, so that he ordered a very great and irresistible hosting upon Leth-Chuinn[g]; i. e. a hosting of the Cinel-Eoghain[h], Cinel-Conaill[i], and Airghialla[j], and of the men of Meath, in the fourth year of his reign, or in the thirteenth, as some will have it, to levy the Borumean tribute.

Long, indeed, was this muster of forces being carried on, for each man of Leth-Chuinn to whom the order came used to say: "If Donnbo[k] come on the hosting, I will." Now Donnbo was a widow's son of the Fera-Ross[l], and he never went away from his mother's house for one day or one night, and there was not in all Ireland one of fairer countenance, or of better figure, form, or symmetry, than he; there was not in all Erin one more pleasant or entertaining, or one in the world who could repeat more amusing and royal stories[m], than he; he was the best to harness horses, to set spears, to plait hair, and he was a man of royal intelligence in his countenance: of whom was said—

> Fairer than sons was Donnbo.
> Sweeter his poem than all that mouths rehearse.
> Pleasanter than the youths of Innis-Fail[n],
> The brilliancy of his example took the multitude.

His mother did not permit Donnbo to go with Fergal, until Mael-mic-Failbhe,

the old vellum Book of Nehemias Mac Egan from some romantic historical tale on the battle of Almhain, now unknown.

[l] *Fera-Ross.*—The name of a tribe inhabiting the district around the present town of Carrickmacross, county of Mo-naghan, whose territory extended into the present county of Louth.

[m] *Royal stories.*—i. e. stories relating to kings.

[n] *Innis-Fail.*—This was one of the most ancient names of Ireland.

mic Failbe mic Erannain mic Cromtainn, comarba Colaim Cille, fria airic beo ⁊ go ttuccraide Colam Cille ono dia cionn go mired Donnbo rlán da taiġ féin a crié Laiġfi.
Tocomla ono Feargal fori réd. Ra battur ona luct eolair reime, nír bú mait an t-eolur do radrad do .i. i ccuingaib gaca conaire ⁊ in-aiṁrédaib gaca conaire go raincuttur Cluain Dóbail i n-Almain. Ar ain buí Aodan claṁ Cluana Dobail ar a cinn. Do ronrat ono na fluaiġ a micortad .i. a aon bó do ṁarbad ⁊ a fuine ar brraib na riagnairi, ⁊ a tfc do breit da cinn, ⁊ a lorccad; confibfft an claṁ com ba digal go brát for Uib Néill an digal do berred an coimdid fairrin, ⁊ tainice an claṁ reime go rubal Ffrgail, ⁊ battur riograid Leite Cuinn uile ar a cinn i fin rubal in can fin. Ro baoi an claṁ ag acaoine a imnid na ffriagnairi; ní tainig cride neić dib fair, act cride Conbrftan mic Congura ri ffri Rorr, ⁊ a red ón ná ba haitreć do Coinbrftan, uair ni terma fi do ufć ro baoi irin ruball act Cubrftan mac Congura a aonar ar in cat. Conad ann adbert Cubrftan:—

Ad agar cat for dearg flaind
A fir Ffrġaile ad glionn;
bad bronaiġ muintir mic Maire
Ar mbreit an taiġ dar cionn,
bó an claṁ ro gaod a nofgaid a daim,
Maing láiṁ ra toll a mbrad
Ar ní rimcomarc mac brain, ⁊rl.
                                                    Ar

" *Mael-mic-Failbhe*.—This may be intended for *Conamhail mac Failbhe*, tenth Abbot of Hy, who was of the Airghialla. Tighernach calls him Conmael, and it is not impossible that our author, who is not very precise, may have called him Mael mc Failbe. His date comes very near this period, for he died 710.
ᵖ *Cluain-Dobhail*.—This name is now forgotten.
ᵠ *Cubretan*—This name is not to be found in any of the published Irish An-

Mael-mic-Failbhe°, son of Erannan, son of Criomhthann, successor of Colum Cille, was pledged for his return alive, and until he pledged Colum Cille for himself that Donnbo would return safe to his own house from the province of Leinster.

Fergal proceeded upon his way. Guides went before him, but the guidance they afforded him was not good; i. e. through the narrowness of each road, and the ruggedness of each pass, until they reached Cluain-Dobhail^p, at Ahnhain. And Aedhan the Leper of Cluain-Dobhail was there before them. The hosts ill-treated him: they killed his only cow, and roasted it on spits before his face, and they unroofed his house and burned it; and the Leper said that the vengeance which God would wreak on the Ui-Neill, on his account, would be an eternal vengeance; and the Leper came forward to the tent of Fergal, where the kings of Leth-Chuinn were before him. The Leper complained of the injuries done him, in their presence; but the heart of none of them was moved towards him, except the heart of Cubretan^q, son of Congus, King of Fera-Ross; and for this Cubretan had no reason to be sorry, for of all the kings who were in the tent, none escaped from the battle except Cubretan, son of Congus, alone. On which occasion Cubretan said:

> A red bloody battle was waged,
> O good Fergal, in thy valley;
> The people of the son of Mary were sorrowful
> After taking the roof off the house.
> The cow of the Leper was killed, after its ox.
> Woe to the hand that pierced their neck,
> For the son of Bran did not defend, &c.

Then

nals. *Cubretan* signifies dog or hero of Britain. The ancient Irish had many names of men compounded with *cu*, a dog; as *Cu-mara*, dog of the sea; *Cu-Uladh*, Canis Ultoniæ, *Cu-Muman*, dog of Munster, *Cu-Caisil*, dog of Cashel, &c.

Ar andsin arbert Fergal fria Donnbó; déna airfided dúin, a Doinnbá, ro bid ar tu ar deaċ airfide fuil i n-Eirinn .i. i cúirig, agar i cuirlendoib, ⁊ i cruitib, ⁊ randaib, ⁊ paidreċoib, ⁊ fiġrġé-laib 'Eirenn, ⁊ ir in maidiri i mbárać do béram-ne caċ do Laiġ-nib. Aċ, ar Donnbo, ní ċumġaimri airfide duitri anoċt, ⁊ imtéa aon ġníom ṫib rin uile do taidbrin anoċt, ⁊ cirri airm i rabairi a márać, ⁊ imbeora, do dénra airfide duitri. Dénaḋ imurro an riogḋruċ hua Maiġléine airfide duit anoċt. Tugaḋ hua Maiġléni ċuca iarttain. Ro ġabraiḋe oġ moirin caċ ⁊ comrama leiċe Cuinn ⁊ Laiġen ó toġail Tuama Tenbat, .i. Deanda riġ, in ra marbaḋ Cobṫaċ Caolbreġ, conigi an amrir, rin, ⁊ ní bá mór codalta do rinneḋ leo in aiḋchi rin ra méd eagla leo Laiġin, ⁊ la méid na doininne, .i. uair aiḋċe féle Phinniain ġaimriḋ rin.

Imṫiġ Laiġin do loiturraide i eCruaċán Claonta, dáiġ ní maiḋ ror Laiġniu da ndearnat a comairle ann, ⁊ ġur obar tiuraḋ do ċum an ċaṫa. Lottur iarrain ġo Dinn Canainn, araiḋe do ċum an ċaṫa.

Conrancuttur tra ir in maidin ar na márać na caṫa ċé-taiḋa, naoi míle do Laiġnib, míle ar fiċit imurro do Leiṫ Cuinn. Ar cruaiḋ ⁊ ar feoċair ra cuireḋ an caṫra leiṫ for lṫé, ⁊ ra ġaḃ caċ na ċomraicib ann.

Ra

' *Maighléine.*—This personage is not mentioned in any other known Annals.

' *Tuaim Tenbath,* i.e. *Dinnrigh.*—O'Fla-herty places this event so far back as A. M. 3682. This was the name of the ancient palace of the Kings of Leinster. The re-mains of its earthen works are situated on the west side of the River Barrow, in the townland of Ballyknockan, about a quar-ter of a mile south of Leighlin Bridge.

For a notice of the burning of this palace, see "Leabhar na g-Ceart," pp. 15, 16. The ancient Irish poets had a great many stories of this description which they used to recite to their kings and chieftains. See Campion's "Historie of Irelande," chap. vi.

' *The eve of the festival of Finnian.*—i.e. the 11th of December. The Annals of Clonmacnoise make it the 3rd of the Ides

Then Fergal said to Donnbo: "Show amusement for us, O Donnbo, for thou art the best minstrel in Eriu at pipes, and trumpets, and harps, at the poems and legends and royal tales of Erin, for on tomorrow morning we shall give battle to the Leinster-men." "No," said Donnbo, "I am not able to amuse thee to-night, and I am not about to exhibit any one of these feats to-night; but wherever thou shalt be to-morrow, if I be alive, I shall show amusement to thee. But let the royal clown, Ua Maighleine^r, amuse thee this night." Ua Maighleine was afterwards brought to them. He commenced narrating the battles and the valiant deeds of Leth-Chuinn and Leinster from the demolition of Tuaim Tenbath, i. e. Dinn-righ^s, in which Cobhthach Cael-mBreagh was killed, unto that time; and they slept not much that night, because of their great dread of the Leinster-men, and of the great storm, for it was the eve of the festival of Finnian^t, in the winter.

With respect to the Leinster-men, they repaired to Cruachan Claenta^u, for the Leinster-men would not be defeated if they should hold their council there, and proceed from thence to battle. They proceeded thence to Dinn-Canainn^v, and thence to the battle.

On the following morning the battalions of both sides met: nine thousand of the Leinstermen, and twenty-one thousand of Leth-Chuinn. Vigorously and fiercely was this battle fought on both sides, and all showed equal fight.

The

of December, which would be the 11th.

^u *Cruachan Claenta*.—i. e. the round Hill of Clane, situated about five miles to the north-east of Allen, where this battle was fought. The Leinster-men believed that whenever they could hold their council of war here, they should not be defeated.

The origin of this belief is not yet discovered, nor is this superstition noticed in "Leabhar na gCeart," among the *Geasa* and *Urgartha* of the Kings of Leinster.

^v *Dinn-Canainn*. — Now Duncannon, nearly midway between Clane and the Hill of Allen.

Ra ba uimóp pa innipi compama na Laoć Laiʒen ⁊ Laoć Leite Cuinn. Apbept ʒo ppacap bpiʒio op cionn Laiʒen; auéfp ono Colum Cille op cionn hua Néill. Ra meamuib iapam an caċ pia Mupchab mac mbpain, ⁊ pe n-Cob mac Donncaba, mic Colʒan pí Laiʒen Dcapʒabaip. Ra mapbab Peapʒal ann Cob m̄o ⁊ Donnchab mac Mupchaba po mapbpat Pfpʒal pauepin, ⁊ bile mac buain, pí Alban, ap uaib aimnniʒtep Coppbile, ı n-Almaine. Ap é ono Cob menb pa mapb Donnbó. Ní topcaip imuppo Peapʒal ʒo ttopchaip Donnbó. Ra mapbab ono pepca ap céb amup ın bú pın. A coimlín péin po mapbaıb Laiʒın pan ċaċ pın bo Leit Cuinn .ı. naoı mıle ; ⁊ naoı nʒeltı bıb bo bol pop ʒeltaċt, ⁊ ċétpıʒ bo pıʒaıb. Ata Cnoc Pfpʒaıl annpın; pa ċuippıot Laıʒın ılaıʒ commaıbmı anb bno, unbe bıcıtup :—

> Deoblaite Almaine,
> Ap copnam buaıp bpfʒmaine
> Ro la baub bélbeapʒ bıopaċ,
> Iolaċ ım cfhn pPfpʒaıle.

Scapapp

* *Valorous.*—The Irish word compama, deeds of valour or prowess. The substantive compuma is glossed copcup, victory, in II. 3, 18, p. 536.
* *Brigit.*—She was the patroness of all Ireland, but particularly of Leinster. See under A. D. 605, where St. Mura is represented as saying that St. Bridget was greater than he, and her prayers more powerful than his prayers.
⁷ *Colum Cille.*—He was the principal patron of the Cinel Conaill. St. Mura was the patron of the Cinel-Eoghain, but Colum was the greater saint of the two, and is therefore introduced as contending with St. Bridget in protecting his kinsmen of the race of Niall.
¹ *Son of Bran.*—King of Leinster.
² *Fergal.*—King of Erin.
ᵛ *Bile, son of Buan of Albain.*—i. e. of Scotland. No account of this Scottish champion has been found in any of the authentic Irish Annals, and it is very probably that he is a mere fictitious character introduced here among the historical chiefs who really flourished at this time

The valorous[w] deeds of the heroes of Leinster and of Leth-Chuinn are very much spoken of. It is said that Brigit[x] was seen over the Leinster-men; Colum Cille[y] was seen over the Ui-Neill. The battle was gained by Murchadh, son of Bran[z], and Aedh, son of Donnchadh, son of Colgan, King of South Leinster. Fergal[a] himself was killed in it; and it was Aedh Menn, and Donnchadh, son of Murchadh, that slew Fergal himself, and Bile, son of Buan, of Albain[b], from whom Corrbile[c], at Almhain, is named. Aedh Menn was also the person who slew Donnbo. Fergal was not killed till Donnbo had first fallen. One hundred and sixty soldiers were killed on the occasion. The Leinster-men killed an equal number of Leth-Chuinn in this battle; i. e. nine thousand and nine of them ran mad[d], and one hundred kings. The hill of Ferghal[e] is at the place. The Leinster-men raised shouts of exultation there, *unde dicitur:*

> At the end of the day at Almhain,
> In defending the cows of Bregia,
> The red-mouthed, sharp-beaked raven,
> Croaked over Fergal's head.
>   Murchadh,

and fought in this battle.

[c] *Corrbile.*—i. e. Bile's Pit, would now be anglicized Corbilly; but there is no place of the name in the neighbourhood of the Hill of Allen.

[d] *Ran mad.*—Connell Mageoghan translates this—"There were nine persons that flyed in the ayre as if they were winged fowle." But this is hardly correct. For the Irish ideas about *gealtacht* and panic, the reader is referred to the "Buile Shuibhne," to the romantic tale called the "Battle of Finntraighe," or Ventry, and "Battle of Magh Rath," p. 231, and p. 234, note [n]. It is still believed in many parts of Ireland that all the lunatics of Ireland would make their way, if unrestrained, to a valley in the county of Kerry, called Gleann na nGealt, and remain there feeding on the herbs and water-cresses of the valley until they should recover their former sanity.

[e] *The hill of Ferghal.*—No hill of this name is now pointed out in this neighbourhood. The name would be now anglicized Knockfarrell.

G

Scapaŗŗ Muŗchaḋ ŗa miḋlaiġ,
bŗoġaiŗ a tŗiuna i ttalmuin,
Do ŗoi ŗaoḃaŗ ŗŗia Ƒeaŗġal,
Ġo ŗŗein ḋeaŗmaŗŗ ḃʃŗ Almain.
baṫ ann céḋ ŗuiŗeṫ ŗaṫaṫ,
Cŗuaḋaṫ, coŗtaḋaṫ, caŗnaṫ,
Im naoi nġelta ġan míne,
Um naoi míle ŗeaŗ n-aŗmaṫ.
Ceitŗi ṫéḋ caḃŗaiḋ a Cŗuaiṫ .i. Cŗuaṫain,
Laŗ an amŗaiġ ġaoḋ ŗan ġliaiḋ,
La tŗí céḋoiḃ Conaill cŗuaiḋ,
A ŗé   *   *   *   *   *

Ra ġaḃaḋ annŗain an ḋŗuth hua Maiġléine ⁊ ḋo ŗaḋaḋ
ŗaiŗ ġéim ḃŗuit ḋo ḋénaṁ, ⁊ ḋo ŗiġne; bá maŗ ⁊ ba binn an
ġéim ŗin, ġo maiŗiḋ ġéim hUi Maiġléine ó ŗin a le oc ḃŗutaiḃ
'Eiŗenn.

Ra ġaḋaḋ a cʃnn iaŗttain ḃ'Ƒeaŗġal, ⁊ ŗa ġaḋaḋ a cʃnn ḋon
ḃŗuṫ. Ro baoi macalla ġeimi an ḋŗúiṫ ŗin aieoŗ ġo cʃnn tŗí la
⁊ tŗí noíḋṫé. Aŗ ḋe aŗ mbeŗaŗ ġéim hUí Maiġléine oġ taŗann
na ŗʃŗi 'ŗan móuaiḋ.

Do luiḋ ḋno Aoḋ Laiġen mac Ƒitṫeallaiġ, ŗí hUa Maine
Connaṫt i ŗaon maḋma ⁊ teiṫin, ġo neḃeŗt ŗŗia macoiḃ: naṫ
ma ŗáccḃaiḋ, a ṁacca, buó ŗeŗŗḋe buŗ máṫaiŗ ŗŗiu mo ḃŗeiṫ ŗi
liḃ. Nit beŗaḋ, oŗ Laiġin, conaḋ ann ŗin ŗo maŗḃaḋ Aoḋ Laiġen,
ŗí hUa Máine. Ra ŗiaṫtattuŗ imuŗŗo, a ṁic [coŗŗ] Aoḋa Laiġin
im Aoḋ Alláin mac Ƒeaŗġaile, ġo Lilcaṫ, aiŗm a mbuí Moḋićiu,
mac

¹ *Aedh Laighean.*—i. e. Aedh, or Hugh of Leinster. He is not mentioned in the pedigrees of the Ui-Maine, printed for the Irish Archæological Society; but his brother Dluthach is set down as chief of Ui-Maine, and as dying in 738.

ᶠ *Aedh Allan.*—He was afterwards monarch of Ireland from A. D. 734 to 743.

Murchadh, no companion of cowardice,
Brings his numerous heroes on the ground;
He turns his weapons against Fergal,
With great heroes, south of Almhain.
There perished there an hundred chieftains, prosperous,
Vigorous, contentious, victorious,
With nine gone mad without mildness,
With nine thousand men of arms.
Four hundred fell at Cruach, i. e. Cruachain,
By the soldiery, wounded in the conflict,
With three hundred of the hardy Cinel Conail;
And six   *   *   *   *   *   *

The clown, Ua Maighleine, was taken prisoner, and he was asked to give " a clown's shout," and he did so. Loud and melodious was that shout, so that the shout of Ua Maighleine has remained with the clowns of Erin from that forth.

Fergal's head was afterwards struck off, and the clown's head was struck off. The reverberation of the clown's shout remained in the air for three days and three nights. From which comes [the saying] " the shout of Ua Maighleine chasing the men in the bog."

Aedh Laighen[f], son of Fithcheallach, King of Ui-Maine, in Connaught, was routed, and fled from this battle; and he said to his sons: " Do not leave me, O my sons; your mother will be the better of it, if you bring me with you." " They shall not bring thee," said the Leinster-men; so that then, Aedh Laighen, King of Ui-Maine, was killed. But his sons carried the body of Aedh Laighen, with Aedh Allan[g], son of Fergal, to Lilcach[h], where Modichu, son of Amairgin, and the Gall Craibhthech[i] were; and it was on this occasion that the Ui-Neil

[h] *Lilcach.*—A place near Slane, in East Meath, not yet identified. See Annals of the Four Masters, A. D. 512, 723.
[i] *Gall Craibhtheach.*—i. e. the pious or

mac Aṁaiṛgin, ⁊ an Ġall Craiḃḋeaċ, conaḋ ann ṛin claiḋiṛit hUí
Néill ⁊ Connachta claḋ na cille, ⁊ iaḋ i ṛioċt na ġcléiṛeaċ, ⁊
aṛ amlaiḋ ṛin ṛa ṛaoṛaiḋ tṛi mioṛḃuile na naoṁ, ġo ḟṛail cotaċ
hUa Néill ⁊ Connaċt ó ṛin ale 'ṛin cill ṛin : unḋe Aoḋ Allain
cecinit :—

Ní ḟṛuaṛamaṛ aṛ talṁain Almain baḋiḋ ṛéḋitiṛ;
Ní ṛanġamaṛ iaṛ ṛin caċ Lilcaċ baḋiḋ neṁṡċaṛ.

Ḃa buaḋaċ tṛa an lá ṛin ḋo Laiġniḃ. Ra hanaiceḋ imuṛṛo
Cubṛetan mac Conġuṛa ṛi ḟḞeaṛ Roṛṛ aṛ na ṛunna ḋo ṛiġne
an aiṫḟċe ṛeiṁe.

I Conḋail na ṛíoġ ḃáttuṛ Laiġin an aiḋċi aġ ol ḟína ⁊ mḃa
aṛ ccuṛ an caṫa ġo ṛubaċ ṛoimṡnmaċ, aġuṛ cáċ ḋíoḃ aġ innṛin
a coṁṛaṁa, iṛ iaḋ mḃoṛaiġ meaḋaṛċaoin. Aṛ anḋ ṛin ṛa ṛáiḋ
Muṛchaḋ mac Ḃṛain : " Ḋo ḃéaṛainn caṛṛat cetṛe cumala, ⁊
mo eaċ ⁊ m'ṡṛṛaḋ ḋon laoċ ṅo ṛaġaḋ iṛin áṛṁaċ, ⁊ ḋo ḃéṛaḋ
coṁaṛċa cuġainn aṛ." Raġaḋ-ṛa, aṛ baoṫġalaċ laoċ ḋim
Muṁain. Ġeḃiḋ a ċaṫeṛṛaḋ caṫa ⁊ coiṁlanna uime, ġo ṛáiniġ
ġo haiṛm i mḃaoí coṛṛ Ḟeaṛġaile, ġo ccuṛla ní i nṡaġaiṛġaiṛe iṛin
iṛin aeoṛ óṛ a cinn, conḋeṛeṛt. Aṛ cloṛṛ uile, timaṛnaḋ ḋuiḃ ó
ṛiġ ṛṡċt niṁe. Ḋénaiḋ aiṛṛiḋe ḋá ḃuṛ ttiġeaṛna anoċt .i.
ḋ'Ḟeaṛġal mac Maolḋúin, cia ḋo ṛoċṛaṛaiṛ ṛunn uile in ḃaṛ
naoṛ ḋuna einiṛ cuiṛleanḋċu, ⁊ coṛnaiṛe, ⁊ cṛuitiṛe, ná taiṛ-
mṡṛeca eṛṛuaċ no héġ comnaṛt ṛiḃ ḋ'aiṛṛiḋeḋ anoċt ḋ'Ḟeaṛġal.

Ġ°

religious Gall, or foreigner, probably a
Saxon or Englishman. This was the same
Gall who gave name to Inis an Ghaill
(Inchaguile) in Lough Corrib, county of
Galway.

ⁱ *The part he took.*—i. e. in sympathiz-
ing with the leper, whose hut the army of
the Hy-Neill had pulled down.

ᵏ *Condail of the Kings.*—Now Old Connell, in the county of Kildare, about
five miles to the east of the Hill of
Allen.

Ui-Neil and the Connaught-men erected the wall of the church, they being in the disguise of the clergy, and they were thus saved through the miracles of the saints, so that the friendship of the Ui-Neill and the Connaught-men is in that church from that forward. Unde Aedh Allan cecinit :—

We did not find on earth a smoother place than Almhain,
We did not reach, after this, a place more sacred than Lilcach.

Now, the Leinster-men were victorious in this battle. Cubretan, son of Congus, King of Fera-Ross, was protected in consequence of the part he took[j] the night before.

It was at Condail of the Kings[k] the Leinster-men were that night drinking wine and mead, merrily, and in high spirits, after gaining the battle; and each of them was describing his prowess, and they were jolly and right merry. Then Murchadh, son of Bran, said: "I would give a chariot of [the value of] four cumhals, and my steed and battle-dress, to the hero who would go to the field of slaughter, and who would bring us a token from it." "I will go," said Baethgalach, a hero of Munster. He puts on his dress of battle and combat, and arrived at the spot where the body of [King] Fergal was, and he heard a noise in the air over his head, and he said, on hearing it: "All praise be to thee, O King of the seven heavens! ye are amusing your lord to-night; i. e. Fergal, son of Maelduin, though ye have all fallen here, both poets, pipers, trumpeters and harpers, let not hatred or ability prevent you to-night from playing for Fergal." The young warrior then heard the most delightful and entrancing piping and music in the bunch of rushes next him, a Fenian melody sweeter than any music. The young warrior went towards it. "Do not come near me," said a head to him. "I ask who art thou?" said the young warrior. "I am the head of Donnbo," said the head, "and I made

Go ccualа іарам an toglác an cuirig ⁊ an ceol pípeactaċ, go ccuala ban 'ran tum luaépa ba nírɑ bó an tópu pіanra ba binne ceolaıḃ. Luıb an toglać na bóćını; na taıp ap m'amup ap an cfnn ppıp. Cfpc, cıa ṫu? ap an tóglaċ. Nıñ, mıpı cfño Ouınnbó, ap an cfnn, ⁊ naıoın po naıbmfŏ ppım a péıp aıppıbeŏ an pí anoċt, ⁊ ná epcóıtoıŏ ḃam. Caıbe copp Ffıɼgaıl punn, ap an t-óglać? Ap é bo aıṫtne ppıt anall. "Ceıpc anbab béı lfın," ap an tóglać ? "Ap tú ap bеaċ lım:" Nom bépa, ap an cfnn ; aċt pat Cpípt bou ċınn ba nom puga, go btuga mé ap amup mo colla bo píòıpı. Oo béı égın, ap an tóglać, ⁊ ımpoı an tóglać ⁊ an cfnn laıp conıgе Conbaıl, ⁊ puaıp Laıgın ag ól ap a cfnn 'pın aíòċı cétna. An ttugaıp comapéa lat? ap Mupchaò. Tugap ap an tóglać, cfnn Ouınnbo. Fopaım ap an puaıtne úo ċall, ap Mupchaò. Tugrab an pluag uıle aıtne paıp gup bé cfnn Ouınnbó, ⁊ apeò po páıòpıb uıle : bıppan ŏuıt a Ouınnbó, bá caom bo bealḃ, béna aıppıbе búınn anoċt, pеḃ bo pıgnıp bot tıgeapna ımbuapaċ. Impoıgtep a aıgıò bono, ⁊ attpaċt a bopb pіanra attpuag ap áıpb, go mbáttup uıle ag caoı ⁊ ag tuıppı. Iònaıcıò an laoċ ċébna an cfnn bo ċum a colla amaıl po geall, ⁊ coıpgıò é ap a mеıbe. Cıttpaċt páıtıc Donnbó go tfċ a máċtap, uaıp appıab tpí ıongancta an catа pa .ı. Donnbo bo poċtaın na ḃfcaıb go nıge a ṫfċ bap cfnn bpeıṫpe Coluım Cılle, ⁊ géım an trpuıṫ hUí Maıgléıne tpí la ⁊ tpí haıòċe 'pan aeop, ⁊ na naoı mıle bo popnaıpłıg an pıċıt, unbe bıcıtup :

   Caṫ Almaıne, áp gеın
   Móp an gníom Decembeıp

                Ro

---

[1] *If thou bring me.*—i.e. if thou art minded to bring me at all, find my body, and bring my head and body together.

[m] *To its body.*—Stories of this kind are very common in Irish. See the Registry of Clonmacnoise, printed in the "Transactions of the Kilkenny Archæological Society," for the story of Coirpre Crom,

made a compact last night that I would amuse the King to-night, and do not annoy me." "Which is the body of Fergal here?" said the young warrior. "Thou mayest observe it yonder," said the head. "Shall I take thee away?" said the young warrior; "thou art the dearest to me." "Bring me," said the head; "but may the grace of God be on thy head if thou bring me¹ to my body again." "I will indeed," said the young warrior. And the young warrior returned with the head to Condail the same night, and he found the Leinster-men drinking there on his arrival. "Hast thou brought a token with thee?" said Murchadh. "I have," replied the young warrior, "the head of Donnbo." "Place it on yonder post," said Murchadh: and the whole host knew it to be the head of Donnbo, and they all said: "Pity that this [fate] awaited thee, O Donnbo! fair was thy countenance; amuse us to-night, as thou didst thy lord last night." His face was turned, and he raised a most piteous strain in their presence, so that they were all wailing and lamenting! The same warrior conveyed the head to its body[m], as he had promised, and he fixed it on the neck [to which it instantly adhered, and Donnbo started into life]. In a word, Donnbo reached the house of his mother. The three wonders[n] of this battle were: the coming of Donnbo home to his house alive, in consequence of the pledged word of Colum Cille, and the shout of the clown Ua Maighleine, which remained [reverberating] three days and three nights in the air, and nine thousand prevailing over twenty-one thousand; *unde dicitur*:—

  The battle of Almhain, great the slaughter,
  Great the deed of December
               Which

whose head was put on by St. Ciaran of Clonmacnoise.

ⁿ *Three wonders*.—Three wonders are usually introduced into Irish romantic stories. Compare with the three wonders of the battle of Magh-Rath.

Ro bpıp Mupchaḋ mopḃa cpeać
Mac bpaın la laocpaıḋ laıġneać.
Meaṁaıḋ ap Feṅgal Faıl
Ap mac Maoılıḃuın ḃſpmaıp
Ḃo meltíp muılle po leıpġ
Ap lıncıḃ pola poıpḃepcc,
Oċt pıġ oċtmoġaḋ ıap ffíop
Naoı mıle, ġan ımappíoıṅ,
Do Leıt Cuınn comal nġnaoı
Do poċaıp ann ap aon ċaoı.
Naoı nġeılte pop ġealtaċt ḃe
Lottup ḃíoḃ pop Fıḃ nĠaıḃle,
Ra claoċloıḋpıc ḃaċ ıapttaın,
Apa ġleċca caċ Almaın.

haec punt nomına peġum quı ınteppectı punt ın hoc bello.
hı punt quıḋem ḋo píol ġCuınn.

Ffpġal mac Maoılıḃuın cum lx. mılıtıbup puıp; Fopbapaċ, pı
boġaıne; Ffpġal hUa Aıtfeḃa; Ffpġal Ua Taṁnaıġ; mac Eaċaċ
Leaṁna; Conġalaċ mac Conaıncc; Eıcneaċ mac Conaınġ; Coıb-
ḃenaċ mac Fıaċaıḋ; Conall Cpau; Ffpġap Ġlut; Muıpġſp mac
Conaıll; Lſtaıceaċ mac Conċapat; Anmċaıḋ mac Concapat; Aeḋ-
ġeın hUa Maıċe; Nuaḋa Uıpc pı Ġuıll ⁊ Ipġuıll, ı-ġ-Cınel Conuıll;
.x. nepotep Maoılpıcpıġ. Ite pın pıġ hUa Néıll an tuaıpcıpc.

hı autem quı pequuntup hUí Néıll an ḋepġıpt:—
Oıleıll mac Ffpaḃaıġ; Suıbne mac Conġalaıġ; Aoḋ Laıġſn
hUa

ᵒ *Of Fail.*—i. e. of Ireland.
ᵖ *Fidh-Gaibhle.*—A celebrated wood of Leinster, situated in the parish of Cloonsast, about five miles north of Portarlington, in the King's County. It is now locally called Fee-Guile, or Fig-Isle!
ᵠ *Boghaine.*—Now the barony of Bannagh, in the west of the county of Donegal.

Which the majestic Murchadh of plunders gained,
Son of Bran, with the heroes of Leinster.
It was gained over Fergal of Fail°,
The son of Maelduin the mighty;
So that mills in the plain did grind
[Turned] by ponds of red blood shed.
Eighty-eight kings, in truth,
Nine thousand [men], without exaggeration,
Of the men of Leth Chuinn, of fair faces,
Fell there in one battle-field.
Nine persons panic-stricken ran mad,
And went into the wood of Fidh-Gaibhle^p.
They changed colour afterwards,
For the Battle of Almhain blenched them.

These are the names of the kings who were slain in this battle. These were some of the race of Conn :—

Fergal, son of Maelduin, with sixty of his knights; Forbasach, King of Boghaine^q; Fergal Ua Aithechta; Fergal Ua Tamhnaigh, the son of Eochaidh Leamhna; Congalach, son of Conaing; Eignech, son of Conaing; Coibhdenach, son of Fiacha; Conall Cran; Fergal Glut; Muirghes, son of Conall; Letaithech, son of Cucarat; Aedhgen Ua Maithe; Nuada Uire, King of Gull and Irgull^r in Cinel-Conaill; ten grandsons of Maelfithrigh. These [foregoing] were the chiefs of the northern Ui-Neill.

The following were of the Ui-Neill of the south :—

Oilell, son of Feradhach; Suibhne, son of Conghalach; Aedh Laighen

^r *Gull and Irgull.*—Two territories in the north of the barony of Kilmacrenan, county of Donegal, more usually called Ros-guill and Ros-Irguill. The name of the former is still remembered, but that of the latter has been long forgotten.

hUa Cṙṁaıġ; Nıa mac Coṗmaıc; Cloëna mac Colġan; Caoġ mac Aıġtıɒe; Ouḃɒaėṗıoċ mac Oṁḃɒaḃaıṗṡın; Mṡcoṗṗaċ mac Ġamnaıġ; Eloḃaċ mac Flaınn 'O'Sġıġı; Ounċhaɒ Ua Fıaċṗaċ; mac Conloınġṗı; mac Maoılemona; Ooıṗıaɒ mac Cunla; Flann mac Aoḋa Oḃḃa; mac Concoınġelc; mac Cuaṫaıl mıc Faoléon; Inɒpṗċcaċ mac Caıöġ; mac Ġaṗbáın; ɒa Ua Maoılċaıċ; ɒa mac Aıleni; Focaṗca Ua Oomnaıll; Aılell mac Conaıll Ġṗaınc; Fıoġal mac Fıȯċheallaıġ; Oınḃoıl hUa Oaınıne ec ṗṗacep cıuṗ; ɒa mac Muıpṡḃaıġ mıc Inɒpṗċcaıġ; Nuaḃa mac Ouıḃɒunċuıṗe; Rṡcaṗṗa hUa Cumuṗcuıġ Ua Maıne; Cṡṗı Cṡṗa; Fṡıġaṗ Ua Eoġaın no Leoġaın; Flaıċeamaıl mac Olúṫaıġ; Oonġalaċ hUa Aonġaṗa; Conall Mṡın ṗí Cenıl Caıṗḃṗe; mac Eṗca mac Maoılıḃúın; Cṗí hUı Nuaḃac; Flann mac Ipġalaıġ; Aoɒ Laıġen mac Fıṫċeallaıġ; Nıall mac Muıṗġṗa.

Oolope aucem ec ṗṗıġoṗe moṗcuı ṗunc cl.xxx. caṗ cıṗ caṫa Almaıne ı ccopċmṗ Fṡıġal mac Maoılıḃúın, ꞇca.

Inıcıum ṗeġnı Cıonaɒa, mıc Ipġalaıġ, ṗecunɒum quoṗɒam.

Ral. Ro ġaḃ vno Foġaṗcaċ mac Néıll aınmnuġaɒ ṗıġe 'Eıṗenn ṗo ċéɒóıṗ ı nuṗġaıɒ Fṡıġal, aoın ḃlıaɒaın, no a ɒó ınxca quoṗɒam, ġo maṗḃaɒ la Cıonaoɒ Leıċċaıoċ mac Ipġalaıġ. Aṗ ṗaıṗ ṗo meaṁaıɒ an caṫ ı ꞇCaıltın ṗa Laıġnıḃ.

Cıonaoɒ ımuṗṗo ıaṗccaın cċıṗı ḃlıaḃna ı ṗıġe nEıṗenn. Aṗ ɒoṗaın ɒo ġeall Aḃamnan 7 ṗé a mḃṗoınn a máṫaṗ ġo nġeḃaɒ ṗıġe n-Eıṗenn. ḃa maıṫ vno ṗıġe an Cıonaoɒa. Inɒpaɒ Laıġen laıṗ an
ċéɒ

ᵘ *Odhbha.*—A place near Navan, in East Meath.

ᵗ *Cinel-Cairbre.*—A sept of the south Ui-Neill, situated in the barony of Granard, and county of Longford, to which barony the name is still locally applied.

ᵘ *Aedh Laighen, son of Fáthchellach.*—He was chief of Hy-Many, in Connaught.

ˣ *Lethchaech.*—i.e. half-blind. The word caoċ, written also coeċ or caeċ, as now used, does not always mean blind, though

Laighen Ua Cearnaigh; Nia, son of Cormac; Clothna, son of Colgan; Tadhg, son of Aigthide; Dubhdachrioch, son of Dubhdabhairenn; Mencossach, son of Gammach; Elodhach, son of Flann O'Sgigi; Donnchadh Ua Fiachrach; the son of Culoingsi; the son of Maelmona; Doiriadh, son of Conla; Flann, son of Aedh Odhbha°; son of Cucoingelt, son of Tuathal, son of Faelchu; Indrechtach, son of Tadhg; son of Garbhan; the two Ua Maclenichs; the two sons of Ailen; Focarta Ua Domhnaill; Ailell, son of Conall Grant; Fidhgal, son of Fithchellach; Duibhdil Ua Dainine, and his brother; the two sons of Muredhach, son of Indrechtach; Nuada, son of Dubhdunchuire; Rechtabhra, son of Cumascach Ua Maine; Cer of Cera; Ferghus Ua Eoghain (or Leoghain); Flaitheamhail, son of Dluthach; Donghalach Ua Aenghusa; Conall Menn, King of Cinel-Cairbre'; Mac-Erca, son of Maelduin; the three grandsons of Nuadhat; Flann, son of Irghalach; Aedh Laighen, son of Fithchellach"; Niall, son of Muirghes.

One hundred and eighty died of sickness and cold after the Battle of Almhain, in which Fergal, son of Maelduine, was slain, &c.

[724.] The beginning of the reign of Cinaedh, son of Irgalach, according to some.

[722.] Kal. After Fergal, Fogartach, son of Niall, took the name of King of Erin at once, for one year, or two, according to some, when he was killed by Cinaeth Lethchaech', son of Irgalach. He had been defeated by the Leinster-men in the Battle of Tailtin.

[724.] After him Cinaedh was king of Erin for four years. It was to him, while he was in his mother's womb, Adamnan had promised" that he would attain to the sovereignty of Erin. The reign of this

it is certainly cognate with the Latin *cæcus*. It generally means purblind or one-eyed.

" *Adamnan had promised.*—No notice of this promise has been found in any other Annals or historical tracts.

céo bliaoain ⁊ maiom ꝼoꝑ Ouncháo mac Muꝑchaoa, iꞅ ꝼochaioe oo ꝛaoꝑclanoaib ꝛo maꝑbao cꝛeꝑ an éozao ꝛo.

Inoꝑꝼecaé mac Muiꝑſoaiz, ꝛí Connacc, moꝑicuꝑ. Caé eioiꝑ Ouncháo mac Muꝑchaoa ⁊ Laiozném ꝛí hUa cCionnꝛꞅolaiz, ⁊ maioio an caé ꝼoꝑ Laiozneın.

Kal. Caé Cinnoelzcen i ccoꝛcuꝑ Pozaꝑcaé hUa Cſꝛnaiz. Cionaoo mac Ioꝑzalaiz uiccoꝑ eꝛac ; inoe Rumañ cecinic :—

Meamaio caé Cinn oelzéſn oo ꝛiz Ionó buiꝑꝑ,
Luio ſꝛzall oaꝑ ſꝛzail, caé ceiꝛoꝑeé oeꝛz Oomnaill.

Zo mbao iaꝑ maꝑbao Pozuꝑcaiz no zaĥao Cionaoo ꝛize iaꝑ ꝼꝼaiꝑino.

Cinnolſꝛ ab. Cluana mic Noiꝑ, Paolchu ab. Iae.

Kal. Colman Uamaé, ꝛaoi Oiꝑomaéa moꝑicuꝑ.

Colman banbáin, ꝛaoi Cille oaꝑa moꝑicuꝑ.

Mac Oileꝛain Cille ꝛuaio moꝑicuꝑ.

Kal. Cillene Poca ab. Iae.

Oachonna cꝛáibóeaé, Eꝑꝛcoꝑ Conoeiꝑe, quieuic.

Zuin Cꝑiomcainn mic Ceallaiz, mic Zeꝑcioe, ꝛiz Laizen, i ccaé bealaiz Lice. Zuin Ailella mic boubéaoa Miōe. Caé eioiꝑ

ˣ *Indrechtach, son of Muiredhach.*—His death is entered in the Annals of the Four Masters at the year 718, but it is an interpolation and a mistake.

ʸ *Dunchadh, son of Murchadh.*—Annals of Four Masters, 722 ; Annals of Ulster, 727.

ᶻ *Cenndelgthen.*—Annals of Four Masters, 720, Annals of Ulster, 723. The chronology is confused here. Fogartach Ua Cearnaigh was slain in 724, and was succeeded by Cinaedh, who reigned till 727.

—*Ogygia*, Part iii., c. 93.

ᵃ *Rumann.*—He is usually styled the Virgil of Erin, and died, according to the Annals of Tighernach, in the year 747. —Four Masters, 742 ; Annals of Ulster, 746.

ᵇ *Cuindles, &c.*—The obits of these two Abbots are entered in the Annals of Ulster under A. D. 723, but the true year is 724.

ᶜ *Colman Uamach.*—The death of this Abbot, and also of Banbain of Cill-dara, are

this Cinaeth was good. He plundered Leinster the first year, and defeated Dunchadh, son of Murchadh, and many of the nobles were killed during that war.

Indrechtach, son of Muiredhach[x], King of Connaught, died. A battle [was fought] between Dunchadh, son of Murchadh[y], and Laidhgnen, King of Ui-Cinnselaigh; and Laedhgnen was defeated.

Kal. The Battle of Cenndelgthen[z], in which was slain Fogartach Ua Cernaigh. Cinaedh, son of Irgalach, was the conqueror; on which Rumann[a] sung:

The Battle of Cenn-delgthen was gained by the strong mighty king. Battalion passed over battalion in the bloody battle of Domhnall.

[724.] It was after the killing of Fogartach that Cinaedh assumed the sovereignty, according to some.

Cuindles[b], Abbot of Cluain mic Nois, Faelchu, Abbot of Ia [died].

[725.] Kal. Colman Uamach[c], sage of Ard-macha, died.

Colman Banbain, sage of Cill-dara, died.

Mac Ailerain, of Cill-ruaidh[d], died.

[726.] Cillene[e] Fota, Abbot of Ia [died].

Dachonna[f], the Pious, Bishop of Coinneire, died.

The death of Crimhthann, son of Cellach, son of Geirtide, King of Leinster, in the Battle of Bealach-lice[g]; the death of Ailell, son of Bodhbhcha, of Meath. A battle [was fought] between Ederseel[h], King

entered in the Annals of the Four Masters at 720, but in the Annals of Ulster at 724. The true year, however, is 725.

[d] *Cill-ruaidh.*—Now Kilroot, in the barony of Upper Glenarm, county of Antrim. The obit of Mac Ailerain is not given in any of the published Annals.

[e] *Cillene.*—Four M., 725; Tigh. 726;

Reeves's "Adamnan," p. 382.

[f] *Dachonna.*—He was Bishop of Connor, and died, according to Four M., in 725.

[g] *Bealach-lice.*—i. e. road of the flagstone. See Ann. Four M., A. D. 721.

[h] *Ederseel*, King of Bregia: Compare Ann. Ult., 726.

eioip Eavappgél, pig bpíg, ⁊ Paolán, pí Laigín, ⁊ po meamaid ann pop Eatuppgél, pí bpeag.

Ip in bliadain peo po mapbad Cionaod Caoċ mac Iopgalaig, ⁊ níop gab neaċ va píol pige n-'Eipenn. Plaitbfpitaċ mac Loinpig pop mapb.

Initium pegni Plaitbfpitaig.

Kal. 'San bliadain pi po bpip Aongap, pí Poiptpeann, tpí cata pop Opupt pig Alban. Caċ Opoma Popnoċta eioip Cenel Conaill ⁊ Eogain, i ttopċaip Plann mac Ioptuile, ⁊ Snedgup Deapg hUa bpaċaide.

Adamnani peliquiae in hibepniam tpanpfepuntup, et lex eiup penonatup. bap Mupchada mic bpain, pig Laigín. Caċ Maiptin ioip Laignib péin; meamaid imuppo pé n-Uib Dunlaing pop Uib cCionnpiolaig, i ttopċaip Laodpin, ⁊ mac Conmella, pí hUa g-Cinnpiolaig, ⁊ Aongap mac Paolċon mic Paolain, ⁊ Cfthepnach mac Naoi hUi Ceallaig. Dunchad uictop epat.

Caċ boipne, no Inpi bpeogain, eioip peapaib Life ⁊ peapaib Cualann ⁊ Congal mac bpain. Paolan uictop punt.

Dopinitacio Céle Cpíopo.

Kal. Plann ab. bſinchaip quievit. Leo Aug. mopitup. Caċ Opoma

---

ⁱ *Flaithbhertach.*—The true year of his accession was A.D. 727. The Four M. are wrong in placing it in 723.

ʲ *Fortrenn.*—i. e. Pictland, in Scotland. This entry is not in the published Annals. The Annals of Ulster have at 725—" Nechtain mac Deirile *constringitur apud Druist Regem:*" Reeves's "Adamnan," p. 382.

ᵏ *Druim-fornachl.*—A place near Newry, in the Co. Down. The Four M. place this battle under A. D. 721, but the Ann. Ult. under 726; the true year being 727.

ˡ *Relics of Adamnan.*—Ann. Ult. 726. The law of Adamnan, here referred to, prohibited women from going into battle, or on military expeditions.—Reeves's "Adamnan," p. 383, Pref. l.-liii.

ᵐ *Murchadh, son of Bran.*—Ann. Four M., 721; Ann. Ult., 726.

ⁿ *Maistin.*—Now Mullaghmast, near Athy, in the county of Kildare.

King of Bregh, and Faelan, King of Leinster, in which Edersccl, King of Bregh, was defeated.

[727.] In this year Cinaedh Caech [the blind], son of Irgalach, was slain, and none of his descendants assumed the monarchy of Erin. Flaithbhertach, son of Loingsech, was he who killed him.

The beginning of the reign of Flaithbhertach[i].

Kal. In this year Aenghus, King of Fortrenn[j], gained three battles over Drust, King of Alba [Scotland]. The Battle of Druim-Fornacht[k] [was fought] between the Cinel Conaill and Cinel-Eoghain, in which were slain Flann, son of Irthuile, and Snedhgus Derg Ua Brachaidhe.

The relics of Adamnan[l] were translated to Erin, and his law was renewed. The death of Murchadh, son of Bran[m], King of Leinster; the Battle of Maistin[n] [was fought] between the Leinster-men themselves, in which the Ui-Dunlaing defeated the Ui-Ceinnsealaigh, in which Laidhcenn Mac Connella, King of Ui-Ceinsellaigh, and Aenghus, son of Faelchu, son of Faelan, and Cethernach, son of Nae Ua Ceallaigh, were slain. Donnchadh was the victor.

The Battle of Boirinn, or of Inis-Breoghain[o], was fought between the men of Liffe and the men of Cualann, and Congal, son of Bran. Faelan was the victor.

The rest of Cele-Christ[p].

[728.] Kal. Flann, Abbot of Bennchair[q], died. Leo Augustus died[r]. The

---

[o] *Inis-Breoghain.*—i. e. Breogan's Island. This place has not been yet identified. This battle is entered in the Ann. Ult. at the year 726, but the true year is 727. The Four M. are wrong in placing it under 721.

[p] *Cele-Christ.*—i. e. the servant, or vassal of Christ. His death is entered in the Ann. Ult. at 726; Tighern. 727; Four M. 721.

[q] *Flann, Abbot of Benchair.*—He is called Flann Acntroibh, Four M. 722; Ann. Ult. 727; Tighern. 728.

[r] *Leo Augustus.*—This must be Leo III., "the Isaurian." Died, June, 741, after a reign of 24 years.

Оротa Сорсаіп еібір Flаітвеарсас mас Loіngгіg ⁊ mас Іогgа-
lаіg, і тторесаір Сіопаоє ⁊ Єоѓир mас Аilеllа, ⁊ Маolоúіп mас
Fсаѓраvаіg, ⁊ Dunchаv mас Соѓіпаіс.

Сат́ Аіllіne еіöір vá mас Мuѓрchаvа mіс бpаіп .і. Fаolán ⁊
Dunchаv. Fаоlап іuпіор mісtор fuіт. ет pеgпаuіт. Сат́аl mас
Fіоngаіпe ⁊ Ceallас́ mас Fаоlес́аір, ѓí Оѓраіgе euаrерuпт. Duп-
сhаv mас Мuѓрchаvа, pі Lаіgfп іптеѓѓрестuѓр ерт. Ас́т с́fпа
тéѓпа Dunchаv аѓр ап с́ат́, ⁊ bаоі ѓреастmаіп 'па ufthаіv.
Ѕаbаіv Fаоlап pіgе Lаіgfп, ⁊ атпаіg mпаі ап Dunchаvа .і. Тuа-
lаіт́, іпgfп Сат́аіl mіс Fіоngаіnе, pі Мumhап.

Domnаll, pі Соппас́t, moріturp.

In hoc anno compoѓuiт bеva opuѓр ѓuum magnum, hoc ерт, іп
nono anno Lеопір.

Kаl. Єсbеѓрtuѓр ѓапсtuѓр Сhnіѓртi míleѓ іп hi-Соluіm Сіllі
quіеuіт. bеvа іп Сѓромеір сеѓѓрат.

Kаl. Мас Onс́on ѓеѓрibа Сіlle Daѓра ; Suіbпе ab Арv mас́а
quіеuіt ; Ѕаll ó Lіlсаіg .і. ѓѓрuvеnѓр quіеuіт ; Мас Сопсumbѓі
ѓuí Сluапа mіс Noір ; Аonguѓр mас beссe bаіѓрсе moріturp ;
Сосаll ovaѓр ѓuí bfпс́аір moріtuѓр.

Сат́ Fеарпmаіgе ітіp Сетаmun * *

Kаl. Colman hUа Lіаттаіп ѓеlіgіопір vostop [obіtт].
Eoсhаіv mас Colgáіп, ab Аѓv Мас́hа, moріturp.

Сат́

* *Druim Corcain.*—Ann. Ult. 727; Tighern. 728.

ʰ *Aillinn.*—Now Dun Aillinne, near Old Kilcullen, in the county of Kildare: Ann. Ult., 727. "*Bellum* Ailenne *inter duos germanos filios* Murchada, mic Brain, *et* Duncha, *senior jugulatur; junior Foelanus regnat.* .... Domhnall mac Ceallaig, *rex* Connacht, *moritur.*"

ⁿ *Beda.*—Bede died in the year 734, according to the Saxon Chronicle and the Annals of Ulster, but the true year is 735. No account is given in any other work of the year in which he composed, or put out, his great work. The Emperor, Leo III., succeeded in March, 718, so that the tenth year of his reign was 727, when Bede is said to have composed [i. e. perhaps, pub-

The Battle of Druim Corcain[s] [was fought] between Flaithbhertach, son of Loingsech, and the son of Irgalach, in which were slain Cinaeth and Eodus, son of Ailell, and Maelduin, son of Feradhach, and Dunchadh, son of Cormac.

The Battle of Aillinn[t], between the two sons of Murchadh, son of Brann, i. e. Faelan and Dunchadh. Faelan, who was the junior, conquered and reigned; Cathal, son of Fingaine [King of Munster], and Cellach, son of Faelchair, King of Osraighe, escaped. Dunchadh, son of Murchadh, King of Leinster, was slain; but he survived the battle, and lived for a week after it. Faelan assumed the sovereignty of Leinster, and married the wife of Dunchadh; namely, Tualaith, daughter of Cathal, son of Fingaine, King of Munster.

Domhnall, King of Connaught, died.

In hoc anno composuit Beda[u] suum magnum opus, hoc est in nono anno Leonis.

[729.] Kal. Ecbertus[v] sanctus Christi miles in Hi-Coluim Cille quievit. Beda in Chronicis cessat.

[730.] Kal. Mac-Onchon[w], scribe of Cill-dara, and Suibhne, Abbot of Ard-Macha, quievit; Gall of Lilcach, i. e. the prudent, quievit; Mac-Concumhri, sage of Cluain-mic-nois; Aengus, son of Bec Boirche, died; Cochall Odhar, sage of Benchair, died.

The battle of Fernmhagh[x], between Cetamun * *

[731.] Kal. Colman Ua Altain[y], a religious doctor, died.

Colgu, son of Eochaidh, Abbot of Ard-macha, died.

[733]

lished] his work; for it is not to be supposed that Bede composed his work in one year.

[v] *Ecbertus.*—He died at Hy, according to Bede, and the Saxon Chronicle, on Easter Sunday, the 24th of April, A. D. 729.—Reeves's "Adamnan," p. 379, 383.

[w] *Mac-Onchon.*—Ann. Ult. 729; Tigh. 730.

[x] *Fernmhagh.*—Now Farney, a barony in the county of Monaghan. This entry is not in any of the published Annals. It is left unfinished in our MS.

[y] *Colman Ua Altain.*—A. D. 730. "Col-

Cat do bpipeb do Aod Allan mac Fpiṡail pop Plaitbeaptach mac Loinṡpiṡ, pí 'Eipenn, ṡo otuṡ Plaitbeaptaċ loinṡiup a Poptpcannoib ċuiṡe a n-aiṡib Cinéil Eoṡain, aċt ċfia pa báideab eapṁóp an ċobláiṡ pin. Mopp Plaitbeaptaiṡ péin 'pin bliadain pin, ⁊ pṡaptain piṡe n'Eipenn pe Cenel ṡConaill ṡo pada iaptcain.

Ip in bliadain pi ad ċfp an bó ⁊ pé copa púiċe, ⁊ da copp aice, ⁊ aoin cfin; po bliṡed po tpí hí caċ .í. laoí .i. nDeilṡinip Cualann. Kal. Aod Allain mac Fpiṡail do ṡabáil piṡe n-'Eipenn. Plann Sionna hUa Colla ab Cluana mic Nóip.

Ppincepp no pontipex Maiṡe eo na Saxon ṡapolt obit.

Sebdann inṡen Chuipc, abbatippa Cille dapa [d'écc].

Cat Connacht ittip [. . . . in quo ceciditt] Muipeadaċ mac Indpeactaiṡ.

Cat do bpipiod d'Aod Allan pop Ultoib, itip Aod Róin pí Ulad ⁊ Concad pi Cpuiċne a pPochaipd Muipċeṁne, ttfinpall Pochapd ata opd Aoba Róin.

Cat do pidpi edip Aod Allan ⁊ Cenel Conaill, ittip Conainṡ mac

man *nepos* Littain, *religiosus doctor pausat. Mors* Echdach mic Colggen *Anachorete Ardmache."—Ann. Ult.*

¹ *In that year.*—This battle was fought in 734, in which King Flaithbheartach died. The chronology of the Four Masters is incorrect. For Fortrenn the F. M. and Ann. Clonn. have Dal-Riada.

ª *Deilginis-Cualann.*—Now Dalkey Island, near Dublin. F. M. 727; Ann. Clonm. 730 ; Ann. Ult. 732 ; but the true year would be 734, according to our text.

ᵇ *Aedh Allan.—*F. M. 730 ; Ann. Ult. 733; Tigh. 734.

ᶜ *Flann Sinna Ua Colla.*—This and the two obits succeeding are entered in the Ann. F. M. under 726, and in the Ann. Ult. under 731 ; but the true year is 732 (Tigh.), and they are clearly misplaced above.

ᵈ *Muiredhach, son of Indrechtach.*—The F. M. make him Bishop of *Magh-eo-na Saxon*, and enter his death under 726, but they are totally wrong. In the Ann. Ult. 731, and Tigh. 732, the true reading may be translated thus :—" The battle of Connacht, wherein fell Muireadhach, son of Indrechtach. *Pontifex Maighe heo Sax-*

[733, or 734.] Kal. A battle was gained by Aedh Allan, son of Fergal, over Flaithbhertach, son of Loingsech, King of Erin, so that Flaithbhertach brought a fleet out of Fortrenn [Pictland] to assist him against the Cinel-Eoghain. The greater part of that fleet was, however, drowned. The death of Flaithbhertach himself took place in that year[z], and the sovereignty of Erin was separated from the Cinel-Conaill for a long time afterwards. In this year was seen a cow with six legs under her, and two bodies, and one head. She was milked thrice each day; i. e. at Deilginis-Cnalann[a].

[734.] Kal. Aedh Allan[b], son of Fergal, assumed the sovereignty of Erin.

Flann Sinna Ua Colla[c], Abbot of Cluain-mic-nois [died].

[732.] Gerald, pontifex of Maigheo [Mayo] of the Saxons, died. Sebhdan, daughter of Core, Abbess of Cill-dara [died].

A battle in Connaught between [. . . . . in which fell] Muiredhach, son of Indrechtach[d].

A battle was gained by Aedh Allan over the Ulta, at Fochard-Muirtheimhne[e]; i. e. over Aedh Roin, King of Uladh, and Conchadh, King of the Cruithnigh[f]. In the church of Fochard the Ord [thumb] of Aedh Roin is [preserved].

Another battle was fought between Aedh Allan and the Cinel-Conaill;

onum Garaalt obit."—See Ann. F. M., Ed. J. O'D., p. 324.

[e] *Fochard-Muirtheimhne.*— Now the church of Faughard, in the county of Louth, about two miles to the north of Dundalk. This battle is noticed in the Ann. F. M. at the year 732; Ult. 734; Tigh. 735.

[f] *Cruithnigh.*—i. e. of the Picts, i. e. of the Picts of Ulster. The Ann. Ult. and Tigh. call him "Conchad mac Cuanach rex Coba (ṗ Cobha, *Tigh.*). The F. M. call him chief of East Ulster, Co. Down, and add, that the head of Aedh Roin was cut off on a stone called Clochan-commaigh, in the doorway of the church of Fochard, and that the cause of the battle was the profanation of the church of Cill-Conna [now Kilcoony, in Tyrone] by Ua Seghain, one of the people of Aedh Roin.

mac Congaile mic Feargapa Fánav. Cat Catail vo Domnall i tTailltin.

Kal. Oegsócap Eppcop nGonopoma quieuit.
beva Sapienp lxxxiii anno aetatir ruae quieuit.

[FRAGMENTUM II.]

ALIUD FRAGMENTUM ex eovem Covice extractum pep eunvum; incipienp ab anno cipcitep 661.

Kal. Cuimin Fova quieuit lxxii anno aetatir ruae unve Colman Ua Cluaraig, aive Cuimin cecinit:

 Marb frim anofr, marb antuaiv,
  Nibttup ionmuin aérluaig,
 Do roir a rí nime glair
  An vocairte tatar lair.
 Marbáin na bliavna ra,
  Ní bo caointe ní occa,
 Maolvuin becc mac Feargura,
  Conainn, Cuimin Fova.

           Má

---

[a] *Conaing, son of Congal.*—He was slain in the year 732 [733, *Tigh.*] in the battle of Magh-Itha, according to the Ann. Ult., F. M. 727. "*Congressio iterum inter* Aedh [Allan] mac Fergaile et *Genus* Conaill in Campo Itho, *ubi cecidit* Conaing mac Congaile mic Ferguso [Fanaid] et *ceteri multi.*"—*Ann. Ult.* 732. This battle is misplaced in our text. It was fought in the reign of Flaithbheartach.

[b] *The battle of Cathal.*—This is a mistake. It is entered in the Ann. F. M. at 732, but in the Ann. Ult. at 736. Thus:— "*Congressio invicem inter Nepotes* Aedo Slaine *ubi* Conaing mac Amalgaid *moritur;* Cernach *vicit,* et Cathal mac Aedo *cecidit; juxta lapidem* Ailbe *ab orientali parte gesta est.*" See Tigh. 737.

[i] *Oeghedhchar.*—He was Bishop of Nendrum, an island in Lough Cuan, in the

Conaill; [i. e.] between Conaing, son of Congal[g], son of Fergus of Fanaid. .... The battle of Cathal[h], by Domhnall at Tailltin.
[734.] Kal. Oeghedhchar[i], Bishop of Ocndruim, quievit.
[734, or 735.] Beda Sapiens[k] lxxxiii'., anno ætatis suæ quievit.

[FRAGMENT II.]

ANOTHER FRAGMENT extracted from the same Manuscript, by the same, beginning about the year 661.

[662.] Kal. Cuimin Foda[l] died in the seventy-second year of his age; hence Colman Ua Cluasaigh[m], tutor of Cuimin, sung:

Dead to me is the south, dead the north,
No second host is dear to me;
Relieve, O King of the blue heaven,
The sufferings that are with it.
The deaths of this year,—
Not one of them should be lamented[n],—
[Were] Maelduin Beg, son of Fergus
Conainn, Cuimin Foda.

If county of Down.—*Ann. Ult.* 734; *Tigh.* 735.

[k] *Beda Sapiens.*—Ann. Ult. 734; Tigh. 735. Bede was born in the year 673, and died in the year 735, in the sixty-third year of his age. Therefore, either two of the x's should be struck out of our text, or all English authorities which treat of his age are incorrect, which is not likely.

[l] *Cuimin Foda.*—i. e. Cuimin, the Long or Tall. He was Bishop of Clonfert. See Four M. and Ann. Ult. 661 ; Book of Hymns, p. 84, *sq.*

[m] *Colman Ua Cluasaigh.*—He was the tutor of Cuimine Foda, and died in the same year.

[n] *Should be lamented.*—Because they all went straightways to heaven, and there was no need of sorrowing after them. See Colgan's "Acta SS.," p. 149, Note 7.

Má ro oligthe rri oap muip
  Seirfò irrpuite nGriogoir,
  Mað a h-Eipinn ní baoí ní oó
  Inge Cuinine Poòo.
Seaċ ba heprcoprom rom ba 'pí,
  ba mac tigeapna mo Chuimin
  Tfnoal 'Eirenn ap roar,
  ba h-alainn map ro choar.
Mait a ċeinel, mait a ċput,
  bá lċan a comrlonnaò
  Ua Coirppe ⁊ Ua Cuirc,
  ba raoi, ba hán, ba hoiroerc.

Cat Ogamain, ou i ttorchair Conaing mac Congaile, agur Ultan mac Epinne, pi Ciannachta. blatmac mac Cloòa Slaine uictur ert a rocur Diarmaoa. Maonac mac Pingín pi Muirhan moriturp.

Kal. Seigine .i. Mac hu Cuinio, ab bfnchair quieuit.

Morr Guaire Ciöne, pí Connact, unoc—

  Capn Conaill morpluag pile na comair
  bi marb uile ciata bi,
  Durrann oo Guaire Ciöni.

Guin

ᵃ *A man over sea.*—i. e. a foreigner, viz. in reference to Italy. No Irishman ever yet was Pope of Rome. These lines are given differently by the Four Masters. The Irish, however, claimed Gregory the Great (whom they styled of the golden mouth) as one of their race, and they have engrafted his pedigree on the regal Irish stem of Conaire II., the ancestor of the O'Connells, the O'Falveys, and other families. The O'Clerys give his pedigree as follows in their work on the Genealogies of the Irish Saints :—" Gregory of Rome, son of Gormalta, son of Conla, son of Arda, son of Dathi, son of Core, son of Conn, son of Cormac, son of Core Duibhne, son of Cairbre Muse, son of Conaire." Baronius, however, shows from better evidence that he was born at Rome of a patrician family, being the son of Sylvea and Gordian, the

If it were ordained that a man over sea[o]
   Should sit [as Pope] more learned than Gregory,
   If from Erin, no one for it
   Except Cuimine Foda.
He was not more bishop than king;
   My Cuimin was the son of a lord[p],
   The lamp of Erin for his knowledge,
   He was beautiful, as all have heard.
Good was his race, good his form,
   Extensive was his kindred,
   Descendant of Coirpre, descendant of Core,
   He was a sage, noble, illustrious.

[662.] The battle of Ogaman[q], in which fell Conaing, son of Congal, and Ultan, son of Ernin, King of Cianachta. Blathmac, son of Aedh Slaine, was conquered by the followers of Diarmaid. Maenach, son of Finghin, King of Munster, died.

[663.] Kal. Seigine[r], i. e. Mac hu Cuinn, Abbot of Benchar, died. The death of Guaire Aidhne, King of Connaught, whence [the verses]:

   Carn-Conaill; a great host is near it;
   They were all killed, though lively,
   Sorrowful it was to Guaire Aidhne.

The noblest of the Senate, and the grandson of Felix, who had been Pope himself.

[p] *Son of a lord.*—He was an incestuous child, and his tutor, St. Colman O'Cluasaigh, might well have omitted this boastful allusion to his pedigree. This is quoted in Cormac's Glossary, *sub voce* ꞅaın. Many illegitimate children became distinguished saints, as well as Cuimine Foda. See Dr. Todd's remarks on this subject, *Liber Hymnor.*, p. 92.

[q] *Ogaman.*—Not identified. See Ann. Clon. 658; Ann. F. M. 660; Ann. Ult. 661; Tigh. 662.

[r] *Seigene.*—A. D. 662. "*Quies* Segain mice U Chuinn abb benchoıp et. *Mors* Guaire Aidhne; Jugulatio ii. filiorum Domnaill filii Aedo .i. Conall et Colgu.

Ѕuin ʋa mac Ɗomnaill .i. Conall aɢur Colɢa. Tuaċal mac Moрɢainn moрicuр.
Tuenoc mac Ƒiontain aƀ Ƒeaрna móiрe ꝗuieuit. Ƃaoʋan aƀ Cluana mic Nóiр.
Kal. Moрluiʋ mac Aoʋa Slàine .i. ƀlaċṁac [⁊ Ɗiaрmaiʋ]ꝟ cCalatрuim. Ƃa mapƀ Ɗiapmaiʋ ʋono iрin ionaʋ céʋna, aɢuр ré рince рe Cрoiр na рſjаṁ aɢ рaiɢрin рluaiɢ Laiɢen ċuiɢe ʋa marƀaʋ; рa cnaiʋ a a In ꝗuiƀuрʋaṁ liƀрiр inueniтuр ꝗuoʋ hi ʋuo рeɢeр .i. ƀlaċṁac ⁊ ʋiaрmaiʋ xn. annir, in ꝗuiƀuрʋam — annir ꝗuor nor рeꝗuimuр. Maрƀ tрa ʋon morтlaiʋ рin .i. ʋo'n ƀuiʋe Conaill, na ʋá miɢ рi Єiрenn .i. ƀlaċṁac ⁊ Ɗiaрmaiʋ.
Ƒeċin Ƒoƀaiр; Ailſian an ſɢna; Colmán Caр, aɢuр Aonɢuр Ulaiʋ. Ceiтрe aƀaiʋ ƀſnċaiр .i. ƀſnaċ, Cuimine, Coluim, aɢuр Aoʋán.
Cu ɢan máтaiр, ni Iluṁan, eт cum ceтeрiр тam рluрimir. Єochaiʋ Iaрlaiċe рí Ɗail Aрaiʋe ʋo marƀaʋ ʋo coṁalтoiƀ Maoilрoтhaртaiɢ mic Ronáin. Uaiр inɢſn ʋ'Єochaiʋ Iaрlaiċe рo Ƃaoi aɢ Ronáin aɢ рi Laiɢſn; óɢ an inɢſn, рſn an Ronán, ɢo тtuɢ рí ɢрáʋ ʋo ṁac Ronáin .i. ʋo Maolрoтhaртaiɢ, ⁊ ɢo рaiƀ рí ɢá ɢuiʋe ɢo рaʋa, aɢuр ní рuaiр uaiʋ a рaoṁaʋ, ⁊ óр ná рuaiр aрeaʋ

Mors Gartnaid filii Domnaill, et Domnaill mic Totholain. Mors Tuathail mic Morgaind. Tuenog filius Finntin, abba Fernann, Indereach *episcopus*, Dima *episcopus* *quiescunt.*"—*Ann. Ult.* See Tigh. 663.

ˢ *Baedan.*—Ann. F. M. 663; Ann. Clonm. 660; Ann. Ult. 663; Tigh. 664.

ᵗ *The plague.*—i. e. the Buidhe Chonnaile. See Ann. F. M.; Ann. Clon. 661; Ann. Ult. 664; Tigh. 665.

ᵘ *Caltruim.*—Now Galtrim, in the county of Meath. This plague is also mentioned by Bede, who writes that in the year 664 a sudden pestilence depopulated the southern coasts of Britain, and afterwards, extending into the province of the Northumbrians, ravaged the country far and near, and destroyed a great multitude of men. He also states that it did no less harm in the island of Hibernia, where many of the nobility and of the lower ranks of the English nation were

The mortal wounding of the two sons of Domhnall, i. e. Conall and Colgu. Tuathal, son of Morgann, died.

Tuenoc, son of Fintan, abbot of Ferna-mor, died; Baedan[s], Abbot of Cluain-mic-Nois, died.

[664.] Kal. The death of the sons of Aedh Slaine by the plague[t]; namely, Blathmac and Diarmaid, at Caltruim[u]. Diarmaid died at the same place, while he was standing up with his back against a cross viewing the hosts of Leinster approaching him to kill him. He went, &c. &c. It is found in certain books that these two kings, Blathmac and Diarmaid, reigned twelve years, but in others . . . . years[v], *quos nos sequimur*. Of this plague, i. e. of the Buidhe Chonaill, these two Kings of Erinn, Blathmac and Diarmaid, died.

Fechin of Fobhar[w], Aileran the wise, Colman Cas, and Aengus Uladh, died. Four abbots of Bennchair : viz. Berach, Cuimine, Colum, and Aedhan [died].

Cugannathair, King of Munster, died, with many others. Eochaidh Iarlaithe[x], King of Dal-Araidhe, was slain by the foster-brothers of Maelfothartaigh, son of Ronan ; for the daughter of Eochaidh Iarlaithe was married to Ronan, King of Leinster ; the daughter was young, Ronan was old, so that she loved Ronan's son, i. e. Maelfothartaigh, and she was courting him, but she obtained not his consent, and when she did not, what she did was to tear her head-dress[y], to scratch and bleed her face, and to come into the presence of Ronan in this plight

at that time studying theology or leading monastic lives, the Scoti supplying them with food, and furnishing them with books and their teaching gratis. See also Colgan's "Acta SS.," p. 601.

[v] *Years.*—Here the number of years is left blank in the MS.

[w] *Fobhar.*—Now Fore, in the county of Westmeath. The Four Masters have these entries at the year 664, which is the true year.

[x] *Eochaidh Iarlaithe.*—He is called King of the Cruithnigh, or Picts of Ulster, in the Ann. F. M. 665.

[y] *Her head-dress.*—This story is not found in the other Annals.

K

aɼeaḋ ꝺo ꝑiʒne, cumꝺać a cinn ꝺo ṁionuʒaḋ ⁊ a haiʒiḋ ꝺo
ɼʒɼíobaḋ, ⁊ ꝑuilɼeḋ 'ma haiʒiḋ, aʒuɼ coiḋeaċc ꝺ'ionnɼoiʒ Ronain
aṁlaiḋ ɼin. Cɼſo ɼin? a inʒſn, aɼ Ronán. Ꝺo ṁac ɼuʒać-ɼa,
aɼ ɼí, Maolꝑaċhaɼcaiʒ, ꝺom ɼáꝑuʒhaḋ, ⁊ mo ḃɼiɼioḋ ḋó, ⁊ comꝑac
ꝑɼium. Maɼḃċaɼ Maolꝑoċhaɼcaiʒ la Ronan iaɼ ɼin. Ciaʒaiꝺ
ꝺno comalcaḋa Maolꝑoċhaɼcaiʒ iaɼ ɼin ʒo nuiʒ bail i ꝑaibe
Eoċuiḋ laꝑlaiċe, ⁊ ʒaiɼimio leo amać é o ċáċ, ⁊ maɼḃaiꝺ i ʒcionca
na noſꝑna a inʒſn. Unꝺe Plaiccip cecinic :—

Inꝺiu ꝺellioʒaiɼ liʒe
Eochaḋa mic Piachach Luɼʒan,
I n-uiɼ cille Coinꝺeiɼe
Ro ʒaḃ ꝑoiċſɼ a ʒulban.
Ro ʒaḃ Eochaiḋ aon ċaimɼe
Ina liʒe-leabaiḋ oiɼċċhe.
Ḃɼónan ꝑil ꝑoɼ cċ ḋuine
Acá ꝑoɼ Ꝺun Soḃaiɼce.

Iniċium ɼeʒni Sſenaɼaiʒ mic blaċmaic, u. anniɼ. R. E.

Ḳal. Moɼɼ Oilella mic Ꝺoṁnaill, mic Aoḋa, mic Ainmi-
ɼioc.

Ḳal. Maolċaić mac Scanꝺail, ɼi Cɼuiċne moɼicuɼ. ḃaoiċin
ab ḃſnnċuɼɼ.

Ḳal. Cɼíoċán ab ḃſnꝺcuiɼ quieuic. Cuimin Pionn, ab Iae,
quieuic. Iomɼam Columbani cum ɼeliquiɼ mulcoɼum ɼancċoɼum
ʒo

ᵃ *Conneire.*—Now Connor, the head of an ancient episcopal see in the county of Antrim. The name is still locally pronounced *Connyer,* not *Connor*.

ᵃ *Dun-Sobhairce.*—Now Dunseverick, in the north of the county of Antrim.

ᵇ *Seehnasach.*—He succeeded in the year 665, and died in 671. See " Ogygia," p. 431.

ᶜ *Ailell, son of Dohmnall.*—His death is entered in the Ann. F. M. 665, but the true year was 666.

ᵈ *Maeleaich.*—F. M. 665 [*recte* 667].

ᵉ *Critan.*—Ann. Ult. 668 [*recte* 669].

plight. "What is this, my girl?" said Ronan. "Thy wanton son, Maelfothartaigh," said she, "has violated and forced me, and cohabited with me." After this Maelfothartaigh was killed by Ronan. But the foster-brothers of Maelfothartaigh afterwards came to where Eochaidh Iarlaithe was, and they called him out from all his people, and killed him, in revenge of what his daughter had done. Unde Flaithir cecinit:—

> This day distinguished the grave
> Of Eochaidh, son of Fiacha Lurgan,
> In the earth of the church of Conneire[z],
> Which has received the great heat of his mouth.
> Eochaidh has received one shirt
> In his grave-bed, slaughtered,
> Which has brought sorrow upon every person
> Who is at Dun-Sobhairce[a].

[665.] The beginning of the reign of Sechnasach[b], son of Blathmac, quinque annis, King of Erin.

[666.] Kal. The death of Ailell, son of Domhnall[c], son of Aedh, son of Ainmire.

[667.] Kal. Maelcaich[d], son of Scandal, King of the Cruithne, died. Baithin, abbot of Benchair, quievit.

[669.] Kal. Critan[e], abbot of Benchair, quievit. Cuimin Finn[f], abbot of Ia, quievit. The sailing of Colman[g], with the relics of many saints,

---

[f] *Cuimin Finn.*—i. e. "Comyn the Whyte," Ann. Clonn., Ann. Ult., 668 [*recte* 669]. This is the celebrated Cumineus Albus mentioned by Adamnan as author of a book on the virtues of St. Columbkille. He was also the author of a very curious letter on the Pascal Controversy, published by Ussher in his "Sylloge," No. 11.

[g] *Colman.*—The sailing of Colman to Inis-bo-finne, or *Insula vaccæ albæ* (now Bophin Island, situated off the west coast of the barony of Muresk, in the south-west of the county of Mayo), is given in the

go hImp bó pinne, ubi punoamt ccclepiam. Cat peiptpi icip
Ulcuib ⁊ Cpuitne, in quo cecioit Catupac mac Luippgne, pi Ulaö.
Mopp Ounchaöa hUi Ronáin. Paolan mac Colmain pi Laigen
mopicup. Mopp Maoilpothaptaig mic Suibne, pi hUu tTuiptpe.
Cat Oamoeipg, i ttopchupp Oiocuill mac Eachac, ⁊ Congal mac
Loicine. Zuin bpain pinn mic Maoilóctpaig, pí na nOépi.
Kal. Mopp blatmaic mic Maoilcoba.
Kal. Zuin Scenapaig, mic blatmaic R. E. Ouibouin ⁊c̄a., do
Chaipbpib po mapb i ppill Scenapac: de quo dicitup:

ba pianac, ba heaclapgac
An teac i mbíoö Scenapac,
ba hiomöa puideall pop plaic
I ttig i mbíoö mac blatmaic.

Oppu, pi Saxon mopicup. Conptantinup Aug. mopicup.
Lopgad bfnncaip la bpeatnaib. Lopgad Apomacha.
Mopp Cumapgaig mic Ronáin.
Cat Opoma Coepp. Cat Tolca ápo, ou i ttopcaip Oungaile
mac Maoiletuile, pi bogaine. Loingpioch uictop pint. Copmac
mac Maoilpothaptaig mopicup.

Initium

Ann. Ult. at A. D. 667. See also Bede's
"Eccl. Hist.," lib. iv., c. 4, and Ussher's
"Primordia," p. 825, 964, 1164, and
O'Flaherty's "West Connaught," pp. 115, 294.

ʰ *Fersat.*—Ann. Tigh. 666; Ann. Ult. 667. This was probably the *Fersat*, or ford, which gave name to Bel-ferste, now Belfast.

ⁱ *Ui-Tuirtre.*—A tribe giving name to a territory comprising the present baronies of Upper and Lower Toome, in the county of Antrim.—*Four Masters*, A. D. 668, p. 280, note ᵏ.

ᵏ *Damhderg.*—This was the name of a place in Bregia, but it has not been yet identified. See F. M., A. D. 738.

ˡ *Deisi.*—i. e. Decies, in the present county of Waterford.

ᵐ *Seehnasach.*—Ann. Ult. 670. The true year was 671.

ⁿ *Ossa.*—i. e. Osney, King of the Northumbrian Saxons, who died, according to the Saxon Chronicle, 15th Feb., 670.

saints, to the island of Inis-bo-finne, where he founded a church. The battle of Fersat[h], between the Ulta [Ulstermen] and the Cruithni, in which was slain Cathasach, son of Luirgne, King of Uladh ; the death of Dunchadh Ua Ronain ; Faelan, son of Colman, King of Leinster, died. The death of Maelfothartaigh, son of Suibhne, King of the Ui-Tuirtre[i]. The battle of Damhderg[k], in which were slain Dicuill, son of Eochaidh, and Congal, son of Loichine. The mortal wounding of Bran, son of Maelochtraigh, King of the Deisi[l].

[670.] Kal. The death of Blathmac, son of Maelcobha.

[671.] Kal. The mortal wounding of Sechnasach[m], son of Blathmac, King of Erin. Duibhduin, and others of the Cairbri, slew Sechnasach by treachery, de quo dicitur :

> Full of bridles and whips,
> Was the house in which Sechnasach was,
> Many were the leavings of plunder
> In the house, in which was the son of Blathmac.

Ossa[n], King of the Saxons, died. Constantinus Augustus died[o].

[672.] The burning of Bennchair[p] in Britain. The burning of Ard-Macha.

The death of Cumascach, son of Ronan.

The battle of Druim Coepis[q]. The battle of Tulach-árd[r], in which fell Dungaile, son of Maeltuile, King of Boghaine[s]. Loingsech was the victor. Cormac, son of Maelfothartaigh, died.

The

---

[o] *Died.*—Wrong; for Constantine lived till 685. See note ", *infra*, p. 70.

[p] *Bennchair.*—i. e. Bangor, in Wales, A. D. 671, " *Combustio Bennchair Britonum.*"—*Ann. Ult.*

[q] *Druim Coepis.*—Not identified.

[r] *Boghaine.*—Now the barony of Bannagh, in the west of the county of Donegal.

[s] *Tulach-árd* (i. e. high hill), not identified.

Initium ɼeʒni Cinɒfaolaɒ mic Cɼuinnmail, mic blaitmic. in annɼ.

Kal. Conɼtantinuɼ filiuɼ Conɼtantini impeɼauit xuiii. annɼ.

Kal. Ʒuin Conʒaile Cſnnfoɒa mac Ɒunchaɒa, ɼi Ulaɒ, becc boiɼċe ɼoɒ nʒon. Ɒoeɼ mac Maoltuile, ɼi Ciannaċta ɒo maɼbaɒ.

Kal. Caṫ in Aiɼċealtɼa i ttoɼchaiɼ Cſnnfaolaɒ mac Cɼuinmail ɼí Eiɼſnn; Fionnachta mac Ɒunchaɒa uictoɼ fuit, unɒe ɒicituɼ :—

Ra iaɒɼaɒ um Fionnaċta ɼiana iaɼtaiɼ tíɼe,
Ro maolaɒ móɼ a ċoiɼe um Cſnnfaolaɒ a ɼiʒe.

Kal. Colmán Inɼi bó ɼinne quieuit. Initium ɼeʒiminiɼ Fionnaċta meic Ɒunchaɒa .xx. bliaɒain.

Kal. Coɼʒɼaɒ Ailiʒ la Fionnaċta. Caṫ eiɒiɼ Fionnaċta ⁊ Laiʒniu aʒ loċ Ʒabaiɼ fe ille fe anonɒ, ɼeɒ tamen Fionnaċta uictoɼ fuit.

Ni ɒo ɼʒéluib Fionnaċta ɼo ſíoɼ. An Fionnaċta tɼa ba ɒaiɒbiɼ ɒoċonáiʒ é aɼ túɼ. Ro baoi tſé ⁊ bſn aiʒe : Ní ɼaibe imuɼɼo ɒo ɼeilb aiʒe aċt aon ɒam ⁊ aon bó. Fſét aon ɒo ɼala ɼí ffſɼ

' *Cennfaeladh, son of Crunnmhael.*—
The Annals of Ulster call him son of Blathmac. "A. D. 671, Ceannfaeladh mac Blathmaic *regnare incipit.*" But our Annals may be right.

" *Constantinus.*—He was the son, not of Constantinus, but of Constans II., whom he succeeded in 668. He died in 685. This entry is therefore inserted in a wrong place.

' *Congal Cennfoda.*—"A. D. 673, *Jugulatio* Congaile Cennfoti mic Duncho, *regis* Ult. Becc Bairche *interfecit cum.*"—*Ann. Ult.*

* *Doer, son of Maeltuile.*—This obit is not in any of the published Annals.

¹ *Aircelltair.*—The situation, or present name of this place, which is somewhere in Meath, has not been yet identified. This entry is given in the Ann. Ult. at 674, more correctly, thus: "*Bellum* Cinnfaelad *filii* Blathmic filii Aedo Slaine *in quo* Cennfaelad *interfectus est.* Finnsneachta mac Duncha *victor erat.*"

The beginning of the reign of Cennfaeladh[t], son of Crummhael, son of Blathmac. [He reigned] three years.
Kal. Constantinus[u], son of Constantinus, governed seventeen years.
[674.] Kal. The mortal wounding of Congal Cennfoda[v], son of Dunchadh, King of Uladh; it was Beg Boirche that slew him. Doer, son of Maeltuile[w], King of Cianachta, was killed.
[675.] Kal. The battle of Aircelltair[x], in which fell Cennfaeladh, son of Crummael, King of Erin; Finnachta, son of Dunchadh, was the victor, unde dicitur :—

> There closed about Finnachta the soldiers of the western territory [i. e. Westmeath].
> They removed, though great his host, Cennfaeladh from his sovereignty.

[676.] Kal. Colman of Inis-bo-finne[y] quievit. The beginning of the reign of Finnachta, son of Dunchadh [R. E.][z] [who reigned] twenty years.

[677.] Kal. The destruction of Ailech by Finnachta. A battle was fought between Finnachta and the Leinster-men on both sides of Loch Gabhair[a], but nevertheless Finnachta victor fuit.

Some of the stories about Finnachta are set down here. At first this Finnachta was poor and indigent. He had a house and a wife, but he had no property but one ox and one cow. On one occasion the

---

[y] *Colman of Inis-bo-finne.*—See Ann. Ult., A.D. 675.

[z] *R. E.*—i. e. *Ri Erinn*, King of Ireland. These letters are in the margin.

[a] *Loch-Gabhair.*—Now Loughgawer, or Lagore, near Dunshaughlin, Co. Meath. This lake is now dried up, and many curious antiquities have been found where it was. See "Proceedings of the Royal Irish Academy," vol. i., p. 424. In the Ann. Ult. this entry is given under the year 676, thus : "A. D. 676, *Bellum inter* Finnsneachta et *Lagenios in loco proximo* Loch Gabair in quo Finusneachta *victor erat.*"

ḃḞir Roiſ ro reacṡan ⁊ mṡiuġaḋ i gcomṡocṡaiḃ ḃoiṫe Ḟinnaċta. Ní ṗaiḃe ṗemṗe ṗiam aḋaiġ ḃú mṡṡa ináṡ an aḋaiġ ṡin, ḋo ġaillim, ⁊ ḋo ṡnſċta, aguſ ḋo ḋoṡċaḋaḋ, ⁊ an tſċ ḋáṡ ḃo ail ḋon ṡí ḋul ⁊ ḋ'á ṁnaoi ⁊ ḋá ṁuintiṡ níoṡ ṡo cumgattaṡ ḋola ṡa méiḋ na ḋoiminne ⁊ na ḋoṡċaḋaiḋ, ⁊ ḃa iaḋ a n-ioṁṡáitc taiṡiṡiom ṡo ḃonaiḃ na ccṡann. Aḋ cuala imuṡṡo Ḟionnaċta iaḋ ṡoṡṡ na hiomṗaitiḃ ṡin, uaiṡ niṡ ḃo ſḋ ṡoḋa ó ḃoiṫ ṡiom ṡo ḃáttuṡ an tan ṡin, ⁊ táinic aṡ a ccionn aṡ an tṡliġiḋ, ⁊ aṡċḋ ṡo ṡáiḋ ṡiu, ḃa ċóṡa ḋóiḃ toiḋeaċt ṫá ḃoiṫṡiom; Ciḃinniṡ ṡa ḃaoi ṡí, ina imṫſċt na haiḋċe ḋoiṗċe ḋoiminne. Aṡſḋ a ḋuḃaiṡt an ṡí ⁊ a ṁuinṅtiṡ, iſ ṡíoṡ aṡ cóṗa aṡ ṡiaḋ, ⁊ aṡ maiṫ linn euiṗ a ṗaḋa ṗinn. Tangattuṡ iaṡ ṡin ḋá ṫaiġ ⁊ ṡo ḃa moḋ méiḋ an taiġi ioná a ṡaiḋḃṡe. Do ṡaḋ imuṡṡo Ḟionnaċta buille a ccionn a ḋaim, ⁊ buille oile a gcſnn na ḃó. Ro ioṗlaṁaiġṡit muinnteṡ an ṡí ṡéin go tṡic ⁊ go tinnſṡ- naċḋ ḋo ḃioṗ ⁊ ḋo ċoiṡe, ⁊ ṡo ċaiṫṡioḋ guṡ ḃa ṡáiṫġ. Ra coḋlat- tuṡ go maiṫ iaṡttain go ttáinig an ṁaiḋin. Ro ṡáiḋ ṡi ḃḞir Roiſ ṡa ṁnaoi ṡéin iſ in maiḋin. Naċ ṡetaṡ, a ḃſn, géṡ ḃo ḋaiḋḃiṡ a nallana an tſéṡa, coniḋ ḋaiḋḃṡe anoṡṡa, aṡ maṡḃaḋ a aon ḃó ⁊ a aon ḋaṁ ḋúinne. Aṡ ſioṡ tṡa ṡin, aṡ an ḃſn. Aṡeḋ aṡ cóiṡ anoſ a ṡaiḋḃṡiugaḋ uainne. Ciḃé méiḋ laiġſḋ ḋo ḃéṡaṡae ḋon ṡioṡ ḋo ḃeṡṡa a cuṡṡuma ḋá ṁnaoi. Aṡ maiṫ na naḃṡae, aṡ an ṡí. Do ṡaḋ tṡa an ṡí aiṡge lán móṡ ḃó ⁊ muca iomḋa ⁊ caoiṡiġ co na mḃuaċaillḃ ḋ'Ḟionnaċta. Do ṡaḋ ḋno ḃſn an ṡiġ ḋo ṁnaoi Ḟionaċta an cuṡṡuma céḋna. Do ṡaḋṡaḋ ḋno éḋaiġe ṡaineaṁla, ⁊ eich maiṫe ḋóiḃ, aguſ gaċ ní ṡangattuṡ a lſṡ ḋon tṡaoġal.

Níoṡ ḃo cian iaṡttain tṡa go ttáinic Ḟionaċta maṡſluaġ móṡ ḋo ṫoiġ ṡſtaṡ ḋó, aṡ na ċuiṡeḋ ḋon tṡiaiṗ, ⁊ ṡṡiṫaiġiḋ aice ṡaiṗ.

^b *Fera-Ross.*—A tribe and territory comprising the county around Carrickma- cross, in the county of Monaghan, and a part of the county of Louth.

the King of Fera-Ros[b] happened to wander and stray in the neighbourhood of Finnachta's hut. There never was before a worse night than this for storm, and snow, and darkness, and the King and his wife, with their numerous people, were not able to reach the house which they desired to reach, in consequence of the intensity of the cold and the darkness; and their intention was to remain under the shelter of the trees. But Finnachta heard them express these intentions—for they were not far from his hut at the time—and he came to meet them on the way, and said to them that they had better come to his hut—such as it was—than to travel on that dark, stormy, cold night. And the King and his people said: "It is true it were better," said they, "and we are glad, indeed, that thou hast told us so." They afterwards came to his house; and the size of the house was greater than its wealth. Finnachta, moreover, struck the ox on the head, and struck the cow on the head, and the King's own people actively and quickly prepared them on spit and in cauldron, and they ate thereof till they were satiated. They slept well afterwards till the morning came. The King of Fera-Ros said to his own wife, "Knowest thou not, O woman, that this house was at first poor, and that it is now poorer, the owner having killed his only cow and his only ox for us?" "This is indeed true," said the wife: "and it behoves us now to enrich it; whatever much or little thou wilt give to the man, I will give the same amount to his wife." "Good is what thou sayest," said the King. The King then gave a large herd of cows, and many pigs and sheep, with their herdsmen, to Finnachta; and the King's wife gave the same amount to the wife of Finnachta. They also gave them fine clothes, and good horses, and whatever they stood in need of in the world.

It was not long after this until Finnachta came with a great troop of horse to the house of a sister of his, who had invited him, to be invited

ꝼaıp. Αʒ ταıḋecτ ḋóıḃ na n-ınıpım, αꞃ ann ꝺo ꞃala ꝺo Αḋaṁnán na ꞃʒolaıʒe óʒ ḃeıτ αʒ ımτſċτ na ꞃlıʒſo céꝺna, ⁊ ballán lan ꝺo lomom αꞃ a ṁuın, ⁊ oʒ τeıcſḃ ꝺo ꞃéꞃ an maꞃcꞃluaʒ ꝺon τꞃlıʒıꝺ ꝺo ꞃala a ċoꞃ ꝼꞃıa cloıċ, ⁊ τoꞃchaıꞃ ꝼéın, ⁊ ꝺno. an ballán ʒo noſꞃ-naꝺ bꞃıoꞃʒ bꞃuaꞃ ꝺe, ⁊ ʒéꞃ bo luaċ ꝺo na heochaıḃ níoꞃ bó nſṁ, luaıċe ꝺo Αꝺaṁnán ʒo na ballan bꞃıꞃτe ꝼoꞃ a ṁuın, ⁊ ꞃé ꝺuḃaċ ꝺoḃꞃónaċ. O ꞃo conꝺaıc Ꝼıonnaċτá é ꞃo ṁaıꝺ a ꝼaıτḃıuꝺ ʒáıꞃe ꝼaıꞃ, ⁊ ꞃo ḃaoı ʒá ꞃaꝺ ꞃe hΑꝺaṁnán, ꝺo ʒéna ꞃın ꞃúḃaċ ꝺíoτ, uaıꞃ aꞃum comꞃaıċnſċꞃa ꝼꞃıa ʒaċ n-ınınſḃ ꝺo cumanʒ : ꝼoʒeḃꞃa a ꝼoʒlaıınτıꝺ, aꞃ Ꝼıonnaċτa coımꝺíoḋnaꝺ uaımꞃı, ⁊ na ḃí ʒo ꝺuḃaċ. Αꞃeꝺ ꞃo ꞃaıꝺ Αḋaṁnán, a ḃſʒ ꝺuıne, aꞃ ꞃé, aτá aꝺḃaꞃ ꝺuḃ aʒam, uaıꞃ τꞃí meıc léıʒınn maıτe aταıꝺ a naoınτıʒ, ⁊ αταımne ꝺá ʒıolla aca ⁊ aꞃeꝺ ḃíoꞃ ʒıolla aꞃ τıməıoll uaınn aʒ ıaꞃꞃaıꝺ ḃſτamnaıꞃ ꝺon ċoıʒıoꞃ, ⁊ ꝺamꞃa ꞃáınıʒ ıaꞃꞃaıꝺ neıτe ꝺáıḃ anıu : ꞃá ċuaıꝺ an τıoꞃḃalτa ꞃá ḃaoı aʒamꞃa ꝺóıḃ ꝼo láꞃ, aʒuꞃ an ní aꞃ ꝺoılʒe ann .ı. an ballán ıaꞃaċτa ꝺo ḃꞃıꞃıoꝺ, ⁊ ʒan a íoc aʒom. 'Ιcꝼaꝺꞃa an ballán, aꞃ Ꝼınnaċτa, ⁊ τuʒꞃa laτ an cuıʒſꞃ ꝼuıl aꞃ ꝺo ꞃʒáċꞃa anoċτ ʒan ḃıaꝺ ʒo nuıʒe an τſċ ꝺ'á ττıaʒaımne ; ꝼo ʒeḃaıꝺ ḃıaꝺ ⁊ lıonn aʒaınne. Ꝺo ꞃıʒnſꝺ aṁlaıꝺ ꞃın, τuʒꞃaτ an coıʒıoꞃ cléıꞃſċ, ⁊ ꞃo coıꞃʒſꝺ an τſċ leanna, lſτ an τoıʒe ꝺo cléꞃċıḃ ⁊ an leτ aıle ꝺo laochaıḃ. Αıτe Αꝺamnáın ꞃo líonaꝺ é ó ꞃaċ an ꞃꞃıoꞃaꝺ naoıḃ, ⁊ ꞃꞃıꞃıτ ꝼaıꞃτıne, ⁊ aꞃeꝺ ꞃo ꞃáıꝺ : ḃuꝺ aıꞃoꞃí Εıꞃeann, aꞃ ꞃé, an ꞃſꞃ ꝺá ττuʒaꝺ an ꝼlſʒꞃa : ⁊ ḃuꝺ cſhꝺ cꞃaḃaıꝺ ⁊ eaʒna Εıꞃſhn Αḋaṁnán, ⁊ ḃuḋ e anmċaꞃa Ꝼıonnaċτa, ⁊ ḃıaıꝺ Ꝼınnaċτa ı ꞃſτnaıʒe móıꞃ, co ꞃo oılḃeımnıʒ ꝺo Αḋaṁnán.

Níoꞃ

---

c *Broken vessel on his back.*—It appears from a passage in Bede's "Eccl. History," lib. iii., c. 27, that the sons of the Saxon nobility who were studying in Ireland in 646 " went about from one master's cell to another, the Scoti willingly receiving them all, and taking care to supply them with food, and to furnish them with books to read, and their teaching gratis." It is curious how much this re-

vited by him in his turn. As they rode along they met Adamnan, who was then a young school-boy, travelling the same road, having a vessel full of milk on his back; and as he ran off out of the way before the horsemen, his foot struck against a stone, and he fell with the vessel, which was broken to pieces, and, though the horsemen rode swiftly, they were not swifter than Adamnan with his broken vessel on his back[e], and he being sad and melancholy. When Finnachta perceived him, he burst into a fit of laughter, and he said to Adamnan: "That shall make thee glad, for I am willing to repair every injury in my power: thou shalt receive, O school-boy," said Finnachta, "shelter from me, and be not sorrowful." What Adamnan said was:—"O good man," said he, "I have cause for being melancholy, for there are three good school-boys in one house, and they have us as two messengers, and there is always one messenger going about seeking food for the five; and it came to my turn to-day to seek for them. The gathering I had fell to the ground, and, what I grieve for more, the borrowed vessel has been broken, and I have not wherewithal to pay for it." "I will pay for the vessel," said Finnachta; "and do thou bring with thee the five who are without food depending on thee, to the house to which we are going, and you shall receive food and drink from us." This was done accordingly: the four clerics were brought; and the ale-house was prepared, half the house for clerics, and the other half for laics. The tutor of Adamnan was filled with the grace of the Holy Spirit, and with the spirit of prophecy, and he said: —"The man by whom this banquet is given shall be supreme monarch of Erin, and Adamnan shall be the head of the piety and wisdom of Erin, and he shall be the spiritual adviser of Finnachta, and Finnachta shall be in great repute until he shall offend Adamnan."

Not sembles the modern "poor scholar of our own times," who went about on foot, and was everywhere entertained by the Irish peasantry on account of his learning.

Níop bo cian v'aimpip iap pin co ttáinic Fionnacta ⁊ ꝑi ꝑꝼꞅi Roꝼ a éapa péin leiꝼ v'ionnpaigiv bpácap a acap, .i. Cionnꝼaolav, vo iappaiv ꝼꞅꝛainn ꝼaiꝑ. Do pav Cꞅnoꝼaolav ápvmoepaigeacc na Míbi uile ó Sionumn go ꝼaiꝑge vó, .i. aꝑ céiéꝑi cuacaib ꝼiéꞅc. Ro baoi Finacta ꝼꝛi ꝯe n-aimꝛꝛꝑe ainlaib pin. Táinic v'á coṁaiꝑle ꝼꝛi a éaꝑuiv ꝼén .i. pi Feꝑ Roꝼꝼ, cia vo géuaiv, ucuꝑ níꝑ bó loꝑ laiꝑ map po boi. Do pavꝛaibe vna coṁaiꝑle epuaib epóba vó, ⁊ aꝑév po ꝑéav ꝑꝑ: Naé ꝑoinnꝼb Slige Apail Míve ꝼoꝑ vó? Oꞅnapa an vapa leit vo'n Mꞅive copoꝑ taiꝑꝑꝛi vucꝛacaé vuit, ⁊ map búꝑ taiꝑꝛꝛi vuic an let pin, vꞅna comval ꝼꝑꝛ in lꞅt eile, ⁊ maꝑb a nvꞅgoaome a ꝑuinn eaéa ꝛaibe, ⁊ ní namá biaꝑ lainꝑige na Míve agat, ací biaib eiv ꝑige Tꞅmꝑaé beóꝑ, máv cul lꞅt. Do ꝑꞅgne iaꝑaṁ Fionnatta an comaiꝑle pin, ⁊ ꝑa ꝼuagaiꝑ cat iap pin ꝼoꝑ bꝛácaiꝑ a atap .i. ꝼoꝑ Cꞅnoꝼaolav. O vo cuala bꞅn Cinoꝼaolav pin ꝯo boí ag béim ꝼoꝑ a ꝼꞅi 'man maopaigeaét vo ꝛav v'Finacca; aꝑ ann ꝑo éan an bꞅn: Ra iavꝛav, ut ꝛuꝑꝛa. Do pavav eaé go epuaib epóba ꞅtoꝑꝑa iaꝑ pin .i. eivip Cionnꝼaolav ⁊ Fionnatta i n-Aiꝑceallcꝛa, ⁊ ꝯo maꝑbav Cinoꝼaolav ann ⁊ ꝛoch- aive maille ꝼꝛiꞅ. Ro gab Fionnatta iaꝑ pin ꝑige n-Eiꝑꞅnn pa ꝯeiv bliavain.

Aꝑ é an Fionnatta pin ꝑo ṁait an mboꝑama vo Moling, aꝑ na tobaé la eꞅtꝛaéaiv pí pémi pin anall, .i. ó Thuatal Tꞅécṁap

go

ᵃ *Sinainn.*—i. e. the River Shannon. Ancient Meath extended from the River Shannon to the sea.

ᵉ *Slighe-Asail.*—An ancient road extending from the Hill of Tara in the direction of Lough Owel and the Shannon. It divided ancient Meath into two equal parts, not east and west, as at present, but north and south. See Ann. Four M.,

A. D. 157, p. 104.

ᶠ *Ut supra.*—See above, under A. D. 675.

ᵍ *Twenty years.*—This is correct. He succeeded in 675, and was slain 14th Nov., 695.

ʰ *Boromha.*—This was an exorbitant tax, said to have been originally imposed on the Leinster-men by the monarch Tua-

Not long after this, Finnachta and his friend the King of Fera-Ros came to his father's brother, Cennfaeladh, to ask land of him, and Cennfaeladh gave him the head stewardship of all Meath from the Sinainn[d] to the sea, i. e. over twenty-four territories. Finnachta was thus situated for some time. He came to consult with his own friend, the King of Fera-Ros, as to what he should do, for he was not satisfied with his station. His friend gave him a hard and wicked advice, and he said to him: "Does not Slighe-Asail[e] divide Meath into two equal parts? Make thou one half of Meath faithfully loyal to thee; and when this half is loyal to thee, appoint a meeting with the other half, and kill their chieftains who are their leaders in battle, and thou shalt not only have the full sovereignty of Meath, but also of Teamhair, if thou wilt." Finnachta followed this advice; and he afterwards challenged his father's brother to battle, viz. Cennfaeladh. When Cennfaeladh's wife heard this, she was reproaching her husband for having given the stewardship of Meath to Finnachta. It was then the woman sung: "There closed," &c., *ut supra*[f]. After this a battle was vigorously and bravely fought between them; viz. between Cennfaeladh and Finnachta, at Aircealtra, where Cennfaeladh and numbers of others were slain along with him; after which Finnachta assumed the monarchy of Erin [and reigned] twenty years[g].

It was this Finnachta that remitted the Borumha[h] to Moling after it had been levied during the reigns of forty kings previously, viz. from

thal Techtmhar in the second century. It was the cause of many battles, but was at at length remitted by Finnachta at the request of St. Moling, who is represented in the text as having deceived him by a mental reservation. See Ann. F. M.,

696, p. 298. Acts of this kind attributed to the Irish saints, as if laudable, by their biographers, are a curious evidence of the rudeness of the times, and have been censured by the earlier Bollandists in the severest terms.

go Ḃionnacṫa, Táiniġ iaraṁ Moling ó Laiġniḃ uile ḋ'iarraiḋ maiṫime na boroṁa ḟor Ḃionnacṫa. Rá iarr ṫra Moling ar Ḃinnacṫa maiṫim na boroṁa ḟria lá ⁊ aiḋċe. Rá ṁaiṫ iaraṁ Ḃinacṫa an boroṁa ḟria la ⁊ aiḋċe. Roḃ ionann aġ Moling rin aġar a maiṫiṁ ṫre ḃíṫe : uair ní ḟḟuil 'ran aimrir aċt lo ⁊ aiḋċe. ḃá ḋoiġ imurro la Ḃinnacṫa ar aon lo ⁊ aon aiḋċe namá. Táiniġ Moling reiṁe amaċ, ⁊ arṡó ro ráiḋ; Ṫuġair cáirḋe impe tré ḃíṫe ⁊ ané; ro ġeall Moling nṡiṅ oḂionnacṫa. Ro ṫuiġ ḋno Ḃinacṫa ġur ro ṁeall Moling é, ⁊ aḋruḃairt ḟria a ṁuinṫir : eirġíḋ ar ré i noṡġaiḋ an ḋuine naoiṁ ḋo ċuaiḋ uaim, ⁊ aḃraiḋ rir naċ ttuġura aċt cáirḋe aon laoi ⁊ aon aiḋċe ḋó; uair an ḋar lḟn, ro meall an ḋuine naoṁ mé, uair ní ḟḟuil aċt la ⁊ aḋaiġ ir in inḃioṫ uile. Ó ro ḟuir Moling imurro ġo ttiocraiḋe na oṡġhaiḋ rá rioṫ ġo tric tinnearnaċ ġo ráiniġ a ṫṡċ, ⁊ ní ruġraḋ ioir muin. ṫir an rí ḟair.

Aḃ beiraiḋ arailc ġo ruġ Moling ḋuan lair ḋ'Ḃionnachta .i. Ḃionnacṫa ḟor Uiḃ Néill ⁊c (atá rin 'rin boroṁa 'rin liobuṗra rġrioḃṫa). Ro maiṫḃ ṫra an boroma ḋo Moling ó rin ġo bráṫ, ⁊ ciar bo haiṫreaċ la Ḃionnacṫa níor ḟṡ a toḃaċ, uair ar ḋo ċionn niṁe ro ṁaiṫ. Et hoc ert uerrur.

In xu°. anno ab hoc anno ro ṁaiṫ Ḃionnacṫa an boruṁa tainiġ Aḃaṁnáin ṡó céḋóir ḋ'ionnraiġiḋ Ḃinacṫa tar éir Moling, ⁊ ro ċuir clércaċ ḋ'á muinnṫir ar cionn Ḃionnacṫa ġo ttíoraḋ ḋa aġ allaṁ. Ar ann ro ḃoí Ḃinnacṫa aġ imirt ḟitċille. Tair ḋ'aġallaṁ Aḃaṁnáin, ar an clércaċ. Ní raċaḋ ġo ḋtair an cluiċí ri, ar

---

[1] *The book called the Borumha.*—There is a copy of this historical tract preserved in the Book of Lecan, and another in Trinity College, Dublin, II. 2, 18. See Ann. F. M., A. D. 106, p. 100. It is much in the style of this story, but less modernized. It is interspersed with quotations from ancient Irish poems adduced in proof of the historical facts related by its author.

from Tuathal Techtmhar, to Finnachta. Moling came [as an ambassador] from all Leinster to request a remission of the Borumha from Finnachta. Moling asked of Finnachta to forgive the Borumha for a day and a night. Finnachta forgave the Borumha for a day and a night. This to Moling was the same as to forgive it for ever, for there is not in time but day and night. But Finnachta thought it was one [natural] day and night. Moling came forth before him, and said: "Thou hast given a respite respecting it for ever, and yesterday;" Moling promised heaven to Finnachta. But Finnachta conceived that Moling had deceived him, and he said to his people: "Go," said he, "in pursuit of this holy man, who has gone away from me, and say unto him that I have not given respite for the Borumha, to him, but for one day and one night, for methinks the holy man has deceived me, for there is but one day and one night in the whole world." But when Moling knew that they were coming in pursuit of him, he ran actively and hastily till he reached his house, and the people of the King did not come up with him at all.

Others say that Moling brought a poem with him to Finnachta, beginning: "Finnachta over the Race of Niall," &c. (and this poem is written in the book called the Borumha)[1]. However, the Borumha was forgiven to Moling from that till judgment; and though Finnachta was sorry for it, he was not able to levy it, for it was for the sake of [obtaining] heaven he had remitted it. *Et hoc est verius.*

In the fifteenth year from the year in which Finnachta had forgiven the Borumha, Adamnan came to Finnachta after Moling, and he sent a cleric of his people to Finnachta that he might come to converse with him. Finnachta was then playing chess. "Come to converse with Adamnan," said the cleric. "I will not till this game is finished," said Finnachta. The cleric returned to Adamnan, and told him the answer of Finnachta. "Go thou to him, and say to him

ap Pionnacta. Táinig an cléipeac d'ionnpoigiò Aòamnain, ⁊ po innip ppígpa Pionnacta dó. Eipgiò-pi da ionnpoigiò piom, ⁊ abaip piip: gebav-pa caogav palm anaipfo pin, ⁊ atá palm 'pan caogaid pin, ⁊ guiòpfo-pa an coimòfo pin tpalmpain conaċ geba mac na ua duitpi no pfi do comainina go bpát pige n-Eipenn. Ra cuaiò ono an cléipeać, ⁊ po pàiò pe Pionnacta pin, ⁊ ní tapad Pionnacta da uide, aċt po imbip a pitéill go ttapnaig an cluice. Taip d'agallaiii Aòaninain, a Pionnacta, ap an cléipeaċ. Ni pag, ap Pionnacta, go ttaip an cluicipi. Ro innip an cléipeaċ pain do Aòamnán. Abaippi ppippiom, ap Aòamnán, gebaopa caogaò palm an aipfo pin, ⁊ atá palm 'pan caogaid pin, ⁊ iappfaopa ipin palm pin, ⁊ cuingpfopa ap an ccoimòfo gaipde paogail dopam. Ra innip an cléipeaċ pin d'Pinaċda, ⁊ ní tapad Pionnacta da paoide, aċt pa imbip a pitéill go ttapnaig an cluice. Taip d'agallaò Aòamnáin, ap an cléipeaċ. Ní pag ap Pionnacta go ttaip an cluicipi. Táinic an cléipeaċ, ⁊ pa innip do Aòamnán fpeagpa Pionnacta. Eipgpi dá ionnpoigiò, ap Aòamnán, ⁊ abaip ppip, gebaopa an tpfp caogaò, ⁊ ata palm 'pan caogaid pin, ⁊ guiòpfopa an coimòfo 'pan tpalm pain na fuigpiom plaiċiup nime. Táinic an cléipec peme go Pionnacta, ⁊ pa innip pin. Map po évala Pinnacta pain po énip an pitéill go hobann uad, ⁊ táinic d'ionnpoigiò Aòaninain. Ci dod tug annopa cugam, ap Aòamnán, ⁊ na ttángaip pip na tettaipeaċtaib eile? Apeò po depa uam, ap Pionnacta, an tomaoiòfm do poinip peme po opin .i. gan mac na ua naim do gabáil pige, ⁊ gan peap mo comainina i pige n-Eipfun, no gaipde paogail uaim; éopom popom paiò, an tan imippo po geallaipi nfm do gaid popm, ap uine tánag go hobann do d'agallaòpi; uaip ní ffuil a fulaingpaide agam-pa.

An píop, ap Aòamnan an bhopaina do maiteeann òuit lá ⁊ aiòce do Moling? Ap píop, ap Pionnacta. Ro meallaò tu, ap
Aòamnan,

him that I shall sing fifty psalms during that time, and that there is a psalm among that fifty in which I shall pray the Lord that a son or grandson of his, or a man of his name, may never assume the sovereignty of Erin." The cleric accordingly went and told that to Finnachta, but Finnachta took no notice, but played at his chess till the game was finished. "Come to converse with Adamnan, O Finnachta!" said the cleric. "I will not go," said Finnachta, "till this [next] game is finished." The cleric told this to Adamnan. "Say unto him," said Adamnan, "that I will sing fifty psalms during that time, and that there is a psalm among that fifty in which I will ask and beseech the Lord to shorten his life for him." The cleric told this to Finnachta, but Finnachta took no notice of it, but played away at his chess till the game was finished. "Come to converse with Adamnan," said the cleric. "I will not," said Finnachta, "till this game is finished." The cleric told to Adamnan the answer of Finnachta. "Go to him," said Adamnan, "and tell him that I will sing the third fifty psalms, and that there is a psalm in that fifty in which I will beseech the Lord that he may not obtain the kingdom of heaven." The cleric came to Finnachta and told him this. When Finnachta heard this, he suddenly put away the chess from him, and he came to Adamnan. "What has brought thee to me now, and why didst thou not come at the other messages?" "What induced me to come," said Finnachta, "was the threats which thou didst hold forth to me, viz., that no son or grandson of mine should ever reign, and that no man of my name should ever assume the sovereignty of Erin, or that I should have shortness of life. I deemed these [threats] light; but when thou didst promise me to take away heaven from me, I then came suddenly, because I cannot endure this."

"Is it true," said Adamnan, "that the Borumha was remitted by thee for a day and a night to Moling?" "It is true," said Finnachta. "Thou

Aḋaṁnán, aɼ ionann ɼin ┐ a maiṫſṁ ṫɼé ḃiṫċ, ┐ aɼ aṁlaiḋ ɼo ḃoí ʒa aṫċoɼɼán, ┐ ɼo ɼáiḋ an laoiḋ:—

Aniu ʒe cſuʒlaiḋ cuaċa an ɼí cɼinléiṫ ʒan ḋéḋa,
An buaɼ ḋo ṁaiṫ ḋo Moliṅʒ ḋeṫḃiɼ ḋon ciṅʒ niɼ ɼéḋa;
Ḋamaḋ miɼi ɼionnaċta, ɼʒo maḋ mé ɼlaiṫ Ṫeṁɼa,
Ʒo ḃɼáṫ noċa aṫṫiḃeɼainn, ní ḋiṅʒenainn a noſɼina.
Ʒaċ ɼí naċ maiṫſinn a ċiuɼ aɼ ɼaḋa ḃíḋ a ɼʒéla.
Maiɼʒ ḋo ɼaḋ an ḋail, an tí aɼ laʒ aɼ ḋo aɼ méla.
Ḋo aɼnaċtaɼ ḋo ɼaoɼa, aɼ aɼi baoɼa ʒo mḃinne,
Maiɼʒ ɼiʒ ɼo ṁaiṫ a ċiuɼa, a Íoɼa nſṁḋa niṁe.
Soċla ʒaċ nſċ o ṫɼeaḃuɼ, aɼ maiɼʒ lſnaɼ ḋo liaċa,
Aɼ ɼaḋa an ḋalɼa macaiṫe, ba ɼaiṫe ʒomba ɼiaċa.
Ḋáṁɼa ɼíɼi ɼuaḋuɼ cɼu, ɼo ṫaiɼnɼinn mo ḃíoḋḃaḋa
Ro ṫoiʒeḃainn mo ḋionʒna, ɼoḃɼaṫ iomḃa m'ioɼʒala
Roḃuíɼ iomḃa m'ioɼʒala, mo ḃɼiaṫɼa niḃuiɼ ʒuaċa.
Roḃuíɼ ɼíoɼa mo ḋala, ɼoḃuíɼ lána mo ṫuaċa.
Roḃuíɼ iomɼoiʒɼi m'aiɼḋe, mo ḋala ɼoḃuíɼ ḋaiṅʒne.
An ḋál ɼa, cia ciam ba ṫeċinaiṅʒ, ní léċɼaíñ ɼe Laiʒne.
Ʒuiḋimɼi iṫʒe ɼoɼ Ḋlia, náċum ṫaiɼ ḃáɼ ɼo bɼoʒal,
Ʒuɼ ɼo ṫeɼno aniu Moliṅʒ, ní ḃſċ ḋo ɼinn ɼo ḋɼaoḃaɼ.
Mac ɼaillen ɼſi ḋaɼ ṁ, ní claiɼiḋſi ḋaɼa naɼa.

Ro

' *Thou hast been deceived.*—This story is found in the tract called the "Borumha Laighen," but the antiquity of that tract, in its present form, cannot be very great. A writer in the "Dublin University Magazine" for Feb., 1848, p. 225, says "that it would have been better for the people of Leinster to have continued to pay the Borumean tribute to this day than that their St. Moling should have set an example of clerical special pleading and mental reservation, in the equivocation by which he is represented to have procured their release from that 'impost." The whole story is, however, a mere bardic fiction as regards Adamnan and Moling; but it must be confessed that it was universally read and received as true in ancient times by the people of Leinster and Ulster, and must have exercised a

"Thou hast been deceived"ᵏ, said Adamnan, "for this is the same as to remit it for ever." And he went on scolding him, and sung the lay:—

To-day, though they bind the locks of the white-haired toothless King,
The cows which he forgave to Moling are due to a wiser head.
If I were Finnachta[1], and that I were chief of Teamhair,
Never would I forgive it; I would not do what he has done.
Of every king who remits not his tribute, long shall the stories remain.
Woe to him who gave this respite; to the weak it is sorrow!
Thy wisdom has ended, and given way to folly.
Alas for the King who forgave his tributes, O heavenly Jesus of heaven!
Weak is every one who is anile; woe! who follow grey-beards!
Long is this bargain to last; longer till the debts are due!
Were I a king who sheds blood, I would humble my enemies,
I would raise up my fortresses, many would be my conflicts.
Many would be my conflicts: my words would not be false.
Just would be my compacts, full would be my territories.
Visible would be my qualities, firm would be my treaties.
This treaty should it happen to me, I would not cede to Leinster-men.
I ask a petition from God, that death or danger may not overtake me,
That Moling may this day escape, may he not perish by point or edge [of weapon].
Mac Faillen, from beyond the sea, will not be driven over sea.

He

demoralizing effect upon their minds.

[1] *If I were Finnachta.*—These lines were evidently fabricated by some warlike poet who wished to stimulate the race of Tuathal to renew this tribute. In one of the poems addressed to Turlough Luinech O'Neill, he is advised to renew the Borumha.

Ro ṗíoıṗ ṗuna mıc Dé, ṗo ṗíoıṗı mac Dé aṗúna.
Tṗí caoġaıı̀ ṗalm ġać Dıa, aṗeı̀ ġebıuṗ aṗ Dlıa.
Tṗí caoġaıı̀ boċt ṗeolṗoıṗće, aṗeı̀ bıaċuṗ ġać noíı̀ce.
Qn bıle buaı̀a bıṗıġ, an ṗıṗıı̀ ġuṗ na ṗṡṗaıb
Loṅġ lṡṗoa ṗo ṗuaıṗ ṗáılte, conn beaṗba baıṗce bṗeaṗaıl,
Qn lon óıṗ aṗ an ınne, an cláṗ óıṗ oṗ na clannaıb,
'Éıġne Dubġlaıṗı ouınne, ṗuaım coınne coın ṗṡṗıa halla. Qmu.

Ro ċaṗınn cṗa ıaṗ ṗın Fıonnaċta a ćṡın a n-uċt Qı̀aṁnáın,
⁊ oo ṗıġne aıċṗıġe 'na ṗıaı̀naıṗı, ⁊ ṗo loġ Qı̀amnan oo maıċṡṁ na
boṗaṁa.

Ṗal. Moṗṗ Colġan mıc Faılbe Flaınn, ṗí Muman. Caċ euıṗ
huıb Cınnṗılaıġ ⁊ Oṗṗaıġıb, ın quo Tuaım ṗnáṁa .ı. Cícaıṗe, ṗí
Oṗṗaıġe occıṗuṗ eṗc. Faolán Sṁcuṗtul, ṗí hUa cCınnṗıolaıġ
ınċcoṗ ṗuıc. Unoe—

Qn caċ la Tuaım ṗnáṁa níṗ éıoıṗ [.ı. níṗ ba éıoıṗ]
Dıambeṗc ṗeaċcuṗ nao ecaıl [.ı. naoṡcoıl leıṗ a ċabaıṗc]
Faolan cáıṗoe aṗ éıġın

Dó

^m *Berbha.*—i. e. the River Barrow, on the banks of which St. Moling erected his monastery. Breasal, here referred to, was Breasal Breac, one of the Pagan kings of Leinster, who is much celebrated by the Irish poets for his naval exploits. He is the ancestor of all the great families of Leinster and Ossory. See Reeves's " Eccl. Antiq. of Down, Connor, and Dromore," p. 200.

ⁿ *Dubhghlaise.*—Now Douglas, a stream in the east of the Queen's County, which falls into the River Barrow.

^o *Forgave him.*—Finnachta had committed a great sin against the race of Tuathal by forgiving the Borumean tribute to gain heaven for himself, or by allowing himself to be outwitted by St. Moling. To remit the Borumha in order to gain heaven for himself was doubtless to deprive the race of Tuathal Teehtmhar of a great revenue for a selfish purpose; but to allow himself to be outwitted by St. Moling was scarcely a sin on the part of the King, for it appears that Finnachta had no notion of remitting the Borumha at all. He merely promised to stay the levying of it for one natural day and night, which St. Moling, by a kind of logic not very intelligible, interpreted to mean *for ever,* and this interpretation Adamnan

He knows the secrets of the Son of God; the Son of God knows
his secrets.
Thrice fifty psalms each day he sings to God;
Thrice fifty paupers, worthy deed, he feeds each night.
The virtuous, productive tree, the seer with the visions,
The foreign ship which has found welcome,
The wave of Berbha[m] of the ship of Breasal,
The golden treasure from the centre, the golden board over the tribes,
The salmon of the brown Dubhghlaise[n], the wave-sound, the wave
against the cliff.

After this Finnachta placed his head in the bosom of Adamnan,
and he did penance in his presence, and Adamnan forgave him[o] for
the remission of the Borumha.

[678.] Kal. The death of Colgu[p], son of Failbhe Flann, King of
Munster. A battle [was fought] between the Ui-Ceinnseallaigh and
the Osraighi, in which Tuaim-snamha, i. e. Cicaire, King of Osraighe,
was slain. Faelan Senchustal, King of Ui-Ceinnsealaigh, was the
victor. On which was said:—

The battle by Tuaim-snamha could not be gained[q];
Which he fought against his will,
Faelan respite, with difficulty,

To

is represented as having approved of. In
the historical tract called the "Borumean
Tribute," St. Moling is represented as requesting the King to forgive the Borumha
till *Luan*, i. e. Monday, in the ordinary
sense of the word, but it appears that
Luan also meant the Day of Judgment;
and St. Moling insisted on this being the
true meaning of the word as used in the
compact between him and the head of the

race of Tuathal Techtmhar on this occasion, although the latter had no idea that
the word was to be used in that sense.
See Ann. F. M., A. D. 106, p. 99, and
A. D. 593, p. 216, *et seq.*

[p] *Colgu.*—A. D. 677. "Toimsnama, rex
Osraigi, *quievit. Mors* Colggen mic Failbei
Flainn, *regis* Muman."—*Ann. Ult.*

[q] *Gained.*—The words within brackets
in the Irish text are given as a gloss over

Dó dor pad po copmaile ba bpat a bpionnad ʒo ttuʒ ʒialla Orraiʒe o ta buana ʒo Cumap.

Cat Dúin loca. Cat Liaʒ Maoláin. Cat i Calatpor in quo uictur ept Domnall bpeac. Paolan (.i. dalta Caoimʒin) mac Colmain, pí Laiʒean mopitup. Cuier Pailbe ab Iae.

Kal. Cat etir Fionnacta ⁊ becc mboipce. Incipit Fianamail peʒnape por Laiʒnib.

Kal. Colman ab bfincair quieuit.

Lorʒad na piʒ i nDun Ceitrin .i. Dunʒal mac Sʒanail, pi Cpuitne, ⁊ Cfinpaolad mac Suibne, pi Ciannacta Glinne Gaimin; la Maoldúin mac Maolpitpiʒ po lorʒad.

Ciap inʒfn Duibpea.

Kal. Guin Cinnfaolaid mic Colʒain, pí Connact.

Cat Rata móipe Maiʒe line fpi bpeatnu, du i ttopcaip Catupac mac Maolduin, pí Cpuitne, ⁊ Ultán mac Diocolla.

Mopp

nip eidip and na detail respectively.

ᶠ *From Buana to Cumor.*—This is probably a mistake for, "from Bladma to Cumar," i. e. from Slieve Bloom to the Cumar, or Meeting of the Three Waters, which was the extent of the ancient Ossory, and is still that of the diocese of Ossory.

ᵍ *Dun-locha.*—Probably Dunloe, in the county of Kerry. This entry, and the following, are not to be found in any of the other Annals.

ᵗ *Liag-Maelain.*—Not identified.

ᵘ *Calatros.*—A place in the west of Scotland. See Reeves' "Adamnan," p. 123, and Ann. Ult., A. D. 677. Domhnall Brec was King of Scotland.

* *Faelan.*—His death is entered in the Ann. Clonm. at the year 663, and in the F. M. at 665. St. Caeimhghin, the tutor of this king, died in the year 618.

ˣ *Failbhe.*—Ann. Ult. 678, Tigh. 679. He was the immediate predecessor of Adamnan, who makes a distinct allusion to him in his "Vit. Columbæ," lib. i., c. 3 (Reeves, p. 26).

ʸ *Bec Boirche.*—"A.D. 678, Bellum contra Bec mBoirche."—*Ann. Ult. Tigh.* 679.

ᶻ *Colman.*—"A.D. 679 [*Tigh.* 680]. Colman, abbas Bencbair, pausat."—*Ann. Ult.*

* *Dun Ceithirn.*— Now called the Giant's Sconce. It is an ancient cyclopean fort situate in the parish of Dunbo,

To him gave, in appearance, his grant was betrayal,
So that he took the hostages of Osraighe from Buana to Cumor'.

The battle of Dun-locha". The battle of Liag-Maelain'. A battle was fought in Calatros", in which Domhnall Breac was conquered. Faelan' (the alumnus of Caimlighin), son of Colman, King of Leinster, died.

[679.] The death of Failbhe', Abbot of Ia.

Kal. A battle between Finnachta and Bec Boirche'. Fianamhail began to reign over Leinster.

[680.] Kal. Colman², Abbot of Benchair, died.

[681.] The burning of the kings in Dun-Ceithirn^a, i. e. Dunghal, son of Sgannal, King of the Cruithni, Cennfaeladh, son of Suibhne, King of Ciannacta-Glinne Gaimhin^b; by Maelduin, son of Maelfithrigh, they were burnt.

Ciar^c, daughter of Duibhrea.

[682.] Kal. The killing of Cennfaeladh^d, son of Colgan, King of Connaught.

The battle of Rath-mor of Magh-line^e against the Britons, in which were slain Cathasach, son of Maelduin, King of the Cruithni^f, and Ultan, son of Dicolla.

The in the north of the county of Londonderry. "A. D. 680 [*Tigh.* 681.] Combustio Regum in Dun-Ceithirn," &c. —*Ann. Ult.*

^b *Ciannachta-Glinne Gaimhin.* — Now the barony of Keenaght, in the present county of Londonderry.

^c *Ciar.*—She is the patroness of the parish of Kilkeary, in the barony of Upper Ormond, county of Tipperary. See Colgan's Acta SS., p. 14-16, at 6th

January, and Ann. F. M., A. D. 679; Tigh. 681.

^d *Cennfaeladh.*—A. D. 681 [*Tigh.* 682. Jugulatio Cinnfaela mic Colgen, regis Connacie."—*Ann. Ult.*

^e *Rathmor of Magh-line.*—Now Rathmore, a townland containing the remains of a large earthen rath with a cave, situate in the parish of Donegore, near the town of Antrim. See Ann. F. M., A. D. 680.

^f *Cruithni,*—i. e. the Picts of Dalaradia.

Moṗṗ Suiḃne mic Maeluṁa pṗincepiṗ Coṗcaiġe [ı. ponṫiṗiciṗ Coṗcaġienṗiṗ].

Ḳal. Ḋunchaḋ Muıṗıṗġe mac Maoılḃuıḃ ıuġulaṫuṗ eṗt.
Aḋamnan ḋo ġabaıl abḋaıne lae.
Caṫ Coṗaınn ı ṫṫoṗchaıṗ Colġa mac ḃlaṫmaıc, ⁊ Ḟṗıġuṗ mac Maolḋúın, ṗı Cıneıl Caıṗṗṗe.
Inıṫıum moṗṫalıṫaṫıṗ ṗueṗoṗum ın menṡe Oṫṫoḃṗıṗ, quae ṗuıṫ ṫṗıbuṗ annıṡ ın Ḣıbeṗnıa.
Quıeṡ Aıṗmḃ́aıġ na Cṗaıḃe.
Ḳal. Moṗṫalıṫaṡ ṗılıoṗum ın qua omneṡ ṗṗıncıṗeṡ eṫ ṗeṗe omneṡ nobılaṡ ıuuenum Scoṫoṗum ṗeṗıeṗunṫ.
Ḳaḷ. Saxoneṡ campum ḃṗeaġh ḋeuaṡṫanṫ, eṫ pluṗımaṡ Eccleṡıa.

Ḳal. Ḋomnall ḃṗeac mac Eaṫaċ ḃuıḋe moṗṫuuṡ eṗt.
Quıeṡ banḃáın ṗġṗıba Cılle ḋaṗa.
Ḳal. Quıeṡ Ḋoċuma Chonoc, ab ġlınne ḋa loċa.
Quıeṡ Roıṗene ab Coṗcaıġe.
Iṡ ın ḃlıaḋaın ṡı ṡo ṗuaṡlaıġ Aḋaṁnán an ḃṗaıḋ ṗuġṗaḋ Saxoın a hEıṗınn.
Caṫ Ḋuın Neaċṫaın ıṫṫıṡ mac Oṡṡa, ⁊ ḃṗuıṫe mac ḃıle uıc-ṫoṗ ṗuıṫ [ṗıc].

Sancta

ᵍ *Suibhne.*—Ann. Ult. 681; Tigh. 682.

ʰ *Cork.*—The words in brackets in the Text are written as a gloss over the words "Princepis [*sic*] Corcaighe."

ⁱ *Dunchadh Muirisge.*—Ann. Ult. 682; Tigh. 683; F. M. 681.

ᵏ *Adamnan.*—This entry is out of place here. It should have been inserted after the death of Failbhe, A. D. 679. See Reeves's "Adamnan," page xliv.

ˡ *The battle of Corann.*—Ann. F. M. 681; Ann. Ult. 682; Tigh. 683.

ᵐ *Mortality of children.*—Ann. Ult. 682; Tigh. 683; Brut y Tywysog. and Ann. Cambr. 683.

ⁿ *Airmeadhach of Craebh.*—i. e. Abbot of *Craebh Laisre*, a place near Clonmacnoise. Ann. Ult. 682; F. M. 681; Tigh. 683.

The death of Suibhne^g, son of Maelumha, prince [i.e. abbot] of Cork^h.
[683.] Kal. Dunchadh Muirisgeⁱ, son of Maeldubh, was killed. Adamnan^k assumed the abbacy of Ia.

The battle of Corann^l, in which were slain Colga, son of Blathmac, and Fergus, son of Maelduin, King of Cinel-Cairbre.

The beginning of the mortality of children^m in the month of October, which continued for three years in Ireland.

The repose of Airmeadhach of Craebhⁿ.

[684.] Kal. The mortality of the children, in which all the princes and almost all the nobles of the youth of the Scoti perished.

[685.] Kal. The Saxons^o devastated the plain of Breagh, and many churches.

[686.] Kal. Domhnall Breac, son of Eochaidh Buidhe [King of Scotland], died.

The repose of Banbhan^p, scribe of Cill-dara.

[687] Kal. The repose of Dochuma Chonoe^q, Abbot of Gleann-da-locha.

The repose of Roisene^r, Abbot of Corcach.

In this year Adamnan ransomed the captives^s whom the Saxons had carried away from Erin.

The battle of Dun Neachtain^t, between the son of Ossa and Bruide^u, son of Bile, in which the latter was the victor.

The

^o *The Saxons.*—Ann. Ult. 684; Tigh. 685; Ann. F. M. 683; Saxon Chron. 684.
^p *Banbhan.*—Ann. Ult. 685; Tigh. 686.
^q *Dochuma Chonoy.*—Ann. Ult. 686; Tigh. 687.
^r *Roisene.* — "A. D. 686 [*Tigh.* 687]. Dormitatio Rosseni, abbatis Corcaidhe mare" [great Cork: *mare* for *móre*].—*Ann. Ult.*

^s *Ransomed the captives.*—A. D. 686, or 687, Ann. Ult., and 689, Tigh. See Reeves's "Adamnan," pp. 186, 187, notes.
^t *Dun Neachtain.*—Now Dunnichen, a parish in Forfarshire. The Ann. Ult. 685, and Tigh. 686, say that this battle was fought on Saturday, 20th May, which agrees with 685. See Sax. Chron. 685.
^u *Bruide.*—He was King of the Picts;

Sancta Evelopioa, Chpipci pesma, pilia Annae pesip Anglopum, et ppimo et altepi uipo pepmasnipico, et poptea Evelppioo pesi, comux vata ept; popcquam xii anno thopim incoppupta pepuaint mapitalem popt pesinam pumpto uelamine pacpo uipso pancțimonialip eppicitup, quae popt xui. pepultupae cum vepte qua inoluta ept incoppupta pepepitup.

A. D. 686. Kal. Cat Imbleacha Phich, i ttopchaip Oubvaínbfp, pi Apva Ciannacta, ¬ Uapcpaite hUa Oippin: unve Zabopefin cecinit:—

Bpónac Conailli moin vetbip vóib iap n-Uapepibiu,
Ní ba eallma biap sfn, i n-apu iap n-Oubva inbfp.

In hoc bello alienam pațienp vominationem Ciannachtea senp ppimata ept pesno.

Sesine Epp ab Apomacha.
Cuțbeptup Epp quievit.
Cana mac Zaptnain moptup. Conptantinup Impepator moptup.

Kal.

"Rex Fortrenn;" Tigh. 686; Ult. 685. Ecfrid, son of Ossa (i. c. Ecgfrith, son of Oswin) is called King of the Saxons. Reeves's "Adamnan," p. 186, note. Lappenberg (Hist. of Engl.). "Geneal. of the Kings of Bernicia," vol. i., 289 (Thorpe's Transl.).

ʸ *Etheldrida.*—Or Aedilthryd. Bede, "Eccl. Hist.," lib. iv., c. 19. She is often called St. Audry in England. She died A.D. 679, according to the Saxon Chronicle.

ˣ *Ethelfrid.*—More correctly Ecgfrid, or Ecgfrith. He was King of Northumbria. This paragraph is extracted from Bede's *Chron. sive de sex ætatibus sæculi,* A.D. 688 (Works, ed. Giles, vol. vi., p. 327), and is very corruptly transcribed. Bede's words are: "Sancta et perpetua virgo Christi Ædilthryda, filia Annæ regis Anglorum, et primo alteri viro permagnifico, et post Ecfrido regi conjunx data, post quam xii. annos thorum incorrupta servavit maritalem, post reginam sumpto velamine sacro virgo sanctimonialis efficitur: nec mora etiam virginum mater et nutrix pia sanctarum, accepto in construendum monasterium loco quem Elge vocant: cujus merita vivacia testatur etiam mortua caro, quæ

The Queen of Christ, St. Etheldrida[r], daughter of Anna, King of the [East] Angles, who had been first given in marriage to another nobleman, and afterwards to King Ethelfrid[s]; after she had preserved her marriage-bed incorrupted for twelve years, the holy virgin, after she had become Queen, took the sacred veil, and became a nun; who sixteen years after her interment was found uncorrupted, as well as the shroud in which she had been wrapt.

[687.] A. D. 686. The battle of Imblech Phich[y], in which were slain Dubhdainbher, King of Ard-Cianachta[z], and Urchraithe Ua h-Ossin[a]; whence Gabhorcheun cecinit :—

Sorrowful are the Conailli this day; they have cause after Uarcraithe.
Not in readiness shall be the sword in Ard, after Dubhdainbher.

In this battle the race of the Cianachta passed under the dominion of another family, and was deprived of its power.

Segine[b], Bishop, Abbot of Ard-macha [died].

Cuthbertus, bishop, quievit.

Cana[c], son of Gartnan, died. Constantine, the Emperor, died. [689.]

post xvi. annos sepulturæ cum veste qua involuta est incorrupta reperitur."

[y] *Imblech Phich.*—Now Emlagh, near Kells, county of Meath. Ann. F. M. 686; Ann. Ult. 687; Tigh. 688.

[z] *Ard Cianachta.*—Now the barony of Ferrard, Co. Louth. The Cianachta were of the race of Cian, son of Oilioll Olum, King of Munster. Tadhg, son of Cian, obtained this territory in the third century from Cormac Mac Airt, King of Ireland; the district extended from the River Liffey to near Drumiskin, Co. Louth.

[a] *Urchraidhe Ua h-Ossin.*—"Huarcride nepos Osseni."—Ann. Ult. 687. "Uarcridhe hUa hOssine, righ Conaille."—Tigh. 688. See F. M. at A. D. 686.

[b] *Segine.*—F. M. 686; Ann. Ult 687; Tigh. 688. Cuthbert was Bishop of Lindisfarne. Ussher's "Primordia," pp. 944, 945; Bede, "Hist. Eccl.," iv. 27.

[c] *Cana.*—See Tigh. 688; Ult. 687. The Emperor Constantine IV., surnamed *Pogonatus*, died in 685.

Kal. Ʒuin Diarmada Miḋe, mic Airmḋaiʒ Chaoic; de quo bancáinte i nAonac Tailltĕn cecinit :—

Sia Diarmaid dor ror rḗin, rion ʒabla ro lenaiḋ laoich, ba hḟó uball abla óir, rian mara móir mac an Chaoic.

Kal. Aimer beccáin ab Cluana iraird.
Ʒnatnat abbatirra Cille dara.
Ʒuin Conʒaile mic Maoileduin, mic Aoḋa bḟnnáin, rí Muṁan.
Iurtinianur minor imreiat annir x.
Kal. Cronán mac hUa Cualna ab bḟnnċair quieuit. Fiṫ-ciollaċ mac Flainn rí hUa Máine moritur. Ailill mac Dunʒaile rí Crnitne moritur.

Kal. Adamnanur xiii anno port obitum Failbe ab. Iae ad Hibermam uenit. Fṡiʒar mac Aoḋáin, rí an ċúiʒiḋ moritur.
Ʒuin Faolċair rí Orraiʒe. Ʒuin Cinnfaolaiḋ mic Maoilbrea-rail la Laiʒniḃ.

Kal. bruide mac bile rí Fortrean moritur.
Maiṫim na borama la Fionnaċta do Moling, ar na breiṫ la xl. ri, unde dicitur :—

Cṡraċa

ᵈ *Diarmaid Midhe.* — Or Diarmait of Meath, i. e. King of Meath. "Jugulatio Diarmata mⁱ. Airmethaigh, .i. r. Midhi, la h Aed mⁱ. nDluthaigh r. Fercul."—Tigh. 689; Ult. 688. The female poet here quoted is unknown.

ᵉ *Becean.*—Ult. 689, where he is called "Dobeeog of Cluain Aird," which is correct. Tigh. 690, and F. M. 687, have Cluain Iraird. The devotional name *Do-beeog*, or *Dabeog*, instead of the diminutive *Becean*, is used by Ult. and Tigh.

ᶠ *Congal, son of Maelduin.*—Ann. F. M. 687.

ᵍ *Justinianus minor.*—Began to reign 685, and reigned ten years, when he was deposed, and his nose cut off. This entry is out of its proper place.

ʰ *Cronan Mac Ua Cualna.*—Ann. F. M. 688; Ann. Ult. 690; Tigh. 691.

ⁱ *Fithchellach, son of Flann.*—Ann. F. M. 688; Ann. Ult. 690; Tigh. 691.

ᵏ *Ailell, son of Dunghal.*—Not in the published Annals.

[689.] Kal. The slaying of Diarmaid Midhe[d], son of Airmheadhach Caech [i. e. blind], of whom the female satirist said at the fair of Tailtin :—

Diarmaid placed a bush on himself; he of the fair arms who destroyed heroes.
He was the apple of the golden orchard; the King of the great sea was this son of the Caech [i. e. the blind].

[690.] Kal. The repose of Beccan[e], Abbot of Cluain-Iraird. Gnathnat, Abbess of Cill-dara, [died.]
The slaying of Congal, son of Maelduin[f], son of Aedh Bennan, King of Munster.
Justinianus minor[g] reigns ten years.

[691.] Kal. Cronan Mac Ua Cualna[h], Abbot of Benchair, died.
Fithchellach, son of Flann[i], King of Ui Maine, died. Ailell, son of Dunghal[k], King of the Cruithni, died.

[692.] Kal. Adamnan[l] came to Ireland in the thirteenth year after the death of Failbhe, Abbot of Ia. Fergus, son of Aedhan, King of the province[m], died. The slaying of Faelchar[n], King of Osraighe. The slaying of Cennfaeladh, son of Maelbresail, by the Leinster-men.

[693.] Kal. Bruide, son of Bile[o], King of Foirtreann, died.
The remission of the Borumha[p] by Finnachta to Moling, after it had been levied by forty kings, on which was said—

Forty

---

[l] *Adamnan.*—See Adamnan's "Vit. Columbæ" (ed. Reeves), p. 378.

[m] *King of the province.*—i. e. of the territory of Uladh. "Fergus mac Aedain rex in Coicidh," [i. e. of the province] "obiit."—*Ann. Ult.*, A. D. 691.

[n] *Faelchar.*—"Faelchar hua Mailodrai." Tigh. 693. "Faelcar nepos Maele ordae." Ult. 692. "Faolcar Ua Maolodra." F. M. 690; Clonm. 688.

[o] *Bruide, son of Bile.*—He was King of Fortrenn, or Pictland, and died in 693.— Reeves's "Adamnan," p. 378.

[p] *The remission of the Borumha.*—See note °, p. 84, *supra*, and F. M., A. D. 106, p. 99, and A. D. 593, p. 216.

Cfpaċa pí do pala, lapa puzaḃ an ḃopaṁa
'O aimpip Tuaṫail Tlaċtga zo haimpip piop Pionnaċta.

Cetepa ppepcpipmup.

Mopp Fianaṁla mic Maoilecuile, pi Laiġṅ. Poiépċan da ṁuincip péṁ pod mapḃ; unde Moling:—

An can ċonzaip Fianaṁail ċuzċa a caoṁa uile,
A pomḟiad Poiépfċán, bad beo mac Maolcuile.

Kal. Ḃpan mac Conaill incipic pezṅape pop Laiznib. .
Cponán aḃace ab Cluana mic Nóip.
Mochua ballna quieuic.
huiopine Maize bile quieuic.
Zuin Cpiḃaill mic Maoile oḃpa pí hUa Néill.
Cat eidip Oppaiże ⁊ Laiznu, in quo cecidic Paolċaip hUa Maoile oḃpa.
Kal. Mapḃaḋ Pionnaċta mic Ounchaḋa, pí 'Epfin, dá ḃpáiṫpiḃ pén ⁊ ḃpeapal a ṁac maile ppip. Ap aṁlaiḋ po po mapḃaḋ .i. in can po paoid Pionnaċta a ṁac ḃpeapal ip in puball i n-Zpeallaiz Oollaid, canzaccap a ḃpaiṫpe pobccup auḃapcnaiżefċa dó .i. Aod mac Oluċaiz ⁊ Conzalac mac Conaing, gan aippizaḋ dóiḃ ipin
puball

ᵃ *Fianamhail.*—This entry is out of place. It is given by the F. M. at 678, Ult. 679, the true year being 680, as in Tigh.

ᵗ *Bran, son of Conall.*—Ann. Clonm. 685; F. M. 687.

ˢ *Cronan the Dwarf.*—See F. M. 692, and Ann. Ult. 693, where he is called Cronan Bec, i. e. the Little. Tigh. 694.

ᵗ *Mochua of Balla.* —This obit appears to be out of place here. It is entered in the Annals of Clonmacnoise, and in the Ann. F. M. at the year 637. St. Cronan, of Balla, died in 693, according to the Annals of Ulster. Tigh. 694; F. M. 692; so that there is probably confusion.

ᵘ *Huidhrine.*—F. M. 691; Ult. 693.

ᵛ *Cearbhall.*—Ann. Ult. 693.

ˣ *Faelchair.*—See above at A. D. 691.

ʸ *Finnachta.*—Ann. Clonm. 690; Ann. F. M. and Tigh. 693; Ann. Ult. 694.

Forty kings there were, by whom the Borumha was levied,
From the time of Tuathal of Tlachtgha, to the exact time of
Finachta.

Cætera præscripsimus.

The death of Fianmhail[q], son of Maeltuile, King of Leinster. Foichsechan, one of his own people, killed him, of which Moling [said]—

When Fianamhail cried out, "At them, ye nobles all!"
Had Foichsechan withheld, the son of Maeltuile would have
lived.

[694.] Kal. Bran, son of Conall[r], began to reign over the Leinster-men.

Cronan the Dwarf[s], Abbot of Cluain-mic-Nois, [died].

Mochua, of Balla[t], quievit.

Huidhrine[u], of Maghbile, quievit.

The slaying of Cearbhall[v], son of Maelodhra, King of the Ui-Neill [of Leinster(?)].

A battle [was fought] between the Osraighi and the Leinster-men, in which Faelchair[x], grandson of Maelodhra, fell.

[695.] Kal. The slaying of Finnachta[y], son of Dunchadh, King of Erin and of Breasal, his son along with him, by his own brethren. This is the manner in which he was killed: when Finnachta sent his son Breasal into the tent at Greallach-Dollaidh[z], his brethren, who were opposed to him, viz. Aedh, son of Dluthach, and Conghalach, son of Conaing, came, without being perceived by them, into the tent, and

---

The true year is 695. See O'Flaherty's "Ogygia," Part iii., c. 93. p. 432.

[z] *Greallach Dollaidh.*—This is probably the place now called Grellach, Anglice Girley, near Kells, in the county of Meath. See Ann. F. M., A. D. 693, note ᵑ, p. 297.

puball ⁊ ɼa maɼbɼac Fionnaċca ⁊ a mac, ⁊ ɼa bɼɼac a ccionna úíob; unbe bicicuɼ:—

   ba buiɼɼan bFionnaċca aniu laiʓe i ccɼoiliʓe
   Ron bé lá ɼɼiaib nime biolʓab ionna bóɼaime.

Oɼʓain Cainʓ mic Failbe i nʓlionn ʓaimin.ᵃ
Quieɼ Minbbaɼɼɼ, ab Aċaib bó.ᵇ
Ʒaimine Lúʓmaiʓ moɼicuɼ.
Moɼɼ bɼain, mic Conaill biʓ.ᶜ
Kal. Loinʓɼċé mac Aonʓaɼa ɼo ʓab ɼiʓe n-Eɼeann i nuɼʓaib
Finnacca ɼe hoċc mbliabnaib. Fionʓuine mac Con ʓan máċaiɼ moɼicuɼ.ᵈ Fɼiʓal Aibne, ⁊ Fianamail mac Maonaiʓ moɼiuncuɼ.
Conʓalaċ mac Conainʓ mic Aiba moɼicuɼ.
Loiċine Mɼnb Sapienɼ, ab Cille bapa, inʓulacuɼ eɼc.
Cunimeni Muʓbopna quieuic.
Kal. Abamnanuɼ uenic in Hibeɼniam, ec inoicic leʓem inno-centium populiɼ hibeɼniae .i. ʓan maca ʓan inná bo maɼbab.ᶠ
Caɼán ɼeɼba ó Luɼca quieuic.
Molinʓ Luaċɼa, plenuɼ bieɼum quieuic.
Maolɼaċuɼcaiʓ ɼiʓ na n-Aiɼʓiall quieuic.
Iomaiɼɼʓ Cɼanbċa, i ccoɼċaiɼ Feaɼċaiɼ mac Maoil buin.
bɼɼcnai ⁊ Ulaib bo ɼáɼuċċab Maiʓe Muiɼċemne.

                                                        Kal.

ᵃ *Tadhg, son of Failbhe.*—Ann. F. M. 693. Glenn Gaimin was the ancient name of the vale of the River Roo, near Dungiven, in the barony of Keenaght, county of Londonderry. It is called by Tighernach, A. D. 695, "Glen in Croccind;" translated "vallis pellis," by the Ann. Ult. 694.

ᵇ *Mennbairen.*—Ann. F. M. 693; Ult. 694. *Achadh-bo* is the present Aghabo, in the Queen's County. *Lughmhagh* is the present town of Louth.

ᶜ *Bran.*—Ann. F. M. 687; Tigh. 690.

ᵈ *Loingsech, son of Aenghus.*—Ann. Ult. and Tigh. 695, which seems the true year. But he reigned nine, not eight years. See O'Flaherty's "Ogyg.," p. 432.

ᵉ *Finguine.*—Ann. Ult. 695; Tigh. 696.

ᶠ *Law of the Innocents.*—There are two copies of this *Lex Innocentium*, called *Cain Adamnain*, still preserved, one in a

and killed Finnachta and his son, and cut off their heads, on which was said—

Pitiful for Finnachta this day, to lie in death.
He will be with the men of heaven for remitting the Borumha.

The slaying of Tadhg, son of Failbhe[a], in Glenngaimhin.
The death of Mennbairen[b], Abbot of Achadh-bo.
Gaimide, of Lughmhagh, died.
The death of Bran[c], son of Conall Beg.

[695.] Kal. Loingsech, son of Aenghus[d], took the government of Erin, after Finnachta, for eight years. Finguine[e], son of Cu-ganmathair, died. Ferghal Aidhne [King of Connaught], and Fianamhail, son of Maenach, died. Conghalach, son of Conaing, son of Aedh[Slaine], died.

Loichine Menn the Wise, Abbot of Kildare, was killed.
Cummeni, of Mughdhorna, quievit.

[696.] Kal. Adamnan came to Erin, and promulgated the "Law of the Innocents"[f] to the people of Erin, i. e. not to kill children or women.

Casán[g], scribe of Lusca, quievit.
Moling Luchra plenus dierum quievit.
Maelfothartaigh[h], King of the Airghialls, quievit[i].

The battle of Crannach [was fought], in which was slain Fearchair, son of Maelduin. The Britons and Ultonians devastated Magh Muirtheimhne[k].

[697.]

MS. in the Ambrosian Library at Brussels, and another in the Bodleian Library at Oxford, Rawl. 505.--See Ann. Ult. 696. and Reeves's "Adamnan," p. 179.

[g] *Casán.*—"Cassan scriba Luscan, quievit. Moling Luachra dormitavit."—*Ann. Ult.* 696. See F. M., 696; Tigh. 697.

[h] *Maelfothartaigh.*—See Ann. F. M. 695; Ann. Ult. 696.

[i] *Quievit.*—The word "moritur" is written over this word as a gloss, probably because *quievit* was properly applied only to the death of a saint.

[k] *Magh Muirtheimhne.*—This was the

Kal. Mopp Popanoain, ab Cille oapa.

Cat Fspnmaige i ttopcaip Aoö mac Maolouin, ⁊ Concobap Aipfo, pí Dáil Apaioe, qui cecinit:—

Ap mé Concopup speacac, pop Loc Eacac iomaoßal.
Mspclé pia gail impetiup, ip poptecsut oon aobut.

Kal. Tpep papmae in coelo quapi bellantep uipae punt ab opiente in occioentem in modo inoapim, pluctuantium in tpan-quillippima nocte Apcenpiomp Domini. Ppima niuea, pecunoa ignea, teptia panguinea. Quae, ut apbitpatup, tpia mala pequentia ppaepigupabant. Nam in eodem anno aipmenta bouilia in tota hibepnia pepe oeleta punt, [et] non polum in hibepnia, peo etiam pep totam Eupopam. In altepo anno peptilentia humana tpibup continuit annip. Poptea maxima pamep, in qua hominep ao inpamep epcap peoacti punt.

Cat Fiannamla mic Opene.
Mopp Muipgiupa mic Maoilouin, pí Cineil Caipppe. Iup-timanup Augurtur pellitup.
Kal. Leo impepat annip iii.
Kal. Quiep Aoöa Eppcoip Slebte.

Fiannamail

level part of the present county of Louth. "Britones et Ulaid vastaverunt Campum Muirtheimhne." Ann. Ult. 696; Tigh. 697.
¹ *Forannan.*—Ann. F. M. 697; Tigh. 698.
ᵐ *Loch Eachach.*—Now Loch Neagh.
ⁿ *Three shields.*—This prodigy is not recorded in any of the published Irish Annals, nor in the Saxon Chronicle.
ᵒ *Herds of cows.*—"Accensa est bovina mortalitas in Hibernia in Kal. Februarii in Campo Trego i Tethbai."—*Ann. Ult.* 699; *Tigh.* 700.
ᵖ *Unmentionable foods.*—"Fames et pestilentia tribus annis in Hibernia facta est, ut homo hominem comederet."—*Ann. Ult.* 699; *Tigh.* 700.
ᑫ *Fianamhail.*—He was probably the Fianamhail Ua Dunchadha, chief of Dal Riada, mentioned in the Ann. F. M. as slain in 698; vide *infra*, p. 100, note ᵃ.
ʳ *Muirghes.*—Ann. Ult. 697.

[697.] Kal. The death of Forannan[l], Abbot of Cill-dara.
The battle of Fearnmhagh, in which were slain Aedh, son of Maelduin, and Conchobhar Aired, King of Dal Araidhe, who said—

"I am the plundering Conchobhar, on Loch Eachach[m] mighty. Rapid they run before valour, they fly to the fortress."

[698.] Kal. Three shields[n] were seen in the heavens, as it were warring from the east to the west, after the manner of undulating waves on a very calm night, being that of the Ascension of the Lord. The first was snowy, the second fiery, the third bloody; which prefigured, as is thought, three succeeding evils: for in the same year the herds of cows[o] throughout Ireland were nearly destroyed, and not only in Ireland, but also throughout the whole of Europe. In the other year there was a human pestilence [which continued] for three successive years. Afterwards the greatest famine [set in], during which men were reduced to devour unmentionable foods[p].

The battle of Fiannamhail[q], son of Oisen.

The death of Muirghes[r], son of Maelduin, King of Cinel-Cairpre.

Justinianus[s] Augustus is expelled.

Kal. Leo reigned three years.

[700.] Kal. The death of Aedh[t], Bishop of Sleibhte.

Fiannamhail

[s] *Justinianus.*—This refers to the banishment of Justinian II., by the usurper Leontius, here (as well as by Bede, *Chron. in an.* 701) called Leo: who after having cut off his predecessor's nose, and banished him to the Chersonese, A. D. 694, occupied the throne until 697, when his own nose and ears having been cut off, he was imprisoned in a monastery by his successor Tiberius Absimarus; at length, in 704 or 705, Justinian recovered the throne, and put both Leontius and Absimarus to death.

[t] *Aedh.*—He is called "Anchorita," not *Bishop*, of Slebhte: Tigh. 700; Ult. 699; F. M. 628. Sleibhte, now called Slatey, is situated in the Queen's County, near Carlow.

Fiannamail hUa Dunchaḋa, ri Dail Riaṫa moriṫur.

Irin bliaḋainri do rala eirir Iorgalaċ mac Conaing ⁊ Aḋaṁ-
nan ar rárugaḋ Aḋaṁnain do Iorgalaċ im marbaḋ Néill a bráṫar
dó ar comairge Aḋamnáin. Areaḋ do gníoḋ Aḋamnan trorgaḋ
gaċ n-oíḋċe, ⁊ gan coḋla, ⁊ beiṫ i n-uirgiḃ uariḃ, do ċimḃiḋe rao-
gail Iorgalaiġ. Ar eaḋ imurro do gníoḋ an córaiḋ rain .i. Iorgalaċ
a riarraigiḃ do Aḋaṁnán, "Créd do ġénara anoċt a cleirig?"
Ní ba hail do Aḋamnán brég do ráḋa rriṫ. Ro imirċd dó go
mbiaḋ a ttorgaḋ gan ċoḋlaḋ i n-uirge uar go maiḋin. Do gníoḋ
an t-Iorgalaċ an céḋna .i. da raoraḋ ar rrguine Aḋamnáin. Aċt
ċṁa ro ṁeall Aḋamnan ériom .i. ro ḃoí Aḋamnan 'ga ráḋ ra
cléreaċ dá ṁuintir, "bíri runna anoċt im rioċt-ra ⁊ ṁéḋaċ-ra
ioman, ⁊ da ttí Iorgalaċ dá iarraigliḋ ḋíot, créd ra ġena anoċt,
abairre buḋ frḋugaḋ, ⁊ coḋlaḋ do ġena, ar ḋaig go nḋearnaroṁ
na céḋna, uair arru ra Aḋaṁnán brġ da rior muintire quam do
rén. Tainig iaram Iorgalach dionroigiḃ an cléirig rin, ⁊ an dar
leir, ba é Aḋamnán baoi ann, Ro iarraig Iorgalaċ ḋe, créd do
ġénara anoċt, a cléirig? Frḋugaḋ ⁊ coḋlaḋ, ar an cléreaċ.
Do roine ono Iorgalaċ frḋugaḋ ⁊ coḋlaḋ an aiḋċe rin. Do rine
imurro Aḋamnan aoine, ⁊ ḟriotaire, ⁊ beiṫ 'r an ḃóinn go maiḋin. An tan ono ro ḃaoi Iorgalaċ 'na ċoḋlaḋ a reaḋ aḋ ċonnairċ
Aḋamnán do ḃeiṫ go nuige a ḃragaiḋ ir in uirge, ⁊ ro bíog go mór
trín rin ar a ċoḋlaḋ; ⁊ ra imir dá mnaoí. An ḃrṁ imurro, ba
huṁal

ᵘ *Fiannamhail Ua Dunchadha.*—Ann. F. M. 698; Ann. Ult. 699.

ᵛ *Irgalach, son of Conaing.*—The cursing of this chieftain by Adamnan at Rath-na Seanadh, at Tara, is mentioned in an ancient poem published in Petrie's "Antiquities of Tara Hill," p. 122-148. See Reeves's "Adamn.," liii., liv., 179.

ˣ *Should tell a lie.*—Adamnan (according to this story) did not wish to tell a lie himself, but he had no objection that one of his clergy should tell a lie to screen him. This is a mere legend, and much more modern than the Age of Adamnan. It

Fiannamhail Ua Dunchadha", King of Dál-Riada.

In this year a dissension arose between Irgalach, son of Conaing[v], and Adamnan, after Adamnan had been sacrilegiously violated by Irgalach, by killing his brother Niall, who was under the protection of Adamnan. What Adamnan used to do was to fast every night, and remain awake, and stay [immersed] in cold water to cut short the life of Irgalach. And what this champion, i. e. Irgalach, used to do was to ask Adamnan, "What wilt thou do to-night, O clerk?" Adamnan did not like to tell him a lie. He used to tell him that he would be fasting without sleep in cold water till morning. Irgalach used to do the same to free himself from the curse of Adamnan. But, however, Adamnan deceived him. He said to a clerk of his people: "Be thou here to-night in my stead, with my clothes upon thee, and if Irgalach should come to ask thee what thou wilt do to-night, say thou unto him that thou wilt feast and sleep, in order that he may do the same, for Adamnan had rather that one of his people should tell a lie[x] than himself. Irgalach afterwards came to that clerk, and thinking that it was Adamnan who was there, he asked him, "What wilt thou do to-night, O clerk?" "Feast and sleep," replied the clerk. Irgalach, therefore, feasted and slept that night. But Adamnan fasted, and watched, and remained in the Bóinn[y] till morning. Now when Irgalach was asleep, he saw [in a dream] that Adamnan was immersed to the neck in the water, and he started violently from his sleep in consequence of it, and told it to his wife. The wife, however, was humble and submissive to the Lord and to Adamnan,

occurs in the Irish Life of Adamnan. See Reeves, p. liv., and note ". Stories of this nature in the lives of Irish saints are severely censured as *fabulæ futiles* by the early Bollandists. They are evidence, not of lax morality in the saints, but of the rude ignorance of the times in which such tales were invented and told as not inconsistent with a saintly character.

[y] *The Bóinn.*—i. e. the River Boyne.

huṁal ınírıl í ꝺon coıṁoꝛꝺ, ⁊ ꝺo Aꝺaṁnán, uaıꝛ ba coꝛꝛac í, ⁊ ba híꝟaıl lé a clann ꝺo loꞅ ꞅꝛé ꝛꝟuıne Aꝺaṁnáın, ⁊ ꝛa ꝟuíṁeaꝺ ꟾo meınıc Aꝺamnán ꟾan a clann ꝺo loꞅ no ꝺ'eꝛꟾuıne. Ra eıꝛıꟾ ıaꝛaṁ loꝛꟾalac moccꝛác aꝛ na báꝛac, ⁊ ꝺo ꝛala Aꝺamnán na aıꟾıꝺ. Aꝛeaꝺ ꝛa ꝛáıꝺ Aꝺamnán ꝛıꝛ; "a ṁıc ṁallıꟾꞅe (aꝛ ꝛé), ⁊ a ꝺuıne aꝛ cꝛóꝺa, ⁊ aꝛ mꞅꝛꝛa ꝺo ꝛıꟾne Ꝺıa, bıoc a ꝛıoꝛ aꟾac ꟾuꝛ ob ꟾaıꝛıꝺ ꟾuꝛ ꝛoꝺꝛꟾeꝛcuꝛ ꝛıc ꝛlaıcıuꝛ, ⁊ ꝛaꟾa ꝺo cum n-Iꝛꝛınn." O ꝺo cuala bín loꝛꟾalaıꟾ ꝛın, caınıꟾ aꝛ aınuꝛ Aꝺamnáın, ⁊ ꝛo luıꟾ ꝛo coꝛꝛaıb Aꝺamnáın, ꝛa accaıꟾ Ꝺıa ꝛıꝛꝛ ꟾan a clann ꝺ'eaꝛ- ꟾuıne, ⁊ ꟾan an ꟾeın ꝛo baoı'na bꝛoınn ꝺo loc. Aꝛeaꝺ ꝛo ꝛáıꝺ Aꝺamnán, buꝺ ꝛı ꟾo ꝺeıṁın, aꝛ ꝛé," an ꟾen ꝛaıl ıꝺ bꝛoınn, ⁊ aꝛ bꝛıꝛce a líꞅꝛúıl anoꝛꝛa cꝛe eaꝛꟾuıne a acaꝛ. Aꟾaꝛ aꝛ aṁlaıꝺ ꝛın ꝺo ꝛála. Ruꟾaꝺ ꝛo céꝺoıꝛ ıaꝛꝛaın an mac, ⁊ aꝛ aṁluıꝺ ꝛo baoı ⁊ ꝛé leacćaoc.

Féıꝺlımıꝺ mac Maoıle cacaıꟾ. Aılell mac Con-ꟾan máċaıꝛ, ꝛí Muman (ꝺéc.).

Oꝛꟾaın Néıll mıc Cꝛꝛnaıꟾ, uc Aꝺamnanuꝛ ꝛꝛoꝛhecauıc.

Oꝛꟾaın Néıll oc Ꝺꝛꝛıꝛ Eaꝛꝛꝛaıꟾ,
Ꝺıa láıꝛꝛ ꝺáıꟾ ꝺo Mullac ꝛı,
Ꝺıa ꝛꝛꝛı aꝛ ꝛoꝛ ꝛoꝛbaꝛ cuan
Ꝺıa Luaın ı n-Imlıoc Fích.

Iꝛꟾalac mac Conaınꟾ [occıꝺıc ıllum].

Kal. Faolꝺobaꝛ Chlocaıꝛ obııc.

Cıbeꝛıuꝛ

ᵃ *Shall verily be a king.*—He was Cinaedh, son of Irgalach, who reigned as monarch of Ireland from 724 to 727. It does not appear from any other authority that he was a one-eyed king.

ᵃ *Feidhlimidh, son of Maelcothaigh.*—Not in the published Annals.

ᵇ *Ailell, son of Cu-gan-mathair.*—Ann. F. M. 699; Ann. Ult. 700; Tigh. 701.

ᶜ *Niall.*—" *Occisio* Neill mic Cearnaig. Irgalach ucpos Conaing *occidit illum.*" Ann. Ult. 700; Tigh. 701. Reeves's "Adamnan," p. liii., liv. Here the compiler of these Annals mixes up two entries,

Adamnan, for she was pregnant, and she was afraid that her child might be destroyed through Adamnan's curse, and she often besought Adamnan not to injure or curse her child. Irgalach rose early the next morning, and Adamnan came to meet him. What Adamnan said was : " O cursed man" (said he), "and thou bloodiest and worst man that God hath made, be it known unto thee that in a short time thou shalt be separated from thy kingdom, and shalt go to hell." When the wife of Irgalach heard this she came to Adamnan, and, prostrating herself at his feet, she besought him, for God's sake, not to curse her children, and not to destroy the infant she had in her womb. Adamnan said: "The child that is in thy womb," said he, " shall verily be a king"; but one of his eyes is now broken in consequence of the cursing of his father." And thus it came to pass. The son was born immediately afterwards, and it was found that he was half blind.

Feidhlimidh[a], son of Maelcothaigh, Ailell, son of Cu-gan-mathair[b], King of Munster, [died].

The killing of Niall[c], son of Cearnach, as Adamnan had prophesied.

> The plundering by Niall at Dris-Easfraigh,
> As he burned to Mullach-ri,
> As he inflicted slaughter on numerous troops
> On Monday at Imleach-Fich.

Irgalach, son of Conaing [killed him].
[702.] Kal. Faelcobhar[d] of Clochar died.

Tiberius

—one relating to the triumph of Niall, the son of Cearnach Sotal, over his enemies at Imlech Phich, which actually took place in the year 687, and which our compiler has noticed at the proper place—and the other, his death, which occurred in 701. The verses here quoted belong properly to the year 687. See p. 91.

[d] *Faelcobhar.* — Faoldobhair. Ann. F. M. and Ann. Ult. 701 ; Tigh. 702.

Tiberiur impepac annrp un.

Ir in mbliaöainri ro marbaö Iorgalac mac Conaing .i. ı rſct-
maö bliaöain flaċa Loingrig, cre frguine Aöamnáin, 7 ro connairc
fén ı n-airlinge a naöoig fé na marbaö amail ro marbaö. Tainig ıariam lorgalac an la ıar ffaigrin a airlinge ar carraig amac,
7 aö cuala an guc áro .ı. fá na fſrannaib coṁfoıgri öuib (ar ré)
7 öooíö 7 loırgıö 7 airgıö ıaö: 7 ra connaic ar a haıċle rin na
fluaig 7 na roćuıöe og ınnreaö an fſrainn; 7 cáinigrıom reṁe go
hairö ra ınır mac Nerain aniar, 7 ır ın uair rin öo fála coblac
Lrſcnac öo ċor ı rorc ann, 7 anraö lán mór öoíb; Ro connaic miliö
öıbrıöe airlinge an aöaıg reime, .ı. créö öo ċorcuıb öo crıoéugaö
uime, 7 an corc ba móó ann öo marbaö öo ö'aonöuille raıgöe;
agar arcaö ón fá ríoraö, uair ba hé lorgalac an corc mór rain,
7 ba hé a fluag rſcac mallaccnacrom an créö úö. 'On miliö rin
cra aö connairc an airlinge ro marbaö lorgalac.

Kal. Colman mac Fıonnöair ab lir mór moricur.

Mórfluag la Loingrıoć, mac Aongura, ı g Connaccaıb, ö'argain
agar ö'innrfö Connacc. Ro baccuır filiö loingrıg ag aoraö rí
Connacc .ı. Ceallac, mac Ragallaıg, 7 öo bíöír ga fáöa, nár bo
cuburö öo fſurıg crıocánac mar Ceallac comcógbail no combuar-
cur re rıg n-Eırſın, 7 gé öo nſċ, ro ba fair buö maıöm. Acc
ċna, ni haṁlaıö rin öo fála, acc a coöarrna, uair ó öo connairc
an Ceallac ri Connacc a ċır 7 a ċalaṁ ga locc 7 öa hinnrſö, ro
gairm cuıge na öá Dúnċaö ı. Dúnċaö Muırırge, 7 an Dúnċaö
eile

e *Tiberius.*—This was Tiberius Apsimarus. See note 8, p. 98, *supra.*

i *Irgalach.*— " *Irgalach Nepos* Coning
a Britonibus jugulatus in Insi mic Nesan."
—*Ann. Ult.* 701; *Tigh.* 702.

g *Loingsech.*—Loingsech began his reign
in the year 795, and the true year of Irgalach's death was 702.

h *Inis-mac Nesain.*—i. e. the island of
the sons of Nesan, now Ireland's Eye,
[i. e. Ireland's Island], near the Hill of
Howth, in the county of Dublin.

Tiberius[e] reigned seven years.

[702.] In this year Irgalach[f], son of Conaing, was slain, i. e. in the seventh year of the reign of Loingsech[g], in consequence of the curse of Adamnan. And he himself had seen in a dream, the night before his death, how he was [to be] killed. Irgalach came the day after he had seen this vision out upon a rock, and he heard a loud voice, saying, "Into the nearest lands go ye, and burn, consume, and plunder them;" and he saw, after this, hosts and troops plundering the land; and he came forward to a hill to the west of Inis-mac Nesain[h]; and at that time there came a British fleet into port there, being overtaken by a very great storm. A hero of these had seen a vision on the night before, viz., that a herd of swine made an attack upon him, and that the largest boar of them was killed by him with one blow of a dart; and this was indeed verified, for Irgalach was that great boar, and his sinful and cursed host was that herd. By that very champion who had seen this vision was Irgalach slain.

[703.] Kal. Colman[i], son of Finnbhar, abbot of Lis-mor, died.

A great host was led by Loingsech, son of Aenghus, into Connacht, to plunder and waste that province. The poets of Loingsech were satirizing the King of Connacht, i. e. Ceallach, son of Raghallach, and they used to say that it was not proper for a palsied old king like Ceallach to vie or contend with the King of Erin, and that, if he did, he would be defeated. But, however, this did not happen to be the case, but the very opposite: for when Ceallach, King of Connacht, had perceived that his territory and land were being injured and plundered, he called unto him the two Dunchadhs, i. e. Dunchadh Muirsa, and the other Dunchadh, and he determined beforehand that they should succeed to the kingdom of Connacht after

---

[i] *Colman.*—Ann. Ult. 702; Tigh. 703; F. M. 702. See Colgan, Acta SS., pp. 154, 155. He was commonly called *Mocholmoc*, i. e. "my little Coluin," accord-

oile, ⁊ na cinoaiġe peiṁe ꞅo maḃ iaḃ na ꞅeḃaḃ niġe Connachꞇ na
ḃꞅaiḃ ꝑéin. Ro ḃaoi ꝑén imunno an na poꞇnuccaḃ, ⁊ an ccun ola
⁊ luiḃe ioinḃa pioġḃa paoi. Do naḃ ꝑꞅn ḃon ḃíꞅ pꞅṁnáiꞇe (.i. ḃo
na ḃá Dunċaḃ) ḃá lnċ ḃein ⁊ ꝑꞅn ḃa leiꞇ clí, ⁊ na ċonaiġ Connaċꞇa uinne ḃo ċum an ċaꞇa. Rá linꞅ ꝑén .i. Ceallaċ an a ċaꞃḃaḃ
amaċ ꞅo ꞇnic, ⁊ ꞅo ꝑaḃa ón ċanꞃaḃ, ⁊ aḃ cualaḃ ḃninꞅleaċ ċnáṁa
an ꞇꞃṁóꞃaċ oꞅ léim an an ċanḃaḃ, ⁊ ꞅo ꞅaiḃ ian ꞃin ó ġuċ móꞃ,
oꞅ léim ḃo ċum an ċaꞇa coṁaiꞇiġ: a Chonnaċꞇa, an ꝑé, ḃíḃmḃ ⁊
coiṁéḃoiġ ꝑén ḃun ꞅaoine, uain ní huainꞃu ⁊ ní ḃeoḃa an cinꞅḃ ꝑail
in ḃun n-aiꞅiḃ ionḃáꞇíꞃi, ⁊ ní mó ḃo nonꞅaḃ ḃo ṁaiꞇ ꞅun aniu; ⁊
aṁlaiḃ na ḃaoi ꞅá náḃ, ⁊ a ġuċ ꞃo cnioꞇ ⁊ a ꝑúile ꝑon laꞃaḃ. Do
naḃꞃaḃ ianam Connaċꞇa ḃá nuiḃ ꞃin, ⁊ na ꞅaḃ an ꞃí cnioꞇánaċ ꞃin
neampa a ꞅeꞅḃn ċaꞇa ní Einꞅnn, ⁊ na ṁaiḃ nenṁe ꝑon ní Einꞅnn, ⁊
ꞅo manḃaḃ Loinꞅnoċ in Einꞅnn ann, ⁊ ḃꞅnꞅán a ṁuinꞇine, ⁊ a ꞇnní
mac, ⁊ ḃá mac Colꞅán, ⁊ Duḃoiḃenꞅ mac Dunꞅaile, ⁊ Eochaiḃ
ꞅnnna, ⁊ Ꝑꞅnꞅun Ꝑoncnaiḃ ⁊ Conall Ꞅhaḃna. I quanꞇ luil ꞃo
cuinꞅn an caꞇ ꞃo .i. caꞇ Conainn. Aꞃ ꞇniaꞅ na nannaiḃ ꞃi imunno
na cuinꞃḃ an caꞇ. Conall menḃ cecinniꞇ:

    ḃáꞃa aḃaiꞅ i ccoꞃann, ḃaꞃa uaċꞇ, ḃaꞃa omunn,
    Manaḃa ḃaꞅocu laꞃ niḃa i Coꞃann mac nDunchaḃa,
                                                    Da

---

ing to the Irish mode of expressing per-
sonal devotion to a saint. See Colgan's
Acta SS., p. 71, notes 2 and 3.

ᵏ *King of Erin.*—" *Bellum* Corain, *in
quo cecidit* Loingsech mac Oengusa *rex Hiberniæ*," &c. Ann. Ult. 702; Tigh. 703;
F. M., A. D. 701, p. 302.

ˡ *Fourth of July.*—Tigh. and the Ann.
Ult. say: " 4° id. Julii, 6° hora diei Sab-
bati hoc bellum confectum est." Therefore the year must have been 704, as

O'Flaherty remarks (Ogyg., p. 432), not
703, as in Dr. O'Conor's edition of Tighernach. The Chron. Scotor. has "Id. Julii,"
or July 15, which corresponds to 703.

ᵐ *Coranna.*—" Coranna regio olim Ga-
lengam in agro Mayoensi, Lugniam, et ho-
diernam Corannam in agro Sligoensi com-
plexa est."—O'Flaherty's *Ogyg.*, p. 334.

ⁿ *Conall Menn.*—In the Leabhar Ga-
bhala of the O'Clerys (p. 194), and in the
F. M. (p. 303), the last two lines of this

after himself. He himself was after bathing, and after applying oil, and many precious herbs. He placed one of the two aforesaid, i. e. of the two Dunchadhs, on his right, and the other on his left, and he arrayed the Connacht-men about him for the battle. Ceallach himself rushed from his chariot actively, and he went a far distance from it, and the crackling of the bones of the old man was heard as he leaped from the chariot; and he after this said in a loud voice, in springing to the battle: "O men of Connacht," said he, "do you yourselves preserve and defend your liberty, for the people who are against you are not nobler or braver than you, and they have not done more good to this day." And he said these words with a trembling voice, and with eyes on fire. The men of Connacht took heed of this, and this palsied king proceeded at their head to meet the army of the King of Erin, and he drove the King of Erin[k] before him; and Loingsech, King of Erin, was killed there, and his people were dreadfully slaughtered, and his three sons were killed; as were the two sons of Colgan; and Dubhdibherg, son of Dunghal; and Eochaidh Leamhna, and Fergus Forcraidh, and Conall Gabhra. On the fourth of July[l] this battle was fought, i. e. the Battle of Corann[m]. It was in consequence of these verses this battle was fought. It was Conall Menn[n] that composed them:

I was a night in Corann; I was cold, I was timid,
Were it not for the goodly youths who were with him in Corann of the sons of Dunchadh.

If poem are attributed to Cellach himself. The F. M. quote also the 3rd, 4th, 5th, and 6th lines, and attribute them to Conall Menn, chief of the Cinel Cairbre. The Dublin copy of the Ann. Ult. has in the margin the following second account of the battle:—Cat Copainn in quo cecidit Loingреé mac Oengupa pi Cpeno cum tribus filiis suis, ⁊ pi Caipppi Opoma cliab [Drumcliff] ⁊ pi hUa Conail Ṡabpa, ⁊ .x. piġ do piġaib Epenn imaille piu pein hi cloinpino hi cinn oenaiġ

Da ttí Loingrioć no bannaι, co na tṗι céoιιιḃ céo ιme,
ʒιallp̣aιṫ cιṫ leaḃop̣ a ḃlιać, Ceallać lιać Loċa Cιme.
Teacp̣aιʒ Ceallać cειp̣clι ćp̣uιnnι cp̣o tṗι p̣ιnne
ḃoṫḃ moṗlιnʒι, la p̣ιʒ lánṁöſaṗʒ Loċa Cιme,
ḃa huιlʒ ċuιlʒ maιṫſn p̣a ḃaoι aʒ Ʒlaιp̣ṗ Chuιlʒ
ḃeop̣a Loingṗιoć an ṫo ċaιlʒ aιp̣ṫp̣ιʒ 'Eιp̣ſnn ιιne cuιp̣ṫ.

Ra ćuaιṫ ιap̣ttaιn Ceallać mac Raʒallaιʒ ṫ'ſcclaιp̣, ⁊ p̣o p̣á-
ʒaιḃ an ḃá Ounċaṫ 'na p̣ιʒe, ⁊ ba map̣ḃ an Ceallać ι ʒcιonn ṫa
ḃlιaṫaιn ιap̣ttaιn.

Caṫ Maιʒe Cuιllιnn eιoιp̣ Ultuιb ⁊ ḃp̣eatnuḃ ι n-Ap̣ṫ hua
n-Eaċṫać, ι ttop̣ċaιp̣ mac Ranʒunṫ, aṫueṗp̣ap̣ιιup̣ ecclep̣ιap̣um
Oeι. Ulaιṫ uιctop̣ep̣ ep̣ant.

Ḃp̣an mac Conaιll, p̣í Laιʒſn, moṗιtup̣.

INITIUM REGNI FOGARTAIG·

Kal. Ceallać mac Ʒeιp̣ćιoe ι p̣ιʒe Laιʒſn.

Foʒap̣taċ aṗíp̣ ṫo ʒaḃáιl p̣ιʒe aoιn ḃlιaṫaιn ʒo tcop̣ċaιp̣ ι ccaṫ
Cιnnṫelʒtιn la Cιnaoć mac Ιop̣ʒalaιʒ.

Sluaʒ la Foʒap̣taċ ι Laιʒnιḃ, ʒo ttuʒp̣aṫ Laιʒιn caṫ ṫú.ι. caṫ
Claonta, ⁊ p̣o ṁaιṫ p̣e Laιʒnιḃ an caṫ, ⁊ p̣o map̣ḃaṫ ṫeap̣ʒáp̣
muιntιp̣e

Loʒa ιtep̣ Conaιll ⁊ Connaċta.

"*If Loingsech.*—O'Reilly quotes this line and the next from O'Clery, but reads *Cellach* instead of Loingsech.—*Dict., voce* biaċ. See note ⁿ, F. M., p. 303.

ᵖ *Loch Cime.*—Now Lough Hacket, in the parish of Donaghpatrick, barony of Clare, and county of Galway.

ᵠ *Glais-chuilg.*—Situation unknown. It was probably the name of a stream in this barony.

ʳ *Into the Church.*—i. e. took the monastic habit.

ˢ *Two years.*—"Ceallach mac Ragallaigh, rex Connacht, *post clericatum*, obiit."—*Tigh.* 705; *Ult.* 704.

ᵗ *The Battle of Magh Cuillinn.*—Tigh. 703: Ult. 702.

If Loingsech° should come to the Banna, with his three hundred
hundreds about him,
He will make submit, though large his parts, Ceallach the Gray of
Loch Cime;
Ceallach of the round balls was active, a circle of spears,
Terrible, was leaped over by the red-handed King of Loch Cime^p.
Ambitious were his deeds, the morning he was at Glais Chuilg^q.
I slew Loingsech there with a sword, the arch King of Erin all round.

Ceallach, son of Raghallach, afterwards went into the Church^r,
and left the two Dunchadhs in his kingdom, and this Cellach died at
the end of two years^s afterwards.

The Battle of Magh Cuillinn^t [was fought] between the Ultonians
and the Britons in Ard Ua n-Eachdhach, in which Mac Radgund, the
adversary of the Churches of God, was slain. The Ultonians were
the victors.

Bran, son of Conall^u, King of Leinster, died.

THE BEGINNING OF THE REIGN OF FOGARTACH^v.

[722.] Kal. Ceallach, son of Geirtide, in the kingdom of Leinster.

Fogartach again assumed the sovereignty for one year, when he
fell in the Battle of Cenndeilgtin^x by Cinaeth, son of Irgalach.

A hosting by Fogartach into Leinster; and the Leinster-men
gave him battle, i. e. the Battle of Claenadh^y. The battle was gained
by

^u *Brann, son of Conall.*—Ann. F. M.
787; Tigh. 690. This entry is out of
place here.

^v *Fogartach.*—He began his reign in
722, and was slain in 724 by Cinaedh,
son of Irgalach, his successor.

^x *Cenndeilgtinn.*—Ann. Ult. 723; Tigh.
724. The place is now unknown. See F.M.
719, 720. Tigh. says that this battle was
fought on Saturday, the Nones of Oct. (or
Oct. 7), which agrees with A. D. 724.

^y *Claenadh.*—Now Clane, county Kil-

muinntipe Rozaptaiz im boobcap mac Diapmaoa Ruanaio unoe
Optanać :

Uinće [.1. cat] copzap cpuaib, paon poclaontaip cata zpáin
ʒo ttopćaip lap an pluaʒ boobćap bile buiofn báin.

Mopp Flainn Fíona mic Oppa pi Saxan, in tʒnaib ampa,
nalta Aoamnáin, oe quo Riaʒuil bfnncuip cecinit:

Iniu pfpap bpuioe [.1. m⁰oepil] cat, in popba a pfnatap,
Manao alʒap la mac Dé, coniné ao ʒfnatap
Iniu po bit mac Oppa a ccat ppia claibme ʒlapa
Cia oo paoa aitpiʒe, ip hí ino hí iap nappa.
Iniu po bit mac Oppa, lap ambiíp buba beoʒa
Ro cuala Cpípt áp nʒuíoe poipaopbut bpuioe bpfʒa.

Ip in bliaoainpi po paomrao pip 'Eipfnn aon pmatt ⁊ aoinpia-
ʒail oo ʒabail ó Aoamnán um ceile abpao na Cápʒ ap Domnach
an ctpamao oéc epʒa Appil, ⁊ in copónuʒ Pfoaip oo beit pop
cléipcib Eipfnn uile. Uaip bá móp an bucaiopfo pá baoi i n-Eipinn
ʒo mʒe pin .1. buiofn oo cléipcib 'Epfnn aʒ celeabpao na Cáipce ap
Ohomnaé an ctpamao ofʒ Epʒa Appil, ⁊ copónuʒao Pfoaip app-
toil, ap pluott Pháopice ; buiofn eile uno óc pechim Choloim
Cille, .1. Caipce oo ceileabpao ap ctpamao oéce epʒa Appil ʒibé
látte pfpmuine ap a mbeit an ctpamao oécc, ⁊ copónuʒao Simoin
Opuao poppa. An tpfp buiofn, níop b'ionann uile iao pe peittóib
Patpaice, no pe peittóib Choloim Cille, ʒo mbiuíp peanaoa iomba
oʒ cléipcib Eipfnn, ⁊ ap amlaio tiʒuíp na cléipiʒ pin na pfnaoaib,

⁊ a

dare.—F. M. 702; Ult. 703; Tigh. 704.
¹ *Flann Fionn.*—See Tigh. 704, and Reeves's "Adamnan," p. 185. His real Anglo-Saxon name was Aldfrith. He was King of Northumbria.—Lappenberg. Hist. of Engl., vol. i., p. 187 *n*.
² *Bruide.*—The words .1. M⁰Oepil are in the margin of the MS. See Tigh. 706.

by the Leinster-men, who cut off the people of Fogartach with great slaughter, with Bodhbhchar, son of Diarmaid Ruanaidh. Unde Orthanach [said]:

A battle, a hard victory; lowly they prostrated the battalions of triumph,
And there fell by the host Bodhbhchar, the scion of the white troop.

[704.] The death of Flann Fiona^a, son of Ossa, King of Saxonland, the famous wise man, the pupil of Adamnan, of whom Riagail of Bennchair sung:

This day Bruide^a fights a battle for the land of his grandfather,
Unless the Son of God wish it otherwise, he will die in it.
To-day the son of Oswy was killed in a battle with green swords,
Although he did penance, he shall lie in Hi after his death;
This day the son of Oswy was killed, who had the black drinks;
Christ heard our supplications, they spared Bruide the brave.

In this year the men of Erin consented to receive one jurisdiction and one rule from Adamnan, respecting the celebration of Easter^b, on Sunday, the fourteenth of the moon of April, and respecting the tonsuring of all the clerks of Erin after the manner of St. Peter, for there had been great dissension in Erin up to that time; i. e. some of the clergy of Erin celebrated Easter on the Sunday [next after], the fourteenth of the moon of April, and had the tonsure of Peter the Apostle, after the example of Patrick; but others, following the example of Columbkille, celebrated Easter on the fourteenth

^a where we have his death—"Bruide m^c Derile mortuus est."—*Ull.* 705.

^b *Easter.*—The scribe has written in the margin—Ceileabpaö na Capʒ po. "The celebration of Easter, here." See Reeves's "Adamnan," p. 26 n., and Introd., p. liii.

⁊ a ttuata leo go mbíóip compaicte cata, ⁊ mapbťa iomba eatoppa; go ttangattcap uile iomba i n-Eipinn tpío pin .i. an bó áp mór, ⁊ an gopta pó mór ⁊ tíomanna iomba, ⁊ eattupćinīboig bo lot na h-'Eipīn. battup amlaib pin go paba .i. go hainpip Abamnán. 'Eipibe an nomab abb po gab la tap éip Coluim Cille.

Ópab mór bo bpeit bo Saxonéaib a hEipinn: Abamnán bo óul bo hatċuingib na bpaite, ⁊ amail inntpip béib 'pan ptaip bhéib ṗá tionoilpit ṗmóp eppcop Eoppa uile bo baɨnnab Abamnán ap an caipg bo celeabpab ap phoćt Coluim Cille, ⁊ ap coṗónugab Śímoin Opuab bo beit paip .i. ab aupe ab aupem. Abbeip béib gép ba hiombba ṡgnaibe pan tp.hab paɨn po popuaiphg Abamnan iab uile a híṡna, ⁊ a híplabpa, ⁊ apeb po pāib Abamnán, ní ap aťipip [Simoin Opuab] po baoi an coṗónugab ub paip, aċt ap aitipip Iohannip bpuinne, balta an tSlainicioba, ⁊ ap é pub coṗónugub po baoi paippibe, ⁊ ciap bo annpa pe Pībap a Slainicib pob annpa pip Slainicib Iohan; ⁊ bno ap ap cśṫpaṁab béce ep̃ga Appil, gibé la pīctmaine ap a mbeit, po celeabpattup na happtail an cáipg. Ap ann pin po eipig pīnóip ann, ⁊ po pāib: cia é Colom Cille péin? bia po beit ap áipb punna, ní gebmaoipne uab go mbeit po aoinṁpiagaɨl pinne. Sibpe inuppo, ní gebtua uaib go mbeití po aoinṁpiagail
pinn.

^c *Simon Magus.*—The scribe writes the Latin word "calumnia" in the margin. On this subject see note to the first Fragment of these Annals, under A. D. 718.

^d *Battles.*—Here again the scribe has written "calumnia" in the margin.

^e *Bede.*—The scribe writes in the margin—"Non legit Scuip béib" [Historiam Bedæ] "et si legerit non intellexit." See Bede, H.E., v., c. 15.

^f *Europe.*—Bede does not say a word about this. The compiler of these Annals here confounds the dispute which Colman, Bishop of Lindisfarne, had with the English clergy about the tonsure (Bede, iv., c. 25), with the dispute about Easter.

^g *Excelled them all.*—Bede says the very contrary; viz., that Adamnan, being admonished by many who were *more learned* than himself, not to presume to live contrary to the universal custom of the Church, &c., he changed his mind, and readily

teenth of the moon of April, on whatever day of the week the fourteenth should happen to fall, and had the tonsure of Simon Magus^c. A third party did not agree with the followers of Patrick, or with the followers of Columbkille; so that the clergy of Erin used to hold many synods, and these clergy used to come to the synods accompanied by the laity, so that battles^d and deaths occurred between them; and many evils resulted in Erin in consequence of this, viz., a great murrain of cows, and a very great famine, and many diseases, and the devastation of Erin by foreign hordes. They were thus for a long time, i. e. to the time of Adamnan, who was the ninth abbot that took [the government of] Ia after Columbkille.

A great booty was carried off by the Saxons from Erin, [and] Adamnan went to demand the booty, and, as Bede^e relates in his History, the greater part of the bishops of all Europe^f assembled to condemn Adamnan for celebrating Easter after the manner of Columbkille, and for having the tonsure of Simon Magus upon him, i. e. from ear to ear. Bede says that though many were the wise men [assembled] at that synod, Adamnan excelled them all^g in wisdom and eloquence; and Adamnan said that it was not in imitation of Simon Magus that he had this tonsure, but in imitation of John the Beloved, the alumnus of the Saviour; and that this was the tonsure which he had upon him; and though Peter loved the Saviour, the Saviour loved John; and [he urged] that it was on the fourteenth of the moon of April, whatever day of the week it should fall upon, the Apostles celebrated Easter. It was then a certain senior rose up there, and said, "Who was Columbkille himself? If he were here present, we would not part from him until he should be of the same rule with us; but we shall not part from you until you are of the same

preferred those things which he had seen and heard in the English churches to the customs which he and his people had hitherto followed.

ꞅꞃꞁꞃ. Tuᵹ Aꝺaṁnán ꞅꞃꞇᵹꞃa ꞅaꞁꞃ, ⁊ a ꞃé ꞃo ꞃáꞁꝺ; ꝺꞁaꝺꞃa, ꞅo aoꞁꞃꞃꞁaᵹuꝉ ꞃꞃꞁꝺ. Cóꞁꞃꞃꞁᵹéꞅꞃ éu ꝺeꞃꞁꝺe, aꞃ na heꞃꞃꞅoꞁꞃ. Aꞃ ꝉóꞃ, aꞃ Aꝺaṁnaꞃ acoꞃꞃ ꞃꞃaꞁꞃꞃꞇꞁꞃ ꞅén: acc, aꞃ ꞁaꝺꞃoṁ, aéꞇ a céꝺóꞁꞃ. Ꝺo níéꞅꞃ ꞇꞃa cóꞁꞃꞃꞁuᵹaꝺ Aꝺaꞃꞃꞃaꞁꞃ aꞃꞃ ꞃꞁꞃ, ⁊ ní ꞇuᵹaꝺ ꝺo ꝺuꞁꞃe óꞃoꞁꞃ aꞃ ꞃꞃoo ꞁꞃa aꞃ ꞇꞇuᵹaꝺ ꝺo Aꝺaꞃꞃꞃaꞃ aꞃꞃꞃꞃꞁꞃ, aᵹuꞃ aꝺꞃaᵹuꞃ aꞃ ꝺꞃꞁaꞁꝺ ꞃꞃóꞃ ꞃaꞁꞃ ꝺó, ⁊ ꞇꞁᵹ ꞃeꞁꞃꞃe ᵹo ꞃuꞁᵹe a ꞃꞃaꞁꞃꞃꞃꞇꞁꞃ ꞅéꞃ ᵹo ꝉꞁa. Ꞃo ꝺá ꞃꞃaéꞇꞃuᵹaꝺ ꞃꞃoꞃ ꞃa coꞁꞃꞃéꞁoꞃoꝉ a ꞅaꞁᵹꞃꞁꞃ ꞅoꞃ coꞃoꞃuᵹaꝺ ꞃaꞁꞃ. Ꞃá ꝺaoꞁꞃꞁoꞁꞃ ᵹá ꞁoꞃaꞁꝉ aꞃ aꞃ coꞁꞃꞃéꞁoꞃoꝉ aꞃ coꞃoꞃuᵹaꝺ ꝺo ᵹaꝺáꞁꝉ, ⁊ níꞃ ꞅéꝺ uaéa. Ꞅeꝺ Ꝺeuꞃ ꞃeꞃꞃꞁꞃꞇ coꞃueꞃꞇuꞁ ꞃeccaꞃe .ꞁ. ꞁꞃꞅuꞃꞃ Aꝺaꞃꞃꞃaꞃuꞃꞃ eꞃꞃꞃeꝉꝉeꞃe quꞁ ꞃꞃꞁꞃeꞃꞇuꞃ eꞃꞇ hꞁꝺeꞃꞃꞃꞁae. Ꞅꞁc ꝺeꝺa ꝺꞁꞅꞁꞇ. Uaꞁꞃ ꞃa ꝺaoꞁ ꝺéꞁꝺ ꞃꞃaꞁꝉꝉe ꞃe hAꝺaꞃꞃꞃáꞃ céꞁꞃ ꞃo ꝺaoí ꞁꞃ Saꞃaꞁꞃ.

Táꞁꞃꞁᵹ ꞇꞃa Aꝺaꞃꞃꞃáꞃ ꞁ ꞃ-Éꞁꞃꞁꞃꞃ ꞁaꞃꞇꞇaꞁꞃ ⁊ ꞃo ꞁoꞃꝺaꞃꞅaꞁᵹ ꞃaꞁꞃ ꞅoꞃ 'Éꞁꞃꞁꞃꞃ, ⁊ ní ꞃo ᵹaꝺaꝺ uaꝺ aꞃ ꞇaoꞃꞃꞃꞃaéꞇ ꞃaꞁꞃ ꞃa Caꞃec ⁊ aꞃ coꞃóꞃaꞁᵹéé ᵹo ꞃuꞁᵹe aꞃꞃ ꝺꝉꞁaꝺaꞁꞃꞃꞁ.

Ꝺa ꞃꞃaꞃꝺ oꞃo Aꝺaꞃꞃꞃáꞃ ꞃꞁꞃ ꝺꝉꞁaᵹaꞁꞃꞃꞁ, ꝉꞃꞃꞃꞁꞁꞁ°. aeꞇaꞇꞁꞃ ꞃuae.

[FRAGMENTUM III.]

Ceꞃꞇꞁuꞃꞃ ꞅꞃaᵹꞃꞃeꞃꞇuꞃꞃ eꞃ eoꝺeꞃꞃ Coꝺꞁce ꞃeꞃ euꞃꝺeꞃꞃ Ꝼeꞃꝺꞁꞃꞁuꞃꞃ eꞃꞇꞃacéuꞃꞃ, ꞁꞃcꞁꞃꞁeꞃꞃ ab anno 5°, ꞃeᵹꞃꞁ Maoꞁꝉꞃeachꝉoꞃꞃꞃ ꞃꞃꞁc Maꞁꝉꞃuaꞃaꞁᵹ, ꞅeu (uꞇ habent A. Ꝺuꞃᵹ.), 849.

Ꝼoꞃéoꞁꞃꞃeꝺaꞁᵹé ꞁꞃꞃuꞃꞃo ꞃa Ꝉoéꝉaꞃꞃ ꞃꞃaꞃ ꞃo ꝺáéꞇaꞃ ᵹo ꞅꞃꞁéᵹꞃaꞃꞃaé

[h] *Compassion.*—" Misertus est Hiberniæ," i. e. honoured Ireland with his presence.

Thus Bede says.—One would think from this that the Irish writer was telling the story exactly as Bede has it, but this is not so. He tells the story after his own bardic manner, exaggerates the whole affair, and confounds what Bede says of Colman with what he says of Adamnan. Comp. Bede, H. E., v., c. 15.

[k] *Eighty-third.*—See Reeves's " Adam-

same rule with us." Adamnan made answer to him, and said, "I will be of the same rule with you." "Be thou, therefore, tonsured," said the bishops. "It will be sufficient," said Adamnan, "at my own monastery." "Not so," said they, "but at once." Adamnan was, therefore, tonsured there; and no greater honour was ever given to a man than was given to Adamnan there. And the great booty was restored to him; and he came forward to his own monastery to Ili, and his congregation marvelled much to see him with this tonsure. He was requesting of the congregation to take the [same] tonsure, but God permitted the convent to sin, and to expel Adamnan, who had compassion[h] upon Ireland. Thus Bede says[i]; for Bede was along with Adamnan while he was in England.

Adamnan afterwards came to Erin, and he excelled all Erin; and that one regulation of Easter was not received from him, nor the tonsure, until this year.

[704.] Adamnan died in the eighty-third[k] year of his age.

[FRAGMENT III.]

A third fragment, extracted from the same manuscript by the same Firbissius, beginning at the fifth year of the reign of Maelsechlainn, son of Maelruanaigh, or (as the Annals of Donegal have it) 849.

[A. D. 851.] As now the sentinels of the Lochlanns[l] were vigilantly

nan," p. xl., note ᶠ. Tigh. records his death at A. 704, and says his age was 77.

[l] *Lochlanns*.—These were the Norwegians, who were settled in Ireland for about half a century previously. This extract, which is evidently a continuation of a long story, seems to have been taken from some history of the Danish invasions now lost.

gnaṁaċ aġ ríġaḋ an mapa uaċa aḋ ċonncaṫṫap an muṗċoḃlaċ mór muiṗiḋe ḋ'á n-ionnroiġlaḋ. Ro ġaḃ uaṁan mór ⁊ ſġla iaḋ: aċṫ ḋpfin ḋib aiſo aḋbepḋíp, conio Loċlannaiġ ḋa ffupṫaċṫpam ⁊ ḋa ffoipiġin. Oṗeam oile, ⁊ aṗ ffiṗ pa ṫuiġpioṫṫpaiḋe; coniḋ Ḋauniṫeṗ .i. Ḋanaiṗ pa ḃáṫṫuṗ ann ḋá n-aṗġaipiom ⁊ ḋa n-moṗíḃ; ⁊ aṗeaḋ ón ḃá ṗíṗe ann. Ra ċuiṗṗioṫ na Loċlonnaiġ long lánluaṫ na n-aiġiḋ ḋá fṗiuṗ. Ṫainiġ ḋna long lánluaṫ an ġiolla óiġ ṗeim· pioḋṫe, aenaṗ pép na longoi ḃoile, ġu ṫṫáplaṫṫuṗi na ḋá loing ḋ'aiġiḋ iṫ'aiġiḋ, ġo neḃepṫ Sṫiupuṗman na loinġe Loċlannaiġe; ṗiḃṗi, a ṗiuṗa, aṗ ṗé, ġa ṫíṗ aṗ a ṫṫanġaḃaiṗ aṗ an muiṗṗi? an ṗa ṗíḋ ṫanġaḃaiṗ, no an ṗa coġaḋ? Aṗé fṗeaġṗa ṫuġaṫṫuṗ na Ḋanaiṗ faiṗṗin, fṗoṗṗ póṁóṗ ḋo ṗaiġḋiḃ ṗoċa. Cuiṗiḋ a ṫċeḋóiṗ eſin i ċeſin luċṫ na ḋa long ṗin; ṗo ṗopuaiṗliġ long na nḊanaiṗ long na Loċlannaċ, ⁊ maṗḃaiḋ na Ḋanaiṗ luċṫ loinġe na Loċlannaċ. Lin· ġaiṫ a n-aoinṗeaċṫ uile na Ḋanaiṗ i ċeſin na Loċlannaċ, ġuṗ po ḃáṫuṗ ṗin ṫṗáiġ. Cuiṗiḋ ċaṫ ġo ċṗuaiḋ, ⁊ maṗḃaiḋ na Ḋanaiṗ a ṫṗí coimlíon fén ḋíoḃ, ⁊ ṗa ḋíċſinṗaṫ ġaċ aon ṗo maṗḃṗaṫ: Ṫuġṗaṫ na Ḋanaiṗ longa na Loċlannaċ leo ġo ṗoṗṫ. Raġaḃṗaṫ ṫṗa na Ḋanaiṗ aṗ ṗain mná ⁊ óṗ ⁊ uile maiṫiuṗ na Loċlannaċ; ġo ṗuġ an coimḋċ uaċa amlaiḋ ṗin ġaċ maiṫ ṗuġṗaṫ a ċeallaiḃ, ⁊ neṁfḃaiḃ ⁊ ṗġṗíniḃ naoṁ 'Eiṗeann.

Iſ in aimṗiṗ ḋno ṗa ċuiṗ Maoilſeaċloinn ṫeaċṫa aṗ ċſin Cionaoiṫ mic Conainġ, ṗí Cianaċṫa, ⁊ aṗ éiṗiḋe ṗo loiṗġ Cealla ⁊ ḋiṗṫiġe na naoṁ (aṁail ṗo inniṗiomaṗ ṗſinaiñ) aṁail ḃiḋ ḋo coṁ-aiṗle

---

ᵐ *Young man.*—i. e. who was in the command of the Lochland ship, and mentioned, perhaps, in the former part of the narrative.

ⁿ *Steersman.*—Sṫiuṗaṗmann. This is a Teutonic word, and is probably derived from the Danish, *To steer*.

ᵒ *Maelsechlainn.* — Maelsechlainn, or Malachy I., began his reign in 846, and died on the 13th of November, 863.

ᵖ *Cianachta.*—A territory in the east of ancient Meath, in which a sept of Munster-men of the race of Cian, son of Oilioll

lantly observing the sea, they saw a great marine fleet coming towards them. They were seized with great fear and terror. Some of them said that they were Lochlanns who were coming to aid and assist them; but others, who understood better, said that they were Daunites, i. e. Danes, who came to plunder and rob them; and this was indeed the truth. The Lochlanns sent a very swift ship towards them to know who they were, and the swift ship of the young man[m] aforesaid came alone to one of the other ships, and the two ships met face to face; and the steersman[n] of the Lochlann ship asked, " Ye, O men," said he, " from what country have ye come upon this sea? Have ye come with peace, or with war?" The answer which the Danes gave him was to discharge a large shower of arrows at him! The crew of the two ships set to at once: and the ship of the Danes overcame the ship of the Lochlanns, and the Danes killed the crew of the ship of the Lochlanns. The Danes then altogether made for the place where the Lochlanns were, and arrived at the shore. They fought a battle fiercely, and the Danes killed thrice their own number of them, and they beheaded every one they killed. The Danes brought the ships of the Lochlanns with them to a port, and they also took the women, the gold, and all the property of the Lochlanns with them; and thus the Lord took away from them all the wealth which they had taken from the churches, and sanctuaries, and shrines of the saints of Erin.

Now at this time Maelsechlainn[o] sent messengers for Cinaeth, son of Conaing, King of Cianachta[p], and it was he who had burned the churches and oratories of the saints (as we have narrated before[q]), as if to consult with him how they should act with respect to the cause

Olum, were seated at this period. Duleek was its principal church. They were soon after overwhelmed by the southern Ui-

Neill, who detested them.

[q] *Narrated before.*—Not narrated in this Fragment, although it was, no doubt,

aiple iip cionnap vo ġenvaoip im caingin na nOanap, uaip pá baoi aṁail bív pív eivip Maoilpeacloiñ ¬ Cionaoc, ¬ cia pa baoi Cionaoc ı ngalap púla, acc vo pigne cuibeacc v'ionnpoiġ Maoilpeachloinn, ¬ pluaġ uime map bav va coiṁſv.

Ra coṁpaiġpioc iapaṁ Maoilpſclainn ¬ Cionaov a n-aoinionav ¬ Ciġſpnac, ın bpiſġ; apeav pob áil vo Maoilpeacloinn é pén ¬ pí bpiſġ vo mapbav pí Cianacca. Ní vſpna vno Maoilpeacloinn a ccévóip pin, uaip ba pocaive vo Chionaov, ¬ pab ſġail leip coṁiṁapbav vo vſnaṁ ann. Apeav vo poine a puipeac ġo maivſn ap na bápac. Ro veilb vno Maoilpſcloinn cúipi bpeaġaca ġo ccíopvaoip ġo niġe a n-ionav cévna ap na bápac, ¬ pa puaġaip vo na pluaġaib imceacc. O pa imtiġ a pluaġ ón Chionaov, táiniġ Maoilpſcloinn ġo pluaġ móp laip v'ionnpoiġ an Chionaov, ¬ níop bo lá ġo maic ann, ¬ apeav po páiv Maoilpeacloinn ó ġut móp cpóva náiṁvige pna Chionaov. Civ, ap pé, 'mapa loipġip vipciġe na naoṁ, ¬ civ ma pa pa ṁillip a neṁava, ¬ pġpeappa na naoṁ ¬ Loclannaiġ lac? Ra piviꝑ imupꝑo an Cionaov na capmnaiġpeav ní vo eaplappa caoin vo vſnaṁ, apeav vo piġne beic na cocc. Ra capipnġſv iap pin an mac paopclannac, poicinelac, ꝑonaipt pin amac, ¬ po báivhev é cpé coṁaiple Maoilpeacloinn ı ꝑpucán palac, ¬ puaip bás aṁlaiv pin.

Ip ın bliavain-pi, .i. an coiġſv bliaġain platta Mhaoilpeaclainn, pa tionolpac vá coipſc loipġpi na Loclonn .i. Ġain ¬ laꝑġna plóiġ móꝑa ap ġac áiꝑv a n-aiġiv na n-Oanaꝑ. Cionolaiv iapaṁ ġo pabavap

---

narrated in the original work from which this extract was taken.

Breagh.—A large territory comprising the greater portion of East Meath, and of which Cianachta was a subdivision.

Dirty streamlet.—The Ann. Ult. 850,

say that he was "demersus in lacu crudeli morte." According to the Four Masters (A. D. 849), he was drowned in the River Ainge, now the Nanny Water, a river flowing through the very middle of Cianachta, and dividing the barony of

cause of the Danes, for there was a kind of peace between Maelsechlainn and Cinaeth, and though Cinaeth was labouring under a disease
of his eye, he nevertheless came to meet Maelsechlainn with a host
about him, as if it were to guard him.

After this, Maelsechlainn, and Cinaeth, and Tighernach, King of
Breagh[r], met together: and Maelsechlainn's desire was that he and
the King of Breagh should kill the King of Cianachta. Maelsechlainn, however, did not do this at once, for Cinaeth had more forces,
and he was afraid that mutual slaughter might take place. What
he did was to wait till the next morning. Maelsechlainn feigned
false reasons, for which they should come to the same place the next
morning, and he ordered the forces [of Cinaeth] to go away. When
his army went away from Cinaeth, Maelsechlainn came with a great
host to meet Cinaeth before it was clear daylight, and Maelsechlainn
said with a loud, fierce, and hostile voice to Cinaeth: "Why," said
he, "hast thou burned the oratories of the saints, and why hast thou
destroyed their sanctuaries and their writings, the Lochlanns assisting thee?" Cinaeth knew that it would be of no avail to him to
make use of fair speeches; what he did was to remain silent. That
noble, goodly born, brave youth was afterwards dragged out, and
drowned in a dirty streamlet[s], by advice of Maelsechlainn, and thus
he perished!

[851.] In this year, i. e. in the fifth year of the reign of Maelsechlainn[t], the two chiefs of the fleet of the Lochlanns, i.e. Zain and Iargna,
collected great hosts from every quarter against the Danes. They
afterwards assembled to the number of threescore and ten ships, and
proceeded

Upper Duleek from that of Lower Duleek, in the county of Meath. See the "Tripartite Life of St. Patrick," Part I., c. 54.—Colgan, *Triad. Thaum.*, p. 125.

[t] *The fifth year of the reign of Maelsech-lainn.*—This king succeeded in 846, so that this battle between the Norwegians and Danes took place in the year 851.

ṗaḃaḋaṗ ḋeć longa ⁊ ṫṗí ṗićiḋ, ⁊ ṫṡ̇ain go Snáṁ aiġnṡ̇ ⁊ aṗ annṗaiḋe ḃaṫṫuṗ na Ḋanaiṗ an ṫan ṗin. Comṗaiciṫ ann ṗin leiṫ̇ ḟoṗ leaṫ̇, ⁊ cuiṗiḋ caṫ̇ cṗuaiḋ ḋuaiḃṗioṫ̇ lṡ̇ ḟoṗ lṡ̇ : naiṗ ní ċualamaṗ ṗeiṁ ṗin a n-ioṅaḋ oile ṗiaṁ aṗ muiṗ an áṗ ṗo ċuiṗṗioṫ̇ ṡ̇tuṗṗa annṗo .i. eiḋiṗ Ḋanaṗa ⁊ Loċlannaiġ. Aċṫ̇ ċṡ̇na aṗ ḟoṗṗ na Ḋanaṗoiḃ ṗo ṁaiḋ. Ra ṫionóilṗioṫ̇ na Ḋanaiṗ iaṗ ṗin, aṗ mḃṗiṗeaḋ maḋma ḟoṗṗa, ⁊ an goṗṫa ga maṗḃaḋ, ⁊ aṗeḋ ṗo ṗáiḋ a ṫṫiaġaṗna .i. hoṗm ḃṗin, ⁊ comġe ṗo ḃa ḃṡ̇i cṗuaiḋ coṗgṗaċ eiṗiḋċ : Ruġṗaḃaiṗ-ṗi comġe ṗo (aṗ ṗé) coṗgaiṗ imḋa cia ṗa ṗoṗuaiṗliġeaḋ ṗiḃ ṗonn ṫṗé iomaṗca ḃluaiġ. 'Eṗṫiḋ ṗiṗ na ḃṁaṫṗaiḋ aoḃéṗṗa ṗiḃ : "gaċ ḃuaiḋ ⁊ gaċ coṗġuṗ ⁊ gaċ ḃlaḋ ḟuaṗaḃaiṗ ṫṗiḋ ṗin, ṗa maṫlaṗṫṡ̇ ṗa ḃloiġ mḃiġ aon laoi ṗin. Ḟéġuiḋ liḃ iaṗaṁ an caṫuġaḋ ḋo ṗiḋiṗi ḋo ġṡ̇ṫaoi ṗiṗ na Loclannċaiḃ, uaiṗ aṫáḋ ḃuṗ mná, ḃuṗ n-uile ṁaiṫiuṗ aca, ⁊ ḃuṗ longa ; ⁊ aṗ ṗuḃaċ iaḋṗim ḋo ḃṗeiṫ ḃuaḋa ⁊ coṗġaiṗ uaiḃṗi aṗeaḋ aṗ ċóiṗ ḋiḃ anoṗa ḋul go haonṁṡ̇maċ ḋa gċṡ̇ṅ aṁail na ṗaoileaḋ ṗiḃ ḟaṗ in ḃṡ̇ṫhaiḋ, aċṫ̇ na ḃeiṫ ṗiḃ og ioṗnaiḋe ḃáiṗ : ⁊ ḟaṗ ḋoiṫ̇gail ḟén ḟoṗṗa, ⁊ gen go ṗaiḃ coṗġuṗ ṗainṁeaċ ḋuiḃṗi ḋeṗin, ⁊ ḃiaiḋ a m-ḃéṗaḋ aṗ nḋeé ⁊ áṗ ṫṫóicṫe ḋúin ; muna ṗaiḃe maiṫ̇ ḋúin ann, ḃiaiḋ commaṗḃaḋ coiṫ̇ċṡ̇n leiṫ̇ ḟoṗ lṡ̇ ann.

Ag ṗo comaiṗle oile leam ḋuiḃ : an Ṗáṗṗaicc naoṁ ṗa aṗ aiṗḋ eṗṗċoṗ ⁊ aṗ ċṡ̇n naoṁ na h'Eiṗṡ̇n, ṗiṗ a nḋeaṗnṗaṫ na naṁuiḋṗailṡ̇ oġainne uile imḋa, guiḋmiṫne go ḋíoċṗa, ⁊ ṫaḃṗam almṗana onóṗaċa ḋó, aṗ ḃuaiḋ ⁊ coṗġuṗ ḋo ḃṗeiṫ ḋo na náiṁḋiḃ ṗin.

Ro ḟṗeaġṗaṫṫuṗ uile é, ⁊ aṗeaḋ ṗo ṗáiḋṗiḋ : "aṗ comaiṗcce," aṗ ṗiaḋ, an ṫí naoṁ Ṗáḋṗaicc ⁊ an ċoimḋe aṗ ṫiġeaṗna ḋo ṗin ḟén.

" *Snámh Aighnech.*—Now Carlingford Lough, near which, at a place called Linn-Duachaill, the Norwegians had a fleet and strong fortress. Ann. Ult. 851; F.M. 850.

proceeded to Snámh Aighnech^u where the Danes were [stationed] at that time. There they fought on either side, and engaged in a hard and stubborn battle on either side, for we have never heard before this time of so great a slaughter at sea as was caused between them, i. e. between the Danes and the Lochlanns. But, however, it was against the Danes the defeat was. The Danes, after being defeated in this battle, being sore oppressed by famine, assembled their people, and what their Lord, Horm, who hitherto had been a firm, victorious man, said to them was,—" Hitherto," said he, " ye have gained many victories, although ye have been defeated here by superior forces. Listen to the words which I shall say unto you: 'Every victory, every triumph, and every fame which ye had gained was obscured by the little fame of that day.' Look ye sharp to the battle which ye shall next make with the Lochlanns, for your women and all your property are in their hands as well as your ships; and they are rejoicing for having gained victory and triumph over you! What is proper for you now to do is to go unanimously against them, as if ye did not think of life, but not to be waiting for death, and to revenge yourselves upon them, and though ye may not gain a prosperous victory thereby, ye shall have whatever our gods and our fate will give us; if it be of no advantage to us, there shall be at least equal slaughter on either side.

"This is another advice of mine to you: 'This Saint Patrick, against whom these enemies of ours have committed many evils, is archbishop, and head of the saints of Erin. Let us pray to him fervently, and let us give honourable alms to him for our gaining victory and triumph over these enemies."

They all answered him, and what they said was: " Let our protector," said they, " be the holy Patrick, and the God who is Lord over him also, and let our spoils and our wealth be [given] to his church."

féin, ⁊ ar ccorguir d'á fglair, ⁊ ar n-ionḋṁnur. Tfgaiḋ iar rin go haonmfninnaċ, ffrḃa, feararṁail i n-aoinf́ſt i gcionn na Loċlannaċ, ⁊ cuirit caṫ.

If in uair rin táinig Ẑain leitrí na Loċlann, ⁊ Matoḋan rí Ulaḋ d'ingrim na nDanar do ṁuir ⁊ tír, gion go raḃa a fior rin reṁe ag Ẑain Loċlannaċ, táinig ⁊ an t-uaitfḃ ro ḃaoi na farrraḋ d'ionfuigh na nDanar don ḋara leiṫ agar iargna leitrí oile na Loċlann don leiṫ eile do na Danaroiḃ. Ar cruaiḋ tra ra cuirfḃ an catra. Ra ċlor ar leiṫ rgfingail na flẑ, agur gloinnbémnfḋ na ccloiḋfṁ, ⁊ tuairgnfḋ na rgiaṫ gá mbualaḋ, ⁊ béicfḋaċ na mileḋ ag imirt éccoṁloinn orra. Aṫt trá cíḋ fada rá bár imi rin, ar forr na loċlannaiḃ ro maiḋ, ⁊ ir iaḋ na Danair rug ḃuaiḋ ⁊ corgar tra raṫ Ráḋraice gé ro ḃáḋar na Loċlannaig trí ċuttroma jur na Danuroiḃ, do ceiṫre cuḋruma. Tiagaiḋ na Danair iarrin foj longrort na Loċlann, ⁊ marḃaiḋ dream ann, gaḃaiḋ dream eile, ⁊ cuirid dream eile i tteitfḃ, ⁊ gaḃaiḋ gaċ maitiur óir ⁊ airgid, ⁊ gaċ maitiur ar ċna, ⁊ amná ⁊ a longa. Aṫt ċna ní raiḃ Ẑain féin ag cur an ċatra, uair ní táinig maille ra ṁuintir ar ammur an longruirt, uair ro ḃaoi aige coṁairle a n-ionaḋ oile. An uair táinig do ċum an longruirt arriaḋ na náṁuiḋ aḋ ċonnairc ann, ⁊ ní hiaḋ a ṁuintir féin. A n-égmair anneoḋ ro marḃaḋ do na Danuraiḃ féin, areaḋ ra marḃaḋ do na Loċlannaiḃ cúig ṁíle fear roiċinelaċ : roċuiḋe imurro do míleaḋaiḃ ar ċna, ⁊ do ḋaoiniḃ in gaċ áiḃ ra marḃaḋ a n-éginair na nuiṁire rin.

Ar in tan rin ra ċuir Maoilreaċloinn, rí Tfṁra teaċta d'ionnruige na nDanar. Ar aṁlaiḋ ro ḃáttur na Danair ag luċtairfḋt

---

¹ *Fire thousand.*—This is perfectly incredible.

² *Heaps of the bodies.*—This presents a curious picture of the ferocity of the Scan-

They afterwards came unanimously, bravely, and manfully together against the Lochlanns, and joined battle.

At this time Zain, half king of the Lochlanns, and Matodan, King of Uladh, came to attack the Danes by sea and land; although Zain, the Lochlann, had not known of this before, he came with the party who were with him to harass the Danes on the one side, and Iarguo, the other half king of the Lochlanns, came to attack them on the other side. This battle was a hard fought one. The whizzing of lances, the clashing of swords, the clattering of shields when struck, and the shrieks of soldiers when subdued, were heard! But, however, though long they were *at it*, the Lochlanns were defeated, and the Danes gained victory and triumph, on account of the tutelage of Patrick, though the Lochlanns were three or four times their number! The Danes, after this, entered the camp of the Lochlanns, killed some of them, made prisoners of others, and put others to flight; and they possessed themselves of all their treasures of gold and silver, and other property, as well as of their women and ships. Zain himself, however, was not present at this engagement, for he did not come towards the camp along with his people, for he was holding a council elsewhere. When he had arrived at the camp, it was his enemies he saw there, and not his own people! Independently of those killed by the Danes, there were slain of the Lochlanns five thousand[x] goodly-born men; also many soldiers and people of every grade were slain in addition to this number.

Now, at this time Maelsechlainn, King of Teamhair, sent ambassadors to the Danes. And at their arrival the Danes were cooking, and the supports of their cauldrons were heaps of the bodies[y] of the Lochlanns,

dinavian nations, who were Pagans at this period. The favourites of their god Odin were all those who died in battle, or, what was considered equally meritorious, by their own hand. The timid wretch, who allowed himself to perish by disease or age, was considered unworthy of the joys of their paradise. These joys were fight-

luċtaiɼṡċt aɼ a ʒcionn, ⁊ aɼ iaᴅ ba ʒabla ᴅá ccoiɼcᴅaiḃ cáiɼn ᴅo
ċoɼɼaiḃ na Loċlann ⁊ ciᴅ na bṡɼa aɼ a mbíoᴅ an ḟeoil, aɼ ḟoɼ
coɼɼaiḃ Loċlann no ḃíḋiɼ a leiċcinn, ⁊ an cine aʒ loɼʒaᴅ na coɼɼ,
ʒo mbíoᴅ an ḟeoil ⁊ an méaċɼaᴅ ɼa ċaiċɼioc an aᴅaiʒ ɼeṁe aʒ
inaiḋm aɼ a nʒailiḃ amaċ.
    Ra baccuɼ ᴅna cṡċta Maoilɼeaċloinn ʒá ḟɼéʒaᴅ aṁlaiᴅ ɼin,
⁊ ɼa báccuɼ ʒa ccaċaoiɼ um na Ꝺanaɼaiḃ ɼin. Aɼeaᴅ ɼa ɼáiᴅ-
ɼioc na Ꝺanaiɼ; aɼ aṁlaiᴅ buᴅ maiċ leoɼum áɼ mbeiċne. Claɼ
móɼ lan aca ᴅo óɼ, ⁊ ᴅa aiɼʒeaᴅ ᴅá ċabaiɼc ᴅo Ráᴅɼaicc, uaiɼ
aṁlaiᴅ ɼa báccuɼ na Ꝺanaiɼ ⁊ cinéle cɼabaiᴅ aca .i. ʒaḃaiᴅ
ɼealaᴅ ḟɼi ḟeoil, ⁊ ḟɼi mnáiḃ aɼ cɼabuᴅ. Cuʒ cɼa an caċ ɼo
mṡnma maiċ ᴅo Ꝋaoiḃealaiḃ uile aɼ an ɼʒɼioɼ ɼo ᴅo ċabaiɼc aɼ
na Loċlannaiḃ.
    'S in bliaᴅain ɼeo ᴅna ɼo ḃɼiɼ Mooilɼeaċlainn caċ ḟoɼɼ na
ɼaʒánaiḃ, ⁊ ᴅna ɼo ḃɼiɼiɼic Ciannaċta caċ ḟá ᴅó ḟoɼɼ na
ʒeɼciḃ.
    Ral. Foɼbaiɼi Maoilɼeaċlainn i cCɼuɼaic unᴅe Maoilɼċini
cccinic :—
        Miċhiᴅ ᴅul caɼ ḃóinn mḃáin, i mᴅail moiʒe Mᴅe mín,
        Aɼ anᴅɼa beiċ ḟɼi ʒaoiċ nʒluaiɼ iɼinᴅ uaiɼ i cCɼuɼaiᴅ cɼín.
    Inᴅɼṡċaċ, aḃ la, ᴅo ċiaċcain i n-Eiɼinn ʒo mionnaiḃ Coloim
Cille Laiɼ. Iɼ in mbliaᴅain ɼi ḃeoɼ .i. in ɼexto anno ɼeʒni Maoil-
                                                                ɼeaċlainn,

ing, ceaseless slaughter, and drinking beer
out of the skulls of their enemies, with a
renovation of life to furnish a perpetuity
of the same pleasures. The Scandinavians
placed their whole delight in war, and
entertained an absolute contempt of danger
and of death; and their glory was esti-
mated by the number they had slain in
battle. Of this we have a faithful picture
in the death-song of Regner Lodbrok (who
was probably the Turgesius of Irish history). This great conqueror comforts himself in his last agonies by recounting all
the acts of carnage he had committed in
his lifetime. See Mallet's "Northern Antiquities," Bohn's edition, pp. 105, 383;

Lochlanns, and one end of the spits on which the meat was hung was stuck into the bodies of the Lochlanns, and the fire was burning the bodies, so that they belched forth from their stomachs the flesh and the fat which they had eaten the night before.

The ambassadors of Maelsechlainn beheld them in this condition, and they reproached the Danes with this [savage conduct]. The Danes replied: "This is the way they would like to have us!" They had a great wide trench [filled] with gold and silver to give to Patrick, for the Danes were a people who had a kind of piety, i. e. they gave up meat and women awhile for piety! Now this battle gave good courage to all the Gaeidhil[z] on account of this destruction brought upon the Lochlanns.

In this year Maelsechlainn gained a battle over the pagans, and the Cianachta[a] defeated the Gentiles a second time in battle.

[852.] Kal. The encampment of Maelsechlainn was at Crufait[b], unde Maelfeichine cecinit:—

Time to cross the fair Boinn to the plain of smooth Meath;
It is difficult to be in the pure wind at this hour in withered Crufait.

Indrechtach, Abbot of Ia, came to Erin with the relics of Colum Cille. In this year also, the sixth year[c] of the reign of Maelsechlainn, Amhlaeibh

and Tytler's "Elements of General History," p. 136.
[z] *The Gaeidhil.*—i. e. the Scoti, or native Irish, in contradistinction to Gaill, i. e. Galli, or foreigners.
[a] *Cianachta.*—Ann. Ult. 851; F. M. 850.
[b] *Crufait.*—Ann. F. M. 847. The present name is unknown unless it be Cro-

boy, in Meath.
[c] *The sixth year.*—This was the year 852.—O'Flah. Ogyg., p. 434. Indrechtach, Abbot of Hy, appears to have come to Ireland with the relics of St. Columbkille so early as the year 849 or 850; he was killed in 854 by the Saxons. See Reeves's "Adamnan," p. 390, and Ann. Ult., A. D. 853.

ｐeaċlaınn, ċáınıẓ Aṁlaoıḃ Conung, .ı. mac ṗıẓ Loċlann, ı n-'Éıｐınn, ⁊ ｔuẓ leıｐ eｐｐuaẓｐa cíoｐa ⁊ cánaḃ n-ımḃa ó a aċaıｐ, ⁊ a ṗáẓḃaılｐıḃe ẓo hobann. Táınıẓ ｄno loṁaｐ an bｐáċaıｐ ba ｐoo 'na ḃｆẓaıḃｐıḃc ｄo ċoḃaċ na ccíoｐ cｆｄna.

Kal. Loċ Laoıẓ ı eｐıċ Uṁaıll ｄo éloḃ.

Kal. Ríoẓḃal ｐｆｓｐ n-'Éıｐｆnn ın Aｐｄmaċa eıoıｐ Maoılｐeaċlaınn ⁊ Maｔｄｄan ｐí Ulaḃ, ⁊ Ｄıaｐmaıｄ ⁊ Ｆeｔẓna ẓo ｐaṁaḃ Paｄｐaıcc, ⁊ Suaıｐleaċ ẓo ccléıｐcıḃ Míḃe.

Ínｄｐeaċｔaċ Úa Ｆınnaċｔa Comaｐba Colum Cılle, ⁊ Ｄıaｐmaｄa ｐaｐıenｔıｐｐımı, ｄo ṁaｐḃaḃ ｄo ｊlaｄaıẓıḃ Saxanaċa oẓ ｄol ｄo Róıṁ, ⁊ maıｐıḃ a ｆuıl eannaẓ ｐaın ḃeoｐ ıｐ ın ıonaｄ ın ｐo maｐḃaｄ ı ẓcoṁuｐｔa a ḃıoẓalｔa ｄo Ｄhıa ｐoｐ an luċｔ ｊoｐ maｐḃ.

Íｓ ın ḃlıaḃaınｐı ｐa ｔoċuıｐeaḃ ｐıẓ Loċlann ｄo cum Maoılｐeaċlaınn ｄ'ól, ⁊ ｐo ḃoí ｆleaḃ lánṁóｐ aｐ a cıonn, aẓaｐ ẓaċ ní ｐa ẓeall ｊıı Loċlann ｄo ċomall co na luıẓc ; aċｔ cｆna ní ｐa ċoṁaıll a ḃｆẓ aｐ ｄoul a ｔıẓ Maoılｐeaċlaınn aımaċ, aċｔ ｐa ẓaḃ a ẓcéｄóıｐ aẓ ıonnｐaḃ ｆeaｐaınn Maoılｐeaċlaınn. Aċｔ cｆna ní ｆｆċｔnac ｐáınıẓ leıｐ an coẓaḃ ｐın.

Íｓ ın ḃlıaḃaınｐı ｄno ｐo ｔｐéıẓｐıoｔ ｐochaıḃe a ınḃaıċıｐ Cｐíoｐｔaíḃaċｔa ⁊ ｔanẓaｔｔaｐ malle ｐıｐ na Loċlannaıḃ, ẓuｐ aıｐẓｒıoｔ Aｐｄmaċa, ⁊ ẓo ｐuẓｐaｔ a maıċıuｐ aｐ. Seｄ ｑuıｄem ex ıｐｓıｓ poenıｔenｔıam eẓeｐe, eｔ uenepunｔ aｄ ｒaｔıｓｆacｔıonem.

Kal. Ｄo abb Aｐｄmaċa Ｆoｐannán Eｐｓcop ⁊ ｐẓｐıḃaı ⁊ anchoıｐe ⁊ Ｄıaｐmaıｄ ｓaｐıenｔıｓｓımuｒ Scoｔoｐum qｕıeueｒunｔ.

Cｈıḃall

^d *Amhlaeibh Conung.*—Ann. Ult. 852, where he is called Amlaimh, or Amlaip, son of the King of Lochlinn. *Quare*, is *Conung* an Hibernicized form of the Teutonic *koenig* or *kuenung*, king?

^e *In Umhaill.*—i. e. in Burrishoole,

county of Mayo. Todd's "Irish Nennius," p. 207, and Ann. F. M. 848.

^f *A royal meeting.*—This is noted in the Ann. Ult., A. D. 850; F. M. 849.

^g *Indrechtach Ua Finnachta.*—Ann. Ult. 853, "iv. *Id. Martii*;" F. M. 852.—

Amhlacibh Conung[d], i. e. the son of the King of Lochlann, came to Erin, and he brought with him commands from his father for many rents and tributes, but he left suddenly. Imhar, his younger brother, came after him to levy the same rents.

Kal. Loch Lacigh, in Umhaill[e], migrated.

Kal. A royal meeting[f] of the men of Erin at Ard-Macha, between Maelsechlainn and Matodan, King of Uladh, and Diarmaid and Fethghna with the congregation of Patrick, and Suairlech with the clergy of Meath.

[854.] Indrechtach Ua Finnachta[g], successor of Colum Cille, and Diarmaid, very wise men, were killed by Saxon plunderers on their way to Rome, and their pure blood still remains at the place where they were killed as a sign of the vengeance of God against those who killed them.

In this year the King of Lochlann was invited to [the house of] Maelsechlainn to drink, and there was a great feast prepared for him; and the King of Lochlann [made many promises], and promised on his oath to observe them ; but, however, he did not observe the smallest of them after leaving the house of Maelsechlainn, but he proceeded at once to plunder the land of Maelsechlainn. But, however, this war did not turn out lucky for him.

In this year many forsook their Christian baptism[h] and joined the Lochlanns, and they plundered Ard-Macha, and carried away all its riches; but some of them did penance, and came to make satisfaction.

[852.] Two abbots of Ard-Macha[i], Forannan, bishop and scribe, and Diarmaid, the wisest of the Scoti, died.

Cearbhall,

Reeves's Adamnan, p. 390.

[h] *Many forsook their baptism.*—i. e. many of the Irish joined the Danes, and lapsed into Paganism. This extraordinary fact is not noticed by the Ann. Ult. or by the F. M.

[i] *Two abbots of Ard-Macha.*—"Duo heredes Patricii, viz. Forinnan, Scriba et

Cṙḃall mac Ḋunlaing ṗí Oṗṗaiġe (cliaṁuin Maoilṗeaċlainn .i. ḃeaṗḃṗuiṗ Cṙḃaill og Maoilṗeaċlainn .i. lanḃ ingḟn Ḋunlaing, ⁊ ḃna ingḟn Maoilṗeaċlainn og Cṙḃall) ḃo ċuṗ ḃo Maoilṗeaċloinn i Muṁain ḃo cuinngiḃ giall, aṗ néġ a ṗiġ .i. Ailgṙnán.

Caṫ no ċaḃaiṗṫ ḃ'Aoḃ ḃo ṗiġ Ailiġ .i. ḃon ṗiġ aṗ ḟeṗṗ ṙngnaṁ 'na aimṗiṗ, ḃo loingiuṗ na nGall nGaoiḃeal .i. Scuiṫ iaḃ ⁊ ḃalṫai ḃo Noṗmannoiḃ iaḃ, ⁊ ṫan ann aḃ ḃṙṗaṗ ciḃ Noṗmainniġ ḟṗiu. Maiḃiḃ ḟoṗṗa ṗe nAoḃ, agur cuiṗṫċaṗ a nḃeaṗgáṗ na nGall nGaoiḃeal, ⁊ cinn imḃa ḃo ḃṗeiṫ ḃo [Aeḃ mac] Niall leiṗ, ⁊ ṗa ḃligṗioṫ na h-Eiṗṙinaiġ an maṗḃaḃ ṗoin, uaiṗ aṁail ḃo níḃíṗ na Loċlanr.aiġ ḃo níḃiṗṗioṁ.

Sloigṙḃ la hAoḃ mac Néill ḃo inṗṗaḃ Ulaḃ. Aċṫ eṙna ní ṗeḃ ṗáinig ḃo, uaiṗ ṫugṗaṫ Ulaiḃ maiḃm ḟoṗ Cinél n-Eoġain, ⁊ ṗo maṗḃṗaṫ Flaiṫḃeaṗṫaċ mac Néill, ⁊ Conacán mac Colmáin ann cuin mulṫiṗ aliṗ.

Iṗ in aiṁṗiṗ ṗi aċṫ ḃḟġ ṫáinig Roḃolḃ co na ḟloġaiḃ ḃ'inṗṗaḃ Oṗṗaiġe. Ra ṫionoil ḃno Cṙḃall mac Ḋunlaing ṗloġ na n-agaiḃ, ⁊ ṫug caṫ ḃóiḃ, ⁊ ṗo ṁaiḃ ḟoṗṗ na Loċlannaiḃ. Ra ċuaḃaṗ iṁuṗṗo ḃuiḃṙn ṁóṗ ḃo luċṫ na maḃma ḟoṗ a n-ṙċoiḃ i ṫṫiolaiġ n-áiṗḃ, ⁊ ṗo ḃáṫṫuiṗ aġ ṗéġaḃ an ṁaṗḃṫa iṁṗu, ⁊ aḃ connċaṫṫuṗ a muinċeṗ ṗéin ġá maṗḃaḃ aṁail na maṗḃḃaiṗ caoiṗig. Ra ġaḃ aiṗéḃ moṗ iaḃ, ⁊ aṗeḃ ḃo ṗoiṗaṫ a cclaiḃiḃ ḃo noċṫaḃ, ⁊ a n-aiṗm ḃo

---

Episcopus et anchorita, et Dermaid, sapientissimus omnium doctorum Europæ quieverunt."—*Ann. Ult.* 851; *F. M.* 851. Dermaid is said above to have suffered martyrdom with Innrechtach on their way to Rome; but the F. M. record his death the year before, the Ann. Ult. two years before, the martyrdom of Innrechtach.

ᵏ *Daughter.*—His daughter by a different marriage.

ˡ *Ailghenan*, King of Munster, died, according to the Four Masters, in 851, but the true year is 853.—Ann. Ult. 852.

ᵐ *Gall-Gaeidhil.*—i. e. the Dano-Irish, or rather the Norwegian Irish who had lapsed into paganism, and plundered the churches in as profane a manner as the Norwegians themselves. The Four Mas-

Cearbhall, son of Dunlaing, King of Osraighe (the brother-in-law of Maelsechlainn, for the sister of Cearbhall, *was married* to Maelsechlainn, i. e. Lann, daughter of Dunlaing, and besides the daughter[k] of Maelsechlainn, was married to Cearbhall), was sent by Maelsechlainn into Munster, to demand hostages, on the death of their King Ailghenan[l].

A battle was given by Aedh, King of Ailech, the most valiant king of his time, to the fleet of the Gall-Gaeidhil[m], i. e. they were Scoti and foster-children to the Northmen, and at one time they used to be called Northmen.. They were defeated and slaughtered by Aedh, and many *of their* heads were carried off by [Aedh, son[n] of] Niall with him, and the Irish were justified in committing this havoc, for these were accustomed to act like the Lochlanns.

A hosting was made by Aedh, son of Niall, to plunder Uladh[o], but he did not find this easy, for the Ulidians defeated the Cinel-Eoghain, and slew Flaithbhertach, son of Niall, and Conacan, son of Colman, with many others.

Nearly at this time Rodolph[p] came with his forces to plunder Osraighe. But Cearbhall, son of Dunlaing, assembled a host to oppose them, and gave them battle, and defeated the Lochlanns. A large party of the defeated, however, went on horseback to the top of a high hill, from which they viewed the slaughtered around them, and saw their own people slaughtered like sheep. They were seized with a great desire of revenge, and what they did was to draw their swords

ters state that this victory was gained by Aedh, son of Niall, at Glenufhoichle (now Glenelly, near Strabane, in the county of Tyrone), in the year 854. The Annals of Ulster place it in 855.

[n] *Son of.*—The text has "by Niall," but in the margin are the words "Cloō potius." We ought, therefore, certainly to read Cloō mac Niall.

[o] *Uladh.*—Ann. F. M. 853; Ult. 854.

[p] *Rodolph.*—There is no notice of this chieftain in the published Annals.

oo ʒabail, ⁊ tuiöſġt cum na n-Oppuiʒeaċ, ʒup po mapḃpat opeam ṅíoḃ; ʒineaḋ ap aba pa cuipſo iaupaioe ap ccúla na maiḋm .i. aʒ Áṫ muiceaḋa tuʒaḋ an maiḋm pi. Do pala impuppo Ʒlipic ponn oo Chſpḃall pén .i. anuaip taḃapta an ṁaoma, ⁊ pʒaoileaḋ oa ṁuintip uaḋ; opeam oo na Loċlannaiḃ oo ċoiöſġt cuiʒe ⁊ a eap-ʒabail ṅóiḃ. Áṫt ſpe puptaċt an coimóeaḋ puaip a póipitin: pa bpip pén a eoaċ, ⁊ na cſnʒail pa ḃáttup paip, ⁊ pa ċuaiḋ plán uaiḋiḃ. Áp móp tpá an t-áp tuʒaḋ ann popp na Loċlannaiḃ.

Caṫ no bpipeḋ oo Saxonoiḃ popp na Nopmainnaiḃ.

Iſ in aimpip pi tanʒattup Danaip .i. hopm co na muiṅtip o'iannpoiʒiö Cſpḃaill mic Dunlainʒ, ʒo po conʒnaiḋ Cſpḃall leo i ccſnn na Loċlann, uaip bá heaʒail leo a ffopuaipliuʒaḋ tpe ċeal-ʒaiḃ na Loċlann. Ra ʒaḃ ono Cſpḃall ʒo honópaċ cuiʒe iaḋ, ⁊ po ḃáttup maille pip ʒo mime oʒ ḃpeiṫ ċopʒaip oo Ʒhallaiḃ ⁊ oo Ʒhaoioealaiḃ.

Áp móp la Ciappaiʒiḃ oʒ bealaċ Conʒlaip pop Loċlannaiḃ, uḃi plupimi tpucioati punt pepmippionne Dei.

'Áp ono la h-'Ápaḃa Cliaċ popp na ʒentiḃ ċéona.

Iſ in bliaḋain ċéona pa ċuippiot pip Muṁan teachta o'ionn-poiʒiö Chſpḃaill mic Dunlainʒ, ʒo o-tíopaḋ na Danaip leip, ⁊ tionol Oppaiʒe oa ffuptaċt, ⁊ oa ffóipioin an aʒaiḋ na Nop-mainneċ pa baoap ʒá n-ionnpaḋ ⁊ ʒa n-apʒain an tan poin. Ra ffʒaip ono Cſpḃall pin, ⁊ pa puaʒaip oo na Danapaiḃ ⁊ o'Op-paiʒiḃ toiḋeaċt ʒo léip [ċnóilte] opuptaċt fſp Muṁan, ⁊ ap eaḋ on oo ponoḋ paip. Tainic iapam Cſpḃall peiṁe o'ionnpoiʒhiö na Loċlann

---

ⁿ *Ath muiceadha,*—i. e. ford of the swine-herd. This narrative does not occur in any other Annals known to the Editor.

' *The Saxons.*—This is probably the victory recorded in the Anglo-Saxon Chronicle at the year 851, when King Ethelwulf and his son Æthelbald fought against the Northmen at Ockley, "and there made the greatest slaughter among the heathen army that we have heard tell of unto the

swords and take their arms and come [down] to the Osraighi, a party of whom they slew. They were nevertheless driven back in defeated rout. This defeat was given them at Ath muiccadha⁹. Here Glifit met Cearbhall himself at the time of the defeat, his people having separated from him. A party of the Lochlanns came up with him and took him prisoner; but by the Lord's assistance he was relieved. He himself tore his clothes and the bonds that were upon him, and escaped in safety from them. Great, indeed, was the slaughter that was made of the Lochlanns there.

A battle was gained by the Saxons' over the Northmen. At this time came the Danes, i. e. Horm and his people, to Cearbhall, son of Dunlaing, and Cearbhall assisted them against the Lochlauns [Norwegians], for they were afraid of being overpowered by the stratagems of the Lochlanns. Cearbhall therefore took them to him honourably, and they frequently accompanied him in gaining victories over the foreigners and the Gaeidhil [Irish].

A great slaughter of the Lochlanns was made by the Ciarraighi at Bealach Chonglais⁸, where many were killed by the permission of God.

A slaughter, too, was made by the Aradians of Cliach¹, of the same Gentiles.

In the same year" the men of Munster sent messengers to Cearbhall, son of Dunlaing [to request] that he would come, bringing the Danes with him, and the rising out of Osraighe, to assist and relieve them against the Northmen [Norwegians] who were harassing and plundering them at that time. Now, Cearbhall responded to this [call]

present day."

⁸ *Bealach Chonglais.*—A place near the city of Cork. There is no notice of this battle in the published Annals.

¹ *Aradians of Cliach.*—This entry is not in the published Annals.

" *In the same year.*—Not in the published Annals.

Loclann go rlóg mor Danar ⁊ Gaoiḋeal. Oṫ concattur na Loċlannaiġ Crpḃall co na pluaġ, no muinnċir, ro ġaḃ aḋnaċ ⁊ uaṁan
mor iaḋ. Ra ċuaiḋ Ceapḃall i n-ionaḋ áro ⁊ ro ḃaoi ag agallaḋ
a muinnċire péin ar ċúr; arcaḋ ro ráiḋ, ⁊ ré og régaḋ¹ na ffsrann
frararge imme: Naċ ffaiċtí liḃ, ar ré, mar ra ráruigrioċ na
Loclannaiġ na rcaranna-ra ar mḃreiċ a ċruiḋ ⁊ ar marḃaḋ a
ḋaoine; maḋ creiri ḃáiḃ iniu má ḃuinne, ḋo génaḋ na céċna 'nar
ccír-ne, uair imurro aċáimne rocraiḋc mór aniu, caiċigim go
cruaiḋ na n-aigiḋ. Paċ oile ar noḋ cóir ḋuin saċugaḋ cruaiḋ ḋo
ḋénoṁ, nar rionnaċ na Danair railec maille frinn mrċaċċ ná
mioḋlaecur rorrn, uair ra ċeigéṁaḋ, giḋ maille rinn aċáḋ aniu,
go mḃeḋír 'nár n-agaiḋ ḋoṁrḃir. Paċ oile, gur ro ċugaḋ fir
Muṁan i ccangamar róirioin ár cruar forainn, uair ir minic ar
namaiḋ iaḋ.

Ra agall iarċċain na Danair, ⁊ arcaḋ ro ráiḋ riuraiḋe:
ḋénḃr calma aniu, uair ar namuiḋ ḃunaiḋ ḋuiḃ na Loclannaiġ, ⁊
ra ċuirric caċa eaċċruiḃ, ⁊ ár móra anallána. Ar maiċ ḋuiḃ
rinne maille riḃ aniu na n-agaiḋ, ⁊ ḋna ní eile ann, ní fiu ḋuiḃ
créiċe no laige ḋo ċuigrin ḃuinne forairḋ. Ra freagraċur uile
eoir Ohanaru ⁊ Ghaoiḋealu, ná rionnfaiċe créiċe no mrċaċč
forra. Ro eirgḃur iarċċain eirgċ naoinfir irin uair rin ḋ'ionn-
roigiḋ na Loclann. Na Loclannaiġ immurro ó ḋo concattur
rin, ní caċ ro iomḋruiḋrioḋ ḋo ċaḃairċ, aċċ ar ċeiċḃ ro na caill-
ċiḃ, ar ffágḃail a maiċiura, ḋo ronraċ. Ra gaḃaiḋ na caillċe
ḋá gaċ leiċ forra, ⁊ ra marḃaḋ a nḋeargár na Loclann. Aċċ
ċna conigc ro ní ra fuilngioċċur na Loclannaiġ ḋo'n coiṁ-
líon

¹ *As he looked upon.*—Ag ré og régaḋ.
In modern Irish this would be, agur é
ag féaċain na ḃreapann b-par uime.
² *They were killed with great slaughter.*

—Ro marḃaḋ a nḋearg-ár na Loċlann. The modern construction would
be, Ro marḃaḋar ḋearg-ár na Loc-
lannach, which is better.

[call], and he commanded the Danes and the Osraighi to proceed fully [assembled] to relieve the men of Munster, and this was accordingly done at this summons. Cearbhall afterwards came forward to attack the Lochlanns with a great host of Danes and Gaeidhils. When the Lochlanns saw Cearbhall with his host, or people, they were seized with great fear and dread. Cearbhall went to a high place, and he began to address his own people first, and he said, as he looked upon the deserted lands around him : " Do ye not perceive," said he, " how the Lochlanns have desolated these lands, having carried off their cattle and killed their inhabitants? If they be more powerful this day than we, they will do the same in our territory. But as we are very numerous this day, let us fight bravely against them. Another reason for which it is right for us to fight bravely is, that the Danes, who are along with us, may not perceive cowardice or want of heroism in us, for it may happen that, though they are on our side this day, they may hereafter be against us. Another reason is, that the men of Munster, whom we have come to relieve, may understand our hardihood, for they too are often our enemies." He afterwards addressed the Danes, and what he had said to them was : " Exhibit your bravery this day, for the Lochlanns are your radical enemies, for ye fought battles, and slaughtered one another formerly. It is well for you to have us with you against them this day, and, moreover, it is not worth your while to let us observe dastardliness or cowardice among you." They all made answer, both Gaeidhil and Danes, that neither weakness nor cowardice should be observed in them. They afterwards rose out as one man at that time to attack the Lochlanns. However, when the Lochlanns observed this, they did not close to give battle, but fled to the woods, leaving their property behind. The woods were surrounded on every side upon the Lochlanns, and they were killed with great slaughter[x]. Up to this time

the

líon ꝛo a n-Éiꞃinn uile. A cCꞃuacain i n-Éoꞅanacꞇ ꞇuꞅaᵭ an maiᵭmꞃi.

Ꞇáinic Cꞃᵬall ꞅo mbuaiᵭ ⁊ coꞃꞅuꞃ amlaiᵭ ꞃin ᵭ'á ꞇiꞅ. Ro hiouncaiceᵭ hoꞃm iaꞃꞇꞇain co na mꞃuinnꞇiꞃ ó Cꞃᵬall ꞅo ꞃí Ꞇꞃinꞃac. Rá ꝼꞃi ꞃí Ꞇꞃmꞃac ꝼáilꞇe ꞃiꞃ, ⁊ ꞇuꞅ onóiꞃ móꞃ ᵭó : Rá cuaiᵭ aꞃꞃin ᵭo cum maꞃa. Ra maꞃᵬaᵭ iaꞃꞇꞇain an ꞇhoꞃm ꞃin la Roᵭꞃi, ꞃí ᵬꞃꞇan.

hoc anno quieuiꞇ Mac Ꞅiallain aꞃ mbeiꞇ ꝼꝼꝼ. bliaᵭain i n-aínc.

Niall mac Ꞅilláin iaꞃ mbeiꞇ ꞇꞃioca bliaꞅain ꞅan ᵭiꞅ ꞅan ᵬiaᵭ, ᵭécc A. Ꝺ. 854.

Ꝼal. Ainoli ꞃaꞃienꞃ Ꞇíꞃe ᵭa ꞅlaꞃ moꞃiꞇuꞃ.

Cáꞃꞇac aᵬ Ꞇíꞃe ᵭa ꞅlaꞃ, quieuiꞇ.

Ailꞅꞃnan mac Ꝺonnꞅaile ꞃí Caiꞃil, moꞃiꞇuꞃ. Amlaoiᵬ mac ꞃí Loclann ᵭo ꞇoiᵭeacꞇ i n-Éiꞃinn, ⁊ ꞃa ꞅiallꞃaꞇ ꞅaill 'Éiꞃeann ᵭó.

Ꝼal. Iꞃ in bliaᵭain ꞃi, an ᵭaꞃa bliaᵭainn ᵭécc ꝼlaꞇa Maoilꞃechloinn ᵭo ꞃonaᵭ móꞃꝼluaꞅ la Maoilꞃeacloinn i n-Oꞃꞃaiꞅiᵬ ⁊ im Mumain, aꞃ na ꞃáᵭ ᵭ'ꝼeaꞃaiᵬ Mumon na ꞇiᵬmuíꞃ bꞃaiꞅᵭe ᵭó, ꞅonaᵭ aiꞃe ꞃin ꞃa ꝼuaꞅaiꞃ Maoilꞃeacloinn caꞇ ꝼoꞃꞃa ; ⁊ ꝼáꞇ moꞃ oile aꞅ Maoilꞃeacloinn .i. Cꞃᵬall mac Ꝺunlainꞅ, ꞃí Oꞃꞃaiꞅe, ᵭuine ón ꞅaꞃ ᵬo ᵭinꞅᵬála Éiꞃe, uile Ꝺo ᵬeiꞇ, aꞃ ꝼeaᵬuꞃ a ᵭealᵬa ⁊ a eniꞅ ⁊ a ꞃnꞅnaꞇha, cíꞃa móꞃabliaᵭ naiᵭe ᵭo bꞃeiꞇ ᵭó .i. o na ꞇuaꞇoiᵬ ᵭo Laiꞅniᵬ ꞃa ᵬáꞇꞇuꞃ aiꞅe. In luꞇꞇ imuꞃꞃo ꞃa cuaiᵭ ᵭo ꞇoᵬac

---

¹ *Cruachain Eoghanacht.*—This place is otherwise called *Cruachan Maighe Eamhna*, now Crohane, in the barony of Slievardagh, in the county of Tipperary. It is mentioned in the " Feilire Aeughuis" at 5th October, as in the territory of Eoghanacht-Chaisil.

² *Horm.*—" A. D. 855, Horm, chief of the Black Gentiles, was killed by Ruarai mac Merminn, King of Britain."—*Ann. Ult.* The true year was 856, so that the preceding events must have taken place in the years 854 and 855.

³ *Mac Giallain.*—His death is entered

the Lochlanns had not suffered so great a loss in all Erin. At Cruachain in the Eoghanacht' this victory was gained.

Cearbhall thus returned to his house with victory and triumph. Horm and his people were afterwards escorted by Cearbhall to the King of Teamhair. The King of Teamhair welcomed him, and gave him great honour. He afterwards went to sea. This Horm^z was afterwards killed by Roderic, King of the Britons.

In this year died Mac Giallain^a, after having fasted for thirty years.

Niall Mac Giallain died in the year 854, after having been thirty years without drink, without food.

[853.] Kal. Aindli, wise man of Tir-da-ghlas, died.

Carthach[b], Abbot of Tir-da-ghlas, died.

Ailgenan, son of Dunghal, King of Cashel, died.

[856.] Amhlaeibh, son of the King of Lochlann, came to Erin, and the Galls of Erin submitted to him.

[858.] Kal. In this year, the twelfth[c] of the reign of Maelsechlainn, Maelsechlainn marched with a great army into Osraighe and into Munster, the Munster-men having said that they would not give him hostages, wherefore Maelsechlainn proclaimed battle upon them; and Maelsechlainn had another great cause, which was this: Cearbhall, son of Dunlaing, King of Osraighe, a person who was indeed worthy of possessing all Erin for the goodness of his countenance, hospitality,

in the Ann. F. M. at the year 854, and again at 858; Ann. Ult. 859. "Niall Mac Fiallain [Mac Giallain, F. M.] *qui passus est paralisi* 34 *annis, et qui versatus est visionibus frequentibus, tam falsis, quam veris, in Christo quievit.*" The double entry of his death here (and by the F. M. 854, 858), shows that these Annals were compiled from different sources.

^b *Carthach.*—This and the following entry are given the by F. M. at 851, and are evidently out of place here.

^c *The twelfth of the reign of Maelsechlainn.*—i. e. 858; Ann. Ult. 857.

tobaċ an ċíora rin .i. maoin Cṙibaill mic Dunlaing, imċornaṁ mór do ḋénaṁ dóiḃ aġ tobaċ an ċíora, ⁊ tarcorral mór do taḃairt doiḃ for Laiġniḃ. Laiġin do dola ar roin ġo ġearánaċ d'ionnroiġhio Maoilreaċloinn, ⁊ a inḃrin do Maoilreaċloinn. Fŕiġ mór do ġaḃail Maoilreaċloinn, ⁊ an tionol mórra do ḃreiṫ d'ionnroiġhio Cṙibaill ⁊ fear Muṁan battur aġ congnaṁ la Cṙibaill.

Tangattur iarroin Maoilreaċloinn cona ṗlóiġ ġo Ġaḃrán, ⁊ ar ra ḃruinne Ġaḃrain ra ḃattur na rlóiġ oile. Ġér bo líonṁaire imurro do Maoilreaċloinn, ní hfó ra ċuaid na ceṡin aċt ar conair oile ná ro raoileaḋ a nḋola ra ċuattur, ġo rángattur Cárn Luġaḋa, ⁊ ro ḃaoi Maoilreaċloinn armża éidiġte annrain ar ċṡin ċáiċ. 'Od concaḋar fir Muṁan rin, rá faġrat a longrort ⁊ ra rainrit a fluaġ ar ḋó, ⁊ táinig rí Muṁan .i. Maolġuala co marerluaġaiḃ morait ime in n-aiġid Maoilreaċloinn. Cṙibaill imurro ⁊ a Ḋanair, doneoċ ra ṫairir do ṁuintir horm ra tairir i ffaraḋ Cṙibaill, arfó ba longrort dóiḃ caill uriroe dlúṫ aimréiḃ, ⁊ rá ḃaoi tionol mór ann rin um Cṙibaill. Arfó rá innirit na heolaiġ ġo raḃa ḃuaiḋreaḋ mór annrin for Cṙibaill ar n-iṁirt driaġeaċta do Ṫaircealtaċ mac na Ceartafair, ġo mbaḋ luġaide no diġrid do cum an ċaṫa, ġo nerḃeart Cṙibaill ar coḋlaḋ do ġénaḋ ann rin, ⁊ ní do cum an ċaṫa do raġaḋ. In caṫ tra i raḃa rí Muṁan tuġrat maiḋm ar túr ar muinntir Maoilreaċloinn. Tangaḋar dna a ċoirıġeḋa da róirıṫinrıḋe .i. Maoilreacloinn co na ṁuinntir, ġo ttuġaḋ maiḋm for fearaiḃ Muṁan ⁊ rá cuireaḋ an dearġ ár. Ro marḃaiḋ roċaiḋe do raorċlannoiḃ

^d *Gabhran.*—Now Gowran, in the county of Kilkenny.

^e *Carn Laghdhach.*—i. e. Lughaidh's carn. This place is somewhere near Gowran, but its exact situation or modern name has not been yet determined.

^f *Fircheartach mac na Cearta.*—A famous necromancer often referred to in old Irish romances. He is sometimes called Mac Aenchearda. He seems to have been

lity, and valour, levied great yearly rents from the territories in Leinster, which he possessed; but the people who went to levy the rent, i. e. the stewards of Cearbhall, son of Dunlang, used great violence in levying the rent, and offered great insult to the Leinster-men. The Leinster-men consequently went querulously to Maelsechlainn and told it to him. Maelsechlainn was seized with great anger and led this great muster against Cearbhall and the men of Munster who were aiding him. Maelsechlainn, after this, proceeded with his host to Gabhrán[d], at the confines of which the other hosts were. However, though Maelsechlainn had more numerous forces, he did not go against them, but proceeded by another road where he did not think they would go, until he reached Carn Lughdhach[e], and here Maelsechlainn was armed and accoutred to meet all. When the men of Munster perceived this, they left their camp, and divided their host into two parts, and the King of Munster, Maelguala, came with large squadrons of horse to oppose Maelsechlainn; but Cearbhall and his Danes (such of the people of Horm as remained with him), encamped in a briery, thick entangled wood, and there was a great muster there about Cearbhall. And the learned relate that there was a great trouble on Cearbhall here, Tairchealtach Mac na Cearta[f] having exercised magic upon him, so that he was less inclined to go to battle, and so that Cearbhall said that he would retire to rest and not go to battle! Now, the battalion in which the King of Munster was [the commander] at first defeated the people of Maelsechlainn, but foot soldiers came to their relief (i. e. to the relief of Maelsechlainn and his people), so that the men of Munster were [in their turn] defeated and cut off with dreadful slaughter. Many nobles were killed

the presiding spirit of Carn Lughdhach, where this battle was fought, but the modern name or situation of the place still remains to be determined.

ṗaoṗċlannoiḃ annṗın. Inoıṗıc eolaıġ conaḋ hí numıṗ an cṗlóıġ aṗ a ocuġaḋ an maıḋm ᚏᚏ. milıum.

Aṗ comaıṗle oo ṗınne Cṗḃall, maṗ ṗa ċuala ṗın, bṗaıġoe oo ċaḃaıṗc oo Maoılṗeaċlaınn, ⁊ ġan a cíṗ oo loc, ⁊ ṗo ġaḃ Maoılṗeaċlaınn bṗaıġoe uaḋ, uaıṗ lano ınġṡn Ouṅlaınġ, oeṗḃṗıuṗ Cṗṡṗḃaıll, bṡn Maoılṗeaċlaınn.

Ra ċuaıḋ Maoılṗeaċlaınn oon Mumaın, ġo ṗaḃa ṗe ṗé míṗ oġ ıonnṗaḋ Mumaın ann Eımlıġ, ġo ccuġ bṗaıġoe Mumaın ó Comuṗ cṗí n-uıṗġc ġo hınnṗı Caṗḃna ıaṗ n-'Eıṗınn. Caċ Caıṗn Luġḋaċ ṗaın. Iṗ ın caċ ṗoın ṗo maṗḃaḋ Maolcṗóın mac Muıṗṡoaıġ leıcṗıġ na nÓéıṗı.

Ġen ġo ccíoṗaḋ Maoılṗeaċlaınn an cuṗuṗ ṗo oo ġaḃáıl ṗıġc Mumaın oo ṗéın, ṗo ḃo ċııḃeaċca oo ınaṗḃaḋ an ṗo maṗḃaḋ oo Ġhallġaoıḃealaıḃ ann, uaıṗ oaoıne ıaṗ ccṗéġaḋ a ınḃaıṗce ıaoṗaıḋe, ⁊ aoḃeṗcaıṗ Noṗmannaıġ ṗṗıu, uaıṗ ḃéṗ Noṗmannaċ aca, ⁊ a n-alcṗum ṗoṗṗa, ⁊ ġéṗ ḃo olc na Noṗmannaıġ ḃuıaıḋ oo na hṡġlaıṗıḃ ḃá mṡṗa ġo móṗ ıaoṗaıḋe .ı. an luċc ṗa, ġaċ coṗaıṗ ṗo 'Eıṗınn a ınḃṡoíṗ.

Ṗoġmuṗ ġoṗcaċ ıṡ ın mḃlıaḋaın ṡı.

Inṗıuḋ Laıġṡn uıle la Ceṗḃall mac Ounlaınġ, ⁊ níoṗ ṗṗeṗṗoe bṗaıġoe uaḋ a laıṁ Maoılṗeaċlaınn, ġuṗ ġaḃ Cṗḃall mac Ounlaınġ bṗaıġoe Laıġṡn um Coṗṗmac mac Ounlaınġ, ⁊ ım Suıċṡman ınac

---

ᵃ *Lann.*—The meaning is, that this connexion rendered Maelsechlainn more placable, or that Lann had employed her intercession with her husband.

ᵇ *Imleach.*—Now Emly, in the county Tipperary.

ᶜ *Cumar-na-tri-n-uisce.*—i.e. the meeting of the Three Waters, near Waterford.

ᵏ *Inis Tarbhna.*—Now the Bull, a small island in the barony of Beare, and county of Cork.

ˡ *Gall-Gaidhil.*—The published Annals give us no idea of this class of Iberno-Norwegian or Norwegian-Irish heathens who infested Ireland at this period. O'Flaherty thought that the name was confined

killed there. The learned relate that the number of the army which was there routed was twenty thousand.

When Cearbhall heard of this [defeat], the resolution he adopted was to give hostages to Maelsechlainn, to prevent him from destroying his country; and Maelsechlainn accepted of hostages from him, for Lann[g], daughter of Dunlang and sister of Cearbhall, was the wife of Maelsechlainn.

Maelsechlann then proceeded into Munster, and remained for the space of a month at Imleach[h], plundering Munster, and he obtained the hostages of Munster from Cumar-na-tri-nu-isce[i] to Inis Tarbhna[k], in the west of Erin. This was the battle of Carn Lughdhach. In this battle was slain Maeleron, son of Muireadhach, half King of the Deisi.

Though Maelsechlainn had not come on this expedition to take the kingdom of Munster for himself, he ought to have come to kill all the Gall-Gaidhil[l] who were killed there, for they were a people who had renounced their baptism, and they were usually called Northmen, for they had the customs of the Northmen, and had been fostered by them, and though the original Northmen were bad to the churches, these were by far worse, in whatever part of Erin they used to be.

There was a dearth in the autumn of this year.

[858.] All Leinster[m] was plundered by Cearbhall, son of Dunlang, and his hostages in the hands of Maelsechlainn did not render him the better subject, so that Cearbhall, son of Dunlang, took the hostages of Leinster, together with Cormac[n], son of Dunlang, and Suitheman,

to the inhabitants of the western islands of Scotland, and it is very certain that the mixed race of these islands were so called. See Ann. F. M., A. D. 1154, p. 1113; where they speak of the Gal-Gaidhil of Aran, of Cantire, of the Isle of Man, and of the coasts of Scotland (Alban).

[m] *All Leinster.*—Ann. F. M. 856.

[n] *Cormac.*—The F. M. 856, call him Coirpre, son of Dunlang.

mac Aptúip. Maiṫm pe Cṡpḃall mac Ōunlaing, ┐ pe Niap[f] ꝼo Ġhallġaoiḋealaiḃ i n-Apaḋaiḃ tíre.

Ḱal. Anno Domini, vcccli. Maolġuala, pi Caipil vo ġaḃáil vo Normannoiḃ, ┐ a écc allain acca.[p]

Sluaġ mór la Cṡpḃall mac Ōunlaing ┐ pluaġ Loclan laip i Miḋe ┐ ní pa veiġ . . . . . a ḃpaiġve ḃáttup aġ Maoilpeaclainn, ġo paḃa na tpí míoraiḃ aġ inpaḋ ꝼṡpainn Maoilpeaclainn ┐ ní po an ġup po ꝼolmuiġ an típ uile 'nia maitiup. Ir poċaiḃe tra ṽ'ꝼṡpaiḃ vána Eipeann vo ponpat vuana molta vo Cṡpḃall, ┐ taitnipo ġaċ corġup pnġ inntiḃ; ┐ ap mó vo pine Aonġap an t-áipvġnaiḋ, comapba Molua.

Uċ tra an ní av bṡpam ġo minic : Ap truaġ vo na h-Eipṡnnċaiḃ an mí-ḃép vóiḃ taċup ſtuppa ꝼéin, ┐ nac anaoineaċt uile éipġit a ceṡnn na Loclann. Ra eipġe vna Aoḋ mac Néill, ap na aplaċ vo pí Cianaċta paip eipġe i ceṡnn Maoilpeaclainn, uaip Maoilpeaclainn pa ḃáiḋ veapḃpataip píġ Cianaċta, .i. Cionaoṽ ut ppaepipprimur.

Riġḋail maite 'Eipeann oġ Ráṫ Aoḋa um Maoilpeaclainn, pí Eipeann,[r] ┐ um ꝼeṡġna comapba Pávpaicc, ┐ um Suaiplioḋ, comapba

---

Aradh Tire.—Now the barony of Arra, or Duharra, in the county of Tipperary. Ann. F. M. 857.

[p] *Anno Domini*, 855.—This date is incorrect, and the scribe writes in the margin: (Ip aiḣlaiḋ an nuimipṡ Annopum Domini ┐ ceitṡp bliaḋna vo ḃénam von aoin bliaḋain pṡmunn, in po innapḃ Popannán aḃ cuḃaiḋ Apomacha. "The way that this number Annorum Domini [happened to come here] is, that four years are made of the one year [recte, one year is made of four years] before us, viz. that in which Forannan, legitimate abbot of Ard Macha, was expelled." This remark seems to be out of its proper place, for Forannan was carried off in the year 843.

[q] *Maelguala, King of Cashel.*—Ann. F. M. 857; Ult. 858. The Four Masters tell us that this year coincided with the thirteenth of Maelsechlainn, which would make the true date 859, according to O'Flaherty's Chronology, *Ogyg.*, p. 434.

[r] *In Meath.*—Ann. Ult. 858 (= 859).

Suitheman, son of Arthur. A victory was gained by Cearbhall, son of Dunlang, and by Niar over the Gall-Gaidhil in Aradh Tire°.
[859.] Kal. Anno Domini, 855ᵖ. Maelguala, King of Cashel^q, was taken prisoner by the Northmen, and he died in their hands.

A great hosting [of his own people, and] a hosting of Lochlanns by Cearbhall, son of Dunlaing, into Meath^r, his hostages^s. . . . . . who were in the hands of Maelsechlainn not preventing him, and he continued for three months to plunder the land of Maelsechlainn, and he did not desist until he had stripped all the territory of its property. Many of the literati of Erin composed laudatory poems for Cearbhall, in which they commemorated every victory which he gained, and Aenghus, the high wise man, successor of Molua^t, did so most [of all].

Alas! for the fact which I shall often mention : It is pitiful for the Irish to continue the evil habit of fighting among themselves, and that they do not rise together against the Lochlanns! Aedh, son of Niall^u, at the solicitation of the King of Cianachta^x, rose up against Maelsechlainn, for it was Maelsechlainn that had drowned the brother of the King of Cianachta, as we have written before.

[858 or 859.] A royal meeting of the chieftains of Erin at Ráth-Aedha^y with Maelsechlainn, King of Erin, Fethghna, Comharba of Patrick,

^s *His hostages.*— In the margin of the MS. is this note : ɓeϲρτ ɓeϩɑ́n, " a small portion is wanting."

^t *Successor of Molua.*—i. e. Abbot of Clonfertmulloe, at the foot of Slieve Bloom, in Upper Ossory. It is highly probable that these Annals, so laudatory of the kings of Ossory, were preserved in this monastery, and drawn from the poems here referred to.

^u *Aedh, son of Niall.*— i. e. Aedh Finnliath, who succeeded Maelsechlainn, or Malachy I. in the throne of Ireland. Ann. Ult. 858 ; F. M. 859.

^x *King of Cianachta.*—i. e. Flann, son of Conang, the nephew of Aedh Finnliath, whose brother Cinaedh had been taken in 851, and drowned in the Nanny Water. See note ^s, p. 118, *supra.*

^y *Ráth-Aedha.*— Now Rahugh, in the

apba Finniain do ōſnam ríoda ⁊ caon compaic na h-Eipeann uile, gonaḋ ip in ḋáilpin tuġ Cſpḃall mac Ḋunlaing a oiġpéip do Maoil-peaclainn do péip comapba Phaḋpaice, ap inḃeiṫ do Cſpḃall poimipin i n-Ipapup ⁊ mac pi Loclann maille ppip pa cſṫpaċaic aiḋce og milleaḋ pſpainn Mailpeaclainn.

Aoḋ Finnliaṫ mac Néill do inipaḋ Míḋe, ⁊ Flann mac Co-naing pí Ciannaċta maille ppip, ⁊ ip eipiḋe pa ap laig ap Aoḋ an tinnpiuḋ ḋénam. Fáṫ oile dno, uaip pa inpſptup Maoilpeaclainn peapann Aoḋa pe trí bliaḋnaiḃ diaiḋ indiaiḋ. Mac ingeine dno Neill an Flann. Do póna dna Aoḋ ap an bFlann an cogaḋpa, uaip ní paḃa a piop aca an ní pa ḃaoi ḋe; ⁊ ap eagla na coimcipġe pin do pigne Maoilpeaclainn ríḋ pe Cſpḃall, amail a duḃpamap pomainn.

Opgoin Loca Cſnd iap naigpeaḋ pommop i ttopcáip cxxx. do daoiniḃ.

Kal. Sioc dopolochta go n-imtigtea Loca 'Eipeann cuip coip ⁊ eac.

Deptaċ Lupca do lopccaḋ do Loclannaiḃ.

Suiḃne mac Roicliġ, ab Lipp moip, quieuit.

Copmac Laitpaig bpuin mopitup.

Sodomna Eppcop Sláine do marḃaḋ do Loclannaiḃ.

Caṫapaċ ab Apdamacha, mopitup.

Lucṫ dá coḃlaċ do Nopmannaiḃ do toiḋeaċt i ffeapann Chep-baill

barony of Moycashel, county of Westmeath. Ann. F. M. 857; Ann. Ult. 858 (= 859). This entry is out of place here.

ᵃ *Comharba of Finian.*—i. e. Abbot of Clonard.

ᵃ *Loch Cend.*—Now probably Lough Ki-neel, near Abbeylara, county of Longford. This entry is in the Ann. F. M. at 853.

ᵇ *Frost.*—This frost, and the other entries down to Cathasach, Abbot of Ard-Macha, are given in the Ann. F. M. at A. D. 854, and the Ann. Ult. at 855, the true year being 856. They are clearly out

trick, and Suairlech, comharba of Finian[a], to establish peace and tranquillity throughout all Erin; and it was at this meeting that Cearbhall, son of Dunlaing, gave Maelsechlainn his full demand, according to the decision of the Comharba of Patrick, Cearbhall having been for forty nights previously, accompanied by the son of the King of Lochlann, destroying the land of Maelsechlainn.

Aedh Finnliath, son of Niall, accompanied by Flann, son of Conang, King of Cianachta, plundered Meath. And it was Flann that had solicited Aedh to commit this devastation. There was also another cause, for Maelsechlainn had plundered the land of Aedh three years successively. Flann was the son of Niall's daughter. Now, Niall and Flann entered into this war, not knowing what might result from it, and from fear of this confederacy Maelsechlainn made peace with Cearbhall, as we have said before.

The plundering of Loch Cend[a] after a very great frost, where one hundred and thirty persons were killed.

[856.] Kal. An intense frost[b], so that the lakes of Erin were traversed both by foot and horse.

The oratory of Lusca[c] was burned by the Lochlanns.

Suibhne, son of[d] Roichlech, Abbot of Lis-mor, died.

Cormac, of Lathrach Briuin[e], died.

Sodhomna, Bishop of Slaine[f], was killed by the Lochlanns.

Cathasach, Abbot of Ard-Macha, died.

[860.] Two fleets of Northmen[g] came into the land of Cearbhall, son

of place here.

[c] *Lusca.*—Now Lusk, in the county of Dublin.

[d] *Son of.*—Grandson of Roichlech.—F. M. 854. "Nepos Roichlich."—Ult. 855.

[e] *Lathrach Briuin.*—Now Laraghbrien,

near Maynooth, in the county of Dublin.

[f] *Slaine.*—i. e. Slane, in the county of Meath.

[g] *Two fleets of Northmen.*—The arrival of these fleets is not noticed in any of the published Annals. They must have put

baill mic Dunlaing ná innraó. Anuair tangur tá innirin do Crr-ball ar ann ro baoi Crrball ror mrrcca. Ra báttur dágbaoíne Orraige ga ráda rir go haloinn 7 go rocraió ga nrrtaó: Ní háb-bar mrrga do beit ror óinne i n-Orraigib do niaó na Loclonnoig anora .i. an tír uile do lot. Att efha go ro coinnéda Dia tura, 7 go ruga buaió 7 corgar dot naimtnib amoil rugair go ninic, 7 amail bera beor. Léig ar tra do mrrga, nair náma an mearga do fngnam. O do cuala Crrball ra cuaió a mrrga uaib, 7 ra gab a arma. Tbinig imurro trian r̥a hoibóe an tan rin. Ar amlaió táinig Crrball immaé ar a grianán 7 rrogcammel mór reime 7 raboí roilri na caindlerin go rada ar gaé leit. Ra gab namán mór na Loclannaig 7 ra teiériot ro na rléibtib raigrib óóib 7 ro na cailltib. An luét imurro ra tairir ra hfngnam óíob ra mar-baó uile. O táinig maioin ammucha ar na márat, ra cuaió Crr-ball go no rocraióe na cernn uile, 7 in ra gab uata, ar marbaó a ndeargáir, go ra cuirr ammaómuim, 7 go ro rgaoilit iad ror gaé leit.

Ra immir Crrball réin go cruaió irin ammur rain, 7 táinig rur go mór a méó att ib an aibóe reime, 7 ra rgé go mór 7 tug ronairte mor dorum rain. Ra grerrr go mór a muinntir go diocra ror na Loclannaib, 7 ar moó na leit an trlóig ra marbaó ann, 7 na teaρna ann ra ceiérit ar ammur a longa.

Og aéaó mic Earclaige tugaó an maiom rin. Ro impa Crr-ball iarttain go mbuaió 7 go neadáil móir.

Irin aimrir rin tainic hona 7 Toimrir Torra dá toireat
roicinelaé

into Waterford harbour, and passed up the Barrow to plunder Ossory.

[h] *Achadh mic Earclaidhe.*—This is probably the celebrated place now called Agha, *alias* St. John's, near the city of Kilkenny. The victory gained at this place by Cearbhall over the Danes of Waterford is entered in the Ann. F. M. at the year 858, but 860 was the true year.

Hona and Tomrir Torra.—There is

son of Dunlang, to plunder it. When messengers came to announce it to Cearbhall, he was intoxicated. The good men of Osraighe said to him gently and kindly, to encourage him : " What the Lochlanns do in Osraighe now is no cause for a person to get drunk, i. e. to destroy the whole country; but may God protect thee, and mayest thou gain victory and triumph over thy enemies, as thou hast often gained, and as thou shalt hereafter. Give up, however, thy drunkenness, for drunkenness is the enemy of valour." When Cearbhall heard this, his drunkenness went off him, and he took his arms. The third part of the night had passed over at this time. Cearbhall came out of his royal chamber with a large, royal candle [carried] before him, the light of which candle shone far on every side. The Lochlanns were seized with great dread, and they fled to the nearest mountains and woods; but such of them as remained through valour were all killed. When the next morning came, Cearbhall set out early in pursuit of them all with his forces, and having dreadfully slaughtered them, he did not leave them until he put them to flight, and until they had dispersed in every direction.

Cearbhall himself acted with great hardihood in this battle, but what he had drunk the night before came much against him ; [however], he vomited much, which gave him great relief. He greatly and vehemently incited his people against the Lochlanns, of whom more than one-half their host was killed in the action, and such as escaped fled to their ships.

At Achadh mic Earclaidhe[h] this victory was gained. Cearbhall returned with victory and great booty.

At this time came Iona and Tomrir Torra[i], two noble chiefs (and

no account of the arrival of these chieftains, or of their battles with the Irish, in the published Annals. Their career appears to have been very brief.

roicinelaċ (⁊ Ōṗuí an clíona), ⁊ ꝼiṗ ḃeoḋa cṗuaıḋe ꝥo niblaıċ moıṗ ıaḋ eıcciṗ aṁuınnciṗ ꝼéın lan ṗaoṗclanna ḋna ıaḋ ḋeṗéıniuḋ Loclann. Tanꝥaccuṗ cṗa an ḋıaṗ ṗın ꝥona ṗoċṗaıḋe ꝥo Luıṁneaċ, ⁊ ó Luıṁneaċ ꝥo Poṗc láıṗꝥe. Aċc éſna aṗ mó ṗa caıṗıṗnıꝥṗıc ına mbṗíóꝥaıḃ ꝼéın ıná 'na ṗoċṗaıḋe. Ra ċıonóılṗıc Eóꝥanacc ⁊ Aṗaıḋ cliaċ ḋóıḃ, ⁊ ṗa ċuıṗṗıc cenń ı ꝥcenn, ⁊ ṗa cuıṗeaḋ cṗíṗ cṗuaıḋ ſccuṗṗa, ꝥo ṗa cuıṗıc na Loclannaıꝥ ı mbaıle bḟꝥ, ⁊ cloċ- ḋaınꝥſn ıme. Ra ċuaıḋ ḋna an ḃṗaoı .ı. hona ⁊ ꝼeaṗ ba ṗıne ḋíoḃ aṗ an ċaıṗıol 'ṗa ḃél oṗlaıꝥce, oꝥ acaċ a ḋee, ⁊ oꝥ ḋénaṁ a ḋṗaoıꝥ- ſċca, ⁊ ꝥa ſṗaıl aṗ aṁuınnciṗ auṗaḋ na nḋee. Taınıꝥ ꝼeaṗ ḋꝼeaṗaıḃ Muṁan cuıꝥe ꝥo ccuꝥ buılle ḋo ċloıċ móıṗ ḋaṗ ṗın a ṁanc ḋú, ꝥo ccuꝥ a ꝼıacla uıle aṗṗ a cſın. Ra ımṗa ıaṗ ṗın a aıꝥıḋ aṗ a ṁuınnciṗ ꝼén, ⁊ aṗṗeḋ ṗo ṗáıḋ aꝥ cuṗ aꝼola cſṗṗaıḋe ḋaṗ a ḃél amaċ: ḋam maṗḃṗa ḋe ṗo aṗ ṗé, ⁊ ṗa ċuıc aṗ aıṗ, ⁊ ṗa ċuaıḋ a anam aṗṗ. Ra ꝥaḃaḋ ḋóıḃ ıaṗccaın ḋo ċloċaıḃ ꝥona ṗa ꝼéḋṗac a ꝼulanꝥ, aċc ꝼaꝥḃaıḋ a n-ıonaḋ ṗın, ⁊ cıaꝥaıḋ ꝼoṗ ṗúṗ- ꝥſın ba nſṗṗa, ⁊ maṗḃcuṗ annṗaıḋe ancaoıṗeċ oıle, ꝥo maṗḃac amlaıḋ ṗın an ḋa ċaoıṗeaċ .ı. hona Luıṁnıꝥ, ⁊ Tomṗıṗ Toṗṗa. Ní ceaṗna ḋna ḋa maıċıḃ aċc ḋıaṗ namá, ⁊ uaıċeaḋ beꝥ Leo, ⁊ ṗuꝥṗac ꝼıṗ Muṁan buaıḋ ⁊ coṗꝥuṗ aṁlaıḋ ṗın.

Iſ ın blıaḋaın ṗı ḋo ṗonaḋ móṗ ṗluaꝥ la Maoılṗeaċlaınń, ıuꝥ 'Eıṗeann, ⁊ Ceaṗḃall mac Ḋunlaınꝥ Laıṗ ꝥo Maꝥ maca. Ra ꝥaḃṗac Lonꝥṗoṗc ann ṗın. Ḃa ſꝥaıl ımuṗṗo la Maoılṗeaċlaınn amuıṗ Lonꝥṗoıṗc ḋo ċaḃaıṗc ḋo Aoḋ mac Néıll ꝼaıṗ; cıaḋ álaım

an

ᵏ *Luimnech.*—i. e. Limerick. The word is here used to denote, not the city, but the Lower Shannon, from the city of Limerick to the sea.

ˡ *Port-Lairge.*—This is the present Irish name of the city of Waterford, but the name is hardly so old as the time here referred to, as Lairge, the chieftain from whom the name was derived, flourished in 951. See Ann. F. M., A. D. 858, note ᵖ.

ᵐ *Eoghanacht.*—i. e. Eoghanacht Chaisil.

(and Iona was a Druid); and these were hardy men of great fame among their own people, and fully noble, of the best race of the Lochlanns. These two came with their forces to Luimnech[k] and from Luimnech to Port-Lairge[l]; but, however, they prevailed more by their own vigour than by their forces. The people of Eoghan-acht[m] and Ara Cliach[n] assembled against them, and they met face to face, and a hard battle was fought between them, in which the Loch-lanns were driven to a small place surrounded by a stone wall. The Druid, i. e. Iona, the elder of them, went up on the wall, and his mouth opened, praying to his gods and exercising his magic, and or-dering his people to worship the gods. One of the men of Munster came towards him and gave him a blow of a large stone on the mouth, and knocked all the teeth out of his head. He afterwards turned his face on his own people, and said, as he was pouring the warm blood out of his mouth: "I shall die of this," said he, and he fell back, and his soul went out of him. They were afterwards so plied with stones that they were not able to bear them, and they quitted that place, and repaired to a neighbouring morass, and here the other chieftain was killed; and thus were the two chieftains killed, i. e. Iona, of Luim-nech, and Tomrir Torra. Of their chief men, only two escaped with a few forces; and thus the men of Munster gained victory and triumph.

[860.] In this year a great hosting[o] was made by Maelsechlainn, King of Erin, accompanied by Cearbhall, son of Dunlang, to Magh-Macha[p]. They encamped there. Maelsechlainn was afraid that his camp should be surprised by Aedh, son of Niall, though fair was the answer

These were seated in the great plain of Cashel, in the county of Tipperary.

[n] *Ara Cliach.*—A territory in the east of the county of Limerick.

[o] *A great hosting.*—Ann. F. M. 858; Ann. Ult. 859 (= 860).

[p] *Magh-Macha.*—Now the Moy, near the city of Armagh.

an ḟleaġra ríoḋa tuġ Aoḋ faip tṙép an ṫuine naoṁ .i. Feṫġna, comaṙba Ṗaṫṙaicc. Aṙeaḋ ṫo ṗiġne Maoilṡeaċlainn Laiġin ⁊ ḟiṙ Muṁan ⁊ Connaċta ⁊ Ulaiḋ, ⁊ ḟiṙ Ḃhṙeaġ ṫo ṫaḃaiṙt a ttiṁċioll a publa, ⁊ a n-aiṙm noċta 'na láṁaiḃ; an ṙíġ ḟéin .i. Maoilṡeaċlainn, ṙo ḃaoi ġo ḟaittṡċ ḟuiṙeċaiṙ ġan ċoṫlaḋ aṙ fġla Aoḋa, ġé ṫo ṙaṫ luiġe a ḟṙiaṫṅaiṙi comaṙba Ṗaṫṙaicc; ġiḋeaḋ táinic Aoḋ ġo na fluaġaiḃ ṫo ṫaḃaiṙt ammuṡ Longṗuiṙt aṙ Maoilṡeaċlainn, ⁊ ní maṙ ṙa faoilṡit ṙa ḟuaṙattuṙ, uaiṙ ṙo ḃattuṙ a n-aiṙm uile a láiṁḃ fluaiġ Maoilṡeaċlainn, aġuṡ ṙa eiṙġiṙit a naoineaċt ḟan luċt táinic ṫá n-ionnṙoiġiḋ ġo ṙo cuiṙṙit amaiḋm iaṙ aṙ maṙḃaḋ a ṅṫeaṙġ-áṙ. Ra ġaḃ ṫna ṫáṙaċt ṡaiṙfin oile ṫíoḃ, ⁊ aṙeaḋ tangattuṙ ṫ'ionnṡoiġiḋ ṗuiḃle Maoilṡeaċlainn, an ṫaṙ leo ṙaḃ iaṫ amuinnteṙ ṡéin; ṙa ḃattuṙ am ġo ṙo maṙḃait uile iaṙttain; ⁊ aṙ an éitioċ ṫo ṙaṫṙat ṫo ṗiġne Ṫia ṙin. Ra iṁṙu Maoilṡeaċlainn ṫ'á tiġ a haitle an ċoṙġuiṙ ṙain. Ra ḃaoi ṫna Aṁlaiḃ i ḟṡaṙṙaḋ Aoḋ 'ṙin maiḋm-ṙa.

Oenaċ Raiġne ṫo ḃénaṁ la Cṙṗḃall mac Ṫunlaing.

Aṙ la Cṙṗḃall mac Ṫunlaing ṡoṙ muinnteṙ Ṙoṫuilḃ i Sleḃ Maiṙġe, ⁊ a maṙḃaḋ uile aċt ṡíṙ uaṫaḋ téaṙna ṫíoḃ i ccailltiḃ: cṙṡċ Leitġlinne, ⁊ ṫna a ḃṙaiṫ ṙa ḃoí aca aṙ maṙḃaḋ ṫṙéime móṙ ṫo muinnteṙ Leitġlinne ṫáiḃ.

Ḳal. Mataṫan mac Muiṙeḋaiġ, ṙí Ulaḋ, in cleṙicatu oḃiit.

Maonġal ab Ḟoḃaiṙ moṙituṙ.

Tṙiaṙ

ⁿ *Amhlaibh was along with Aedh.*—This is not stated in the published Annals.

ᵗ *Raighne.*—This was the ancient name of the chief seat of the Kings of Ossory, situated in the barony of Kells, county of Kilkenny. See Ann. F. M., A. D. 859, p. 494.

ˢ *Sliabh-Mairge.*—Now Slievemargue, a barony in the south-east of the Queen's County. There is no mention made of this Rodolph in the published Annals.

ᵗ *Leithglinn.*—Now Old Leighlin, in the county of Carlow. This entry is not in the published Annals.

answer of peace which Aedh had given him through the holy man, Fethghna, successor of Patrick. What Maelsechlainn did was to place the men of Leinster and Munster, and Connaught and of Uladh and Breagh around his tent, with their weapons naked in their hands. The king himself, i. e. Maelsechlainn, remained vigilantly and warily without sleep from fear of Aedh, though he [Aedh] had taken an oath [of fealty to him] before the successor of Patrick. Notwithstanding, Aedh came with his forces to attack the camp of Maelsechlainn, but they did not find it as they expected, for the forces of Maelsechlainn all had their arms in their hands, and they rose out together against the party who came to attack them, and put them to flight after having cut off many of them with great havoc. One party of them, however, were seized with a panic, and came to the tent of Maelsechlainn, thinking it was that of their own people, and remained there until they were all killed. And God did this in consequence of the falsehood which they had told. Maelsechlainn returned to his house after this triumph. Amhlaibh was along with Aedh[q] in this discomfiture.

The fair of Raighne[r] was celebrated by Cearbhall, son of Dunlang.

A slaughter was made by Cearbhall, son of Dunlang, of the people of Rodolph, at Sliabh-Mairge[s], and he slew them all except very few who escaped to the woods. They had plundered Leithglinn[t], and had [obtained] its spoils after having killed a large number of the people of Leithghlinn.

[857.] Kal. Matudan[u], son of Muiredhach, King of Uladh, died *in clericatu*.

Macnghal, Abbot of Fobhar, died.

Three

[u] *Matudan.*—The obits of this prince, and of the Abbot Macnghal, as also the death of the three men killed by lightning, are dated by the Annals of Ulster 856, which ought to be 857. They are therefore out of place here.

Τριαρ do lorgad do τενιδ ραιζνέν α τΤαιλτεν.

Ϝal. Cιοnαοδ mac Ailpin rex Pictorum, moritur : conad do ρο paideαδ an rann :—

    Nαδ mair Cιοnαοδ ζο líon rgor,
    Po όſρα ζοl in gαċ ταιζ
    Ωon rí α loζα ρο nim,
    Ζο bruinne Romha ní brail.

Cumrud Erρcor η princerr Cluana Ιοραιρδ quievit.
Τιορραιδε banban ab τίρε daζlar quievit.
Maolτuile ab Imlſċα Iobαιr moritur.
Adulphi Saxon Moritur. Ceallaċ mac Ζuaire ri Laiζſn Deαrgabair, moritur. Cſριnaċ mac Ciοnαδα, ri Ua mbairċe τιρε moritur.

Aoδ mac Néill η α cluaṁain .ι. Amlaιδ (ιnζſn Aoδa ρο bαοι αζ Aṁlaοιδ) ζο rloζαιδ móra Ζαοιδιοl η Lοċlann leo ζο maζ mιδe, η α ιοnρραδ leo, η ραορċlanna ιomδa do ṁarbaδ leo.

Mαοιlreaċloιnn mac Maolruanaιδ, rίζ Eireann, í rríδ Callaṅ December defunctur ert, unde quidam cecinit :

    Ar ιomδa mαιrζ in ζαċ du,
    Ar rζel mor la Ζαοιδelu,
    Do móriταδ ríon rlann ρο ζlſnn,
    Do rouba aoιnrι 'Eιrſnn.

Aoδ mac Néill, dearζnaṁa Maolreaċloιnn do ζαbaιl rιζe n-'Eireann ταρ éιr Maolreaclaιnn. Craιbδeaċ roιċnealaċ aιζneaδ

---

* *Cinaedh Mac Ailpin.*—Ann. Ult. 857 (= 858). Ogyg., p. 481.

ʳ *Cumsadh.*—"Cumsuth, Episcopus et anchorita *princeps* Cluana Irairdd *in paco pausavit.* Cinaedh Mac Ailpin, *rex Pictorum.* Adulf *rex Saxan mortui sunt.* Tipraiti Ban, abbas Tire-da-glas."—*Ann. Ult.* 857 (= 858).

ᶻ *Ceallach, son of Guaire.*—Ann. F. M. at 856; but the true year is 858.

Three persons were burned by lightning at Tailten.

[858.] Kal. Cinaedh Mac Ailpin[x], King of the Picts, died, on whom this verse was composed:—

> That Cinaedh with the number of studs liveth not,
> Is the cause of weeping in every house.
> Any one king under heaven of his worth
> To the borders of Rome there is not.

Cumsadh[y], Bishop and Chief of Cluain Iraird, died. Tipraide Banbhan, Abbot of Tir-daghlas, died. Maeltuile, Abbot of Imleach Iobhair, died.

Adolph, King of the Saxons, died. Ceallach, son of Guaire[z], King of South Leinster, died. Cearnach, son of Cinaedh, King of Ui-Bairche-tire, died.

[862.] Aedh[a], son of Niall, and his son-in-law, i. e. Amhlaeibh (the daughter of Aedh was wife to Amhlaeibh), set out with great forces of Gaeidhil and Lochlanus to the plain of Meath, and they plundered it and slew many noble persons.

[863.] Maelsechlainn[b], son of Maelruanaidh, King of Erin, died on the day before the Calends of December, of which a certain poet sung:—

> There is many a moan in every place,
> It is a great cause of grief with the Gaeidhil,
> Red wine has been spilled into the valley,
> The sole king of Erin died.

[863.] Aedh, son of Niall, the mortal enemy of Maelsechlainn, assumed

---

[a] *Aedh, son of Niall.*—F. M. at 860; true year 862.

[b] *Maelsechlainn.*—The Ann. Ult. 861, and F. M. 860, tell us that he died on Tuesday, 30th Nov., and this enables us to correct the chronology of these Annals, for the 30th November fell on Tuesday in 863. O'Flaherty, Ogyg., p. 434.

neaḋ Aoḋa: ѓśc mbliaḋna ḋécc ḋo i ṗiġe ġo ṗíoḋamail, cia ṗo
ġeḃſo imṙſó minic.
Ailill banbain, aḃ ḃioṗaṗ
Aonġaṗ Cluana Pſṗca Molua, ṗaṗienṗ, moṗiċuṗ.
Maoloḋaṗ hUa Ċinoṗiḃ ṗaoi léiġiṗ Eiṗſnn moṗiċuṗ.
Muiṗġiuṗ, anġcoiṗce Aṗomacha, quieuic.
Oálać aḃ Cluana mic Noiṗ quieuic.
Ġoṗmlaiċ, inġſn Oonchaḋa, ṗioġan cſiṗać, in poeniċenċia oḃiċ.
Pionán Cluana caoin, epſcop ⁊ anġcoiṗe quieuic.
Pinnċeallać aḃ Peaṗna moṗiċuṗ.
Séġonan mac Conainġ, ṗi Caiṗṗiġe ḃṗaċaiḋe moṗiċuṗ. Plan-
naġán mac Colmáin moṗiċuṗ. Ġuin Aoḋa mic Ouiḃoaḃaiṗſnn, ṗí
hUa ṗṗioġence, Cſnnṗaolaḋ i ṗíġe Muṁan.
Oomnall mac Ailpin ṗeҳ ṗicċoṗum moṗiċuṗ.

Ƙal. Oſṗiġáṗ ḋo ċaḃaiṗċ ḋo Chſṗball mac Ounlainġ, ⁊ ḋo
Cinnéoe mac Ġáićine .i. mac ḋeiṗḃṗeaċaṗ Cſṗḃaill ṗoṗ lonġuṗ
Roolaiḃ, ⁊ ḃá ġaiṗiḋ ṗeme ċánġaċċuṗ a Loćlann; ⁊ Conall
Ulċać ḋo ṁaṗḃaḋ ann aġuṗ Luiṗġnen, cum pluṗimiṗ aliṗ.

Iṗṗſó ḃṗiġ la Loćlannaiḃ, ⁊ ḋul aṗ uaṁannaiḃ iomḋaiḃ, ⁊ aṗſo
ón na ḃſṗnaḋ ġo minic ṗeime.

Aṗ

' *Seventeen years.*—Aedh died 12th Cal.
Dec., which fell on Friday, as the Chroni-
con Scotorum states. This indicates the
year 879, and makes the length of his
reign 16, not 17 years.—O'Flaherty, *ibid.*
ᵈ *Ailell Banbhan.*—Ann. F. M. 857.
ᵉ *Aenghus.*—Ann. F. M. 858.
ᶠ *Maelodhar O'Tindridh.*—Ann. Ult.
861, where he is called ṗui loiġiṗ ġoiḋcal,
" sage leech of the Gael." This is the
first notice of an Irish physician to be

found in the Irish Annals since the introduction of Christianity. See Ann. F. M.,
A. D. 860, p. 494, note ᵘ.
ᵍ *Muirghius.*—Ann. F. M. 860; Ult.
861.
ʰ *Of Cluain mic Nois.*—The Four Masters call him Abbot of Cluain-Iraird, A. D.
860.
ⁱ *Gormlaith, daughter of Donnchadh.*—
Ann. F. M. 859; Ult. 860.
ᵏ *Finian.*—Ann. F. M. 860.

assumed the kingdom of Erin after Maelsechlainn. The disposition of Aedh was pious and noble. He was seventeen years[c] in the kingdom peaceably, though he often met with annoyance.

Ailell Banbhan[d], Abbot of Biror [died].

Aenghus[e], a sage of Cluain Ferta Molua, died.

[862.] Macolodhar O'Tindridh[f], chief physician of Erin, died.

Muirghius[g], anchorite of Ard-Macha, died.

Dálach, Abbot of Cluain mic Nois[h], died.

Gormlaith, daughter of Donnchadh[i], Queen of Teamhar, died in penitence.

Finian[k], of Cluain-eacin, bishop and anchorite, died.

Finncheallach[l], Abbot of Fearna [now Ferns], died.

Segonan, son of Conang[m], King of Carraig Brachaidhe, died. The killing of Aedh, son of Dubhdabhoirenn[n], King of Ui-Fidhgeinte. Cennfacladh, in the kingdom of Munster.

Domhnall Mac Ailpin[o], King of the Picts, died.

[863.] Kal. A dreadful slaughter was made of the fleet of Rodlaibh[p], by Cearbhall, son of Dunlang, and by Cincide, son of Gaeithin, i. e. the son of Cearbhall's sister; and they [the crews of the fleet] had arrived from Lochlann a short time before; and Conall Ultach and Lairgnen were slain there with many others.

The plundering of Bregh by the Lochlanns, and they entered into many crypts[q], a thing not done often before.

A

[l] *Finncheallach.*—F. M. 860; Ult. 861.

[m] *Seghonan, son of Conang.*—F.M. 857; Ult. 858 (out of place here). Carraig Brachaidhe is in the north-west of the barony of Inishowen, county of Donegal.

[n] *Aedh, son of Dubhdabhoirenn.*—Ann. F. M. 858; Ult. 859.

[o] *Domhnall mac Ailpin.*—He died in 862 (Ann. Ult. 861). Ogyg., p. 484.

[p] *The fleet of Rodlaibh.*—The F. M., at A. D. 860, make it Longphort-Rothlaibh, which may perhaps be a corruption of Longus Rothlaibh, i. e. Rodlaff's, or Rodolph's fleet.

[q] *Crypts.*—See Ann. F. M. 861; Ult. 862; where this account of the plunder-

'Ap ná ngall la Cṙball mac Ounlaing ag Ḟṙta caipeć, ⁊ a
cṙc o'ṗaxḃáil.
Muiṗiogán mac Oiapmaoa, ṗí Naiṗ ⁊ Laigṡn cio oo maṗḃao
la gentiḃ, ⁊ ṗoćaioc moṗ oo ṁaiciḃ Laigṡn.
Kal. Aoḋ mac Cumuṗcaig, ṗi hUa Niallain moṗicuṗ. Mui-
ṗeḋoc mac Maoiluin, ṗi na n-Aiṗcṡṗ iugulacuṗ eṗc ó Oomnall
mac Aoḋa mic Néill.
Cṙball mac Ounlaing oo innṗṙo Laigṡn. Niṗoṗ bó cian iaṗ ṗin
go ṗo tionolṗao Laigin Loclannaig ⁊ iao ṗéin, go ṗo inoṗiṗoṗoḋ
Oṗṗaige na ḃíoganl ṗin. Ḃa ṁoṗ an cṗnaige! oneoć ṗa teić
o'Oṗnaigiḃ im Muṁain ṗa maṗḃaio ⁊ ṗa haiṗgio uile. Ḃa moḋ
ṗo goṗtaig ṗin mṁhma Cṙḃaill .i. an luct ṗogaḃ aige aṁail
caiṗiṗi .i. Eoganact, iaoṗaiḋe oa aṗgain ⁊ oa ṁaṗḃaḋ. Lg aiṗ
imuṗṗo caingṡn na namao : uaiṗ níoṗ bo iongnaḋ laiṗ iaoṗaioe oo
ǵénain na nuṗiṗṗiṗac, uaiṗ ṗa ḃligṗiot. Ro tionol iaṗan ṗloig
Gaoiḋeal ⁊ Loclannaig, agṗ ṗa ṁill na ḟṗanna comṗocṗaiḃe, ṗa
ṁill Mag Ṗeiṁin ⁊ ṗiṗ muige ⁊ ṗug ḃṗaigḋe cimuḋa n-iomḋa laiṗ.
San ḃliaḋainṗi, .i. in cepcio anno ṗegni Aoḋa Ṗinnléit, tangat-
tuṗ Saxain i mḃṗeatnaiḃ Gaimuo, ⁊ ṗa inaṗbaio na Saxain bṙ-
tain aṗ an tiṗ.

Oallaḋ

ing of the caves or crypts is given more
fully.

' *Ferta Caeirech.*—Now Fertagh, near
Johnstown, in the barony of Galmoy,
county of Kilkenny.—See Ann. F. M.,
A. D. 861.

' *Nás.*—Ann. F. M. 861, p. 496, note
'; Ult. 862, where is called King of Naas
and of Airthir Life.

' *Aedh, son of Cumascach.*—Ann. F. M.
861, of the Niallain, in the Co. Armagh.

" *King of Uí-Niallain.*—Now the Oneil-
lands, two baronies in the Co. Armagh.

' *Airthera.*—Now the baronies of Orior
in the county of Armagh. In the Ann.
Ult. 862, he is called ṗecnab aiṗo ma-
cae ⁊ ṗi na naiṗcep—"Sub-Abbot of
Armagh, and King of Orior."

' *Fera-Maighe.*—Now Fermoy, in the
county of Cork.—Ann. F. M. 862 (true
year, 864).

' *The third.*—Aedh Finnliath succeeded

A slaughter of the Galls at Ferta Caeirech[r] by Cearbhall, son of Dunlang, and they left their prey behind.

Muirigen, son of Diarmaid, King of Nas[s] and of Leinster, was killed by the Pagans, and a great number of the chiefs of Leinster.

[864.] Kal. Aedh, son of Cumascach[t], King of Ui-Niallain[u], died. Muiredhach, son of Maelduin, King of the Airthera[x], was killed by Domhnall, son of Aedh, son of Niall.

Cearbhall, son of Dunlang, plundered Leinster. It was not long after this that the Leinster-men assembled themselves and the Lochlanns, and plundered Osraighe in revenge of this. It was a great pity: such of the Osraighi as fled into Munster were all killed and plundered; and this distressed the mind of Cearbhall the more, that the people he took for friends, namely, the Eoghanachts, should plunder and kill them. He thought little of the doings of the enemies, for he did not wonder at their doing what they did, for they were entitled to it. He therefore assembled an army of Gaeidhil and Lochlanns, and spoiled the neighbouring lands [of the Eoghanachts]; he spoiled Magh Feinhin and Fera Maighe[y], and carried off the hostages of many tribes.

In this year, i. e. the third[z] of the reign of Aedh Finnliath, the Saxons came into Britain Gaimud[a], and the Saxons expelled the Britons from the country.

The in the year 863, so that the third year of his reign was 865 or 866.

[a] *Britain Gaimud.*—Perhaps Gwyned (Guenidotia or Venedotia, i. e. North Wales) may be intended. This seems to be the same expulsion of the Britons which is recorded in the Ann. Ult. at 864, in these words: bpeacan ou moapbu apa cιp ɒo ḟaṫanaιb con po ʒaḃaḋ caċc popaιb ιm Maen ċonaιn.—"The Britons were driven from their territory by the Saxons, and were put into bondage in Maen Chonain," i. e. Anglesea, called Mona Conain, from Conan, King of Gwynedd. See Ann. Ult. 815; Brut y Tywysogion, A. D. 817.

Ɖallaɓ Lopcáin mic Catail, ɲɩ Miɓe, la hAoɓ mac Néill. Concopap mac Ɖonnchaɓa, leiṫpi Miɓe ɓo báɓ la hAmlaiɓ i Cluain Ipaipɓ. Inpfɓ na nƉéipi la Cfɲball mac Ɖunlaing, ⁊ lánṁilleaɓ hUi n-Aongupa.

Aɓɓaine Cípe ɓa glap ɓo gaɓail ɓo Maoilpectuip in hoc anno.

Gaɓail Ɖiapmaɓa la gentiɓ.

Eiɓgin bpit Eppcop Cille ɓapa, pcpiba et anachopeta cxiii°, anno aetatip puae quieuit.

Maonaċ mac Conmmaig, ab Roip cpé mopitup.

Ɖomnall hUa Ɖunlaing, pigɓamna Laigfn, mopitup.

Cfpmait mac Cataɲnaig, pí Copca baipcinn, mopitup.

Ral. Caṅg mac Ɖiapmaɓa pi hUa Cinnpiolaig ɓo ṁapɓaɓ ɓá bpáṫpiɓ péin. 'Ap pop Loċlannaiɓ la Flann mac Conaing pí Cianaċt. Ɖeapg áp na Loċlann, ⁊ a mbuaiɓpeaɓ uile pan bliaɓain pi la hAoɓ mac Néill, píg 'Eipeann. Maiɓm lán móp la n-Aoɓ fopp na Loċlannaiɓ ag Loċ Feabaill. Innipit ɓno na h-eoluig gup ob í a bfn ap moó po gpeip Aoɓ i ccfnn na Loċlann .i. Lanɓ, ingfn Ɖunlaing : ⁊ ap pípiɓe ba bfn ɓo Maoilpeaċloinn peiṁe, maċaip mic Maoilpeaċloinn .i. Flaiñ. ba hí máṫaip Cennéɓig mic Gaiṫine í, .i. ɲɩ Laigpi. Ap móp tpa pa pcpíoɓaɓ na ffuapactuip Loċlannaig ɓ'ule 'pan bliaɓain pi [on g-Cenneuigpiɓe] cíɓ moó fuappactuip ó Aoɓ Finnliaṫ mac Néill.

Milleaɓ

ᵇ *Lorcan.*—Ann. F. M. 862; Ann. Ult. 863.

ᶜ *Ui-Aenghusa.*—i. e. the descendants of Aenghus Mac Nadfraich, King of Munster, slain, A. D. 489. See Ann. F. M., p. 499, note ᵐ, A. D. 862.

ᵈ *Maelpetair.*—He died in 890, according to the F. M., who do not give the year of his accession.

ᵉ *Diarmaid.*—Not in the published Annals. It does not appear who this Diarmaid was.

ᶠ *Eidgin Brit.*—Or the Briton. Ann. F. M. 862. His name was probably Edwin, a Briton. Colgan says that he died on the 18th December, probably confound-

The blinding of Lorcan[b], son of Cathal, king of Meath, by Aedh, son of Niall. Conchobhar, son of Donnchadh, half king of Meath, was drowned by Amhlacibh at Cluain Iraird. The plundering of the Desies, and the total spoiling of Ui Aenghusa[c] by Cearbhall, son of Dunlaing.

The abbacy of Tir-da-ghlas was assumed by Maelpetair[d] in this year.

The taking of Diarmaid[e] by the Gentiles.

Eidgin Brit[f], Bishop of Cill-dara, a scribe and anchorite, died in the one hundred and thirteenth year of his age.

Maenach[g], son of Connmach, Abbot of Ros-Cré, died.

Domhnall, grandson of Dunlaing, royal heir of Leinster, died.

Cearmait, son of Catharnach, King of Corca Bhaiscinn, died.

[866.] Kal. Tadhg, son of Diarmaid[h], King of Ui-Ceinnscalaigh, was slain by his own brothers. A slaughter was made of the Lochlanns by Flann, son of Conang, King of Cianachta. A great slaughter was made of the Lochlanns, who were all disturbed this year by Aedh, son of Niall, King of Erin. A complete and great victory was gained by Aedh over the Lochlanns at Loch Feabhail[i], and the learned state that it was his wife that most incited Aedh against the Lochlanns; i.e. Lann, the daughter of Dunlang, and she had been the wife of Maelsechlainn before, and was the mother of Maelsechlainn's son Flann. She was also the mother of Cenneidigh, son of Gaithin, King of Laeighis[k]. It is written that the Lochlanns sustained great evils in this year [from this Cenneidigh], but more from Aedh Finnliath, son of Niall.

[869.]

ing him with Aedan of Ard Lonain.—
Trias. Thaum., p. 629.

[g] *Maenach.*—This and the two succeeding entries are given by the F. M. at 862.

[h] *Tadhg, son of Diarmaid.*—Ann. F. M. 863; Ann. Ult. 864.

[i] *Loch Feabhail.*—Now Lough Foyle.

[k] *Laeighis.*—Now Leix.

Milleaḋ ⁊ innriuḋ Foirtrenn[1] la Loċlannaiḃ go puġrat ḃraiġde iomḋa leo i nġill re cíor; ro bár go faḋa iartéain aġ taḃairt cíora ḋóiḃ.

Ar for Ġallaiḃ oc Minḋroiċit[m] la Cennéidiġ mac Ġaiṫine, ri Laiġri ⁊ la tuairġirt n-Orraiġe.

Ir in aimrir ri tangattur Aunitet[n].i. na Daineir go fluaġaiḃ diairmiḋiḃ leo go Caer Eḃroic[o], ġur ro toġlattur an catraiġ, ⁊ go noṡcattur ruirre, ⁊ da torac imniḃ ⁊ ḋocraċ móir do ḃriṡ- naiḃ rin; uair ní faḋa d'aimrir reiṁe ro ro ḃaoi ġac coġaḋ ⁊ ġac ġlifit i Loċlainn, ⁊ ar ar ro ro fár an coġaḋ rain i Loċlainḋ .i. ḋá ṁac ócca Alḃḋain ri Loċlann ro ionnarḃrat an mac ra rine .i. Raġnall mac Alḃḋain[p], ar eaġla leo é do ġaḃail riġi Loċlann tar éir a n-aṫar; go ttáinic an Raġnall co n-a trí macaiḃ go huiṁriḃ Ore: ro ṫarir iaraṁ Raġnall ann rin, ⁊ an mac da roó do tangattur imorru na mic da rine go hinnriḋ Ḃretan go fluaġ mor leo, ar ttionól an trluaiġ rin ar ġac áirḋ, ar na líonaḋ na mac rin do ḋíomur ⁊ do ṁírratt um eirġe i ccihn Ffrangc ⁊ Saxann. Ra faoilriod a n-aṫair do dol i Loċlainn ro ċéḋóir dar a n-éir.

Ra ṡail iaram an díomur ⁊ a n-óġbaḋata orra iomraṁ rímra dar an ocian Cantaiḃriṡda .i. an ṁuir ful eidir Eirinn ⁊ Ear- páin go rangattur Errain, ⁊ go noṡirraḋ ulca iomḋa i n-Errain eḋir

[1] *Foirtrenn.*—i. e. Pictland.—*Ann. Ult.* 865.

[m] *Mindroichet.*—Now Monadrehid, near Borris in Ossory, in the Queen's County. The Four Masters notice this slaughter of the foreigners at the year 864, but 866 is the true year.

[n] *Aunites.*—This name is perhaps a cor- ruption of *Afnitæ,* or *Hafnitæ,* from Haf- nia (*Höfn,* the haven), called afterwards *Kaupmanna-höfn,* (Merchants' haven), now Copenhagen. But the Editor is not able to quote any other authority for the name of *Hafnites* being applied to the Danes.

[o] *Caer Ebroic.*—i. e. the city of Ebora- cum or York. See " Annal. Cambriæ" and " Brut y Tywysogion" at 866.

[p] *Albdan.*—The Scandinavian form of

[869.] Foirtrenn[1] was plundered and ravaged by the Lochlanns, and they carried off many hostages with them as pledges for rent : and they were paid rent for a long time after.

A slaughter was made of the Galls at Mindroichet[m] by Cenneidigh, son of Gaithin, King of Lacighis, and by the northern Osraighi.

At this time the Annites[n], i. e. the Danes, came with countless forces to Caer Ebroic[o], and destroyed the city, which they took, and this was the beginning of great troubles and difficulties to the Britons. For not long before this time every kind of war and commotion prevailed in Lochlann, which arose from this cause; i. e. the two younger sons of Albdan[p], King of Lochlann, expelled the eldest son, Ragh nall, son of Albdan, because they feared that he would take the kingdom of Lochlann after their father; and Raghnall came with his three sons to Innsi Orc[q], and Raghnall tarried there with his youngest son. But his elder sons, with a great host, which they collected from every quarter, came on to the British Isles, being elated with pride and ambition, to attack the Franks and Saxons. They thought that their father had returned to Lochlann immediately after setting out.

Now, their pride and youthful ambition induced them to row forward across the Cantabrian Sea[r], i. e. the sea which is between Erin and Spain, until they reached Spain[s], and they inflicted many evils in

this name may probably be Halden, or Halfdane. See Saxon. Chron., A. D. 871 ; O'Flaherty's Ogyg., p. 485, A. D. 871.

[q] *Innsi Orc.*—i. e. the Orkney Islands.

[r] *Cantabrian Sea.*—i. e. the Biscayan Sea.

[s] *Until they reached Spain.*—Mallet gives an account of an excursion made by a strong force of Scandinavian rovers into Spain in September, 844, which looks very like the one here described, but he does not mention that they crossed the Gaditanean Straits.—"Northern Antiquities," Bohn's Ed., p. 173, note. See also Depping, "Histoire des Exped. Maritimes des Normands," liv. ii., chap. 3 (p. 121, New. Ed., 1844), who cites the Annal. Bertin. for the statement that the Northmen ravaged the coast of Frisia, and infested the Scottish islands in the year 847.

eoip opgain ⁊ innpeó. Tangattup iaptтain óap an Muincſhn nⰃaóianтa,¹ bail i ттéió muip meóiтeppanian ¹pin Ocian imſċ-тpaċ, go pángattup an Appaic; ⁊ cuipió caт pip na Maupio-тanuib, ⁊ тuiтió óeapgáp na Maupioтana. Aċт cſha ap ag óul i gcſhn an ċaтapa a óuḃaipт an óapa mac pip an mac oile: a ḃpáтaip, ap ſé, ap móp an ṁíċiall ⁊ an óápaċт pil popainn ḃeiт ap gaċ тíp a ттíp ap puó an óoṁuin gáp mapḃaó, a naċ ag cop-naṁ áp n-aтapóa pén aтaáin, ⁊ piap ap n-aтap óo génaṁ, uaip ap a aonap aтá anopa aṁuiċ ⁊ imepтin iттíp naċ leip péin, ap map-ḃaó an óapa inic po pagpoin na pappaó, aṁail poillpigтeap óampa, gomaó i n-aiplinge no poillpigтea óopoṁ pin: ⁊ po mapḃaó an mac oile óó a ccaт pinnḃpſċтain óno, ma тéapna an т-aтaip pén ap an caт pin, que peuepa comppoḃaтum eipт.

In тan po ḃaoi ga páó pin ap ann aó ċonnaipc caт na Maupi-тana ċuca: ⁊ map aó connaipc an mac po páió na ḃpiaтpa pſṁ-ainn pin, po lingg go hoḃañ 'pan ċaт ⁊ тáinic ó'ionnpoig pí na Maupi-тána, ⁊ тug ḃuille óo ċloióſṁ móp óó, go po gaó a láṁ óe. Ro cuipeaó go cpuaió cſċтup an óá lſċ 'pan ċaт pa, ⁊ ní pug nſc óíoḃ copgup óa chele 'pan ċaт pin. Aċт тáinig cáċ óíoḃ ó'ionnpaig a longpoipт, ap mapḃaó poċaióe eттuppa. Ra puagaip imuppo cáċ áp a ċéle тoiḃeaċт ap na ṁápaċ óo ċum an ċaтa. Ro iom-gaḃ imuppo pí na Maupiтana an longpopт, ⁊ pa éla ipin oióċe ap ngaió a láiṁe óe. O тáinig тpa an maióin po gaḃpaт na Loċlañ-aig a n-apma, ⁊ po ċoipigpioт iaó go cpuaió ḃeóóa óo ċum an caтa. Na Maupiтana imuppo ó po aipigpiт a pí ó'elúó, po ċeiċ-pioó ap mapḃaó a nóeapgáip.

Ro

¹ *The Gaditanean Straits.*—i. e. the Straits of Gades, in the south of Spain. The modern Cadiz preserves the name.
² *The external ocean.*—i. e. the Atlantic.
³ *Mauritani.*—i. e. the Moors. Mauritania Proper answers to the modern Morocco.
⁴ *The father himself.*—Meaning, "if our father himself."

in Spain both by killing and plundering. They afterwards crossed the Gaditanean Straits[t], i. e. where the Mediterranean Sea goes into the external ocean[u], and they arrived in Africa, and there they fought a battle with the Mauritani[x], in which a great slaughter of the Mauritani was made. However, on going to this battle, one of the sons said to the other : " Brother," said he, " it is great folly and madness in us to be going from one country to another throughout the world, killing ourselves, instead of defending our patrimony and obeying the will of our father, for he is now alone away from home, and sojourning in a country not his own; the second son, whom we left along with him, having been killed, as was revealed to me (this had been revealed to him in a dream), and his other son was killed in a battle ! It is wonderful, too, if the father himself has escaped from that battle, *que[z] revera comprobatum est*."

As he was saying these words, they saw the battle array of the Mauritani approaching them ; and as the son who said the aforesaid words saw it, he rushed suddenly into the battle, and he came up to the King of Mauritania, and gave him a stroke of a great sword, and cut off his hand. The battle was fought with great hardihood on both sides, although neither party gained the victory in that battle ; but both returned to their camps, after many persons had been killed on both sides. They, however, challenged each other to battle the next day. But the King of Mauritania fled from his camp, and fled at night, after having lost his hand. When the morning came, however, the Lochlanns put on their armour, and prepared themselves with hardihood and vigour for the battle. But when the Mauritani perceived that their king had absconded, they fled, after many of them had been cut off with great slaughter[a].

After

---

[z] *Que.*—Read *quod*. The meaning is, that what had been miraculously revealed to him in a dream, was found to turn out true.

[a] *Great slaughter.*—The editor has not

Ro ċuaccup iappin na Loċlonnaiġ pon cíp ⁊ po aipġpioc, ⁊ po loipġpioo an cíp uile; cuġpao ona pluaġ móp óióƀ a mƀpaic leo ġo hEipinn .i. piao pin na pip ġopma, uaip ip ionann Mauri ⁊ niġpi: Maupicania ip ionann ip niġpicuoo. Ap inbċċain má céapna an cpſſ ouine oo Loċlonnaiƀ eoip in nſċ pa mapƀaio, ⁊ po ƀńóic víƀ pan Muincinn miupiƀe Ġaoicanna. Ap paoa ona po ƀáoap na pip ġopma pin i n-'Eipinn. Ap ann aca Maupicania concpa ba- leapep Inpulap.

Ral. Eclippip polip in Calenoip Iauuapii.
Ceallaċ mac Ailella, ab Cille oapa, ⁊ ab Iae, oopimiuc in peġione Piccopum.
Mainchine Eppcop Lecġline quieuic.
Cuaċal mac Apcġoppa, ppim eppcop Poipcpiſnn, ⁊ ab Ouin Caillen, mopicup.
Ġuin Colmain mic Ounlainġe, pi Poċapc cípe; oo mapƀao é oa ċloinn péin.
Ciġſpnaċ mac Pocapca, pi Peap mƀpeaġ.
Ip in bliaoain pi cainiġ Compap iapla, o Luimnioċ ġo Cluain pſpca bpſnainn, (ouine ainopeannoa aġaiƀ ainoġiƀ eippoe oo Loċ- lannaiƀ) anoap leip oo ġeƀaò bpaò móp 'pin ċill pin, ġioƀ ní map pa paoil puaip, uaip cainiġ peal bſġ piop peimċ, ⁊ po ceiċſo ġo maiċ peimċ i n-eaċpaiƀ, opeam eile i peipcinib, opſm oile 'pin cſm- pul. An opſm imuppo pop a puġpom ap an uplap, ⁊ ip in pelic po mapƀpom. Ro ƀaoi ono Copmac mac Elaċoiġ, paoi eaġna Eipſnn,

been able to find any account of this inva-
sion of Morocco by the Northmen in any
other authority.
[b] *Blue men in Erin.*—No account of
these blue men has been found in any
other Annals or history.

[c] *Balearic Isles.*—Majorca, Minorca, Ca-
brera, Iviza, &c.
[d] *An eclipse of the sun.*—This eclipse
is entered in the Annals of Ulster at the
year 864, but the true year is 865.
[e] *Ceallach.*—Annals of Ulster, A.D. 864;

After this the Lochlanns passed over the country, and they plundered and burned the whole country; and they carried off a great host of them [the Mauritani] as captives to Erin, and these are the blue men [of Erin], for Mauri is the same as black men, and Mauritania is the same as blackness. It is wonderful if every third man of the Lochlanns escaped, between the numbers who were killed and those who were drowned of them in the Gaditanean Straits. Long indeed were these blue men in Erin[b]. Mauritania is situated opposite the Balearic Isles[c].

[869.] Kal. An eclipse of the sun[d] on the Calends of January.

Ceallach[e], son of Ailell, Abbot of Cill dara and Abbot of I, died in the region of the Picts.

Mainchine[f], Bishop of Leithghlin, died.

Tuathal[g], son of Artgus, chief Bishop of Fortrenn, and Abbot of Dun Caillen [Dunkeld], died.

The killing of Colman, son of Dunlang, King of Fotharta-tire[h]: he was killed by his own children.

Tighernach[i], son of Focarta, King of the men of Breagh [died].

In this year came Tomrar[k] the Earl, from Luimnech to Cluain-fearta-Brenainn[l] (he was a fierce, rough, cruel man of the Lochlanns), thinking that he would find a great prey in that church, but he did not find it as he thought, for intelligence had gone a short time before him, and they fled expertly from him, some in boats, others into the morasses, and others into the church. Those whom he caught on the floor

Reeves's "Adamnan," p. 391; F. M. 863.
[f] *Mainchine.*—F. M. 863.
[g] *Tuathal.*—F. M. 863; Ann. Ult. 864.
[h] *Fotharta-tire.*—i. e. the inland Fotharta, now the barony of Forth, in the county of Carlow.—Ann. F. M. 863.
[i] *Tighernach.*—Ann. Ult. 864 [= 865].

[k] *Tomrar.*—This Tomrar is not mentioned in any other Annals, unless he be the same as the Tomrar, son of Tomralt, who was slain 923 (F. M.).
[l] *Cluain-fearta Brenainn.*—Now Clonfert. This attack is not mentioned in any other Annals known to the Editor.

Eippfin, comapba pen Ciapáin Saigpe pin cfinpal pin. Ra paop
Dia ⁊ bpénainn iao amlaig pin. Mapb inoppu do dápacc an
Compaip 'pin bliadain pi, ap n-impipc do bhpénainn miopbal paip.
Ip in bliagain pin po cuadap na pig Loclonnaig im Muṁain
⁊ pluagaa mópa leo, ⁊ pa inopipio go cpoda an Muṁain. Giöfö
cṁa cugaö deapg áp poppa ann, uaip cainig Cinnécig mac
Gaicin, pí Laoigpi (mac épiöe do Laino ingin Ounlainge, ⁊ piöe
ono macaip Flainn mic Maoilpeaclonn ⁊ ap í ba bfin an canpa
d'Aoö mac Néill, pig Tfinpaé), ap é an mac-Gaicin ba gaipge,
⁊ ba copgpaca pop gallaib pan aimpip pin i n-Eipino—cainig
iapam an Cinnécig pi ⁊ Laoigip go nopeim do Oppaigib maille
pip go longpopc na Loclann, gup po niapbpac ofpgáp a nufgoaoine
ap láp an longpoipc. Ip ann pin ao connaipc Cinnédig pfp d'á
ṁuincip péin, ⁊ diap Loclann ag cpiall a cinn do beim de, cainig
go cpic da paopad, ⁊ po bfi an da cfin do'n dip pin, ⁊ po paop a
peap muiñcipe péin. Cainic peṁe Cennédig go mbuaiö ⁊ copgup.
Ap annpaiöc do pala an cpfc Loclannac i. naigiö Cinnédig co
n-édalaib mopa occa. O po cualacup na maiṫc ud do mapbad po
pagpad a gcpeié, ⁊ a n-édala, ⁊ cangaccup go cpuaib, beoda i
n-aigib Cinnécig. Ro cozbaib goca allṁapda bapbapda annpaide,
⁊ pcuic iomda baödpha ⁊ pocuiöe ga páö núi, núi. Ro diodaipgio
iapaṁ paigṫe iomda fcuppa ⁊ lecgae ⁊ pa gabpac pa deoig pop a
ccloiöṁib

---

^m *Cormac.*—He was Abbot of Seirkieran, in the King's County. His death is noticed in the Annals of Ulster at the year 868.

ⁿ *Saved them.*—Something seems to have been omitted here. The narrative is probably abridged from some ecclesiastical legend.

^o *Died of madness.*—This is probably a mistake, confounding this Tomrar with the Tomrar Mac Ailchi, or Elge, who died, or " went to hell with his pains" in 922, according to the Annals of Clonmacnoise.— See "Leabhar na gCeart," Introd., p. xli.

^p *Predatory party.*—A party who had gone forth from the camp for plunder.

floor and in the churchyard he killed. Cormac[m], son of Elathach, chief of Erin for wisdom, the successor of old Ciaran, of Saighir, was in the church. God and Brenann thus saved them[n]. And Tomrar died of madness[o] in this year, Brenann having wrought a miracle upon him.

In this year the Lochlann kings went into Munster, having great hosts along with them, and they bravely ravaged Munster. They were, however, dreadfully slaughtered, for Cennedigh, son of Gaithin, King of Laeighis, the son of Lann, daughter of Dunlang (who was the mother of Flann, son of Maelsechlainn, and at this time the wife of Aedh, son of Niall, King of Teamhair,—and this son of Gaithin was the fiercest and the most victorious man against the foreigners in Erin at this time), —this Cennedigh came with the Laeighis and a party of the Osraighi to the camp of the Lochlanns and made a slaughter of the best of their men in the middle of the camp. On this occasion Cennedigh saw a man of his people between two Lochlann men who were going to cut off his head, and he came actively to his relief, and beheaded the two Lochlanns, and thus saved his own man. Cennedigh then passed forward with victory and triumph. Then the predatory party[p] of the Lochlanns came against Cennedigh, having great spoils in their hands, and when they heard of the killing of the chiefs aforesaid, they left their plunder and spoils and came vigorously and actively against Cennedigh. They raised foreign barbarous shouts there, and blew warlike trumpets, and many said " nui, nui[q] !" Many darts and half javelins were discharged between them, and at last they took to their heavy, strong-striking swords. But God was assisting the son of Gaithin and his

[q] *Nui, nui.*—*Quere*, whether this war-cry is not the Norse *noe, noe* (*now, now !*). This account of the conflict between Kennedy, son of Gahan, King of Leix (a territory included in the present Queen's County), must have been taken from some local Annals, preserved, probably, at Clonenagh or Clonfert-Mulloe. No account

ccloióṁıb ṫroma ċoiṙċḃuillcḃa. Ṡiḃeḃ ṫra ro ḃaí Ḋıa aġ ṗurṫaċṫ ṫo mac Ṡaíṫın co na muınnṫıṙ, ṙo ṙoṙuaıṙlıġṡḃ na Loċlannaıġ, ⁊ ṙa ṗaġṙaṫ a laṫṙaıġ ımḃualṫa: ṙa ċuaḃaṙ arṙ ı mċuṫm aṙ maṙḃaḃ a noṡṙġaṙ. Oṙṡın oıle ní uṡċaṫṫuṙ ı ṗṗaḋ aṙ a ṗṙaınne aṙ ṗṙulanġ ġoṙṫa móıṙe ḃóıḃ, no aṙ a náıṙe leo ṫeċṡḃ. In uaıṙ aḋ concaṫṫuṙ ṙluaġ mıc Ṡaíṫın oċṫ ṫıonol an maıċıuṙa ro ṗaġṙaḋ-ṙuṁ leo, ṫanġaṫṫuṙ na noṡġaıḃ. Maṙ ro connaıṙc mac Ṡaíṫın éṙıḃe, ro ġaḃ ṗoṫa aṁaıl ṙaol ṗo ċaoṙċaḃ, ġo ro ṫeıċṙıoḋ 'ṙan mónaıḃ ġuṙ ro máṙḃaıḋ 'ṙan mónaıḃ uıle ıaḋ, ġo nḃuaṫṫuṙ coın a ccolla. Ro ṁaṙḃṙaṫ ṫno an luċṫṙa .ı. mac Ṡaíṫın co ṁuınnṫıṙ uṡṙġaṙ aoṙa ġṙaḃa ṙıġ Loċlann ı n-áıṙḋ aıle ṙın Muṁaın .ı. maṙeṙluaġ ṙıġ Loclann. Iṙ na ḃıoġaıl ṙa ṁaṙḃṙaṫ na Loċlannaıġ ṙluaġ móṙ cléṙeċ, ṙa ḃaoı [ına lonġṙuṙṫ] ṗéın, aċṫ aṙ ıaṙ mḃuaıḋ onġċu ⁊ aıċṁġe.

Iṙ ı n-aıṁṙıṙ ṙın ṙuġ clú móṙ Maoılcıaṙaın eıḋıṙ Ṡaoıḃealuıḃ aṙ a menċe buaḋa ḋo ḃṙeıṫ ḃó ḋo Loċlannaıḃ.

Iṙ ın bliaḋaıṙı ba maṙḃ Ṫomṙuṙ ıaṙla, náṁa Ḃṙénaınn ḋo ḃáṙaċṫ ı ṙuıṙṫ Manann, ⁊ ba hṡḃ aḋ ċṡu Ḃṙénaınn ġá ṁaṙḃaḃ.

Iṙ ın ṫan ṙo ḋo roıṙaḋ Cıaṙṙuıġe ṗoıḃaıṙı ṗoṙ ṁuınnṫıṙ an Ṫomṙaıṙ ṙın, ⁊ aṙ naṫṫaċṫ ḋóıḃ Ḃṙénaınn aṙ ḃṙú an ṁaṙa, ro ḃaoı an coımḃe aġ ṗuṙṫaċṫ ḋo na Ṡaoıḃıolaıḃ: uaıṙ baoı an ṁuıṙ óġ báḋhaḋ na Loċlann, ⁊ na Cıaṙṙuıġe ġa maṙḃaḋ. Conġal an Sṁóıṙ ṙı Cıaṙṙuıġe ṙuġ buaıḋ ıṙın conġaıl ċaṫa ṙa. Aṙ uaıṫeaḋ ṫṙa lomnoċṫ ⁊ ġonṫa ṫeaṙna ḋo na Loċlannaıḃ; ba móṙ n-óıṙ ⁊ aıṙġıḋ, ⁊ banċaoıṁ ro ṗáġḃaıḋ ann ṙın.

Iṙ ın bliaḋaın ṙı ṫno ṫanġaṫṫuṙ ṙlóıġ Loċlann ó Phuṙṫ Coṙc-aıġe

---

of it is given in the published Annals.

ᵗ *They came.*—i. e. the wounded or wearied Lochlanns rallied, and followed the victorious Irish, to endeavour to recover their spoils.

ᵃ *Maelciarain.*—The death of this champion is entered in the Ann. Ult. at 868; F. M. 867.

his people, and they prevailed over the Lochlanns, who left the field of conflict and fled routed after having sustained red havoc. Some of them had not gone far, in consequence of weakness, having suffered much from hunger, or who were ashamed to fly; when these perceived the host of the son of Gaithin collecting the spoils which they had abandoned to them, they came[r] after them. When the son of Gaithin saw this, he attacked them as the wolf attacks sheep, so that they fled into a bog, and in that bog they were all killed, and dogs devoured their bodies. This party also, i. e. the son of Gaithin and his people, made a great slaughter of the *aes-gradha* [servants of trust] of the King of the Lochlanns in another direction in Munster, i. e. of the cavalry of the King of the Lochlanns; and in revenge of this the Lochlanns killed a great host of clerics who were in their own camp; but it was after the victory of unction and penance.

At this time Maelciarain[s] obtained great fame among the Gaeidhil from his frequent victories over the Lochlanns.

In this year Tomrar, the Earl, the enemy of Brenann, died of madness at Port-Manann[t], and he saw Brenann[u] killing him.

In this year the Ciarraighi [Kerry-men] made an invading camp against the people of this Tomrar, and having supplicated Brenann on the brink of the sea, the Lord was aiding the Gaedhil, for the sea was drowning the Lochlanns, and the Ciarraghi were killing them. Congal, the senior[x], King of Ciarraighe, gained victory in this battle. The Lochlanns escaped, few, naked, and wounded, leaving behind them much gold and silver, and fair women.

In this year also the hosts of the Lochlanns came from the port of

[t] *Port-Manann.*—i. e. the harbour of the Isle of Man.

[u] *Brenann.*—i. e. St. Brendan, of Clonfert. St. Brendan was the navigator of the Irish, and was particularly hostile to the Scandinavians.

[x] *Congal the senior.*—i. e. the aged. There is no account of this destruction of

aige v'apgain Fspmaige Féne, act cfna ní pa cbaig Oia vóib, uaip ip an can pin cangaccup na Oépi ap epfcaib 'pan ppspann cécna cpé pémpégav Oé, uaip ba neapg-namaib peimipin na Oéipi ⁊ Fipmaige. 'O po concaccup iapam na Oépi na Loclannaig og opgain ⁊ og mnpav an cipe cangaccup v'ionnpaigib Feapmuige, ⁊ vo ponpac pib vaingin caipipi, ⁊ po cuavap an aonpsp i ccfnn na Loclann go gaipg, beova, comimbagac, ⁊ pa cuipsb go cpuaib cpova leic pop let scuppa, giósb po nifmaib popp na Loclañaib cpé miopbail an coimvheb, ⁊ pa cuipiob a nveapg ap. Rá cuaib imuppo a ccaoipioc .i. Ƶnimcinnpiolaig la ainim go painig caipcail vaingen baoi a gcómpoépaib vóib, ⁊ po puabaip a gabail, ⁊ apeb ba víomaoin vo, uaip ni pa péb a pulang ap iomab paga ⁊ cloc gá nviubpagab vo. Ipeb vo pignipioni Cfinpaolab vo gaipm cuige, uaip ba vóig leip ba capa é, ⁊ aipgsba iomba vo geallab vo ap a anacal, ⁊ a peb ba víomaoin vopom, uaip po caipingsbpoin amac cpia impibe na pocaibe po pognaiopioc vo peime, ⁊ po maipbab go cpuag é, ⁊ po maipbaib a muinncep uile. Ba gaipic imuppo iapccain go ccangap vo cum an caipceol in po caicpiom a bscaib go papcolac, ⁊ po víorgaoileab uile é. Sic enim placuit Deo.

Ral. Oinspcac, ab Lochpa mopicnup.

Loc Lebinn vo pouv i ppuil, go paibe na paipcib cpó amail pgama.

Spucaip

the followers of Tomrar by field and flood, to be found in the published Annals.

ᵇ *Corcach.*—i. e. from the harbour of Cork. There is no account of this transaction given in the published Annals.

ᶜ *Gnim Cinnsiola.*—It is stated in the Ann. F. M. at the year 865, that Ginimbeolu, chief of the Galls of Cork, was slain by the Deisi, and he was, no doubt, the same person as the Gnim Cinnscalaigh here mentioned.

ᵃ *Castle.*—Caipcial. This is the earliest notice of a Danish castle in Ireland. This entry, however, is not to be found in the other Annals.

ᵇ *Lothra.*—Now Lorha, in the barony

of Corcach[y] to plunder Fera Maighe-Feine [Fermoy]. God, however, did not permit them, for at this time the Deisi had come to plunder in the same land by the providence of God, for before this time the Deisi and the Feara-maighe were mortal enemies. When, however, the Deisi saw the Lochlanns plundering and ravaging the country, they came to the Feara-maighe, and they made a firm and faithful peace [with each other], and they went together against the Lochlanns, fiercely, actively, and unitedly, and a fierce and terrible battle was fought between them; however, the Lochlanns were defeated through God's miracle, and they were cut off with great slaughter. But their chief, Gnim Cinnsiolla[z] by name, went to a strong castle[a] which stood near them, and he attempted to take it, but it was a vain effort for him, for he was not able to bear the number of darts and stones shot at him. He then called Cennfacladh to him, for he thought he was a friend, and promised him many rewards for protecting him; but this was also idle for him, for he was taken out at the request of the hosts who had served him previously, and piteously killed with all his people. Shortly afterwards they came to the castle in which he had passed his time voluptuously, and totally demolished it: *Sic enim placuit Deo*.

[866.] Kal. Dinertach. Abbot of Lothra[b], died.

Loch Leibhinn[c] was turned into blood, so that it was in clots of blood, like *sgama*[d].

Sruthair,

of Lower Ormond, county of Tipperary. See F. M. 864.

[c] *Loch Leibhinn*.—Now Lough Leane, near Fore, in the county of Westmeath. According to the Life of St. Fechin, published by Colgan, Diarmaid, King of Ireland, who died A. D. 664, had lived on

an island in this lake, and, according to the tradition in the country, the Danish tyrant Turgesius had a residence on the same island.—Ann. F. M. 864; Ann. Ult. 865.

[d] *Sgama*.—Scum, dross; the liver, or lights; the scale of a fish. Latin, *squama*.

Sruċaıṗ, ⁊ Sléḃte, ⁊ Aċaḋ Arġlaıṗ ḋ'arġaın ḋo ġentıḃ.

Iṗ ın bliaḋaın ṗı .ı. ṗeẋto anno reġıṁıṁṗ Aoḋa mıc Néıll, maıṫṁ ṗe Laıġnıḃ ṗoṗ Uıḃ Néıll, ı ttorċaıṗ Maolṁnaḋ mac Dunchaḋa, ⁊ Maolṁuıṗteṁne mac Maoılḃṗıġḋe.

Teaġṁaıl cıoıṗ 'Oıṗle, mac ṗí Loċlann, ⁊ Aṁlaıḃ a ḃṗáċaıṗ. Tṗı mıc battuṗ aġ an ṗí .ı. Aṁlaıḃ, ⁊ ıoṁaṗ, ⁊ 'Oıṗle. Oıṗle ba ṗoo a n-aoıṗ ḋıoḃ, ⁊ aṗ é ḃá moó aṗ aoı eanġnaṁa ; uaıṗ ṗuġ ḋeaṗṗġuġhaḋ moṗ ınṫubaṗġaı ṗoġa ⁊ ınṁoṗtġa ḋo Ġhaoıḋealaıḃ. Ruġ ṫno ṫṡıṗġuġhaḋ ḋo Loċlannaıḃ ın ṁuṗt cloıḋım ⁊ ın-ḋıubṗaġaḋ ṗaıġṡo. Ro ḃaoı a ḋuḃṗuat ġo moṗ ġa ḃṗaıċṗıḃ. Aṗeḋ aṗ ṁó ṗo ḃaoı aġ Aṁlaoıḃ. Ní mıṗın cuıṗı na muṗcṅ aṗ a lıbṗı. Ra ċuaḋaṗ an ḋa ḃṗáṫaıṗ .ı. Aṁlaoıḃ ⁊ Ioṁaṗ ı ġcoṁaıṗle ma caınġın ın mıc óıġ .ı. 'Oıṗle, ġé ṗo ḃattuṗ cṁṗı ḋıċealta occa ḋa maṗḃaḋ, ní hıaḋ tuġṗat aṗ áıṗo, aċt cṁṗı eıle ṗo ṫóġbattuṗ aṗ áıṗo aṗ aınleṗıoḋ a ṁaṗḃaḋ, ⁊ ṗá cınṗıot ıaṗaṁ a ṁaṗḃaḋ. 'O ṗo ṗıoṗ Aṁlaoıḃ ḋál an ḃṗáṫaıṗ ba mıoṗġaıṗ leıṗ ḋo ċuıḋeaċt, ıṗṗeḋ ḋo ṗıġne Tíṡtaıṗeuḋa taıṗıṗı ḋo ċuṗ aṗ ċṅn na ṗıtaıṗe ba ṗonaıṗte ⁊ ba beoḋa aıġe, ġo ṁḋeıttíṗ aṗtıġ aṗ ċṅn 'Oıṗle. Táımc ıaṗaṁ an t'Oıṗlı .ı. an ḋuıne aṗ ṗṡıṗı cṁuṫ ⁊ Tnġnaṁ ḃaoı an tan ṗın 'ṗan ḋoṁan; uaıċṡ ḋna taınıġ ı ttṡ aḃṗaċaıṗ ; uaıṗ ní ṗaoıl an ní ṗuaıṗ ann .ı. a ṁaṗḃaḋ. Iṗeḋ ıṁoṗṗo ṗo cuınıġ ann ní naċ ṗo ṗaoıl. Aṗṡ ṗo ıaṗṗ ó tuṗ ḋıolṁaınuṗ laḃaṗta ḋo taḃaıṗt ḋó. Tuġaḋ ḋoṗoṁ ṗaın. Aṗṡ ıṁoṗṗo, ṗolabaıṗṗıoṁ .ı. a ḃṗáċaıṗ

ᵉ *Sruthair*.—Now Shrule, on the east side of the River Barrow, near the town of Carlow. See Ann. F. M., p. 562, note.

ᶠ *Slebhte*.—Now Sleaty, near the town of Carlow.

ᵍ *Achadh arghlais*.—Now Agha, in the barony of Idrone, county of Carlow.

ʰ *By the Gentiles*.—The F. M., at 864, have, "by the Osraighi."

ⁱ *Aedh*.—This was the year 869. This entry is not in the published Annals.

ᵏ *Amhlaeibh*, &c.—These three princes are mentioned in the Annals of Ulster, at the year 862, as having plundered the an-

Sruthair[e], and Slebhte[f], and Achadh Arghlais[g] were plundered by the Gentiles[h].

In this year, the sixth of the reign of Aedh[i], son of Niall, a victory was gained by the Leinster-men over the Ui-Neill; in the battle fell Maelmuaidh, son of Donchadh, and Maelmuirtheimhne, son of Maelbrighde.

A meeting [took place] between Oisle, son of the King of Lochlann, and Amhlaeibh, his brother. The king had three sons, namely, Amhlaeibh[k], and Imhar, and Oisle. Oisle was the youngest of them in age, but the greatest in point of valour, for he gained great celebrity by excelling all the Gaeidhil in shooting darts and javelins, and he excelled the Lochlanns in strength of sword and in shooting darts. His brothers had a black hatred for him, and Amhlaeibh more than the other. The causes of the hatred are not to be told, on account of their complexity. The two brothers, Amlaeibh and Imhar, consulted together about the cause of the young brother, Oisle; and though they had hidden reasons for killing him, these were not what they brought forward, but they dissembled and brought forward other causes for which they ought to kill him; and they afterwards resolved upon killing him. When Amhlaeibh had learned that the party of the brother whom he hated had arrived, what he did was, to send faithful messengers for the stoutest and most vigorous knights he had, that they might be in the house on Oisle's arrival. Oisle afterwards arrived. He was the best shaped and the most valiant man that was then in the world. He came with a small party to the house of his brother, for he did not expect to meet his death there, as he did. He requested a thing which he did not think would be

cient sepulchral caves, as well as the land of Flann, son of Conaing, chief of Cianachta in Bregia; and the murder of

Oisle, or Flosius, is recorded A. D. 866. " Auisle tertius rex Gentilium dolo et parricidio a fratribus suis jugulatus est."

abṗáṫaıṗ (aṗ ṗé) muna ṗṗaıl ṡṗáḋ ḋo ṁná, .ı. ınṡſn Caıṡaoṫ aṡaoṗa, cıṅ na leıṡı ḋaṁṗa uaıṫ í, ⁊ ṡaċ ní ṗo ḋſoṡḃaıṗ ṗıa, ḋo ḃéṗṗa ḋuıṫ, 'O ṗo cualaı an ṫ-Aṁlaıḃ ſın, ṗo ṡaḃ éḋ móṗ é, ⁊ ṗo noċṫ a ċloı-ḋſṁ, aṡuṗ ṫuṡ buılle ḋe ı ṡcſnn 'Oıṗle .ı. a ḃṗáṫaṗ, ṡuṗ ṗoṗ maṗḃ. Ro ċoıṁċıṗıṡ cáċ aṗ aṁuṗ a ċéıle ıaṗṫṫaın .ı. muınṫſṗ an ṗí .ı. Aṁlaoıḃ, ⁊ muınnṫſṗ an ḃṗáṫaṗ ṗo máṗḃaḋ ann; ḃáṫṫuṗ ṗṫuıc, ⁊ coṁaıṗc maṗſċ aınṗaıḋe. Ro ċuaṗ ıaṗṗaın ṗa Lonṡṗoıṫ an ḃṗa-ṫaṗ ṗo maṗḃaḋ ann, aṗ ċcuṗ ḋſṗṡáṗ a ṁuınnṫıṗe. Rob ıoıṁḋa ınaıċıoṗ ıṗ ın Lonṡṗoıṫ ſın.

'Sın ḃlıaḋaın ṗı ḋo ċuaḋaṗ na Daınaıṗ ṡo Caeṗ Eḃṗoıc⁻ ⁊ ḋo ṗaḋṗaṫ caċ cṗuaıḋ ḋo na Saxanaıḃ ann. Ro maıḋ ṗoṗ Saxanuıḃ, ⁊ ṗo ınaṗḃaḋ ṗıṡ Saxan ann .ı. Alle, ṫṗe ḃṗaċ ⁊ meaḃaıl ṡıolla óıṡ ḋa ṁuınṫıṗ ṗéın. Ṫuṡaḋ ṫṗa áṗ móṗ ıṗ ın ċaṫ ſın, ⁊ ṗa cuaṗ ı aṗ ṗaın ṗoṗ Caeṗ Eḃṗoıc, ⁊ ṫuṡaḋ ıoṁaḋ ṡaċ maıċıuṗa eıṗṫe, uaıṗ ḃá ṗaıṅlıṗ an ṫan ſın í, ⁊ maṗḃċuṗ na ṗṗṗıċ ḋo ḋcaṡḋaoıne ınnṫe. Aṗ aṗ ſın ṗo ṗáṗ ṡaċ ḋoconaċ, ⁊ ṡaċ ıṁneaḋ ḋ'ınnṗı ḃṗea-ṫon.

Iſ ın ḃlıaḋaın ſı ṫaınıṡ an Cenneḋıṡ aıṗḋıṗc .ı. mac Ṡaıċın, náṁa clunċ na Loċlann ḋ'ıonnṗoıṡıḋ Lonṡṗoıṫ Aṁloıḃ, ṗí na Loċ-lann (⁊ aṗ eṗḋe ſſṁaınn ḋo maṗḃ a ḃṗáṫaıṗ) ṡuṗ ṗo loıṗċċ . . . . Ṫanṡaṫṫuṗ na Loċlannaıṡ na ḋſṡaıḋ, ⁊ maṗ ṫuṡṗoṁ a aıṡlıḋ ṗoṗṗa, ṗo maıḋ ṗeıṁe ḋıḃ ṡo nıṡe an Lonṡṗoıṫ ⁊ ṗo maṗḃ a nḋeaṗṡáṗ na ṗaoṗclann.

Iſ ın ḃlıaḋaın ſı ṫaınıc ḃaṗṫ ıaṗla, ⁊ ḣaıṁaṗ ḋıaṗ ḋo ċınel ṗoıcıneaıaċ

¹ *Caer Ebroic.*—i. e. the town of York. See Saxon Chronicle, A. D. 867 ; Ann. Ult. 866.

ᵐ *Alle.*—The East Anglians (i. e. Nor-thumbrians), says the Saxon Chronicle, "had cast out their king Osbryght, and had taken to themselves a king, Ælla, not of royal blood." The death of Ælla on this occasion is not recorded ; but Flor. Wigorn. in his Chron. says, " occisis duo-bus regibus," viz. Osbryght and Ælla.

ⁿ *The camp of Amhlaeibh.*—In the Ann.

be granted him. He first requested that freedom of speech should be granted him, and what he said was: "Brother," said he, "if thou art not fond of thy wife, the daughter of Cinaedh, why not give her away to me, and whatever dower thou hast given for her, I shall give to thee." When Amhlaeibh heard this, he was seized with great jealously; he drew his sword and dealt his brother Oislè a blow of it on the head, and killed him. The parties of both then rose up to give battle to each other, i. e. the people of the King, Amhlaeibh, and the people of the brother who was killed. Trumpets were blown, and combats were fought between both parties there. The camp of the slain brother was afterwards entered after his people had been dreadfully slaughtered, and many were the spoils found in that camp.

In this year the Danes went to Caer-Ebroic[l] and gave hard battle to the Saxons there. They defeated the Saxons, and killed the Saxon King there; viz. Alle[m], through the treachery and deceit of a young man of his own people. Great havoc took place in that battle. The city of Ebroc was then entered, and much of every kind of riches was carried out of it, for it was wealthy at this time, and all the good people who were found within it were slain. From this arose every kind of misfortune and trouble to the island of Britain.

In this year the famous Cennedigh, son of Gaithin, the celebrated enemy of the Lochlanns, came to the camp of Amhlaeibh[n], King of the Lochlanns (he who murdered his brother, as we have before mentioned), and burned it . . . . The Lochlanns came in pursuit of him, but he turned upon them and routed them back to their camp, and he made a great slaughter of their nobles.

In this year Barith the Earl[o], and Haimar, two of the noble race of

---

F. M., A. D. 865, Ult. 866, Dun-Amhlaeibh, or Amlaff's fort, is said to have been at Clondalkin.

[o] *Barith the Earl.*—The only Barith

ροιέιηεαλαέ ηα Loclann, τρέ láρ Connact ó'ιοηηροιξιό Luιmniξ, amail ηα οſρηδαίρ ηί δο Conηαἐταιb. Ξιοſb ηί αṁλαιδ δο ράλα, uαιρ ηί 'ραη ιοmαδ ρο ταιριρη·ξριοδ αἐτ ηα mbριξαιb ρέιη. Ro ρυαρραττυρ ηα Conηαἐταιξ τρια ἐέλεε α ρρορυαιρλιυξαδρoṁ: uαιρ δο ράλα αρειλε Mυιṁηεαέ ροηαιρτ, ερυαιδ, ⁊ ξλιε ι η·ιmιρτ αρm, ſτυρρα αη ταη ριη, ⁊ bá ξλιε δηο α εεοmαιρλιb αη Mυιṁηεαέ ριη. Ro ιοραιλſτυρ ιαραṁ Conηαέτα ραιρριδε δολα αρ αmuρ ηα Loclann, mαρ bα δο ἐαbαιρτ εολυιρ δόιb, ⁊ δο mαρbαδ bαριἐ. Mαρ ραηαιξριδε ξο mιξε αη ιοηαδ ι ραbα hαιmαρ τυξ buιλλε δό λεαἐξα ξο ροηαιρτ ιη hαιmαρ, ξο ρορ mαρb. Mιλιδ mυιρρο Conηαἐταἐ δο ἐυαιδ mαιλλε ριρ αρ τί mαρbτα αη bαριἐ, ηί ἐάρλα δοραιδε αṁαιλ bα δύἐραἐτ λαιρ, uαιρ ρο ξοηαδ é τρε ηα ρλιαραιη, ⁊ ρα ἐυαιδ αρ αρ éιξιη ιαρτταιη. Ra ξαbρατ δηο ηα Conηαἐταιξ ρο ηα Loclannαιb ξυρ ἐυιρριοδ δεαρξάρ ηα Loclann, ⁊ ηί hαṁλαιδ ρο bιαδ muna beiἐ αη ἐαιλλ ⁊ αη αδhαιξ ι ρρόςραιb. Iρεδ ρο ἐυαἐτυρ ιαρτταιη coιηιξε αη ιοηαδ αρ α ττανξαττυρ, ⁊ ηί δο Luιmηεαἐ.

Kal. Maolδύιn mac Αοδα Οιρδηιξε, ιη ελερικατυ οbιιτ.

Robαρταἐ, Eριρcοριρ ετ ραριεηρ Fιοηηξλαιρι, mοριτιρ.

Corξραch τιξε Τελλε, ρερiδηιδε ⁊ αηξcοιρε, δ'écc.

Conall Cιλλε Scιρε, εριρcοριρ, quιευιτ.

Cormac hUα Lιαthάιη, εριρcοριρ ετ αηαchορετα, quιευιτ.

Οιξbἐαιρ, αb Coιηδερε ⁊ Laιηηεαλα, quιευιτ.

Ξυαιρε mac Oυbδαbαιρſηη mοριτυρ.

Muιρἐαἐ

mentioned in the Irish Annals is Barith, a fierce champion of the Norsemen, who was slain at Dublin in 878, according to the Ann. F. M.; Ult. 880.

ᵖ *Maelduin, son of Aedh.*—A. D. 866 [= 867] Ann. Ult. He was the son of Aedh Oirdnidhe, who was King of Ireland A. D. 797-820.

ᵠ *Finnglais.*—Now Finglas, near Dublin. Ann. Ult. 866.

ʳ *Tigh Telle.*—Now Tihelly, or Teely, [*the house of St. Telle*, see Mart. Dungal. ad 25 Jan.], near Durrow, in the north of the present King's County. Colgan's Acta SS.,

of the Lochlanns, came through the middle of Connaught towards Luimneach [Limerick], as if they intended to do no injury to the Connaught-men. But this did not happen so, for it was not to numbers they trusted, but to their own vigour. The Connaught-men proposed to cut them off by treachery; for at that time there happened to be a certain Munster-man among them who was brave, hardy, and cunning in the use of arms, and he was also wise in councils. The Connaught-men requested of him to go towards the Lochlanns, as if to guide them, [but in reality] to kill Barith. As he came on to the place where Haimar was, he gave Haimar a strong blow of a half javelin, and killed him. But a Connaught champion, who went along with him for the purpose of killing Barith, did not happen to succeed as he desired, for he was himself wounded through his thigh, and afterwards escaped with difficulty. The Connaught-men, however, attacked the Lochlanns, and made a great havoc of them, but this would not have been the case had not the wood and the night been near them. The Lochlanns then returned to the place from which they had set out, instead of proceeding to Luimneach.

[867.] Kal. Maelduin, son of Aedh[p], King of Aileach, died *in clericatu*.

Robhartach, Bishop and sage of Finnglais[q], died.

Cosgrach, of Tigh Telle[r], scribe and anchorite, died.

Conall, of Cill Scire, a bishop, died.

Cormac Ua Liathain, bishop and anchorite, died.

Oigedhchair, Abbot of Coindeire [Connor] and Lann-Eala [Lynally], died.

Guaire, son of Dubhdabhairenn, died.

Muireadhach,

p. 15, note 10. It is shown on the Ordnance Map under the wrong name of Templekieran. Ann. Ult. 866. The other obits here entered are given in the Annals of the F. M. at 865, and the most of them in the Ann. Ult. at 866, but the true year is 867.

Muirſoac mac Catail, ꞃí hUa Cꞃiomtainn, longa papaliꞃi eꞃtinctuꞃ eꞃt.

Dunchað mac Dungaile moꞃituꞃ.

Canannan mac Ceallaiġ inteꞃꞃectuꞃ eꞃt peꞃ dolum ó mac Ȝaitini.

Connmac ab Cluana mic Noiꞃ.

Maiðm ꞃe mac Ȝaitini ꞃoꞃ Longuꞃ Ata cliat, ɿ ttoꞃchaiꞃ Oðolb¹ Micle.

Duðaꞃtac beꞃꞃac ꞃaoi ſgna quieuit.

Aeðacán mac Fionnacta, ollam leite Cuinn, quieuit.²

Iſ in bliaðain ꞃi .i. in ꞃeꞃtimo anno ꞃeȝni Aoða³, ꞃa ȝꞃennaiȝ-ꞃioð Laiȝin Cſꞃball mac Dunlaing um cat. Ra ioꞃlamaiȝ ðno Cſꞃball aꞃ amuꞃ an cata ꞃain. Ro comꞃaic ða imaꞃꞃꞃluaȝ ȝo noſꞃnꞃað oſꞃaið, ȝo ꞃo maꞃbað ꞃócaiðe eattuꞃꞃa. In tan imuꞃꞃo ꞃo comꞃaic act bſȝ ðon cat cſctaꞃða aꞃ ann tainiȝ Sloiȝſðoc Ua Raitnen, comaꞃba Molaiꞃꞃi Leitȝlinne, ðeocain an tan ꞃoin é, Eꞃꞃcoꞃ imoꞃꞃa, ɿ Comaꞃba Ciaꞃain Saiȝꞃe iaꞃttain; taimcꞃiðe ȝo na . . . . ſgnaið, ɿ ȝo noſꞃnað ꞃið caiꞃiꞃi eattoꞃꞃu.

Iſ in bliaðain ꞃi ðno ꞃonað móꞃꞃluaȝ la hAoð Finnliat, mac Néill, ꞃiȝ 'Eiꞃſnn ð'ionnꞃoiȝið Ciannacta ða n-aꞃȝain, ɿ ða n-inð-ꞃað, uaiꞃ tuȝ ꞃí Ciannacta .i. Flann mac Conaing mac a ðꞃb́-ꞃeataꞃ ꞃéin, ðíꞃꞃiom moꞃ ꞃoꞃ ꞃiȝ 'Eiꞃſnn. Ní ꞃaba imuꞃꞃo ɿ n-Eꞃinn

¹ *Odolbh Micle.*—i. e. Mickle, or the Big. The name is Odulph, Edulph, Adolph, or Adolphus. Frequent mention of a king of Danes of this name occurs in Geffrei Gaimar's "Estoire des Angles."

² *Aedhacan.*—The scribe has added in the margin the following passage from the F. M., A. D. 865 :—Aeðacan mac Finꞃ-necta tanaiꞃi-abbað Cluana ɿ ab cealla n-iomða, ðéc 1. Nou. "Aedacan, son of Finsnechta, Tanist-abbot of Cluan [Cloyne], and abbot of many churches, died 1st Nov."

" *Leth-Chuinn.*—i. e. Conn's half. The northern half of Ireland.

³ *Aedh.*—i. e. the year 870. This battle between the Leinster-men and Cearbhall, King of Ossory, is not noticed in

Muireadhach, son of Cathal, King of Ui Creamhthainn, died of long paralysis.

Dunchadh, son of Donnghal, died.

Canannan, son of Ceallach, was slain by treachery by the son of Gaithin.

Conmnhach, Abbot of Cluain-mic-Nois, [died].

A victory was gained by the son of Gaithin over the fleet of Ath-cliath; in the battle Odolbh Micle[s] was slain.

Dubhartach Berrach, a learned sage, died.

Aedhagan[t], son of Finnacht, Ollamh of Leth-Chuinn[u], died.

[870.] In this year, the seventh of the reign of Aedh[x], the Leinster-men provoked Cearbhall, son of Dunlang, to battle. Cearbhall prepared for this battle. The two cavalries met together and fought, and many were slain between them. Before, however, much fighting had gone on between them, Sloighedhach Ua Raithnen, successor of Molaisse of Leithglinn (who was a deacon at this time, but afterwards a bishop and comharba of Ciaran of Saighir), came with his . . . . wise, and he made a sincere peace between them.

[868.] In this year a great hosting was made by Aedh Finnliath, son of Niall, King of Erin, against the Cianachta[y] to plunder them, for the King of Cianachta, i. e. Flann, son of Conang, his own sister's son, had offered a great insult to the King of Erin. There was not in all Erin

the published Annals. ·Sloighedhach Ua Rathnen, successor of St. Ciaran of Saighir, died in the year 885. F. M.

[y] *Cianachta.*— i. e. the Cianachta of Bregia. This hosting by King Aedh is noticed by the F. M. at 866, which they make the sixth of the reign of Aedh, and in the Ann. Ult. at 867, but the true year is 868 or 869. The F. M. have quoted several

ancient verses composed on the subject of this battle, which are referred to by the scribe of our MS., who writes in the margin, " Vide carmina de hoc prælio in Ann. Dungal. an. 866." The account here given is the fullest that has yet been discovered. It appears to be perfectly authentic, and seems to have been written immediately after the event had taken

2 A

n-Eipinn uile bá moo enfch na caonpuapapcaib ionáp an Flanopa, ⁊ ono gen pobuibfc Aob an can pain be, ⁊ Aob na ápopig Eipeann, po ba maic gpeim Flainn bó an can páinig a lfp .i. an can po baoi cogab fcoppa ⁊ Maoilpelainn mac Maolpuanaib: uaip ip cpfo pin po innapb Maoilpeclainn an Flann ap a cíp. An cpa imuppo oo pab an Flann mac Conaing an oinpiompi oo pig Eipfhn ap ann pin po boí Flanoa ingen pi Oppaige .i. Ounlaing, ⁊ ip ipibe ba bfn o'Aob Finnliac ancanpa, ap mbeic peme ag Maoilpeclainn, ⁊ ip í pug Flann oó, an mac ón ip fíip cáinig i n-Eipinn 'na aimpip, ⁊ ba apopí Eipeann iapccain. Api an Lano cécna mácaip Cennéoig fioaipe mic Gaicíni. Ip ann aobeipim po boi an piogapa ag oénam cfmpuil oo naoim bpigio i cCill oapa, ⁊ paoip ioma aice ipin caille og cfpgab ⁊ ag pnaibe cpann. Ra cuala cpa an piogapa coiipab ⁊ uga Laigfn má fíp .i. um Aob Finnliac ⁊ ima mac .i. im Flann mac Maoilpeclainn, ⁊ ní paba ap mac oile piam a cló na a allab an can pin, ⁊ ó po ficip coineipge Laigfn la Flann mac Conaing pí Ciannacca, cáinig peimpe go nige bail i paba a fíp, ⁊ pa inuip bó, ⁊ po nfic go pofpaibe é, im cionól caca na n-agaib. Cuipfb cpa Aob iap pin a fluag po Ciannacca, ⁊ aipgio ⁊ loipgio go n-áp móp baoine oo maibab nóib. Ní cáinig imuppo Flann po céóip ba n-ionnpoigib, uaip pabaoi coblac móp an can pin ag inbfp bóinne, ⁊ po cuippiom fiop ap a n-amup paibe go oriopbaoip ná pópibin, ⁊ cangaccuppom ón, ⁊ ono cangaccup Laigin o'foipigin an Fhlann. Cangaccup uile iapccain i nofgaib pig Eipeann ⁊ a epfca peime. Ro cuaib Aob ap ápo po baoí ag ffgab na móp focpaibe baoi na ofgaib. . . . . . ré ⁊ a lucc comaiple, ní ap líon óg bpipcean eac, acc ip cpé fupcacc an coimbeab,

⁊ cpé

place, by some Leinster historian who was opposed to the Hy-Niall race; and who may probably have been an eye-witness of the events which he has recorded.

¹ *Fleet.*—i. e. a fleet of Norsemen or Lochlanns.

Erin, at this time, any one of greater valour or renown than this Flann, and although Aedh was not very thankful to him at this time, he being supreme King of Erin, Flann had afforded him aid when he required it, i. e. when there was a war between him and Maelsechlainn, son of Maelruanaidh, for it was in consequence of this that Maelsechlainn had expelled Flann from his territory. When, however, Flann, son of Conang, offered this insult to the King of Erin, then Flanna, daughter of the King of Osraighe, i. e. of Dunlang, the wife of Aedh Finnliath at this time, she having been previously married to Maelsechlainn, to whom she bore Flann, the best man in Erin in his time, and who was monarch of Erin afterwards. This same Flanna was also the mother of the famous Cennedigh, son of Gaithin. This queen, I say, was then erecting a church to Brigit at Cill-dara [Kildare], and she had many tradesmen in the wood felling and cutting timber. Now, this queen had heard the conversation and talk of the Leinstermen about her husband, i. e. Aedh Finnliath, and her son, i. e. Flann, son of Maelsechlainn, whose fame and renown at this time had never been enjoyed by any son before,—and when she had learned that the rising out of Leinster was going to aid Flann, son of Conang, King of Cianachta, she came forward to where her husband was, and told it to him, and she exhorted him heartily to assemble his forces to give them battle. After this Aedh sent his army throughout Cianachta, which they plundered and burned, and they made a great havoc of the people. Flann himself did not, however, come to attack them immediately, for there was a large fleet[z] at this time in the mouth of the Boinn [Boyne], and he sent for them, requesting that they would come to his relief—and so they did; and the Leinstermen also came to relieve him. They all set out in pursuit of the King of Erin, who had sent his spoils before him. Aedh ascended a hill which commanded a view of the great hosts which were in pur-

⁊ τρé ϝípınne ρlατα;ª an οíomuρ ımuρρo ⁊ an ıoταρcραιο ϝluαξ, ní
híο αρ ıonṁαın ρα Οια, ατ́ ıṁρlé αιξnıο ⁊ cραιοe οαınξṁ. So-
τ́uıοe ıαραṁ οo'n luτ́τ ϝo, ⁊ αρ υíoṁρατ́ τ[ξαıυ. Τıonoılíoρı uıle
ımumρα αnoρα, ⁊ nα bíoο mṁnmα τeıτ́ıο αξαıb, uαıρ αρ ϝαοα uαıb
ξo n-uıξe bαρ ττıξτ́ ϝéın, ⁊ ní cαρcnο lṁρaρ ριb, ní hαnαcαl nα
coıξıll ϝoξeb́τ́αoı. Οénαıο τρα nα nοṁρηραο báρ n-αıτ́ρṁα ⁊ bαρ
ρṁαıτρeατ́α, ϝuılnξío τρα ϝρoρα ı n-αınm nα τρíonoıοe οo τ́eαlξuο
οuıb. ϺΜαραο α τ́ıτ́ıρτ́ı ınıρı αξ eıρξe, eıρξío uıle ı n-αoınρϝ́τ́τ
ϝoτα ṁαρ ϝαıllρτ́uρ Οια οuıb. Οια luαın αρ αoı láıτ́e ρϝ́τ́ṁαıne
ρın. In Ρlαnn ımuρρo ṁαc Coṁunξ ıρın ραınn eıle, αρ fο ρo ραıο-
ρíοe ρρıα ṁuınnτıρ. Αρ uατhαο an luτ́τ úο, ⁊ αρ líonṁαρ ατ́άıṁne,
⁊ cρuτ́αıοιξıοιρι τ́eím οά n-ıonρoιξío, ⁊ οo ριξne τρí cóıρıξτ́e οe .ı.
é ϝéın αρ τúρ, ⁊ Lαıξın ıαρτταın, nα Lοτ́lαnnαιξ ϝα οeoιξ; ⁊ ρο
báoı ξα n-αξαllαο uıle. Τuıτρıο an luτ́τ úο líbρı, αρ ρé, ⁊ beρ-
τ́αoı buαıο ⁊ coρξuρ οíοb, αρ ní buο ϝıu leo τeıτ́eο ρṁαıbρı, ⁊
ατ́αoıρı líon αρ moó. Uαıρ ní αρ ϝατ oıle ατúρα αξ an cατ́uξαορα,
ατ́τ οo ξαbáıl ρıξe Τ(ṁρατ́, nο οoṁ ṁαρbαο. Roβττuρ áılle τρά
nα τρí coıρıξτ́ı ρın, ρob ıoṁοα meıρξe álαınn ıolοατ́ατ́ αnn, ⁊ ρξıατ́α
ξατ́α οατ́α. Τanξαττuρ ıαρuṁ ϝón ccuma ραın ο'ıonρoıξıο ρıξ
'Gıρeαnn.

Ρo bαoı ımuρρo ρí 'Gıρeαnn ξα n-ıoρnαıοe, ⁊ ρé meıρξe ρo bαoı
αıξe, cρoτ́ an τ́oıṁoρ, ⁊ bατ́αll loρα.

'Ó τanξατταρ τρα nα ϝluαıξ ńάıṁοιξe ı ξcoṁρoτ́ραιο οo Ἀοο,
ρά ρuıο ⁊ ρα coρuıξ uıme ρí Ulαο οo'n οαρα leıτ́, ⁊ ρí Ṁíοe οon
leıτ́ oıle ⁊ ρo ρáıο ρıu: Ńά h-ıoṁράıοíο τeıτ́fο, ατ́τ τaıρıρnıξιο
ıρın coıṁoρ ó ϝρuıl coρξuρ οonα Cρíoρτaıοıο, nαρ αb bαnοα bαρ
n-αıξínτα,

ª *Showers.*—i. e. Showers of darts or ja- our Lord Himself to St. Patrick. See Col-
velins. gan's Trias Thaum., p. 263, and Dr.
 ᵇ *Staff of Jesus.*—This was the celebrated Todd's Introd. to the book of "Obits of
Baculus Jesu, said to have been given by Christ Church," p. viii., *sq.*

suit of him . . . . and by the advice of his councillors, he said: "It is not by force of soldiers that a battle is gained, but by the aid of God, and the righteousness of the prince. Pride, and superfluous forces, are not pleasing to God, but humility of mind and firmness of heart [are]. These people have great hosts, and they advance proudly. Assemble ye all around me now, and have no intention of flying, for far from you are your own houses, and they are no friends who will follow you; it is not protection or quarter ye shall receive. Do, however, as your fathers and your grandfathers have done; in the name of the Trinity suffer showers[a] to be discharged at you. When you see me rising, rise ye all to attack, as God will show unto you." Monday was the day of the week. Now Flann, son of Conang, on the other hand, said to his people: "These people are few, and we are numerous; harden your steps against them." He then divided his forces into three divisions, in the first of which he was himself, in the second the Leinster-men, in the last the Lochlanns, and he harangued them all, saying: "This people will fall by you," said he, "and ye shall gain victory and triumph over them, for they are too proud to fly before you, and ye are more numerous. I am not engaged in this battle with any other view except to gain the throne of Teamhair, or be killed." These three divisions were indeed beautiful; many were the beautiful parti-coloured standards that were there, and shields of every colour. They afterwards came in this order to meet the King of Erin.

The King of Erin was awaiting them, having six standards, the cross of the Lord, and the staff of Jesus[b].

When the enemies' forces came close to Aedh, he placed and arrayed around him the King of Uladh on the one side, and the King of Meath on the other, and he said to them: "Think not of flight, but trust in the Lord, who gives victory to the Christians; let not your

n-aiġṡnta, aċt ġup ob ḟpba, ⁊ bpiṗiú ġo hobann caṫ ap bup naim-
oiḃ, ġup po mapa ḃup cclu cṗé ḃioċu. Arṡo po pȧoṗio uile ġo
noionġnaioṡíp. Ní ċainiġ impppo oo piġ 'Eipeann oeipeaḃ na mbpia-
ċap pin oo ṗaḃ an uaip canġaccup a námaicc i ḟḟocup, ⁊ po oiu-
baipġpiou ḟpoppa oíomópa oo ṗaiġoiḃ ap cúp ⁊ ḟpoppa o'ṗaġaiṗ
iapccain, ⁊ an cpiṡp ḟpopp oo leċġaiḃ, ionnup ġup eipġe an piġ co
naa ṁuincip na n-aiġio, ġup caiċiġpiou oo cpoḃa ḟpiu.

Popíop ní ṗaġhim ap in cpeinhoḃap acá bpipce, iomlaine na
himċċċa oo ponpac caċ 'pan caċhpo Cille hUa nOaiġpe, nȧio
na bpiaċpa bpṡġȯa oo laḃaip piġ 'Eipṡn ġo huihoḃe oo oiopġaȯ
aṁuinċipe ṗéin. Ġioḃo caċam ġup bpipioḃ leipin piġ ap a ná-
ṁaio.

Aġup annpin po ṗaiḃ an piġ (an can baoí an ṁaiȯm ṗé na
ṁuinnċip): a ṁuinncip ionṁain, léġio oo na Cpíopcaioiḃ, ⁊ impio
ḟop ioualaḃapċaiḃ ó caio a mauṁaimm pṡnaiḃ. Níop bú oíoṁaoin
oopoṁ pin oo ṗaḃ, uaip oo pónṗau pin paippioṁ, ionnup nać moó
ioná cṡchpamhaḃ oíoḃ paimġ ṗlán. Ċéppaccup Laiġin iomlán uá
n-achapḃa ṗéin, uaip oo ponpau cipe oainġen cṡnġailce oíoḃ ṗéin
cpe coṁaiple an caoipiġ cpeaḃaip bui aca, .i. Maolċiapain mac
Rónain. Plan imippo mac Conaing, po ċeiċ co na ṗocpaiṡe, ⁊
pugpac muinncip an píġ paip, ⁊ po ṗaġaiḃ a cṡnn, ⁊ cuġau é oo
laċaip aipṡċa an piġ, ⁊ po baoi an pí ann pin aġ ioṁċaoíṅḃ paip,
⁊ po baoí caċ ġá ṗaḃa pip náp bo cóip oo a ċaíṅḃ cpe ġoipe a
nġaoil, ⁊ ap auḃapaiḃ eile naċ ḟṗaġuim ap in cpenleaḃap, ⁊c.

Kal. Niallan Eppcop Slaine, obic.

Copmac

<small>ᵉ *The old book.*—A marginal note says: "Sunt verba Firbisii," meaning that this lamentation over the defects of the old book was that of Dudley Firbis, the scribe, who had deciphered "the old vellum book," and who also adds in the margin that *Cill Ua nDaighre*, where this battle was fought, is situated one mile to the north of Drogheda, "Cill hUa n-Oaiġpe mile ó cuaiḃ oo Opoiċṡc Ȧċa." It is</small>

your minds be effeminate, but manly, and suddenly put your enemies to flight in the battle, that your fame may last for ever." They all replied that they would do so. The King of Erin had not finished the delivery of these words when the enemy came near him, and first discharged great showers of darts, and afterwards showers of javelins, and thirdly a shower of half javelins, so that the king and his people rose up against them, and fought bravely with them.

Alas! I do not find in the old book[c] which is broken, the whole of the proceedings of both parties in this battle of Cill Ua nDaighre, nor all the fine words which the King of Erin spoke to direct his own people; however, we find that the enemy were defeated by the king.

And then the king said (when the enemy was routed by his people), "Beloved people," said he, "spare the Christians, and fight against the idolaters, who are now routed before you." These words were not spoken by him in vain, for they did this at his bidding, so that not more than one-fourth of them escaped scathless. The Leinster-men escaped in safety to their own patrimony, for they formed themselves into a solid, compact phalanx, by advice of their prudent leader, i. e. Maelciarain, son of Ronan. But Flann, son of Conang, fled with his forces, and was overtaken by the king's party; he lost his head, which was carried before the King's Council, and the king lamented over it then, and all told him that he ought not to lament over it merely on account of the nearness of their relationship, and for other reasons which I cannot get from the old book, &c.

[869.] Kal. Niallan[d], Bishop of Slaine, died.

Cormac,

the place now called Killineer, which is a townland of St. Peter's parish, Drogheda, on the road leading N. W., about half way towards Monasterboice. See the Ordnance Map of Louth, Sheet 24.

[d] *Niallan.*—This and the succeeding obits are given in the Ann. F. M. at 867, and in the Ann. Ult. at 868.

Coṗmac mac Eloċaiġ, ab Saiġṗe, ⁊ ṙġṗiba moṗicuṗ.
Ailill Cloċaiṗ, ṗeṗiba ec epiṗcopuṗ ec ab Cloċaiṗ. Duḃcac
mac Maoilcuile docciṗṗimuṗ Lacinoṗum cociuṗ Euṗopae in
Chṗiṗco quieuic.
Maṗcṗa Eoḋuṗa mac Donnġaile ó ġenciḃ i nDiṗiuṗc Diaṗ-
maḋa.
Dunlainġ mac Muiṗċḋaiġ, ṗí Laiġċn moṗicuṗ.
Maolciaṗain mac Rónáin, ṗiġ-nia aiṗciṗ Eiṗċnn, moṗicuṗ.
Oṗġain Aṗomaca ḋ'Aṁlaoiḃ, ⁊ a loṗccaḋ co na oḟṗṗciġiḃ .i.
oḟṗċac móṗ mic Anḋaiġc. Deic cceḋ eicciṗ ḃṗaiḋ ⁊ maṗḃaḋ;
ṗlaḋ móṗ olċena.
Donnaġan mac Ceḋṗaḋa, ṗi hUa Cenṗiolaiġ; Cian mac Cu-
maṗġaiġ ṗi hUa m-baiṗṗiche ciṗe moṗicuṗ.
Iṡ in bliaġainṗi .i. in occauo anno ṗeġni Aoḋa Finnléic ṗa ion-
naṗbṙaḋ Laiġin caoiṗioc ḋa ccaoiṗiocaiḃ ḋaca, uaiṗ ba mioṗġaiṗṡ
leo é .i. baoi ṗoṗmaḋ aca ṗiṡ aṗ meḋ na ccoṗġuṗ no beiṗeḋ ḋo na
Loċlannaiḃ, no ḋno, uaiṗ ba cuilice aca é, uaiṗ ḋo Ciaṗṗaiḋiḃ
Luacṗa a ḃunaḋ, no ḋno aṗ meḋ a ḋiomaiṗ ba mioṗġaiṗ leo é;
uaiṗ na ṗo ṗeḋ ḋin ḃeic i ccinn maice Laiġċn ⁊ ṗi Laiġċn, cainiġ
ṗa ṁuiñciṗ leiṡ aṗ ionnaṗba ḋ'ionnṗoiġiḃ ṗiġ Eiṗċnn, ⁊ aṗ meḋ a
ḃlaiḋc ċnġnaṁa ṗo ġaḃ an ṗí ċuiġe ġo honóṗuc é, ⁊ cuġ a inġin ḋó
ḋo ṁnaoi .i. Eicne. Ro bé meḋ imuṗṗo an ṗmacca ⁊ annṗic caṗṗaiḋ
ṡé ṗoṗ Loclannaiḃ, conac lamḋaoiṡ naċ ġnioṁ moġḋa ḋo ḋénaṁ iṗ
na ḋomnaiġiḃ: ṗo ba ṗġel móṗ ṗia innṗin na ccaḃṙaḋaoiṡ ḋo ciuṗa
ḋó

Clochar.—" Clochar mic nDaimen."—
Ann. Ult., A. D. 869.

ᶠ *Eodhus.*—No mention of this Eodhus, or of the circumstances of his martyrdom, is found in the Irish Martyrologies.

ᵍ *Died.*—"Moritur." This should be,

" was slain," as in the F. M. The Ann. Ult. have "jugulatus est."

ʰ *Ard-Macha.*—Ann. Ult. 868; F. M. 867. But neither Annals mention the "Oratory of Mac Andaighe."

ⁱ *The eighth.*—i. e. 871. The chieftain

Cormac, son of Elothach, abbot of Saighir [Seirkieran], and a scribe, died.

Ailell of Clochar, scribe, and bishop and abbot of Clochar[c]; Dubhthach, son of Maeltuile, the most learned of the Latins of all Europe, in Christo quievit.

The martyrdom of Eodhus[f], son of Dunghal, by the Gentiles at Disert-Diarmada.

Dunlaing, son of Muireadhach, King of Leinster, died.

Macleiarain, son of Ronan, royal champion of the East of Erin, died[g].

The plundering of Ard-Macha[h], by Amhlaeibh, and its burning with its oratories, i. e. the great oratory of Mac Andaighe. Ten hundred persons were taken captives or killed; a great plunder also.

Donnagan, son of Cédfad, King of Ui-Ceinnselaigh; [and] Cian, son of Cunnas-cach, King of Ui-Bairrche-tire, died.

[871.] In this year, the eighth[i] of the reign of Aedh Finnliath, the Leinster-men expelled one of their chieftains because they hated him, that is, they envied him in consequence of the many victories which he had gained over the Lochlanns, or else they regarded him as illegitimate, for he was of the Ciarraighi-Luachra as to his origin, or they hated him in consequence of his great pride. When therefore he could not be at the head of the chiefs of Leinster, he came with his followers in banishment to the King of Erin, and in consequence of the fame of his valour the King of Erin received him honourably, and gave him his daughter Eithne to wife. So great was the control and the sway which he gained over the Lochlanns, that they durst not perform any servile work on Sundays. It was great news

here referred to was Macleiarain, son of Ronan, whose obit has just been given (Ann. Ult. 868). He commanded the Leinster-men in their retreat from the

óó . . . . Iſ aſ tnut ⁊ aſ ꝼoꞃmaꝺ ꞃo ıonnaꞃbꞃaꝺ Laıġın uata ꝼéın é, ⁊ ꝺno aꞃ a beıt oꝼꞅꞃuıb Muṁan.

Táınıg tꞃa ıaꞃ ꞃın go ꞃocꞃaıꝺe leıꞃ ı Laıgnıb, go nꝺꞅꞃna aıꞃgne ⁊ ıonꞃꞃaꝺa ıomꝺa, ⁊ loıꞃgte ⁊ maꞃbta mıntıb. Aċt éꞅna ata a ꝼꝼagbaluıb naoṁ, ná bán péıꝺ ꝺo tí no ꞃɪgaꝺ a Laıgnıb amaé aꞃ ıonnaꞃba tuıoꞅét aꞃ ccula ꝺo éogaꝺ ıntıb ꝺo ꞃıgna na baꝺ péıꝺ, ꝺo . . . . ꝼıꞃı ꝼꞅı no coṁlann óó, aét ꞃo gabaꝺ ꝺo aꞃ gué aꞃꞃo ꝺo gaıb ⁊ ꝺo tuagaıb, ⁊ ꝺo cloıꝺmıb, go nꝺꞅꞃꞃat mıonta bꞅcca be, ⁊ guꞃ ꞃo bꞅnaꝺ a éꞅın ꝺe. Ro maꞃbaıt ꝺın a muınıtıꞃ uıle. Ruxaꝺ a éꞅın ıaꞃꞃın ꝺo éum na Loélann, ⁊ ꞃo cuıꞃꞃıoꝺꞃaıbé ꝼoꞃ énaılle é, ⁊ ꞃo gabꞃat ꞅeal ꝼoꞃa a ꝺıubaꞃgan, ⁊ ꞃo éuıꞃꞃıot 'ꞃın muıꞃ ıaꞃttaın é.

Kal. Suaıꞃleé Ineıꝺneın, Eꞃꞅcoꞃ ⁊ anéoıꞃe, ⁊ ab Cluana Ioꞃ-aıꞃꝺ, oꞃtımuꞃ ꝺoctoꞃ ꞃelıgıoꞃuꞃ totıuꞃ hıbeꞃnae, quıeuıt.

Geꞃan mac Oıocoꞃca ab Saıġꞃe.

Oıaꞃmuıꝺ ab Ꝑꞅꞃına quıeuıt.

Oubꝺaéuıle, ab léıt Mocaoṁog.

Maoloꝺaꞃ eꞃꞅcoꞃ ⁊ ancoıꞃe, ab Oaımınꞃı, quıeuıt.

Cumꞃuꝺ, ab Oıꞃıꞃt Cıaꞃaın bealaıġ ꝺuın, eꞃꞅcoꞃ et ꞅcꞃıba quıeuıt.

Comgan Foṫa, ab Ṫamlaéta, quıeuıt.

Cobṫaé mac Muıꞃꞅbóıg, ab Cılle ꝺaꞃa, ꞅaꞃıenꞃ et ꝺoctoꞃ, ꝺe quo ꝺıcıtuꞃ:—

Cobṫaé

battle of Cill Ua nDaighre the year before.

ᵏ *Curses.*—Ꝑáꞃbala, i. e. things left fixed and immutable by the saints. St. Patrick left success of fish and curse of drowning on several rivers; for example, the curse of drowning on the River Dineen in Idough, &c. St. Columbkille left it as a curse on the family of Magniggan, in Ulster, that there should never be a priest of the name; which caused them to change it to Goodwin. St. Nia left success of fish and curse of drowning on the River Sileece, in Fermanagh.

¹ *Suairlech of Inedhnen.*—These obits

to be related all the rents which they paid him .... It was out of envy and hatred the Leinster-men expelled him away from themselves, and because he was of the men of Munster.

After this he came with an army into Leinster, and committed many plunders and depredations, many conflagrations and slaughters therein. But, however, it is among the curses[k] of the saints that it will not be safe for one banished out of Leinster to come back to make war therein again. This was the case with him .... They observed not the rights of men, or combat towards him, but they attacked him on every side with javelins, and axes, and swords, so that they hacked him into small pieces, and cut off his head. They also killed all his people. His head was afterwards brought to the Lochlanns, who placed it on a pole, and continued for some time to shoot at it, and afterwards cast it into the sea.

[870.] Kal. Suairlech of Inedhnen[l], bishop and anchorite, and abbot of Cluain-Iraird [Clonard], the best doctor of religion in all Erin, quievit.

Geran, son of Dicose, Abbot of Saighir, quievit.

Diarmaid, Abbot of Fearna [Ferns], quievit.

Dubhdathuile, Abbot of Liath Mochaemhog, [quievit].

Maelodhar, bishop and anchorite, Abbot of Daimhinis [Devenish], quievit.

Cumsudh, Abbot of Disert Chiarain of Bealach-dúin [Castlekieran, in Meath], bishop and scribe, quievit.

Comhgan Fota, Abbot of Tamhlacht, quievit.

Cobhthach[m], son of Muireadhach, Abbot of Cill-dara [Kildare], a sage and doctor [dormivit], of whom is said:—

Cobhthach

are given in the Ann. F. M. at 868, and in the An. Ult. at 869, but the true year is 870.

[m] *Cobhthach.*—" Princeps cille daro."— *Ann. Ult.* 869. Comp. F. M., 868, where the following verses are also given.

Cobṫac Cuirpiġ cuirċaiġ,
Daṁna riġ Liṗe lṁnaiġ:
Durran mac mór Muirḃcaiġ
baliac hua caoinṗionn Ceallaiġ.
Cleṫe Laiġſi leiġniḋe,
Saoi rlan reġainn roċlać,
Reċla ruirſė rėiṁriġe
Conarba Conlaiċ Cobṫac.

Maonġal, Erſcop Cille ḋara, quieuiṫ.

Iſ in bliaġainſi ṫainiġ Aoḋ mac Néill illaiġniḃ, ġo maḋ do
dioġal an óġlaoic a ḋubramur romuinn, do marḃaḋ do Laiġniḃ, no
dno ġo maḋ do ṫoḃać cíora. Ro ṁurṫar Laiġne o Aṫ cliaṫ ġo
Ġaḃrán. Ṫainiġ dno Cſiball mac Dunlainġ, ri Orraiġe ⁊ Cen-
neiḋiġ mac Ġaiṫin, ri Laoiġri do'n leiṫ oile do Laiġniḃ, ⁊ an méd
ro ſéḋaḋar eiriſ lorġaḋ ⁊ arġain ⁊ marḃaḋ do ronraṫċiſ, ġo
ranġaṫċuir Dun inbolġ, ⁊ ro ġaḃſac lonġroiſc annrain, .i. Cſiball
⁊ Cennetiġ.

Ra cionolſaḋ Laiġin iarċċain 'má riġ .i. má Muirḃać mac
mḃrain, ⁊ ciḋ eiriḋe ba ri criaiḋ, corġrac, ġlic, uair ar ſaḋa ro
baoi ſor ionnarba a n-Albain, ba aicincciḋe do cruar ⁊ ſiġnaiṁ, ⁊
arſi ro ſmuainſeaḋar aca ġur ab córa ḋóiḃ ḋol a ccſin Laiġri
⁊ Orraiġe báċċuir i nDún bolġ ionár ḋola i ġcſin riġ 'Eiriſin baoi
oġ bealać Ġaḃráin, ⁊ ḋola 'rin aiḋċe ſon lonġroiſc. Cſġain iarain
Laiġin, ⁊ a ri maille riu, ġo cruaiḋ ronaiſſ na ccoruġaḋ ġu Dun
inbolġ, bail a raḃaċċuir a námaiḋ. Boiſ a met! Iſ ionġnaḋ an
cuinġioll

ⁿ *Cuirreeh.*—Now the Curragh of Kildare.
° *The youth.*—viz. Maelciarain, son of Ronan. See p. 184, n. ʳ.

ᵖ *Dunbolg.*—In the margin of the MS. the scribe has written toġail duin bolġ, "Destruction of Dunbolg." This was the name of a fort near Donard, in the county

Cobhthach of Cuirrech[n] of races,
Heir apparent of the King of Liffe of tunics:
Alas for the great son of Muireadhach,
Ah! grief: the descendant of the fair Ceallach.
Chief of scholastic Leinster,
A perfect, comely, prudent sage,
A brilliant shining star,
Was Cobhthach, the successor of Connlath.

Maenghal, Bishop of Cill-dara, died.

Aedh, son of Niall, came into Leinster to avenge the youth[o] whom we have mentioned before as killed by the Leinster-men, or indeed it was to levy rent. He plundered Leinster from Ath-cliath [Dublin] to Gabhran [Gowran]. On the other side of Leinster came Cearbhall, son of Dunlang, King of Osraighe, and Cennedigh, son of Gaithin, King of Laeighis, and did all they could effect by burning, plundering, and killing until they arrived at Dun-Bolg[p], where they encamped, i. e. Cearbhall and Cennedigh.

The Leinster-men afterwards gathered round their king, i. e. round Muiredhach, son of Bran, who was a hardy, victorious, prudent king, for he was for a long time in exile in Alba [Scotland], where he distinguished himself by his hardihood and bravery. And they thought among themselves that they should rather go against the men of Laeighis and Osraighe, who were at Dunbolg, than against the King of Erin, who was at Bealach Gabhrain[q], and to enter their camp at night. The Leinster-men then proceeded, with hardihood and courage, along with their king, arrayed in regular order, to Dunbolg, where their enemies were fierce and numerous! Prodigious was their

of Wicklow. Ann. F. M. 868; Ult. 869.
[q] *Bealach Gabhrain.*—i. e. the road or pass of Gowran, in the county of Kilkenny.

cuinʒioll ꝏonꝏa, uaip po cuaccup Laiʒin ı muiniʒin Naoiṁ ḃpiʒioe ʒo puʒꝏaoıp ḃuaıꝏ ⁊ copʒup ꝏo Oppaiʒıḃ ⁊ ꝏo Laoıʒıp. Ro cuac‑
cup ꝏno Oppaiʒe ı muinʒin Naoiṁ Ciapáin Saiʒpe ma ḃuaıꝏ ⁊
copʒup ꝏo ḃpeıc ꝏo Laiʒıṁ. Ro ḃaccap Laiʒin ʒo ꝏíocpa oʒ acac
Naoiṁ ḃpiʒioe, ʒup po mapḃꝏaoıp a náiṁꝏe .... Ipeꝏ cpa can‑
ʒaccup Laiʒin ꝏon leıc a paḃa mac Ɠaicíin ꝏon lonʒpopc.¹ Nı a
n‑imʒaḃaıl ꝏo piʒne mac Ɠaicin, acc ap na n‑aʒaıꝏ ʒo cpuaıꝏ peoc‑
aıp caimʒ, amuıl ba ḃép ꝏó. Do ʒnícḣep cpa cacuʒaꝏ cpuaıꝏ
cpoꝏa leċ pop leċ anu pın. Ap cıan po clop ʒáıp na ppṡı oʒ iuupc
ꝏıocumainʒ poppa, ⁊ poʒap na pcoc nꝏeaḃca, ⁊ po ʒaḃ an calaṁ
cpiocnuʒaꝏ ʒo nofcaccup a n‑fépaḃa ⁊ a n‑iomáince ı nʒealcaċc, ⁊
ba caipmpʒ míp ꝏ'fıʒnpaıṅ na luoc pın, acc cfna an luċc po ḃoí
ꝏon cpluaʒ ı pcalpıḃ cappaıʒ, canʒaccup anaʒıꝏ na n‑iumáıncı,
ʒo po popaccup míp ꝏíoḃ. Ba mop an muipn pın, ⁊ ba mop a
ppoʒup 'pın aeıp uapca. Imıpın po ḃaoı Ceṅḃall oʒ cfʒapʒ a
ṁuinncıpe, uaıp ba copac oíꝏcı pıaıp, ⁊ po pıaıꝏ; ʒıḃeꝏ ó ccíopaꝏ
na naiṁaıo cuʒaıḃ, na ʒlupaꝏ nfc uaıḃ ap a ımċıo cacaıpı, ⁊ conʒ‑
ḃaꝏ pıḃ ʒo cpuaıꝏ pıp na naiṁoıḃ. Ro cuaıꝏpıoṁ Cṡıḃall ⁊ poc‑
paıoe laıp ꝏ'ıonnpoıʒıꝏ ṁıc a pfċap .ı. Cenneoıʒ, po ḃaoí ı n‑eıʒfn
mop eoıp a náiṁoıḃ, ⁊ po ċoʒuıḃ a ʒuċ cpuaıꝏ ap áıpꝏ, ⁊ po ḃaoı
aʒ nfpcaꝏ a ṁuinncıpe a ccfnn Laıʒen (⁊ pa cualaccup Laıʒin
pın) ⁊ ꝏno po ḃáccup an muinncıp ʒa nfpcaꝏ pom. Ro fıḃ pa ꝏíp
ꝏá ṁuinncıp paıpe ꝏpopcoımeꝏ ꝏo. Ro ꝏıuḃaıpʒ pí Laıʒın leıċʒa
pocaıpṡe ʒup po mapḃ an ꝏapa pfı ꝏıḃ .ı. Polocċac,² pecnaḃ Cille
ꝏaıpe. Ap mop cpa an coıpm ⁊ an pocpom ḃaoı fcuppa anuaıp
pın, ⁊ pa cóʒaıḃ ḃaꝏḃ cfnn fcuppa, ⁊ ḃaoı mapḃaꝏ mop fcuppa
pán cán. Ro pcuícpıoc cpa Laıʒın on Lonʒpopc, ⁊ po ḃáccup aʒ
ḃpeıċ

¹ *The clamour.*—ḃamop an muıpn pın. See a similar expression used by the F. M. at the year 1504, p. 1278.

² *Badhbh.*—This was the name of a sort of fairy goddess of war, the *Bellona* of Irish mythology. But the name was also given

their number! Wonderful was the human condition! for the Leinster-men placed all their hope in St. Brighit that they should gain victory and triumph over the men of Osraighe and Laighis, and the men of Osraighe placed their hope in Ciaran of Saighir, for gaining triumph and victory over the Leinster-men. The Leinster-men fervently prayed to St. Brighit that they might kill their enemies . . . . . The side of the camp to which the Leinster-men came was that in which the son of Gaithin was. The son of Gaithin did not avoid them, but he opposed firmly and fiercely, as was his wont. A stubborn, fierce battle was fought there between them. Far were heard the cries of men suffering discomfiture, and the sound of the martial trumpets, and the earth shook, so that their horses and cattle ran terrified, which was a great hindrance to the valiant deeds of heroes. But, however, such of the host as were in the clefts of the rocks came down to the cattle and stopped many of them. Great was the clamour[r], and great was the noise in the air over them. Therefore Cearbhall was instructing his people, for it was the beginning of the night, and he said: "Wherever the enemy come from us to you, let not one of you move from his place of battle, and keep firmly to the enemy." Cearbhall went with a force to his sister's son, Cennédigh, who was in great jeopardy among his enemies, and he raised his firm voice aloud, and encouraged his people against the Leinster-men (and the Leinster-men heard it), and his people were encouraging him. He ordered two of his people to keep watch for him. The King of Leinster aimed a half javelin at them, and killed one of them, i. e. Folachtach, vice-abbot of Cill-dara. Great indeed was the din and tumult that prevailed between them at this time, and Badhbh[s] showed herself among them, and there was a great massacre

to the Royston, or carrion crow; so that the meaning may, perhaps, be that birds of prey began to appear on the field of battle, attracted by the dead bodies.

bρeiċ a pi leo, ⁊ ó nap féo an pí a ḟluaġ o'popċao na pappaò po liηg ap a eaċ ⁊ ċáiniġ anoiaiġ a ṁuinnpipe. Ap oeiṁin linn ġonaò τpe miopḃail naoiṁ ḃpiġoe ⁊ Sein Ciapáin po pġaoilpioc aṁlaiò pin; ⁊ cia po mapḃaò paopclanna fcuippa, ní paḃa áp móp ann. Ní pa léiġ Cfpḃall ná Cennéoiġ na muinnċip lṁṁuin Laiġfn ap ḟaiċ-énip. Ro mapḃaò 'pan ló ap na ṁápaċ opfin oo Laiġniḃ po ḃaċċup pop pfépán. Cáηġaccup Cfpḃall ⁊ Cennéoiġ na ccač efn-ġailce cópaiġċe τpé láp a náṁao ġo Ġaḃpán, o'iopnpoiġiò pi 'Eipfnn .i. Qoòa Pinnléić, (oeipḃpiup Cfpḃail a t́fipaoe, ⁊ máċaip an Cennéoiġ f) ⁊ innipio oo pí 'Eipfnn aṁail oo pala oóiḃ .i. lonġpopc oo ġaḃail poppa ⁊ċa. Oo ponpao compáò ċaipipi, ⁊ po oeiġlipioo iapccáin.

Rí Laiġfn ní hfó oo piġne pfpġpa maič oo ċaḃaipc pop pí 'Eipfnn, aċc ip cuiṁṁuġaò na nofinpao pip oo piġne, ⁊ ni ċapao efop no ġiall.

Ip in bliaòain pi oo ponpao na piġ Loċlann popḃaipi pop Spiač Cluaiòe i mḃpeačnaiḃ; pé ceċpe miópaiḃ aġ popḃaipi oóiḃ puippe, pa oeoiġ ċpa iap ppoppaċ an loċċa po ḃaoi innċe oo ġopτa ⁊ o'íoċċaiò, ap ċτpaġaò ġo hioiġnaiò an ċoḃaip po ḃaoi aca ap méòon: po cuap poppa iapcca n. Ruġaò ċpa ap ċúp ġaċ maičup po ḃui innce. Ruġaò plóġ móp eipτe i mḃpiaio [Oupalcaċ Pipḃipiġh po pġpioḃ 1643] inġuič ċpanpepipτop ppimup.

Kal. Maoiiġal, ab bfinčaip, quievic.

Ouḃčač,

* *Srath-cluaide*.—This is the Irish name for Strathclyde in Scotland, but it is evidently a mistake for Ailech Cluathe, which was the old name of Dunbarton. This entry is given in the Annals of Ulster at the year 869 [870] as follows :—" Obsessio Ailech Cluathe, a Norddmannis, i. e. Amlaiph et Imhar duo reges Norddmannorum obsederunt arcem illum et distruxerunt in fine .iiii. mensium arcem et predaverunt."—*Dublin MS*. So also the Welsh Annals, e. g. the Annales Cambriæ, A. D. 870, " Arx Alt-Clut a gentilibus fracta est."—Brut y Tywysogion, A. D. 870, ae y torret Kaer Alclut y gan y Paganyeit; "and Caer Alclut was demolished by the Pagans."

" *Dubhaltach Firbisigh*.—The meaning

massacre between them to and fro. The Leinster-men slipped away from the camp, and were carrying off their king, and when the king could not stop his men from flying, he mounted his horse and followed after his people. We are certain that it was through a miracle of St. Brighit and the Old Ciaran that they separated in this manner; for although nobles were slain between them, there was no great slaughter. Neither Cearbhall nor Cennédigh permitted their people to pursue the Leinster-men, through fear. On the next day some of the Leinster-men who had gone astray were slain. Cearbhall and Cennédigh came in a solid arrayed phalanx through the middle of their enemies to Gabhran [Gowran] to meet the King of Erin, i. e. Aedh Finnliath (the sister of Cearbhall was his wife, and she was the mother of Cennédigh), and they told the King of Erin what had happened to them, i. e. how their camp had been entered, &c. They conversed affectionately, and then separated.

The King of Leinster did not give the King of Erin a good answer, but reminded him of all they had done to him, and gave him neither tribute nor hostages.

In this year the Lochlann King laid siege to Srath-cluaide[t] in Britain, and they continued the siege for four months; at length, however, after having wasted the people who were in it by hunger and thirst, having wonderfully drawn off the well they had within, they entered [the fort] upon them. At first they carried off all the riches that were within it, and afterwards a great host of prisoners were brought into captivity. [Dubhaltach Firbisigh[u] wrote this, 1643] Inquit transcriptor primus.

[871.] Kal. Maenghal[x], Abbot of Beannchar [Bangor], died.

Dubhthach,

is, that the note, "Dubhaltach Firbisigh ro ρεροιδ 1643," was made by Mac Firbis's, the first *transcriber* of these Annals, from whose autograph the Brussels copy was made. See "Introd. Remarks," pp. 1, 2.

[x] *Maenghal*.—Ann. F.M 869; Ult. 870;

Dubtac, ab Cill Acaiḋ epircopur, rcpiba et anchopita quieuit.
Ailill, epircop ⁊ ab Foḃaip, quieuit.
Cupui, ab Inpi Cloṫpann, raoi rṁcura 'Eipſn, quieuit.
Aṁlaoiḃ ⁊ Imap do ṫoiḃeċt apíḃpi a hAlbain ⁊o- h-'Aṫcliaṫ, ⁊ bpaḋ mór bpiſtan ⁊ Alban, ⁊ Saxon leó, ḋá ċéd long a líon.
To⁊ail Ohuin Soḃaip⁊e, quod antea nunquam factum ept.
Ailill mac Ounlain⁊, pi Lai⁊ſn ⁊ Nopthmann interfectur ept.
Maolmuaḋ mac Finnaċta pí Aipṫip Life mopitur. Plaitſṁ mac Faolċaip do ḃáḋaḋ do ṁuinntip Leiṫ⁊linne.
Inpſḋ Connaċt la Crṗḃall ⁊ Ounċaḋ, i ttopċaip buaċail mac Ounaḋai⁊. Inpſḋ Muiṁan ona la Crṗḃall ḋap Luaċaip piap.
Aṁlaoiḃ do dol a h-'Eipinn i Loċlainn do ċo⁊aḋ ap Loċlanḋaiḃ ⁊ do ċon⁊naṁ rá a aṫaip .i. ⁊orrid, uaip no Loclannai⁊ a⁊ co⁊aḋ na cſinpaiḋe ap ttiaċtain ó a aṫaip ap a cſnn, ⁊ apa ba faḋa ra inipin cúip a ċo⁊aiḋ ⁊ apa lai⁊rḋ tpemḃip⁊rp cu⁊ainn cid a⁊ainn no beiṫ a fiop, rá⁊ḃam ⁊an a r⁊pnḃrnn, uaip atá áp n-oḃaip im neoċ ap o"Epinn do rcpiḃrnn, ⁊ cid ní iaḋpaiḋe uile, uaip ní namá fuil⁊iḋ na h'Epſnnai⁊ uile na Loċlann, aċt fuil⁊iḋ uile iomḋa uata féin.
Ir in ḃliaḋain ri .i. an ḋcſmaḋ bliaḋain flaṫa Aoḋa Finnléiṫ, ro ṁrerttar Iomap mac ⁊oṫrraiḋ, mic Ra⁊naill, mic ⁊oṫrraiḋ Conun⁊, mic ⁊oṫrraiḋ, ⁊ mac an rip ra ċuaiḋ a h'Eipinn .i. Aṁlaoiḃ, Eipe o iapṫup ⁊o haipṫeap, ⁊ ó der⁊capt ⁊o tuip⁊eaat.

Kal.

but the true year is 871.

ʲ *Cill-achaidh.*—Now Killeigh, a village in the barony of Geashill, King's County.

ᶻ *Amhlaeibh and Imhar.*—Ann. Ult., A. D. 870 [871].

ᵃ *Family.*—i. e. the monks of Leighlin.

ᵇ *From Erin to Lochlann.*—There is no account of this in the published Annals.

ᶜ *The tenth.*—i. e. the year 873. This plundering is not noticed in the published Annals.

Dubhthach, Abbot of Cill-achaidh[y], bishop, scribe, and anchorite, died.

Ailell, Bishop and Abbot of Fobhar [Fore], died.

Curui, Abbot of Inis Clothrann [in Loch Ribh], the most learned of all the Irish in history, died.

Amhlacibh and Imhar[z], came again from Alba [Scotland], to Ath-cliath [Dublin], having a great number of prisoners, both British, Scottish, and Saxon. Two hundred ships was their number.

The demolition of Dún-Sobhairce [Dunseverick], which was never done before.

Ailell, son of Dunlang, King of Leinster and of the Norsemen, was slain.

Maelmuadh, son of Finnachta, King of Airther-Liffe, died. Flaithemh, son of Faelchar, was drowned by the family[a] of Leithglinn.

Connaught was plundered by Cearbhall and Dunchadh, on which occasion Buachail, son of Dunadhach, was slain. Munster was also plundered beyond Luachair westwards by Cearbhall.

Amhlacibh went from Erin to Lochlann[b] to wage war on the Lochlanns, and to aid his father Goffridh, for the Lochlanns had made war against him, his father having come for him; but as it would be tedious to relate the cause of the war, and besides it appertains but little to us, though we have a knowledge of it, we forbear writing it, for our business is not to write whatever may belong to Erin, nor even all these; for the Irish suffer evils, not only from the Lochlanns, but they also suffer many injuries from one another.

[873.] In this year, the tenth[c] of the reign of Aedh Finnliath, Imhar, son of Godfraidh, Conung, son of Godfraidh, and the son of the man who went away from Erin, i. e. Amhlacibh, plundered all Erin from west to east, and from south to north.

[872.]

Kal. Ṡnia ab Daimliaġ Cianain, epircopur et reṗiba et anachoṗeta, quieuit :—

Uair Ṡnia ṡrian ar ccaoméḃainne.
Cḟnn craḃuiṗ inri 'Emir
Do ġaḃ narap naomrainne,
Comarba Cianain caliṡ.
Céin máir raṁaṗ ṗoriciaibe
Dia mba cḟnn céim ġan cina
Dirran minv már molḃrariġe
'Ar cara caoiṁrionn Ṡniaa.

Cḟnraolaṗ Ua Muiétiġḟrna, rí Cairil, ⁊ comarba Aiḃve,
Fḟrvoimnaé ab Cluana mic Noir.
Loinṡrioé mac Foillen, rrinceṗr Cille Auraille, et. m.
Robarcaé Dḟirmaiġe, reṗiba moriéur.

Orġain rḟr na ctrí maiġe ⁊ na ṡ-Comanv ṡo Sliaḃ blaṗma
vo riaogaiḃ Ṡall i rnḟéta na ṗele briġve.
Ir in bliaġain ri .i. unvecima anno reġni Aoṗa, ra écarrriṅṡ
báirié, ⁊ vna aitté é vo mac an riġ, lonṡa ioinva ó muir riar ṡo
Loé Ri leir, ṡo ro imll ailéna Loéa Ri eroiḃ, ⁊ na feṗanna comṗoéruibe, ⁊ Maġ luirṡ. Ir anrain ro faor Dia comarba Columi
a láṁaiḃ na Loélann, ⁊ mar ro éuaiṗ ar a láṁaiḃ, an vaṗ leo bu
coiṗte cloiéé é.

'Eġ

ᵈ *Gnia.*—The death of this bishop and the succeeding obits are entered in the Ann. F. M. at 870; Ann. Ult. 871. The verses on the death of Gnia are also quoted, with some variations of reading, by the Four Masters.

ᵉ *Emhir's Island.*—i. e. Ireland, the island of Emhir, Eber, or Heber, the celebrated Milesian chieftain.

ᶠ *Of Ailbhe.*—i. e. Bishop of Emly.

ᵍ *Three plains.*—This entry is given in the Ann. F. M. at 870: where, see note.

ʰ *The eleventh.*—i. e. the year 874.

ⁱ *Barith.*—There is no account of this

[872.] Kal. Gnia[d], Abbot of Daimhliag-Cianain [Duleek], bishop, scribe, and anchorite, died.

For Gnia was the sun of our fair race,
Head of the piety of Emhir's Island[e],
He celebrated the festivals of the saints,
The successor of the wise Cianán.
For a long time the bright congregation,
Of which he was head, had dignity without obscurity.
Alas! for the great precious gem,
Our fair, bright friend, Gnia.

Cennfaeladh Ua Muichtigherna, King of Caisel, and successor of Ailbhe[f] [died].

Ferdomhnach, Abbot of Cluain-mic-Nois [died].

Loingsech, son of Foillen, chief [abbot] of Cill Ausaille [Killossy], died.

Robhartach, of Dearmhach [Durrow], a scribe, died.

[872.] The plundering of the men of the Three Plains[g], and of the Comanns as far as Sliabh Bliadhna [Slieve Bloom], by the Kings of the Galls in the snow of Bridgetmas.

[873.] In this year, the eleventh[h] of the reign of Aedh, Barith[i], who was tutor to the King's son, drew many ships from the sea westwards to Loch Ri[k], and he plundered the islands of Loch Ri out of them, and the neighbouring lands, and also Magh Luirg[l]. On this occasion God saved the successor of Columb from the hands of the Lochlanns, and when he escaped from their hands they thought that he was a pillar-stone.

The

Barith, or his expedition, in the published Annals.

[k] *Loch Ri.*—Or Loch Ribh, now Lough Ree, an expansion of the Shannon between Athlone and Lanesborough.

[l] *Magh Luirg.*—Moylurg, i. e. the baro-

Ex ɼíg Loċlann, .i. Goɼɼaiḋ, ꝺo ti ꝋmaimm gɼána opoṅꝺ, ɼic enim Ꝺeo placuit.
Imnḟoa ḃɼſcan in hoc anno.
Ꝺeeɼc ciɼciceɼ aḃ anno 871 aꝺ ann. 900.
Ḳal. Inoɼṡċcaċ mac Ꝺoḃailén, aḃ ḃſiṅċaiɼ quieuic.

Tɼí ċéꝺ ḃliaʒain caꝺa cuiɼ
O éicɼioċc Comgaill ḃſiṅċaiɼ,
Go ɼé ɼo maiꝺ ɼuaċaɼ nʒle.
Inoɼſċcaiʒ aiɼꝺ oiɼoniꝺe.

Maolɼóil, pɼincepɼ Spuɼɼa Guaiɼe, moɼicuɼ.
Ƒuɼaꝺɼán mac Gaɼḃáin, ɼecnaḃ Cille aċaiḋ, moɼicuɼ.
Ċéle mac Ioɼċuile, ɼecnaḃ Aċaiḋ ḃó Cannig, moɼicuɼ.
Ƒlann mac Ꝺoṁnaill, ɼigḋamna an cuaiɼʒiɼc, moɼicuɼ.
Ecenſcan mac Ꝺálaiʒ, ɼí Cinel Conaill moɼicuɼ.
Ciaɼmac hUa Ꝺunaꝺaiʒ, ɼí Gaḃɼac, moɼicuɼ.
Guin Muiɼſḋaiʒ mic Ꝺoṁnaill, ɼiogḋamna Laigſi.
Ciaɼoꝺaɼ mac Cɼunnmaoil, ɼi hUa Ƒelmſḋa moɼicuɼ.
Moɼɼ Ślaiɼine mic Uiɼine, ɼí hUa Maccaile. Aɼ ꝺo ḃaɼ
Eiccneċáin, Inoɼſċcaiʒ, Ƒlainn, ⁊ Ciaɼmaċáin, ac ɼuḃɼaꝺ:—

Ecc aɼ eiciʒ ƒoɼaccaiḃ
Sluaʒa ɼaigſɼ iaɼ ɼſccaiḃ

Maɼꝺ

ny of Boyle, in the county of Roscommon.

ᵐ *The King of the Lochlanns.*—The death of this King is noticed in the Ann. F. M. at 871, Ult. at 872; but no mention is made of the ugly disease. The Ulster Annals say: "Imhar *Rex Normannorum totius Hiberniæ et Britanniæ vitam finivit.*"— *Dublin MS.*

ⁿ *A chasm.*—The words "Deest circiter," &c., are a note by the transcriber in the margin of the MS.

º *Indrechtach.*—These entries are given in the Ann. F. M. at 901; Ult. 905; but the true year is 906.

ᵖ *Ui-Felmedha.*—i. e. the barony of Ballaghkeen, in the county of Wexford, now

The King of the Lochlanns[m] died of an ugly, sudden disease. *sic enim Deo placuit.*
Britain was much annoyed this year.
A chasm[n] from about the year 871 [873] to the year 900.
[906.] Kal. Indrechtach[o], son of Dobhailen, Abbot of Beannchar [Bangor], died.

> One in three hundred fair revolving years,
> From the death of Comhghall of Beanchar,
> To the period of the happy death
> Of the great illustrious Indrechtach.

Maelpoil, chief [i. e. abbot] of Sruthair Guaire, died.
Furadhran, son of Gabhran, Prior of Cill-achaidh, died.
Ceile, son of Urthuile, Prior of Achadh bo Cainnigh [Agabo], died.
Flann, son of Domhnall, royal heir of the North, died.
Egnechan, son of Dálach, King of Cinel Conaill, died.
Ciarmac Ua Dunadhaigh, King of [Ui Conaill] Gabhra, died.
The killing of Muiredhach, son of Domhnall, royal heir of Leinster.
Ciarodhar, son of Crunnmhael, King of Ui-Felmedha[p], died.
The death of Glaisin, son of Uisin, King of Ui-Maccaille[q]. It was of the death of Eignechán, Indrechtach, Flann, and Ciarmacan, was said :—

> Death has left destitute[r]
> The hosts[s] who seek after precious gifts;

If called the Murchoos, or O'Murphy's country.

[q] *Ui-Maccaille.*—Now Imokilly, Co. Cork.

[r] *Destitute.*—These verses are also quo-

ted by the F. M. at A. D. 901, whose chronology is about five years antedated at this period.

[s] *The hosts.*—viz. the poets.

Mapo cloí ven ní péicpec,
Móp liac Eccnec i n-éccaib.
Eccnac ba bubaing b'óccaib
Rí ceinnil Conaill cstaig,
Oippan gnúip cpeobap mibenb
Po cuinn ípenn iap n-éccaib.
Inbpícac bínnéuip buibnig,
Ciapmac Zabpa gaipmpobpaig,
Flann Feabail pial pii bobuing,
'Eccnec pil Conaill caingnig.

Ipce epc cpigepimup annup pegni Flainn mic Maoilpecloinn. Anni Oomini bcccc. Ra cionalab mopfluag ffíp muman lap in oíp ceona .i. la Plaicbípac, ¬ la Copmaic b'iappaib bpáigib Laigín ¬ Oppaige, ¬ pa báccup fip Muman uile i n-aonlongpoipc. Do pala Plaicbeapcac ap a eoc ap fub ppaici 'pin longpopc: copcaip a eac i gclaip noomain paoi, ¬ ba cel olc bopom pain. Sochmbe ba muincip fén, ¬ bon cpluag uile bo náp b'áil bol an cpluagca ap a haicle pin; uaip bá cel buaibpioc leo uile an cuicimpi an buine naoim. Cangaccap cpa cícca uaiple ó Laignib, ó Chípball mac Muipígain, b'ionnpoigib Chopmaic ap cúp, ¬ pa labpaccap

' *Thirtieth year.*—Flann succeeded in the year 879, and the year here intended in 908.

" *A. D.* Dcccc.—This is a mistake for Dccccviii.

' *The same two.*—No reference is made to these two great ecclesiastics in any previous part of these Annals, which shows that there is a chasm of some years here.

' *Flaithbhertach.*—i. e. Flaithbhertach Mac Iumhainen, Abbot of Inis-Cathaigh, now Scattery Island, in the Shannon, near the town of Kilrush.

' *Cormac.*—That is, Cormac Mac Cuilemain, King of Munster and Bishop of Cashel. This battle is given by the F. M. at A. D. 903, and in the Ann. Ult. at 907, but the true year was 908. The scribe writes in the margin of our MS.: " *De morte Cormaci filii Culennani, regis Mo-*

If it has changed the colour of a potent king,
Great grief that Eignech has died.
Eignech, who was the sternest of youths,
King of the populous Cinel Conaill,
Alas! that his face, shrivelled, colourless, is left
Beneath the surface of the clay in death.
Indreachtach of populous Beannchar,
And Ciarmhac of Gabhra, of great fame,
Flann Feabhail, generous, resolute against difficulty,
Egnech of the race of Conall of goodly councils.

[908.] This is the thirtieth year[t] of the reign of Flann, son of Maelsechlainn.

[908.] A. D. DCCCC[u]. The great host of Munster was assembled by the same two[x], i. e. by Flaithbhertach[y] and Cormac[z], to demand the hostages of Leinster and Osraighe, and all the men of Munster were in the same camp. Flaithbhertach went on horseback through the streets of the camp; his horse fell under him into a deep trench, and this was an evil omen[a] to him. There were many of his own people, and of the whole host, who did not wish to go on the expedition after this, for they all considered this fall of the holy man as an ominous presage. But noble ambassadors came from Leinster, from Cearbhall, son of Muirigan, to Cormac first, and they delivered a message of peace from the Leinster-men, i. e. one peace to be in all Erin

moniæ, Archiepiscopi *Casseliensis et Martyris*." Dr. Hanmer says that Cormac was killed by the Danes, but Dr. Keating, in his "History of Ireland," from the historical tract called *Cath Belaigh Mughna*, i. e. the Battle of Ballaghmoon, states that King Cormac was not slain by the Danes, but by the Leinster-men.

[a] *An evil omen.*—Col ole. The scribe glosses the word col by pȧipcino, in the margin. Dr. Lynch, in his translation of Keating's "History of Ireland," translates it *malum omen*. See Ann. F. M., p. 566, note.

2 D

paṫṫaṗ ṫfṫṫaiṗfṫ ṗíoḃa, im méiḋc aṫ ḋfṗṗ ṫo ó Laiġniḃ, .i. aoin ṗiḃc ṫo beiṫ i n-'Eiṗinn uile ġo ḃealṫaine aṗ a cṫionn, uaiṗ ṫoiṫ-ṫiġfṗṗ ṫ'ṗoġṁaṗ an ṫanṗain, a ḃṗaiġṫe ṫo ṫaḃaiṗṫ an fṗláiṁ Maonaiġ, an ṫuine naoiṁ fġnaiṫ ṫṗaiḃṫiġ, ⁊ ṫaoine eile ṫṗaiḃ-ṫeṫa; ṗeoiḋ ⁊ maiṫiuṗa ioṁḋo ṫo ṫaḃaiṗṫ ṫo Plaiṫḃeaṗṫaṫ ⁊ ṫo Choṗmaṫ. Ḃá ṗailiḋ ġo móṗ la Coṗmaṫ an ṫṗíoṗin ṫo ṫaiṗġṗin ṫo, ⁊ ṫáiniġ iaṗṗin ḃá innṗin ṫo Plaiṫḃeaṗṫaṫ, ⁊ ṗa inniṗ ṫo-ṗaiḃe aṁail ṫuġaḋ ṫuiġe ó Laiġniḃ. Aṁail ṗo ṫuala Plaiṫḃeaṗ-ṫaṫ ṗin, ṗo ġaḃ aḋuaṫ móṗ ⁊ aṗeḋ ṗo ṗáiḋ: Pailliṗiġiḋ, aṗ ṗé, ṫo ḃfġinfinamnaiḃe, ⁊ ḋfṗoile ṫo einṫoil ṫṗeoḋ, uaiṗ maṫ ṫomaiṫiġ ṫu; ⁊ ṗa ṗaiḋ ḃṗiaṫṗa ioṁḋa ṗeaṗḃa ṫaṗṫaṗlaṫa aṗ ṗaḋa ṗe n-inniṗin.

Aṗ é ṗṗfġṗa ṫuġ Coṗmaṫ ṗaiṗṗioṁ: Aṗ ṫeṁin lfṁṗa ṫno, aṗ Coṗmaṫ, an ní ḃiaṗ ṫe ṗin .i. ṫaṫ ṫo ṫuṗ, a ṫuine naoiṁ, aṗ Coṗ-maṫ, ⁊ ḃiaṗa ṗo ṁalaṫṫain ṫe, ⁊ aṗ ṫoṫa ḃáṗ ṫṗaġail ṫuiṫ. Aġuṗ ó ṫuḃaiṗṫ ṗin, ṫáiniġ ṫa ṗuḃall ṗéin, ⁊ ṗé ṫuiṗṗioṫ ṫoḃṗónaṫ, ⁊ ó ṗo ṗuiḋ ṗo ġaḃ ṗíoṫal uḃall ṫuġaḋ ṫá, ⁊ ṗo ḃaoi ġa ṗṗoḋail ṫá ṁuinn-ṫiṗ, ⁊ aṗeḋ ṗo ṗáiḋ: A ṁuinnṫiṗ ionṁain, aṗ ṗé, ní ṫioḋnaṫaiḃ-ṗi uḃla ṫuiḃ ón uaiṗṗi amaṫ ġo ḃṗáṫ. Anoṫḋ a ṫiġeaṗna ionṁuin ṫalṁanṫa, aṗ a ṁuinnṫiṗ, ṫiḋ 'ma noṗinaiṗ ḃṗón ⁊ ṫuḃa ṫuinn? Iṗ miniṫ ṫo ġní inoṫélmuine ṫúinn. Aṗeḋ ṫno ṗo ṗáiḋṗioṁ; ṫiḋ óṅ, a ṁuinnṫiṗ ionṁuin, ṫá ní ṫuḃṗioṫ ṗo ṗáiḋiaṗ? Uaiṗ bfġ a n-ioṅġ-naḋ ġen ġo ṫṫuġainnṗi uḃla ṫuiḃ aṗ mo láiṁ ṗéin; uaiṗ biaiḋ nfṫ éiġin uaiḃṗi um ṗaṗṗaḋ ṫioḋnaiṫṗfṗ uḃla ṫuiḃ. Ro óṗṫaiġ ṗoṗ-aiṗeḋ iaṗṫṫain. Ro ġaiṗmfṫ ṫuiġe annṗin an ṫuine naoṁṫa, ṫṗaiḃ-ḋfṫ fġnaiḋ (Maonaṫ maṫ Siaḋail), aṗṫṫoṁaṗba Comġaill, ⁊ ṫo ṗiġne

---

[b] *Séds.*—i. e. jewels, precious stones.

[c] *Apples.*—Keating has the same artless words, but Dr. Lynch, in his Latin trans-lation of Keating, improves the style thus: "Nunquam posthac (inquit) *quid-quam* inter vos, O charissimi, distri-

Erin until May following (it being then the second week in Autumn), and to give hostages into the keeping of Maenach, a holy, wise, and pious man, and of other pious men, and to give séds[b] and much property to Cormac and Flaithbhertach. Cormac was much rejoiced at being offered this peace, and he afterwards came to tell it to Flaithbhertach, and how it was brought to him from Leinster. When Flaithbhertach heard this, he was greatly horrified, and said: "This shows," said he, "the littleness of thy mind, and the feebleness of thy nature, for thou art the son of a plebeian;" and he said many other bitter, insulting words, which it would be tedious to repeat.

The answer which Cormac made him was: "I am certain," said Cormac, "of what the result of this will be; a battle will be fought, O holy man," said he, "and Cormac shall be under a curse for it," and it is likely that it will be the cause of death to thee." And when he said this, he came to his own tent, being afflicted and sorrowful, and when he sat down he took a basinful of apples which was brought him, and he proceeded to divide them among his people, and he said: "Beloved people," said he, "I shall never present you with apples from this hour henceforth." "Is it so, O dear earthly lord," said his people; "why dost thou exhibit sorrow and melancholy to us? It is often thou hast boded evil for us." "It is what I say; but, beloved people, what ominous thing have we said, for it is no great wonder that I should not distribute apples among you with my own hand, for there shall be some one of you in my place who will present you with apples"[c]. He afterwards ordered a watch to be set, and he called to him the holy, pious, and wise man (Maenach[d], son of Siadhal), the chief Comharba of Comhghall, and he made his confession and his will

buam."

[d] *Maenach.*—He was abbot of Disert-Diarmada, now Castledermot in the county of Kildare, which was one of the monasteries founded by Diarmaid, coarb of St. Comgall, of Bangor.

ṗiġne a ḟaoiṗiḋin 7 a ċiomna na ḟiaḋnaiṗi, 7 ṗo ċaiċ Coṗp Cṗíoṗc aṗ a láiṁ, 7 ḋo ṗaḋ láiṁ ṗiṗ an ṗaoġal 'na ḟiaḋnuṗe in Maonaiġ, uaiṗ ṗo ḟicoiṗ ġo maiṗṗiċe 'ṗin caċ é, aċc níoṗ ḃáil ḋo ṗoċuiḋe ḋá ḟioṗ ḟaiṗ. Ṙo ḃaoi ḋno ġá ṗáḋa a ċoṗṗ ḋo ḃṗeiċ ġo Cluain uaṁa ḋa mbeiċ a ṗṗoiṗḃe, muna beiċ ḋno, a ḃṗeiċ ġo ṗelic Ḋiaṗmaḋa mic Aoḋa Ṙóin, bail i ṗaḃa aġ ḟoġluim ġo ṗaḋa. ḃa lánṗainc leiṗ imuṗṗo a aḋnacal i cCluain Uaṁa aġ mac Léinn. ḃa ḟeṗṗ imuṗṗo la Maoñaċ a aḋnacal iṗ in Ḋiṗioṗc Ḋiaṗmaḋa; uaiṗi ba baile la Comġall Ḋiṗioṗc Ḋiaṗmaḋa, 7 ṗa Coṁaṗba Coṁġaill Maonaċ. Aṗ é aṗ fġnaiḋe ṗo ḃaoi na aimṗiṗ, .i. Maonaċ mac Siaḋail, 7 ba móṗ ṗa ṗaoṫṗaiġ an can ṗa aġ ḋénaṁ ṗíoḋa eiḋiṗ Laiġniu 7 ḟioṗa Muṁan ḋa ṗṗéḋaḋ. Ṙo iméiġfccaṗ ṗoċoiḋe ḋo ḟluaġ Muṁan ġo nfṁċumḋaiġċe. Ṙo ḃaoi ḋno ġlóṗ móṗ 7 ṗeṗcan i Lonġṗoṗc ḟḟṗ Muṁan an can ṗa, uaiṗ ċualaḋaṗ Ḟlann mac Maoilṗeaċloinn ḋo ḃeiċ i lonġṗoṗc Laiġṡn ġo ṗlóġ móṗ ḋo ċoiṗ 7 ṗoṗ eoċ.

Aṗ an ṗin ṗo ṗaiḋ Maonaċ: A ḋaġḋoine Muṁan, aṗ ṗó, ba cóṗ ḋuiḃ na bṗaiġḋe maiċe caṗġuṗ ḋuiḃ ḋo ġaḃáil i nfṗláiṁ ḋaoine eṗaiḋḃfċ ġo beallcoine, .i. mac Cṗiḃaill ṗiġ Laiġṡn, 7 mac ṗiġ Oṗṗaiġe. Ṙa báccuṗ ṗiṗ Muṁan uile ġá ṗáḋa ġuṗ ob é Ḟlaiċ-ḃeaṗcaċ mac Ionmainen, a aonaṗ, ṗo coiṁéġniġ iaḋ im ċoiḃfċ i Laiġniḃ.

A haiċle an ġfṗáin móiṗ ḋo ṗonṗac canġaḋaṗ caṗ Sliaḃ Maiṗge iniaṗ ġo Ḋṗoiċḋo Leiċġlinne. Ṙo ċaiṗiṗ imuṗṗo Ciob-ṗaiḋe,

* *Cluain Uamha.*—Now Cloyne, in the county of Cork, of which St. Colman Mac Leinine was the founder and patron.

ᵗ *Diarmaid.*—i. e. to the cemetery of the church of Diarmaid. This Diarmaid was grandson of Aedh Roin, King of Uladh, and founded the Church of Disert Diar- mada, now Castle Dermot, which he dedicated to St. Comgall of Bangor about A. D. 800. He died A. D. 824 (Ann. Ult.). The Macnach here referred to was the successor of Diarmaid rather than the successor of St. Comgall, who does not appear to have ever been at the place.

will in his presence, and he took the body of Christ from his hand, and he resigned the world in the presence of Macnach, for he knew that he would be killed in the battle. But he did not wish that many should know this of him. He also ordered that his body should be brought to Cluain Uamha[e], if convenient; but if not, to convey it to the cemetery of Diarmaid[f], son [read, grandson] of Aedh Roin, where he had studied for a long time. He was very desirous, however, of being interred at Cluain Uamha of Mac Lenin. Macnach, however, was better pleased to have him interred at Disert-Diarmada, for Disert Diarmada was one of Comhghall's towns[g]; and Macnach was successor of Comhghal. This Macnach, son of Siadhail, was the wisest man in his time, and he exerted himself much at this time to make peace (if he could), between the men of Leinster and Munster. Many of the forces of Munster went away without restraint. There was great noise and dissension in the camp of the men of Munster at this time, for they had heard that Flann, son of Maelsechlainn, was in the camp of the Leinster-men with great forces of foot and horse.

It was then Macnach said: "Good men of Munster," said he, "ye ought to accept of the good hostages I have offered you to be placed in the custody of pious men till May next; namely, the son of Cearbhall, King of Leinster, and the son of the King of Osraighe." All the men of Munster were saying that it was Flaithbhertach, son of Ionmainén, alone, that compelled them to go into Leinster.

After this great complaint which they made, they came over Sliabh Mairge[h] from the west to Leithghlinn Bridge. But Tibraide, successor of Ailbhe [of Emly], and many of the clergy along with him, tarried

[g] *Towns.*—i. e. monasteries. See Dr. Todd's Book of Hymns, p. 136.

[h] *Sliabh Mairge.*—This name is still preserved in that of Slievemarague, a barony forming the south-east portion of the Queen's County, but the original Sliabh Mairge extended so far into the county of Kilkenny as to embrace the old church of

paide, camapba Ailbe, ⁊ pochaide do éléipaib ime i Leitȝlinn, ⁊ ȝiollada an tplóiȝ, ⁊ a ccapoill lóin illeitȝlinn. Ro pennid iap pin ptuic ⁊ caipmípta aȝ pípaib Mumcan ⁊ tanȝattup pímpa ȝo Maȝ n-Ailbe. Ro battup imuppo ⁊ a nopuim pa coille ndaingin oȝ iopnaide na námad. Do ponpat pip Mumhan tpí cata commopa commérde díob: Plaitbeaptat mac Ionmainen, ⁊ Ceallat mac Cípbaill pí Oppaiȝe pep in céd cat; Copmac mac Cuilfnáin pí Mumhan pe cat míboin Mumhan. Copmac mac Motla pí na nDéipi, ⁊ pí Ciappaiȝe ⁊ piȝ cinmid eile iombα, iaptap Mumhan ip in tpípp cat. Tanȝattup iapam amlaid pin ap Maȝ n-Ailbe. Ba ȝpánat iad ap iomad a námad, ⁊ ap a n-uaitpít péin. Apcd immpid coluiȝ .i. an lutt po baoi ptuppa ȝo padadap Laiȝin co n-a pocpaidib tpi cudpuma no ceitpe cudpumo, no apliu pe pípaib Mumhan do cum an cata. Ba tpuaȝ mop annuall po baoi ip in cat, amail impid caluiȝ .i. an lutt po baoi ipin cat .i. nuall an dapa pluaiȝ ȝá mapbad, ⁊ nuall an tploiȝ eile aȝ commaoidim an mapbta pin. Dá cuip imuppo po iompolainȝ maidm obann ap pípaib Muman .i. Celfcaip, bpátaip Cinȝeȝain, do leim ȝo hobann ap a eat, ⁊ map do linȝ ap a eat apcd paid: A paopclanna Mu- man, ap pé, teicid ȝo hobann on cat adutmap po, ⁊ léiȝíd eioip na cléipcíb péin na po ȝabpad comnaide eile act cat do tabaipt; ⁊ po téic iaptáin ȝo hobann, ⁊ pochaidc mop maille pip. Aȝap dno pat eile an madma : Ceallat mac Cípbaill, map at connaipc- pide an cat i padattup maite muinntipe piȝ 'Eipfnn aȝ tuapȝain
a cata

Teach Scoithin, now Tiscoffin.

¹ *Magh-Ailbe*.—This was the name of a large plain in the south of the county of Kildare. *Bealach Mughna*, where this battle was fought, still preserves that name, in the anglicized form Ballaghmoon. It is situated in the south of the county of Kildare, and about two miles and a half to the north of the town of Carlow. The site of the battle is still shown, and the stone on which King Cormac's head was cut off by a common soldier is not yet for-

ried at Leithghlinn, and also the servants of the army and the horses that carried the provisions. After this, trumpets were blown and signals for battle were given by the men of Munster, and they came before them to Magh-Ailbhe¹. Here they remained with their back to a fast wood, awaiting their enemies. The men of Munster divided themselves into three equally large battalions: Flaithbhertach, son of Inmainen, and Ceallach, son of Cearbhall, King of Osraighe, over the first division^k; Cormac, son of Cuilenán, King of Munster, over the middle division; Cormac, son of Mothla, King of the Deisi, and the King of Ciárraighe, and the kings of many other septs of West Munster, over the third division. They afterwards came in this order on Magh Ailbhe. They were querulous on account of the numbers of the enemy and their own fewness. The learned, i. e. [the scholars] that were among them, state that the Leinster-men and their forces amounted to three times or four times the number of the men of Munster, or more. Unsteady was the order in which the men of Munster came to the battle. Very pitiful was the wailing which was in the battle, as the learned who were in the battle relate, i. e. the shrieks of the one host in the act of being slaughtered, and the shouts of the other host exulting over that slaughter. There were two causes for which the men of Munster suffered so sudden a defeat, i. e. Céilechar, the brother of Cingégan, suddenly mounted his horse, and said: "Nobles of Munster," said he, " fly suddenly from this abominable battle, and leave it between the clergy themselves, who could not be quiet without coming to battle." And he suddenly fled afterwards, accompanied with great hosts. The other cause of the defeat was: when Cealach, son of Cearbhall, saw the battalion in which were the

gotten by tradition.

^k *Division.*—This agrees with the account of this battle given by Keating from the *Cath Bealaigh Mughna*. It is very probable that both accounts have been epitomized from the same original work.

a catɑ féin, ro ling ar a eaċ ⁊ ro raid re a ṁuinntir féin; Eir-
ġid ar ḃar n-ċaiḃ, ⁊ ionnarḃaid uaiḃ an luċt ruil in ḃar n-aiġid,
⁊ ge adruḃairtrim rin, ní do ċatuġad aḃunad adubairt, aċt ar
do ṫeiċim; aċt trá ro fár do na cauirḃ rin, teiċfo i nainfeċ do
na cataiḃ Muinṁnċaiḃ. Uċ tra, ba truaiġ ⁊ ba mór an t-ár ar
rud Maiġe Ailḃe iarttain. Ní coiġiltea cléirfċ rfċ laoċ ann rin.
Ḃa coimméd ra marḃ daoir, ⁊ ro diéfṅdaoir; an tan ra hainctea
laoċ no cléireċ ann, ní ar ṫrócaire do nítea, aċt rainc ḃa impu-
lanġ d'raġḃail ruarlaiġte uadaiḃ, nó dá mḃreit aġ roġnam ḃóiḃ.
Ṫerna tra Cormac an ri attoraċ an ċéd ċata. Aċt ro ling a
eaċ i cclair, ⁊ ra tuitriom don eoċ: óro ċoncattur dirfm d'á
ṁuinntir rin, ⁊ riad a maidm, tanġattur d'ionnroiġid an rí, ⁊ ra
ċuirftar ar a eaċ é. Ar ann rin ad ċonnairerioṁ dalcu dó fén,
raorclanda d'Eoġanaċt é, Aud a ainm, raoi eaġna ⁊ ḃreitḟiṁ-
naċta ⁊ rṡnċara é, ⁊ laidne; arcd ro ráid an rí fir: A meic ion-
ṁainn, ar ré, na lṡn diom-ra, Aċt nod ḃeir ar aṁail ar fern cot-
niocra. Ro innriura ḃuit-ri reiṁe ro ġo inuirride miri 'rin ċaċ
ro. Ro ċairir uaiṫċfd i frarriad Chormaic, ⁊ táinic reiṁe ar a
rud na rliġfd, ⁊ ba hiomda ruil daoine ⁊ eaċ ar rud na rliġfd
rin. Scicht dno corra deired a ciérioṁ ar an rliġid rleaṁain,
i rliočt na rola rin, tuitid an teaċ ar a hair riar, ⁊ ḃrirfd a
ḃruim ⁊ a ṁuinél ar ḃó, ⁊ ro ráid aġ tuitim: In manur tuar,
Domine, commendo rririrum meum; ⁊ raoiḃid a rriorad, ⁊
tḟġaid na meic mallaċtan eccraiḃḃſċa, ⁊ ġaḃaid ġaae dá colainn,
⁊ ġadaid a cṡn dá ċolainn.

ġér

[1] *Spared.*—Keating has nearly the same words, which Dr. Lynch has improved upon in his Latin translation, quoted in a note to the Annals of the F. M., A. D. 903. "Siquidem in illo conflictu, sacri et profani homines promiscuâ internecione mactabantur, nullâ ordinis aut dignitatis habitâ ratione."—*O'Donovan's Four Masters*, vol. i., p. 568, note.

[m] *His head.*—The F. M. state that it was

the chieftains of the people of the King of Erin cutting down his own battalion, he mounted his horse, and said to his own people: "Mount your horses, and drive the enemy before you." And though he said this, it was not to fight really he said so, but to fly. But, however, it resulted from these causes that the Munster battalions fled together. Alas! pitiful and great was the slaughter throughout Magh-Ailbhe afterwards. A cleric was not more spared[l] than a layman there; they were equally killed. When a layman or a clergyman was spared, it was not out of mercy it was done, but out of covetousness to obtain a ransom for them, or to bring them into servitude. King Cormac, however, escaped in the van of the first battalion, but his horse fell into a trench, and he fell off the horse. When a party of his people who were flying perceived this, they came to the king and put him up on his horse again. It was then he saw a foster-son of his own, a noble of the Eoghanachts, by name Aedh, who was an adept in wisdom and jurisprudence, and history, and Latin, and the king said to him: "Beloved son," said he, "do not follow me, but escape as well as thou canst. I told thee before now, that I should fall in this battle." A few remained along with Cormac, and he came forward along the way on horseback, and the way was besmeared throughout with much blood of men and horses. The hind feet of his horse slipped on the slippery way in the track of blood, and the horse fell backwards, and broke his [Cormac's] back and neck in twain, and he said, when falling, "In manus tuas, Domine, commendo spiritum meum," and he gave up the ghost; and the impious sons of malediction came and thrust darts through his body, and cut off his head[m].

Though

Fiach Ua Ugfadain, of Denlis, that cut off King Cormac's head, but the name of the place, as well as that of the family, is unknown to tradition, and the identification of them has hitherto escaped the ken of our topographical investigators.

Ġép ba iomḋa an marḃaḋ ar Maiġ Ailḃe, ra ḃerḃa a nair, nír bo raitſċ croiḋaċt Laiġſn ḋe rin, ġur ro lſnrat an ṁaiḋm tar Sliaḃ Mairġe riar, ⁊ ro ṁarḃrat raorċlanna iomḋa ḋon lſnṁain rin.

I ffortoraċ an ċaṫa ro ċéḋóir ro marḃaḋ Ceallaċ mac Cſrḃaill, rı Orraiġe, ⁊ a ṁac. Ar rġaoilteaċ imurro ro marḃaiḋ ó rin amaċ etir laoċ ⁊ cléirieaċ: ar mór ḋo cléirċiḃ maiṫe ro ṁarḃaḋ irin ċaṫ ro, ⁊ ar mór ḋo ríoġaiḃ, ⁊ ḋa ṫaoirioċuiḃ. Ro marḃaḋ ann Roġartaċ mac Suiḃne, in ruí reallroṁḋaċta ⁊ ḋiaḋaċta, rı Ciarraiġe, ⁊ Ailill mac Eoġain, an tairoſġnaiḋ óċċ ⁊ an t-árorʻaorċlann, ⁊ Colman, ab Cinnetiġ, áro ollaṁ breieſṁnaċta Eirſnn, ⁊ roċuiḋe ar ċſna, quor longum ert rcriḃere.

Na laoiċ imurro, Cormac rí na nDéiri, Duḃaġán, rı fFſr miaiġe, Cſnnfaolaḋ, rí hUa Conaill, Conn ḋar ⁊ Ainerlir ḋ'Uiḃ Ḟairoealḃaiġ, ⁊ Eiḋean rı Aiḋne, ro ḃaoi ar ionnarḃaḋ a Muṁain, Maolmuaḋ, Maḋuḋán, Duḃḋaḃairſnn, Conġal, Caṫarnaċ, Fſraḋaċ, Aoḋ, rí hUa Liaṫáin, ⁊ Ḋomnall rı Dúin Ceairmna.

Ar iaḋ ḋno ra ḃrir an ċaṫ ro .i. Flann mac Maoilreċloinn, Riġ 'Eirſnn, ⁊ Cſrḃall mac Muirſġan rí Laiġſn, ⁊ Taḋġ mac Faoláin rí hUa ġCionnriolaġ, Témenan, rí hUa nOſġa, Ceallaċ ⁊ Lorċán ḋa rí fear Cualann, Inḋeirġe mac Duiḃġiolla, rí hUa n-Ḋróna

---

ⁿ *Many good clergymen.*—This seems to imply that the clergy were wont to go on military expeditions so late as 908. Fothadh na Canoine had induced the monarch Aedh Oirdnighe (A. D. 804) to release the clergy from this barbarous duty, and Adamnan had made greater exertions, to the same effect, about a century earlier. But the union of the kingly with the episcopal dignity would appear to have encouraged the continuance of this custom to the time of Cormac Mac Cullenan, though, perhaps, not in the northern parts of Ireland, where the influence of the law of Adamnan and Fothadh prevailed at this time.

º *Cenn-Etigh.*—Now Kinnitty in the King's County.

Though extensive was the slaughter on Magh Ailbhe, to the East of the Bearbha [Barrow], the prowess of the Leinster-men was not satiated with it, but they followed up the route west across Sliabh Mairge, and slew many noblemen in that pursuit.

In the very beginning of the battle, Ceallach, son of Cearbhall, King of Osraighe, and his son, were killed at once. Dispersedly, however, others were killed from that out, both laity and clergy. There were many good clergymen[n] killed in this battle, as were also many kings and chieftains. In it was slain Fogartach, son of Suibhne, an adept in philosophy and divinity, King of Ciarraighe [Kerry], and Ailell, son of Eoghan, the distinguished young sage, and the highborn nobleman, and Colman, Abbot of Cenn-Etigh[o], Chief Ollamh of the judicature of Erin, and hosts of others also, of whom it would be tedious to write.

But the laymen were, Cormac, King of the Deisi, Dubhagan, King of Fera-Maighe [Fermoy], Cennfaeladh, King of of Ui-Conaill [Connilloc], Conodhar and Aneslis, of the Ui-Toirdhealbhaigh[p], and Eidhen, King of Aidhne[q], who was in exile in Munster; Maelmuadh, Madudan, Dubhdabhoirenn, Congal, Catharnach, Feradhach; Aedh, King of Ui-Liathain[r], and Domhnall, King of Dun-Cearmna[s].

But the persons who gained this battle were Flann, son of Maelseachlainn, King of Erin; and Cearbhall, son of Muirigen, King of Leinster; and Tadhg, son of Faelan, King of Ui-Ceinnsealaigh; Temhenan,

[p] *Ui-Toirdhealbhaigh.*—A tribe seated in the S. E. of the county of Clare, near Killaloe.

[q] *Aidhne.*—A territory coextensive with the diocese of Kilmacduagh, in the S. W. of the county of Galway. The Eidhen here mentioned was the progenitor of the famous family of O'Heyne.

[r] *Ui-Liathain.*—A tribe and territory nearly coextensive with the barony of Barrymore, county of Cork.

[s] *Dun-Cearmna.*—The ancient name of a fort situated on the Old Head of Kinsale, county of Cork.

n-Opóna, Pollaṁan mac Oilella pí Poṫapta Pea, Tuaṫal mac Uẓaipe pí hUa Muipṡaiẓ, Uẓpan mac Cinnéoiẓ, pi Laoiẓpi,¹ Maoléallann mac Pṡiẓaile, pí na pPopṫuaṫ, Cleipéén pí hUa mbaipce.ᵇ Táinẓ iaptan Plann, pí 'Eipṡnn, mapepluaẓ móp pioẓoa, ẓup po ioḃnaic Oiapmaio mac Cṡiḃaill i piẓe Oppaiẓe.

App ann pin tanẓattap opiṡm a n-aiẓio Plainn, ¬ cṡnn Copmaic an Rí aca: apeo po páiṫpioo pe Plann: "bṡṫa ¬ pláinte, a Rí ćumaċtaiẓ ċopẓpaiẓ, ¬ cṡnn Copmaic aẓain ouit; ¬ aṁail ap bép oo na píoẓaib, tóẓaib oo p'liapao, ¬ cuip an cṡnn po poite, ¬ popḃinẓ é oon p'liapaio. Ap ole, imuppo, aopubaipt Plann piuproiṁ, ní buiṡṡeap oo pao ḃóib. Móp an ẓníoin, ap ré, a cṡnn oo ẓoio oon Eppcop naoiṁ, a onóip imuppo, apeo oo ẓénpa, ¬ ní a ṗoipḃinẓ. Ra ẓaḃ Plann an cṡnn 'na láiṁ, ¬ po póẓ é, ¬ oo pao na timéioll po ṫpí an cṡnn coippeaca, [an naoiṁ eppcoip],ᵈ ¬ in píopmaipṫípeṫ. Ruẓaḃ uaḃ iapttain an cṡnn ẓo honópaċ uionnroiẓiḃ an ċuipp, bail a paḃa Maonaċ mac Siaḃail, coṁapba Coṁẓaill,

¹ *Uí Deaghaidh.*—A territory in the N. W. of the county of Wexford, nearly coextensive with the present barony of Gorey.

ᵃ *Feara-Cualann.*—A territory in the north of the county of Wicklow.

ⁱ *Uí-Drona.*—Now Idrone, county of Carlow.

᾿ *Fotharta-Fea.*—Now the barony of Forth, county of Carlow.

' *Uí-Muireadhaigh.*—A territory comprising the southern half of the present county of Kildare.

ᵏ *Laeighis.*—Now Leix, in the Queen's County.

ᵇ *Fortuatha.*—A territory in the county of Wicklow, comprising Glendalough and the neighbouring districts.

ᶜ *Uí Bairche.*—A territory comprising the present barony of Slievemarague in the S. E. of the Queen's County, and some of the adjoining districts of the county of Carlow.

ᵈ *With thy thigh.*—Keating has: "Here is the head of Cormac, King of Munster, for thee, sit upon it, as is the custom of [conquering] kings; but the monarch, far from complying with their request, reprimanded them, and said that it was very wicked to have cut off the head of the holy bishop; and he refused to treat it with any indignity. He took up the head in his hand, kissed it, and passed it thrice

nan, King of Ui-Denghaidh'; Ceallach and Lorcan, two Kings of Feara-Cualann"; Inneirghe, son of Duibhgilla, King of Ui-Drona˟; Follamhan, son of Oilell, King of Fotharta-Fea˟; Tuathal, son of Ugaire, King of Ui Muireadhaigh˟; Ughran, son of Cennedigh, King of Laeighis˟; Maelehallann, son of Ferghal, King of the Fortuatha⁶; Clereén, King of Ui-Bairche˟.

Flann, King of Erin, came with a numerous royal body of horse, and he escorted Diarmaid, son of Cearbhall, into the kingdom of Osraighe.

Then a party came up to Flann, having the head of Cormac with them, and what they said to Flann was: "Life and health, O powerful, victorious king! We have the head of Cormac for thee, and, as is customary with kings, raise thy thigh, and put this head under it, and press it with thy thigh"ᵈ. Flann, however, spoke angrily to them instead of giving them thanks. "It was an enormous act," said he, "to have taken off the head of the holy bishop; but, however, I shall honour it instead of crushing it." Flann took the head into his hand, and kissed it, and had carried round him thrice the consecrated head [of the holy bishop], and of the true martyr. The head was

around him in token of respect and veneration." Dr. Lynch, in his Latin Translation of Keating's History, improves the style thus :—" Invictissime Rex simul et felicissime, En regis in praelio caesi caput ad tuos pedes projicimus, ei tu inside et totâ corporis mole innitere, (superioribus enim Hiberniae regibus solemne fuit hostici regis in praelio caesi caput femori suppositum duriori sessione premere). Itane orationem et munus non gratulatione aliquâ, sed acerbissimâ deferentium increpa-

tione rex excepit, nec solum sacrum caput tam contumeliosè tractare renuit, verum etiam in percussores acriter invectus quòd sacrato episcopo violentas manus afferre ausi fuerint. Deinde caput ipsum reverenter exceptum osculatus tribus sibi vicibus circumdatum honore debito prosecutus, Mainacho Siadhulli filio, Comgelli successori deferendum dedit, qui caput unà cum trunco corpore justis pro dignitate ritè persolutis, Deserti Diermodi humari curavit."

ꝼaill, ⁊ puȝꞃaiḋe coꞃp Coꞃmaic ȝo Oiꞃioꞃt Ḋiaꞃmata, ⁊ ꞃo [haḋnaiceaḋ ȝo] honoꞃaċ ann ꞃinn é, bail a nḋénann ꝼſꞃta ⁊ mioꞃḃaille.

Cia tꞃa naċ tiȝ cꞃiḋe ⁊ noċ ci an in ȝníoṁ móꞃꞃa, .i. maꞃḃaḋ ⁊ tſꞃcaḋ (ḋ'aꞃmaiḃ aḋétċiṁḃ) an ḋuine naoiṁ aꞃ mo ſnȝnaṁ táiniȝ ⁊ tiocꞃa ḋꝼſꞃaiḃ 'Eiꞃſnn ȝo bꞃaċ Saoi na Ȝaoiḃilȝe, ⁊ na Laiḋne, an t-áiꞃḋeꞃꞃcoꞃ láncꞃaiḃſc, láin-ioḋan, míoꞃbuiḋa, in-ȝſnuꞃ, ⁊ in-ſꞃnaiȝte, an ꞃaoi ꞃſċaꞃḃaċta, ⁊ ȝaċ ſȝna, ȝaċ ꝼſꞃꞃa, ⁊ ȝaċ eolaiꞃ, ꞃaoi ꞃiliḋaċta ⁊ ꝼoȝluma, cſin ḋéꞃeiꞃce, ⁊ ȝaċ ꞃualċa, ⁊ ꞃaoi ꞃoiꞃċſḋail, aiꞃoꞃí ḋá ċoiȝſḃ Muṁan uile ꞃe ꞃé.

Ro iompꞃa tꞃa Flann, Rí 'Eiꞃſnn aꞃ ꝼꝼáȝḃail Ḋiaꞃmaḋa i ꞃiȝe Oꞃꞃaiȝe, aꞃ aꞃ nḋénaṁ ꞃioḋa acoṁaiꞃ ſtuꞃꞃa ⁊ a bꞃaitꞃe. Ra iompattaꞃ ḋno Laiȝin ȝo mbuaiḋ ⁊ coꞃȝuꞃ.

Táiniȝ Cſꞃḃall mac Muiꞃſȝan, ꞃi Laiȝſn, ꞃeṁe ȝo Cill ḋaꞃa, ⁊ buiḋne moꞃa i nſꞃȝaḃail aiȝe, ⁊ Flaitḃeꞃtaċ mac Ionmainén ſttoꞃꞃaꞃaiḋe. Na n-ſꞃbailt aꞃoile ꞃcoluiȝe Laiȝnſc ḋ'uile ꞃa Flaitḃeaꞃtaċ, aꞃ náꞃ ꞃe a ṁnꞃin, ⁊ ni cóiꞃ a ꞃeꞃiḃſin.

Tuȝaiḋ iaꞃttain Flaitḃeaꞃtaċ ȝo Cill ḋaꞃa, ⁊ tuꞃȝaḋ cléiꞃiȝ Laiȝſn aċċoꞃan móꞃ ḋó; uaiꞃ ꞃo ꝼſḋattuꞃ ȝuꞃ oḃ é a aonaꞃ ꞃa nſꞃt an ꞃluaiȝſḃ, ⁊ ȝuꞃ aꞃ a n-aiȝiḋ a ċoile táiniȝ Coꞃmaic. Aꞃ n-éċc imuꞃꞃo Cſꞃḃaill, ꞃi Laiȝſn ꞃa léiccſḃ Flaitḃeaꞃtaċ aꞃꞃ, ⁊ ȝo maḋ i ccionn ḃliaḋna ꞃin iaꞃ ꝼꝼaiꞃiꞃn. Ro ioḋnaic Muiꞃſnn comaꞃba bꞃiȝḋe é, ⁊ ꞃluaȝ móꞃ cléiꞃſc niṁꞃe ⁊ mionḋa ioṁḋa, ȝo ꞃáiniȝ ȝo Maȝ Naiꞃḃ; ⁊ ó ꞃáiniȝ Muṁain ḋo ꞃoine ꞃiḋ innte.

Ra

' *Improper to be written.*—The author of these calumnies (here spoken of as "a certain scholar of Leinster"), as well as the unmentionable crimes themselves, attributed to the royal abbot of Inis-Cathnigh, are unknown.

ᶠ *Muirenn, successor of Brighit.*—i. e. abbess of Kildare. She died A. D. 917.—*Ann. Ult.*

ᵍ *Magh Nairbh.*—This was the name of a plain in the barony of Crannagh, county of Kilkenny. See Ann. F. M., p. 856.

was afterwards carried away from him honourably to the body, where Macnach, son of Siadhal, Comharba of Comhghall, was, and he carried the body of Cormac to Disert-Diarmada [Castledermot], where it was honourably interred, and where it performs signs and miracles.

Why should not the heart repine and the mind sicken at this enormous deed, the killing and the mangling; with horrid arms, of this holy man, the most learned of all who came or will come of the men of Erin for ever? The complete master of Gaedhlic, and Latin, the archbishop, most pious, most pure, miraculous in chastity and prayer, a proficient in law, in every wisdom, knowledge, and science; a paragon of poetry and learning, head of charity and every virtue, and head of education; supreme king of the two provinces of Munster in his time.

Flann, King of Erin, returned home, after having left Diarmaid in the kingdom of Osraighe, and after having ratified an amicable peace between him and his brethren. The Leinster-men also returned home after victory and triumph.

Cearbhall, son of Muirigen, King of Leinster, proceeded directly to Cill-dara [Kildare], carrying with him great troops into captivity, and among the rest, Flaithbhertach, son of Inmainén. What a certain scholar of Leinster has ascribed of evil to Flaithbheartach is shameful to be mentioned, and improper to be written[r].

They afterwards brought Flaithbheartach to Cill-dara [Kildare], and the clergy of Leinster gave him great abuse, for they knew that he alone had invited the expedition and the battle, and that Cormac came against his own will. On the death of Cearbhall, King of Leinter, however, Flaithbheartach was set at liberty, which, according to some, was after the expiration of one year. Muirenn[f], successor of Brighit, accompanied by a great number of clerics, escorted him to Magh Nairbh[g], and when he arrived in Munster he made peace there.

He

Ra cuaið iapttain ðá mainiptip go hInip Catcaig, ⁊ po baoi peal go cráiðbfc inti, go ttáinig amac ðopſóipi ðo gaḃail pige Caipil, go paba ða ḃliagain tpioćað i pige Muṁan. Ap ðo'n cat po pa can Ðallán (mac Moipe) ollaṁ Cheptaill pí Laigfn:—

Copmac Peimin Pogaptac
Colmán, Ceallac cpuaið n-ugpa,
Go ré ṁile ðo poćpattap
I ccat bealuig muaið Múgna.
Ainepliр, ðín Lopuma,
Fſigal péig iomon pepuLinn,
Copmac pionn a Peiṁfnniaig
⁊ Cennpaolað a Fpigpinn.
Connoðap un Aðapṁaig
⁊ Eipfn a h-Aiðne,
La Cfpball ðo poćpattap
Ðia maipt ap Maig Ailḃe.
Maolmuað ⁊ Maðuðán,
Ut pob alainn an paipfnn,
Ðubacan ó Aḃainn Móip,
Ðublaet ⁊ Ðuḃðaboipfnn,
Congal ⁊ Catapnac
⁊ Fſpaðac paraið,

Ðoṁnall

ʰ *Dallan, son of Mor.*—Keating says that he was poet to Cearbhall, King of Leinster, quoted by the F. M., A. D. 903, but their chronology is five years antedated.

ⁱ *Aneslis, shelter of Borumha.*— Now Beal-Borumha, a fort on the west side of the River Shannon, about one mile to the north of Killaloe. This was the residence of the chief of the Ui-Toirdhealbhaigh. This Aneslis was not the ancestor of any line of the Dalcais whose pedigree is known.

ᵏ *Frighrenn.*—This was the name of the chief seat of the Ui-Conaill-Gabhra, now

He afterwards went to his monastery on Inis-Cathaigh [Scattery Island], and spent some time there piously, but he came out afterwards to assume the kingdom of Caisel, and he was in the [enjoyment of] the kingdom of Munster for thirty-two years. Of this battle, Dallan, son of Mor[h], Ollamh of Cearbhall, King of Leinster, sang:—

> Cormac of Feimhin, Foghartach,
> Colman, Ceallach, of hard battles,
> With six thousand, fell
> In the famous battle of Mughain.
> Aneslis, shelter of Borumha[i],
> Fearghal the sharp, of the straight stream,
> Cormac the fair, of Magh Feimhenn,
> And Cennfaeladh, of Frighrenn[k],
> Conodhar, too, of Magh Adhair[l],
> And Eidhen, of Aidhne[m].
> By Cearbhall all were slain
> On Tuesday on Magh Ailbhe.
> Maelmuadh and Madudhan;
> Alas! fair was the host!
> Dubhagan, of Abhainn Mor[n],
> Dubhlach and Dubhdabhoirenn.
> Congal and Catharnach,
> And Feradhach, of the wilderness,

Domhnall,

the baronies of Upper and Lower Conillo, county of Limerick.

[l] *Magh Adhair.*—A level plain in the barony of Tulla, county of Clare. This Conodhar is not the ancestor of any known line of the Dal-Cais.

[m] *Eidhen, of Aidhne.*—He was the an-

cestor of the O'Heynes of Aidhne, a territory in the S. W. of the county of Galway.

[n] *Abhainn Mor.*—Avonmore (or the Great River), now the Blackwater River in the county of Cork. This Dubhagan was the ancestor of the O'Dubhagans [O'Dugans] of Fermoy, county of Cork.

Domnall a Dun Cpimna caoṁ,
⁊ Aoḋ ó Chapn Tapaiġ.
Flann Timpa do'n Tailltṡṁaiġ,
Iſ Cpṫall Dún Capmain ciṫaċ.
I ɼept December cloiɼioḋaɼi
Caṫ go ceḋuib iolaċ,
Tadg mac Faoláin, Temenan,
Ceallaċ iſ Lopcán Loɼiglan;
Indeiɼige mac Duiḃġiolla,
Ro diongḃattuɼi coig nonḃaiɼ.
Maolcallann mac Fɼigaile,
Domnoll iſ Lopcán Liaṁna,
Ugaiɼie no Tuaṫal a Dún Oſɼimaiġe,
Noċaɼi eſtɼiaɼi tiamḋa.
Ugɼian Maiɼige moɼiglonnaċ,
Cleiɼiċen ó Iniſ Failḃe,
Follaṁan mac Aillella,
Duḃdaḃoiɼiſin adaimne.
Tadg an tɼiaċ a Oſɼgaḃaiɼ,
Go ɼuɼtaib bɼiute boɼiɼiɼilat,
Aɼ ɼe caċ ɼio ſɼcoṁail,
Do cloḋ caṫ foɼi Copinac.   Copmac.
Ro ba gníoṁ go ttiumaɼigain
⁊ Aɼ loɼi ɼiaɼi mſbɼiann
Rob

° *Dun Cearma.*—i. e. the old head of Kinsale.

ᵖ *Carn Tnisigh.*—This was the residence of the chief of Ui-Liathain, now the barony of Barrymore, county of Cork; but its situation or modern name has not been yet determined.

ᵍ *Flann, of Teamhair.*—i. e. of Tara and Teltown in Meath.

ʳ *Dun Carman.*—This was the name of an ancient seat of the kings of Leinster, the site of which is now occupied by the

Domhnall, of Dun Cearma°, the fair,
And Aedh, of Carn Tasaigh[p],
Flann, of Teamhair[q], of the plain of Tailltin;
And Cearbhall of the showery Dun Carman[r].
On the seventh[s] of September they joined
Battle with exulting hundreds,
Tadhg, son of Faelan, Temenan,
Ceallach and Lorcan the comely;
Indeirge, son of Duibhgilla,
They discomfited five times nine persons:
Maelcallann, son of Fearghal,
Domhnall and Lorcan of Liamhain[t],
Ugaire, of Dun-Dearmhaigh[u].
They were not a gloomy four;
Ugran, of Mairge[v], the great-deeded,
Cleireen, of Inis-Failbhe,
Follamhan, son of Ailell,
Dubhdabhoirenn we acknowledge,
Tadhg, the lord of Desgabhair[x],
With crushing flails of strong rods,
It is he that discomfited,
That gained the battle over Cormac.
It was a deed of dark plunder,
And it was enough to confuse us,

'Twas town of Wexford.

[s] *The seventh.*—The scribe writes in the margin of the MS., " 17 Sept.," which agrees with the F. M.

[t] *Liamhain.* — Otherwise called Dun Liamhna, and now anglicized Dunlavan, county of Dublin.

[u] *Dun-Dearmhaigh.*—Probably fort of Durrow, on the border of Laoighis and Osraighe.

[v] *Mairge.*—Now Slievemarague, Queen's County.

[x] *Desgabhair.*—i. e. South Leinster, i. e. Ui-Kinsellagh.

Rob uabup, po iomapcpaib,
Tuibíct na ćpíć ap Cpball.
In-tepɼcop, an tanmćapa
An paoi poićɼpna (no ba poćla) popbapc
Rí Caipil, pi Iapmuṁan,
A Dhé, oippan oo Chopmac.
                                   Copmac.

Coṁalta coṁaltpoma ⁊ coimléiġiṁ Copmac mac Cuilennáin ⁊ Cpball mac Muipɼgan, unoe Copmac cecinit :—

Taile oam mo tiompán, go nopnap a heippinm,
Tpe painpeapc oo Ʒhelpeipc ingin Oepill.

1. e. Ʒelpeapc ingɼn Oeipill, pi Fpangc, pa ail iao mapaon unoe Popoo Ʒeilpeipce.

Ʀal. Cpball mac Muipigén, pi Laigɼn mopitup; unoe Oallan cecinit :—

Mop liach Lipe longach,
Ʒan Cpball cubaib ceileać;
Fɼi pial popaib popbapać,
Oia ppognab Eipe éiṁeać.
Liać lɼmpa cnoc Almaine,
⁊ Aillɼnn gan óga,
Liać lioni Capman, noća cél,
⁊ pép oapa póoa.
Níop bo cian a paogalpoṁ
A aitle Copmac po cuillɼb,
                                     Lá

¹ *Gelshere.*—Keating makes no mention of this royal foster-mother of Cormac and Cearbhall.

² *Forod-Geilsheirce.*—*Quære*, whether this is intended for Foradh Geilsheirce, i. e. Geilshere's seat or bench? It was

'Twas pride, 'twas intolerance,
Their coming into his territory against Cearbhall.
The bishop, the confessor,
The famous, (or renowned) illustrious doctor;
King of Caisel, King of West Munster.
O God! alas for Cormac!
                                        Cormac.

Cormac, son of Cuilenan, and Cearbhall, son of Muiregan, were foster-brethren and school-fellows; hence Cormac sung:—

Bring me my tympan, that I may play on it,
For my ardent affection for Gelshere, daughter of Deirill.

i. e. Gelshere^y, daughter of Deirill, King of the Franks, nursed them both, unde Forod Geilsheiree^z.

[909.] Cearbhall^a, son of Muirigen, King of Leinster, died; hence Dallan sung:—

Great grief that Life of ships
Is without Ceallach, her befitting spouse;
A generous, steady, prolific man,
To whom submissive Erin was subservient.
Sorrowful to me the hill of Almhain,
And of Aillen, to be without soldiers;
Sorrowful to me is Carman—I conceal it not—
As the grass is growing over their roads.
Not long was his life
After the dishonouring of Cormac;
                                        A day

probably the name of a place in Ireland where she resided.

^a *Cearbhall.*—The death of Cearbhall, son of Muiregen, is noticed in the Ann. F. M. at 904; Ann. Ult. 908 [909]. The verses which follow are quoted by F. M.

Lá go leić, ní maoilpiaġail,
Ip aoin bliaġain gan puillíb.
Epmać piġc poġlaine,
Rí Laiġín linib laoćpab,
Duppan all ńápo nAlmaine,
Do bul ipéo pípb paoćpać.
Saoć la peoba popćaibe,
Plać náp Náip noićíć iappma,
Ra ćpoć opunga vopćaibe,
Moo liaćaib an liaćpo. Móp.

Gopmplaić ingín Ploinn cecinic:—

ba pobpaiġ Ceapball vo ġpép,
ba pobpaiġ a lép go báp
An po baoi va ćiopc gan ciop
Taipćeall ap a niopc ppi Náp.
Olc opmpa cumaoin va gall
Mapbpac Niall ⁊ Ceapball
Cípball la hUlb comall ngle
Niall Glúnoub la h-Amlaibe.

Dpím ga pába ap amlaib po loicíb Cípball .i. aġ vola vó i cCill vapa ap puo ppáibe in céime cloići paip, ⁊ each biompać paoi, inuaip ćainig aipo an apo pe cípocae ciopmaipe, ann pin uaip pin po ćuip an ciopmaipe a congna amać, ⁊ an cíć na upćomail

[footnote] *Gormflaith, daughter of Flann.*—She was daughter of Flann Sinna, monarch of Ireland, and had been married to Cormac Mac Cullenan, King of Munster, afterwards to Cearbhall, King of Leinster, and after his death to Niall Glundubh, monarch of Ireland. She was the daughter of a king, and had been the wife of three kings. It is stated, nevertheless, in the Annals of Clonmacnoise, that "after all

A day and a half, no wrong calculation,
And one year without addition.
Ruler of a noble kingdom,
King of Leinster, of numerous heroes.
Alas! that the lofty chief of Almhain
Has died in a bitter, painful, manner;
Sorrowful for brilliant jewels,
To be without the valiant, renowned King of Nás.
Although dense hosts have fallen,
Greater than all the sorrows is this sorrow.

Gormflaith, daughter of Flann[b], sung:—

Cearbhall was always vigorous;
His rule was vigorous till death;
What remained of his tributes unpaid,
He brought by his strength to Nás.
Evil towards me [was] the compliment of the two Galls.
They slew Niall and Cearbhall;
Cearbhall was slain by Ulbh, a great deed,
Niall Glundubh, by Amhlaeibh.

Some say that the manner in which Cearbhall was slain was this: As he was going through the street of the stone step eastwards at Cilldara [Kildare], having a proud steed under him, when he came opposite the shop of a fuller, there the fuller[c] sent the Congna[d] out, the horse

these royal marriages, she begged from door to door, forsaken of all her friends and allies, and glad to be relieved by her inferiors."—See Ann. F. M., A. D. 903, 917, 941.

[c] *Fuller.*—Ciopnaipe. The scribe glosses this word in the margin by púcaipe, which is still a living word, meaning, "a fuller."

[d] *The Congna.*—This word is used in the Ann. F. M., A. D. 1499 and 1597, in the sense of a machine or instrument.

mail amaiz, ro rceinn an tfc biomrac bap a hair, zo ttapla a za
fén alláim a ziolla fén baoi na ófzaib (zo mbab é ainm an ziol-
larain Uille, no ainm an ciormaire) ba marb tra Cfpball bon lot
rin i ccionn bliabna, ⁊ ro abnaicfb é inter parcrer ruor i relicc
Náir, unbe bicicur:—

  Failfb naoi ríoz reim naza,
  I ccill Nair ro neim miamba;
  Muirfzan maoin zan mfpball,
  Cfpball, ir Ceallac cialloa.
  Colman, bran beoba,
  Fionn, Faolán, Dúncab vána,
  I cCill Corbain, ro cuala,
  Ro claoicce a n-uaza aza.

 bécc hUa Lectlobair ri Dhail Arnibe moricur; unbe bicicur:—

  'Aro rzél rzaoilce lonz lir
  O ro ruair mor n-imnib
  Nab mair órzar bruac bil
  Clocruire tuace mbir.

 Caicill mac Rutrac ri brftan; Caireoz mac Dunoz, rí
hUa Ffrzura .i. i n-Uib Cinnriolaiz; Muzron mac Soclacáin, rí
hUa Maine, moricur.

 Ro innriomur reme ro .i. rin cftramab bliazain rfmainn na
                     rluaiz

---

f Cill Naas.—Now Kill, a church near Naas, in the county of Kildare, dedicated to St. Corban.

f Bece Ua Leathlabhair.—i. e. Beg O'Lalor. His death is noticed in the Ann. F. M. at 904, where these verses are also quoted, Ann. Ult. 908 [909].

g Tuath-Inbhir.—The ancient name of the mouth of the River Bann, near Coleraine.

h Cadell, son of Roderick.—He died in the year 909, according to the Annales Cambriæ; 907, according to the Brut y Tywysogion.

horse being opposite it outside ; the proud steed started back, so that he [the king] struck against his own javelin, which was in the hand of his own horseboy (whose name was Uille, or this was the name of the fuller), and Cearbhall died of that wound at the end of a year, and he was buried among his fathers in the cemetery of Nás; hence is said :—

> There are nine kings of famous career
> In Cill-Nais[e], of shining lustre:
> Muiregan, a hero without mistake,
> Ceallach and Cearbhall the sensible,
> Colman, Braen, and Bran the lively,
> Finn, Faelan, Dunchadh, the bold,
> In Corban's church, I have heard,
> Their warlike graves were made.

Becc Ua Leathlabhair[f], King of Dal-Araidhe, died; hence was said:—

> Awful news that disperses the ships of the sea,
> Which have braved great dangers,
> That no longer lives, the beloved golden scion,
> The renowned prince of Tuath-Inbhir[g].

Cadell[h], son of Roderick, King of Britain; Caireog, son of Dunog[i], King of Ui Fergusa, in Ui Ceinnscalaigh; and Mughron, son of Sochlachán[k], King of Ui-Maine, died.

We have related before now, i. e. in the fourth year before us[l], how

[i] *Caireog, son of Dunog.*—This obit is not in the published Annals.

[k] *Mughron, son of Sochlachán.*—A. D. 908 [909]. "Mugron mac Sochlachán, rex Nepotum Mainé defunctus est."—*Ann.*

Ult. "Tribes and Customs of Hy Many" (Irish Arch. Society), p. 98.

[l] *The fourth year before us.*—i. e. before the present date. There is no account of the expulsion of the Danes from Ireland

ṗluaiġ Loċlannéa ḋ'ionnaṙba a h-'Éiṗinn τṗe ṗaċ aoine ⁊ ṡṗ-
nuiġċe an ḋuine naoṁ .i. Chéle Ḋaḃaill, uaiṗ ba ḋuine naoṁ
cṗaiḃḃṡċ éṗiḋe, ⁊ éτ móṗ aiġe mana Cṗíoṗḋaiġḋiḃ, ⁊ ṗa ταοḃ nṡṗ-
ταḋα ḋo laoċ n-Éiṗionn i ġcṡnn na ṗáġanḋa ṗo ṗαοτṗaiġ ṗén ṗe
heṗnaiġċe, ⁊ ṗo ċuinġiḋ ṗαοιṗε ḋ'ṡġailṗiḃ 'Eiṗṡnn, ⁊ ḋo ċuṗ ṗeiṗġe
an ċoiṁoḣeḋ uaτa, uaiṗ aṗ aṗ ṗeiṗġ an ċoiṁoḣeḋ ḋo ḃeiτ ṗṁu
τuġaḋ ṡτaiṗċinṡḋaiġ ḋa millṡḋ .i. Loċlannaiġ ⁊ Ḋαnaiṗ ḋo iṁṗḋ
na h'Éṗenn ioiṗ cill ⁊ τuaiτ. Ra cuaḋaṗ τṗa na Loċlannaiġ a
h-Éiṗinn, amuil a ḋuḃṗamuṗ, ⁊ ba ταοιṗιοċ ḋóiḃ hinġamunḋ, ⁊ aṗ
ann ṗa ċuaḋaṗ a n-iniṡ ḃṗṡταn [i mḃṗṡτnuiḃ]. Aṗ é ba ṗi ḃṗṡταn
an ταn ṡin .i. mac Caiτill mic Ruaḋṗaċ. Ro τionoilṗiḋ ḃṗṡτain
ḋoiḃ, ⁊ τuġaḋ ċaτ cṗuaiḋ ṗonaiṗċ ḋoiḃ, ⁊ ṗa cuiṗiḋ aṗ éiġin a
cṗíoċaiḃ ḃṗṡταn iaḋ.

Τainiġ iaṗ ṡin hinġamunḋ co n-a ṗluaġaiḃ ḋ'ionṗaiġiḋ Eḋel-
ṗṗiḋa, ḃainṗioġan Saxan; uaiṗ boí a ṡṡiṗiḋe an ταn ṗa i nġaloṗ .i.
Eḋelṗṗiḋ (na hincṗṡċaḋ nṡċ mé ġé ṗa innιṗιuṗ ṗeaṁain éce Eḋelṗṗiḋ, uaiṗ ταοιṗιοċa ṗo ionáṗ éce Eḋelṗṗiḋ, ⁊ aṗ ḋon ġaloṗṗa aṗ
maṗḃ Eḋelṗṗiḋ, aċτ nṡoṗ ḃáil ḋaiṁ a ṗáġḃáil ġan a ṗeṗíḃṡnn na
nuṡinṗaḋ Loċlannaiġ aṗ noul a h'Éṗinn). Ro ḃaoi iaṗaṁ hinġamunḋ

under the fourth year prior to this, nor in
any other part of this Fragment, from
which it is clear that some portion of the
matter immediately preceding has been
lost. The printed Annals are very meagre
at this period.

ᵐ *Cele-Dabhaill.*—The scribe writes in
the margin, " Cele Ḋaḃaill ab beann-
ċoiṗ ⁊ Comaṗba Coinġaill ṗo Ciṗinn,
obiit Romæ anno Christi 927 die 14.
Septembris Ann. Dung.," i. e. according
to the Ann. of Donegal (or F. M.), " Cele-

Dabhaill, Abbot of Bangor, and successor
of Comhgall, throughout Erin, died at
Rome on the 14th of September, in the
year of Christ 927." See Ann. of Ult.,
A. D. 927.

ⁿ *Hingamund.*—We do not find any
mention of Hingamund in any previous
portion of these Fragments; nor does the
name occur in the Saxon Chron., or other
English historians of the period. But the
Brut y Tywysogion mentions " Igmond,"
who, in the year 900, "came [apparently

how the Lochlann hordes were expelled from Erin through the merits of the fasting and prayers of the holy man, Cele-Dabhaill^m, for he was a holy and pious man, and had great zeal for the Christians, and, besides strengthening the heroes of Erin against the Pagans, he laboured himself by fasting and prayer, and he sought freedom for the churches of Erin, and he strengthened the men of Erin by his strict service to the Lord, and he removed the anger of the Lord from them; for it was in consequence of the anger of God against them that it was permitted that foreign hordes should come to destroy them, i. e. Lochlanns and Danes, to destroy Erin, both church and state. The Lochlanns went away from Erin, as we have said, under the conduct of Hingamundⁿ, their chieftain, and where they went to was to the island of Britain. The King of Britain at this time was the son of Cadell^o, son of Roderick. The Britains assembled against them, and a hard and spirited battle was given them, and they were forcibly driven from the territories of the Britons.

After this Hingamund and his forces came to Ethelfrida^p, Queen of the Saxons, for her husband was at that time in a disease, i. e. Ethelfrid. (Let no one criticise me, because I have mentioned the death of Ethelfrid before, for this [fact, which I now relate] was before the death of Ethelfrid, and it was of this disease he died, but I did not like to leave unwritten all that the Lochlanns did after leaving

from Ireland] to Mona, and fought the battle of Ros-meilon," now Penros, near Holyhead.—*Ann. Cambr.*, A. D. 902.

° *Cadell.*—Clydaug, or Clydog, son of Cadell, son of Rodri Mawr, was slain by his brother Meuruc, A. D. 917.—*Brut y Tywysog.*, or 919, *Ann. Cambr.*

^p *Ethelfrida.*—This was the celebrated Æthelflæd, daughter of Ælfred the Great,

who was married to Æthelred, Ealdorman of the Mercians, who, after her husband's death, defended her territories with great success against the Danes. She died at Tamworth, 19 Kal. Julii, 919.—Henr. Hunting. A double entry of her death occurs in the Sax. Chron. at 918 and 922. The Ann. Ult. give 917 or 918; Ann. Cambr. 917; Brut y Tywys. 914; Lap-

muno ag iappaiö fṡiaiñ ap an piogain atttaipippeö, ⁊ i noingneö cpoaö ⁊ tpṡbaö, ap ba tuippioc é an tan pin bo togaö. Tug iapam Eöelfpioa fṡpainn a ffogup no Captpa öó, ⁊ po an peal ann pin. Apeö po fáp be pin, ó bo conaipc an catpaig lán paiööip, ⁊ an fṡiann togaiöe impe, tugaö mian a tṡctaöa öó. Tainig hingamuno iap pin b'ionnpoigiö taopioc Loclonn ⁊ Oanap, ⁊ po baoi og gṡpán móp na ffiaönuipe, ⁊ apeö po páiö, nac mait po báöap gan fṡiann mait aca, ⁊ gup bo cóip öóiö uile toiöect bo gabáil Captpa, ⁊ öá tṡctaö co na maitiup ⁊ co n-a fṡiannaiö. Rá fáp tpío pin cata ⁊ cogaö iomöa, mópa. Apeö po páiö; guiöfm ⁊ aittefm iaö fén ap túp, ⁊ muna ffagam iaö amlaiö pain ap aip, copnam iaö ap éigin. Ro faoinpattup uile taoipig Loclonn ⁊ Oanaip pin. Tainic Ingamuno iapttain ba taig iap nöál tionóil 'na ofgaiö. Cíö beippiö po ponpaöpom an comaiple pin, fuaip an piogan a fiop. Ro tionoil an piogan iapam plóg móp impe pan cán, ⁊ po líon an catpaig Captpa ó na plógaiö.

Ap bṡg nac ip na láitibpi po cuippfö Foiptpfnnaig ⁊ Loclonnaig cat. Ap cpuaiö imuppo po cuippiot pip Alban an cat po, uaip baoi Colum Cille ag congnam leo, uaip po guiöpioö go bioépa é, uaip ba hé a n-appcol é, ⁊ ap tpíö po gabpaö cpeioṡm. Uaip fṡet oile anuaip po baoi Imap Conung na giolla óg, ⁊ táinig b'inpfö Alban, tpí cata mópa a líon, apeö ba ponpaö pip Alban eibip laot ⁊ cléipfṡ, beit go maibin i n-aoine, ⁊ a n-iopnaiöe pa Oia, ⁊ pa

penberg's Hist. of England (Thorpe's Transl.), ii., p. 95.

ⁿ *Chester*.—York was sometimes called Ceastre, or Ceastrum (Sax. Chron., A. D. 763), and it is possible that our author may intend the treaty made at York between the Danes and Æthelflæd, Queen of the Mercians, in the year 918 (*recte*, 919), according to the Saxon Chron., but we read there also (Petrie's Edit., at the same date), that Queen Æthelflæd also got into her possession the town of *Legra-ceastre*, which may be either Chester or Leicester.

ʳ *Almost*.—The whole of this paragraph

ing Erin.) Hingamund was asking lands of the queen, in which he would settle, and on which he would erect stalls and houses, for he was at this time wearied of war. Ethelfrida afterwards gave him lands near Chester[q], and he remained there for some time. What resulted from this was: as he saw that the city was very wealthy, and the land around it was choice, he coveted to appropriate them. After this, Hingamund came to meet the chieftains of the Lochlanns and Danes; he made great complaints before them, and said that they were not well off without having good lands, and that they all ought to come to take Chester, and to possess themselves of its wealth and lands. From this many and great battles and wars arose. What he said was: Let us ask and implore themselves at first, and if we do not obtain this by their will, let us contend for them by force. All the chiefs of the Lochlanns and Danes approved of this. Hingamund afterwards returned to his house, a host having followed after him. Though they held this consultation secretly, the queen received intelligence of it. The queen collected great hosts about her from every direction, and the city of Chester was filled with her hosts.

Almost[r] at the same time the men of Fortrenn[s] and the Lochlanns fought a battle. Vigorously, indeed, did the men of Alba fight this battle, for Colum Cille was assisting them, for they prayed to him fervently, because he was their apostle, and it was through him they had received the faith. On a former occasion, when Imhar Conung[t] was a young man, he came to plunder Alba with three large battalions. What the men of Alba, both laity and clergy, did, was,
to

has been quoted by Dr. Reeves, in his Edition of Adamnan, p. 332 sq., where, see his notes and references.

[s] *Fortrenn.*—i. e. the country of the Picts. Ann. Ult. 917 (or 918).

[t] *Imhar Conung.*—i. e. Ivor, the king. This is a digression, for he was slain in the year 904, by the men of Fortrenn.— Ann. Ult.; Reeves's Adamn., pp. 333, 392. But the present battle was fought

ꞃa Colam Cille, ⁊ éiġme mópa do ṫénaṁ ꞃiꞃ in coimḋheḋ, ⁊ alm-
ꞃana iomḋa bíḋ ⁊ eḋaiġ do ṫaḃaiꞃt ṽona hꞅġalꞃaiḃ, ⁊ do na boċ-
taiḃ, ⁊ coꞃꞃ an coimḋheḋ no caiṫṡiṁ alláṁuiḃ a ꞃaġaꞃt ⁊ ġeallaḋ
ġaċ maiṫiuꞃa do ġénaṁ amail aꞃ ꞃꞅiꞃ no ioꞃalꞃaiṽiꞃ a ccléiꞃiġ
ꞃoꞃꞃa, ⁊ comaḋ eaḋ ba meiꞃġe ḋóiḃ i ġcꞅnn ġaċ caṫa, baċall Cho-
laim Cille, ġonaḋ aiꞃe ꞃin aḋbeꞃaꞃ Caṫbuaiḋ ꞃꞃia ó ꞃin alle; ⁊ ba
hainm cóiꞃ, ṽaiꞃ iꞃ minic ꞃuġꞃaoroṁ buaiḋ a ccaṫaiḃ lé; aṁail do
ꞃónꞃat iaꞃam an tan ꞃin ḋola a muiniġin Colaim Cille. Do ꞃon-
ꞃaḋ an moḋ céona an tan ꞃa. Ra cuiꞃioḋ iaꞃaṁ an catꞃa ġo
cꞃuaiḋ ꞃeoċaiꞃ; ꞃuġꞃao na h-Albanaiġ buaiḋ ⁊ coꞅġaꞃ; ꞃo maꞃ-
ḃaio imuꞃꞃo na Loċlonnaiġ ġo h-iomḋa aꞃ maiḋm ꞃoꞃꞃa, ⁊ maꞃḃ-
ṫaꞃ a ꞃiġ ann, .i. Oittiꞃ mac Iaꞃnġna. Aꞃ cian iaꞃttain na ꞃo
ꞃaiġꞃioḋ Danaiꞃ na Loċlunnaiġ oꞃꞃa, aċt ꞃo buí ꞃíḋ ⁊ coṁꞃanaḋ
doiḃ; aċt iomꞃam don ꞃġeol ꞃo ṫionꞅġnamaꞃ.

Ro ṫionolꞃat ꞅluaiġ na nDanaꞃ ⁊ na Loċlonn d'ioñꞃoiġiḋ Caꞅ-
tꞃa, ⁊ ó nac ꞅꞃuaꞃattuꞃ a ꞅꞃaoṁaḋ tꞃe ataċ no ġuiḋe, ꞃo ꞅꞃua-
ġꞃattuꞃ caṫ aꞃ ló ḋaiꞃiṫe. Tanġaoaꞃ 'ꞃan lo ꞃin d'ioꞃꞃoiġiḋ na
caṫꞃaċ; ⁊ ꞃo ḃaoi ꞅlóġ móꞃ ġo n-iomao ꞃaoꞃclann 'ꞃan ccaṫꞃaiġ
aꞃ a ccionn. 'O ꞃo concattuꞃ na ꞅluaiġ ꞃaḃattuꞃ iꞃin caṫꞃaiġ,
da ṁúꞃ na caṫꞃaċ, ꞅlóiġ iomḋa na nDanaꞃ ⁊ na Loċlonn ḋá n-ion-
ꞃoiġiḋ,

about the year 918, according to Ann. Ult. See their account, Reeves, ib. p. 332.

" *Cathbhuaidh.*—i. e. battle-victory. In like manner the name of Cathach [prœliosum] was given to the ornamented box of the O'Donnells of Tirconnell, containing a Psalter supposed to have been written by the hand of St. Columba, which was carried before their armies in battle. This valuable relic, through the public spirit of its owner, Sir Richard O'Donnell, is now deposited in the Museum of the Royal Irish Academy.

ˣ *On this occasion.*—i. e. on the occasion of the battle between the men of Fortrenn and the Lochlanns, in 918—the history of the battle with Imhar Conung, in 904, having been introduced merely to record the precedent for the use of the *Cathbuaidh*, or victory-giving crozier of St. Columkille.

ʸ *Otter, son of Iargna.*—Or son of Iargn; Iargna may be the gen. case. The Ann.

to remain untill morning fasting and praying to God and to Colum Cille, and they cried out aloud to the Lord, and gave many alms of food and clothes to the churches, and to the poor, and to take the body of the Lord from the hands of their priests, and to promise to do every good, as their clergy would order them, and that they would have as their standard, at the head of every battle, the crozier of Colum Cille, for which reason it is called the Cathbhuaidh[u] from that time forth, and this was a befitting name for it, for they have often gained victory in battles by means of it, as they did afterwards at that time, when they put their trust in Colum Cille. They acted in the same way on this occasion[x]. This battle was afterwards fought fiercely and vigorously. The Albanachs gained victory and triumph. The Lochlanns were slain in great numbers, and defeated, and their king was slain, i. e. Otter, son of Iargna[y], and it it was long after this until either Danes or Lochlanns attacked them, but they enjoyed peace and tranquillity. But let us return to the story which we commenced.

The hosts of the Danes and the Lochlanns collected to Chester, and when they did not get themselves complied with by entreaty or supplication, they proclaimed battle on a certain day. On that day they came to attack the city, and there was a large host, with many nobles, in the city to meet them. When the hosts, who were within the city, saw, from the wall of the city, the many hosts of the Danes and Lochlanns [coming] to attack them, they sent messengers to the King of the Saxons[z], who was in a disease, and on the point of death

at

Ult., in their account of this battle, mention this chieftain as Ottir, without giving the name of his father.

[1] *King of the Saxons.*—This was Æthelred, Ealdor of the Mercians, whose Queen was Æthelfled, sister of King Edward, and daughter of Alfred the Great. He died in 912.—Sax. Chron. and Flor. Wigorn. in anno; Lappenberg's Hist. of England, ii., p. 90. Therefore, the event here described must have taken place in or before that year. But our author's chrono-

roiʒıð, ɼa ċuıɼɼıoð cſċca ð'ıonɼoıʒıð ɼı Saxan, ɼo baoı a nʒaloɼ, ⁊ aɼ bɼú ċcca an uaıɼ ɼın, ð'ıaɼɼaıð a coṁaıɼlıɼıoṁ, ⁊ coṁaıɼle na ɼıoʒna. Aɼí coṁaıɼle cuʒɼaıðe caċuʒað ðo ʒénaṁ a ɼɼoʒuɼ ðo'n caċɼaıʒ allamaıʒ, ⁊ ðoɼaɼ na caċɼaċ ðo beıċ aıbela, ⁊ ɼloʒ ɼıcaıɼe ðo ċoxa, ⁊ a mbeıċɼıðe ı ɼɼolaċ alla anall, ⁊ man bıð cɼeıɼı ðo luċċ na caċɼaċ aʒ an caċuʒað, ceıcheð ðoıb ðaɼ a n-aıɼ ıɼın ċaċɼaıʒ muɼ ba ı ınaıðın, ⁊ anuaıɼ ðo ċıocɼaıðíɼ ſɼıṁóɼ ɼlóıʒ na Loċlonn ðaɼ ðoɼuɼ na caċɼaċ aɼcíċ, an ɼloʒ bıaɼ a ɼɼolaċ ċall ðo ðúnað an ðoɼuıɼ ðaɼ éıɼ na ðɼeımı ɼın, ⁊ ʒan ní aɼ moo ðo léʒſn oɼɼıa; ʒabáıl ɼon ðɼeım ɼın cıoʒɼaıð ıɼın ċaċɼaıʒ, ⁊ a maɼbað uıle. Ðo ɼonað uıle aṁlaıð ɼın, ⁊ ɼo maɼbað uſɼʒ-áɼ na nÐanaɼ ⁊ na Loċlonn aṁlaıð. Cıð móɼ ðna an maɼbað ɼın, ní hſð ðo ɼonɼað na Loċlonnaıʒ ɼáʒbaıl na caċɼaċ, uaıɼ ba cɼuaıð aınoʒıð ıað, aċc aɼſó aðɼubɼaccuɼ uıle chıaċa ıomða ðo ʒénaṁ aca, ⁊ ʒabla ðo ċuɼ ɼoċa, ⁊ collað an ṁuıɼ ɼoċa; ⁊ aɼſó ón ná ɼa ɼuıɼʒıð, ðo ɼónað na chıaċa, ⁊ ɼo báðaɼ na ɼlóıʒ ɼóċa aʒ collað an ṁúıɼ, uaıɼ ba ɼaınc leo ʒabáıl na caċɼaċ, ⁊ ðıoʒaıl a muınncıɼe.

Iſ ann ɼın ɼa ċuıɼ an ɼí (⁊ é ı ɼoċɼaıb ðo báɼ) ⁊ an ɼıoʒan cſċca uaċa ð'ıonɼoıʒıð na nʒaoıðıol ɼo baccaɼ eıuıɼ na Páʒánaıb (aɼ ba h-ıomða ðalca Ʒaoıðealaċ aʒ na Páʒánaıb), ða ɼáð ɼıɼ na Ʒaoıðealuıb: bſċa ⁊ ɼláıncċ ó ɼı Saxan acá a nʒaloɼ, ⁊ ó n-a ɼıóʒaın, ʒá ɼɼuıl uıle nſɼc Saxan, ðuıbɼı, ⁊ ɼo ðeıṁnıʒɼıoð conað

logy is probably wrong.

ᵃ *Gacidhil.*—i. e. the Irish, or Dano-Irish, called above the Gall-Gacidhil. See p. 128, note ᵐ.

ᵇ *Over all the Saxons.*—In Powell's Hist. of Wales, by W. Wynne (Lond., 1697, pp. 45, 46), this attack upon Chester is referred to in the following words :—" After the death of Anarawd (A. D. 913), his eldest son, Edwal Foel, took upon him the government of North Wales, Howel Dha holding the principality of South Wales and Powis. At what time a terrible comet appeared in the heavens. The same year the city of Chester, which had been destroyed by the Danes, was, by the pro-

at that time, to ask his advice, and the advice of his queen. The advice which he gave was, to give [them] battle near the city outside, and to keep the gate of the city wide open, and to select a body of knights, and have them hidden on the inside; and if the people of the city should not be triumphant in the battle, to fly back into the city, as if in defeat, and when the greater number of the forces of the Lochlanns should come inside the gate of the city, that the hosts who were in ambuscade should close the gate of the city after this party, and not to pretend to any more, but to attack the party who should come into the city, and kill them all. This was all done accordingly, and a red slaughter was accordingly made of the Danes and Lochlanns. Great, however, as was that slaughter, the Lochlanns did not abandon the city, for they were hardy and fierce, but they all said that they should make many hurdles, and that posts should be placed under them, and that they should perforate the wall under [the shelter of] them. This project was not deferred; the hurdles were made, and hosts were [placed] under them to pierce the wall, for they were covetous to take the city, and to avenge their people.

Then the king, who was on the point of death, and the queen sent ambassadors to the Gaeidhil[a] who were among the Pagans (for the Lochlanns, then Pagans, had many a Gadelian foster-son), to say to the Gaeidhil : " Life and health from the King of the Saxons, who is in disease, and from his Queen, who has sway over all the Saxons[b], to

curement of Elfleda, new built and repaired, as the ancient records of that city do testify. This, in the ancient copy, is called Leycester, by an easy mistake for Legecestria or Chester, called by the Romans *Legionum Castra*. The next summer the men of Dublin cruelly destroyed

the island of Anglesey." The "ancient copy" here referred to is probably the Anglo Saxon-Chron., which calls the place *Legraceastre*, A. D. 918. There is great confusion between Chester and Leicester in the Saxon Chron. The former name is written Legaceaster, Leiceaster, Leg-

conaḋ ḟíopċapaiṫ ċaipipi ḋóiḃpioṁ piḃpi: ap amlaiḋ pin ap ġaḃċa ḋuiḃpi iaupoṁ; uaip ġaċ óġlaċ, ⁊ ġaċ cléipċ Ġaoiḋealaċ ċáinig cucapoṁ a h-Éipinn, ní ċuġpaċpom a iomapcpaiḋ onópa ṫ'óġlaċ no cléipeċ Saxon; uaip ap coiṁméċ ap náṁaiṫ ḋuiḃ maille an cineḋ náiṁḋiḋipi na Paġánḋḋa. Ipeḋ ḋin ap liḃpi aṁail ap capaiṫ ċaipipi piḃ, a ḟpopċaċċ poṁ an ċuaipċpi. Aṁlaiḋ po ón a páḋ piupoin, ġoniḋ ó ċaipḋiḃ ċaipipiḃ ḋuiḃ ċaṅġamap-ne ḋa ḃap naġallaṁ, ḋo páḋ ḋuiḃpi pip na Ḋanapaiḃ, cioine comaḋa pṡpainn ⁊ ionnṁaip ḋo ḃeḋḋaoip ḋon luċċ nó ḃpiaiċpṡḋ an caċpaiġ ḋóiḃ. Mapopoemaḋaiċpioṁ pain, a mḃpeiċ ḋo ċum luiġe i ḟḟail i mḃia poipḃe a maṗḃċa, ⁊ map ḃeiopioṁ aġ ċaḃaipċ an luiġe pa cclaiḋṁiḃ, ⁊ pa pġiaċaiḃ, aṁuil ap ḃép ḋóiḃ, cuipġiċċ uaċa an uile apm poiḋioḋpaiġċe. Do piġnḋ uile aṁlaiḋ pin, ⁊ po ċuippioċ a n-apma uaċa, ⁊ ap aipe ip pip na Ḋanapaiḃ ḋo ponpaḋ na Ġaoiḋil pin, uaip ḃa luġ ḃa capaiḋ ḋóiḃ iaḋ ionáiḋ na Loċlonnaiġ. Sochaiḋe iapaṁ ḋíoḃ pa maṗbaḋ aṁlaiḋ pin, ap lécaḋ cappaġ móp ⁊ paḃaḋ móp 'na ġcṡin: Soċuiḋe móp oile ḋo ġaiḃ, ⁊ ḋo paiġḋiḃ, ⁊ ó uile acmoinġc maṗḃċa ḋaoine.

Ro ḃaċċap iniuppo an ṗloġ oile, Loċlonnaiġ póċ na cliaċaiḃ aġ ċollaḋ na múp. Apeḋ ḋo ponpaḋ na Saxoin ⁊ na Ġaoiḋil, po ḃaċċap ċċoppa, caipġe ḋíoṁópa ḋo léċuḋ anuap ġo ċċpaġġpaiḋíp na cliaċa na ccṡin. Apeḋ ḋo ponpaḋpum na aiġiḋ pin, columna mópa ḋo ċup po na cliaċaiḃ. Apeḋ ḋo ponpaḋ na Saxoin na ḟpuapaḋap ḋo lionn ⁊ ḋ'uipġe pin baile ḋo ċup i ccoipiḃ an baile, ⁊ piuċaḋ poppa a léġan i mullaċ in luċċ po ḃaoi po na cliaċaiḃ, ġo po pcoiṁa i lċċap ḋíoḃ. Apé ḟpeaġpaḋ ċuġpaḋ na Loċlonnaiġ

aippin

ceaster (Caer-Lleon, or Caerleon, in the Bret y Tywysogion, *Lleon* being a corruption of *Legionum*); the latter, Legraceaster, Leogereceaster, Ligeraceaster, Leycestre, &c. The fortification of Chester (Ligceaster), by Queen Æthelfled, is recorded in the Saxon Chron. at A. D. 907.

to you, and they are certain that you are true and faithful friends to them. It is therefore meet that you should adhere to them, for they gave to every Gadelian soldier and clergyman who had come to them out of Erin, as much honour as they did to any Saxon soldier or clergyman, for this inimical race of Pagans is equally hostile to you both. It then behoves you, as ye are faithful friends, to relieve them on this occasion." This was the same as if it was said to them: We have come from faithful friends of yours to address you, [to request] that ye should ask the Danes, what gifts in lands and chattels they would give to those who would betray the city to them. If they would consent to this, to bring them to swear, to a place where there would be a facility of killing them; and when they shall be swearing on their swords, and on their shields, as is their wont, they will put away all kinds of missile weapons. They all did accordingly, and they put away their arms; and the reason that the Gaeidhil acted so towards the Danes was, because they were less friends to them than to the Lochlanns. Many of them were killed in this manner, for large rocks and large beams were hurled down upon their heads. Great numbers also were killed by darts and javelins, and by every other kind of apparatus for killing men.

The other hosts, however, were under the hurdles, piercing the walls. What the Saxons and the Gaeidhil who were among them did, was to throw down large rocks, by which they broke down the hurdles over their heads. What the others did to check this was, to place large posts under the hurdles. What the Saxons did next, was to put all the beer and water of the town into the cauldrons of the town, to boil them, and spill them down upon those who were under the hurdles, so that their skins were peeled off. The remedy which the Lochlanns applied to this was to place hides outside on the hurdles. What the Saxons did next was, to throw down all the beehives in

aippin peiéſb do pgaoileb ap na cliaṫaib annap. Aρſb do pónpad na Saxoin gaé a paba do cliab bſé ipin baile do pgaoilſb po luċt na toglu, na po léig dóib copa na láṁa d'iomluad pa hiomad na mbſé ga tſpcad. Ro léigpiod iapttan don ċaṫpaig 7 po págpad í. Ní cian iapttain co ttángatap apipi do caṫughad.

Ip m bliadainpi táinig tionol mop bpeipne ap epſéaib. Ra hinnpiod pin do píg 'Eipſnn, 7 do ṁaccaib. Ap annpin po páid pí 'Eipſnn: ap deipſb n-ainpipe ann, ap ſé, an tan láṁuid coṁ-aitig mup po eipgib a n-aigib páopélann. Do pónad tionól oippſ-gpa po cédóip la pí n-Eipſnn 7 la ṁaccoib, 7 tangattap pſmpa go dpuim éṁiaié, 7 po battup og péccad tionól na mbpéppſé ann pin. Ní pacup peṁe pin tionol do aiefſéuib. Do cuippiod eſnn i gepſn iapttain, 7 gen go paba pi pſmpa do puabpadap go epuaid pig n-'Eipſnn. Ro coñcattup meic pí 'Eipſnn caṫ pealad ó éáé amaé; tangattup dá ionpoigiodpide, 7 po cuippiod ppiu. Ro ṁaid pe macaib an pí ap an ċaṫpin, 7 pomaib ap na caṫaib oile po édóip, po cuipſb a nopipg áp, 7 po gabad pochaide díob gup eſn-naigit iad do éionn ionnṁap.

Táinig an pí go mbuaid 7 copgup do bpeiṫ o na aiṫédaduib, ap mapbad pí na mbpeipnſé .i. Plann mac Tigſpnáin.

Kal. Annup xxxi.up. Plainn, Diapmaid pí Oppaige, 7 Aod mac Duibgiolla,

^c *Druim-criaich.*— Now Drumcree, a townland in the parish of Kilcumny, barony of Delvin, and county of Westmeath.

^d *Attacotts.*—The meaning of this is very doubtful. The term *aitheach tuatha* (attacot) is applied by the old Irish writers to the enslaved descendants of the Firbolgs, and to all those who were not of the royal line of the Milesians or Scoti; but the chiefs of the men of Breifne were descended from as royal a line as the monarch of Ireland himself. The probability, however, is, that the monarch of Ireland spoke in derision on account of the motley appearance presented by these hordes of plunderers. This defeat of the men of Breifne is recorded in the Ann. Ult., A. D. 909 [910]—Caṫpoṁd pe Plonn mac Maelpeénall cum suis filiis pop pipu bpeipne ubi ceciderunt Flann

the town upon the besiegers, which prevented them from moving
their hands or legs from the number of bees which stung them.
They afterwards desisted and left the city. It was not long, however,
until they came to fight again.

[909.] In this year there came a great muster of the Brefnians
[into Meath] to commit depredations. This was told to the King
of Erin and to his sons. Then the King of Erin said, "It is the
end of the world that is come," said he, "when plebeians like these
dare to attack noblemen." An irresistible muster was immediately
afterwards made by the King of Erin and his sons, and they came
forward to Druim-criaich[c], and [thence] they reconnoitered the assembled
forces of Breifnè. They had never before seen a muster of Attacotts[d].
They met each other face to face, and though they had no
king[e] at their head, they attacked the King of Erin with hardihood.
The sons of the King of Erin saw a battalion at some distance out from
the rest; they came towards it, and attacked it. The sons of the king
defeated that battalion, and the other battalions were likewise at
once defeated and dreadfully slaughtered, and many of them were
taken prisoners, who were afterwards ransomed by prices.

The King returned after having gained victory and triumph over
the plebeians, after the King of the Brefnians, i. e. Flann, son of
Tighernan, had been killed.

[910.] Kal. The thirty-first year of Flann[f]. Diarmaid, King of Osraighe,

Mac Tigernain et alii nobiles multi interfecti. "An overthrow of the men of Brefne, by Flann, son of Maelsechlain and his sons, where Flann, son of Tighernan, fell, and many other nobles were slain." The same passage occurs in the Ann. Clonm. at 902, and F. M. at 905 (the true year is 910). But there is no mention of Attacoti or plebeians in any of these Annals.

[e] *No King.*—This looks very strange, for it is stated in the next paragraph that their King Flann, son of Tighernan, was killed. Perhaps there was a body of Attacotts, who were without a king, acting as auxiliaries to Flann and his Breifnians.

[f] *Of Flann.*—i. e. of Flann Sionna (son

Duibġiolla, ꞃí Ua nDꞃona do ṁillſd deiꞃgiꞃc Maiġe Raiġne, ⁊ milliſd dóib Cill na gCailleaċ .i. Finchu, ⁊ Reċtín, ⁊ muinntiꞃ Aoḋa do maꞃbaḋ ꞃagaꞃt an baile, ⁊ aꞃeḋ ón ꞃo díoġail Dia ꞃoꞃ Aoḋ mac Duibġiolla ſain, uaiꞃ ꞃo maꞃbꞃaḋ aꞃaile coṁaitiġ d'Oꞃꞃaiġib é ag iomꞃóḋ da éiġ. Rí hUa nDꞃóna an tAoḋ ſin, ⁊ na tꞃí maiġe, ⁊ ꞃiġḋaṁna hUa Cinnſilaiġ, unde dicitur :—

  A óga Ailbe aine,
  Caoimḋ ꞃiġ Slaine ſaoiꞃe,
  Eꞃcbaiḋ Aoḋ mbuiḋnſċ mbeaꞃba,
  Go ꞃo ſuiḋ Fſiꞃna ſaoine.
  Feaꞃna móꞃ milib doġꞃaċ,
  Niꞃꞃáine aꞃmaḋ cuiṁnſċ,
  Maꞃbán buḋ ſꞃgna allaḋ,
  O ꞃo biċ bꞃan Dub buiḋnſċ.
  Ro ſaoiḋ mo ḋíon mo ḋítte,
  Rí na ꞃíog ꞃedíġ ꞃoḋa.
  Aꞃ ꞃuaiċniġ ꞃoꞃ ꞃaiċ Edain,
  Aoḋ i n-éccaib, a óga.

Uallaċán mac Caċail, ꞃiġḋamna hUa Failġe moꞃituꞃ.
Ugaiꞃe mac Oilella do ꞃioġaḋ ꞃoꞃ Laiġnib.
buaḋaċ mac Moċla ꞃiġḋamna na nDéiꞃi moꞃituꞃ.

of Maelsechlainn), King of Ireland, who began his reign A. D. 879, so that his thirty-first year was 910. See O'Flaherty, Ogyg., p. 434.

ᵍ *Ui-Drona*.—A tribe inhabiting the present barony of Idrone, county of Carlow. See Book of Rights, p. 212, n.

ʰ *Cill-na-gCaillech*.—i. e. the church of the nuns. The founders of this church were the holy virgins Finech and Rechtin.

It is the church now called Killinny [Cill Fhinecca, Ch. of S. Finech], in the parish and barony of Kells, county of Kilkenny. See F. M., A. D. 859, note ᵏ, p. 494.

ⁱ *Ailbhe*.—i. e. Magh Ailbhe, a plain on the east side of the Barrow, near Carlow.

ᵏ *Slaine*.—i. e. the River Slaney.

ˡ *Bearbha*.—i. e. the River Barrow.

ᵐ *Fearna*.—i. e. Ferns, in the county of Wexford.

raighe, and Aedh, son of Dubhghioll, King of Ui-Drona^g, destroyed the east of Magh Raighne, and they destroyed Cill-na-gCaillech^h [i. e. of the nuns] Finech and Rechtin, and the people of Aedh killed the priest of the place, which God afterwards revenged upon Aedh, son of that Dubhghioll, for some plebeians of the Osraighi killed him as he was returning to his house. This Aedh was King of Ui-Drona, and of the Three Plains, and royal heir of Ui-Ceinsealaigh. Unde dicitur :—

O youths of pleasant Ailbhe[i],
Mourn ye the King of noble Slaine[k].
Slain is Aedh of hosts of the Bearbha[l],
The just king of the land of peaceful Fearna[m],
To great Fearna, of the thousand noble graces,
There came not, if I well remember,
A corpse of more illustrious fame
Since Bran Dubh[n] of troops was slain.
My shelter, my protection has departed;
May the King of kings make smooth his way.
It is easily known by Rath-Aedhain[o]
That Aedh is dead, O youths!

Uallachan[p], son of Cathal, royal heir of Ui-Failghe [Offaley], died.
Ugaire, son of Oilell[q], was made King of Leinster.
Buadhach, son of Mothla[r], royal heir of the Deisi, died.

[911.]

---

[n] *Bran Dubh.*—A famous King of Leinster, who was slain A. D. 601. See Ann. F. M., pp. 228, 229, 576.

[o] *Rath-Aedhain.*—i. e. Aidan's Fort, another name for Ferns. So called from St. Aedh or Aidan, alias Mogue, [i. e. mo Aeð óg].

[p] *Uallachan.*—His death is entered in the Ann. Clonm. at the year 902, F. M. 905, but the true year is 910.

[q] *Ugaire, son of Oilell.*—He died in 915, according to the Ann. F. M.

[r] *Buadhach, son of Mothla.*—Ann. F. M. 905.

Kal. Aipóc ionsnaó .i. na uí spén do piot maille in uno die. 1 pjiiu. nom Man. Ounlang mac Coipbpe, pigóamna Laigin, mopituji. Oomnall mac Aoóa, pi Ailig do gabail baéla. Maolmópóa, pjiinceapp [.i. aipéinnce] Tipe oa glap, mopituji.

Gaítin mac Ugpain, pigóamna Laoigipi, mopicup. buaóaé mac Gojigain, pigóamna hUa mbaippce, mopicup. Óianim ingín Ouib-giolla, bín Ounluing, mopicup; unoe oicicup:—

Óianim dion ap noaoine, popcaét gpeim Rig na nóúile,
Ouppan taoó pba puaiéñig, do beié i n-uaiptig úipe.

Inpíó Oppaige la Copmac pig na nÓéipi, 7 cealla iomóa [do] milleó 7 ceall manaé. Ro maptpat Oppaige deapbpatair an Chopmaic .i. Cuilínnan; an tan po baoi Copmac ag milleó Oppaige, táinig Maolpuanaió mac Néill, mac an pí po baoi peime popp na Óéipib, 7 opím do Oppaigib leip, dapéip Copmaic go dúnaó an Copmaic, 7 táinig an Cuileannán a pupppanup pímainn na n-aigió, 7 do pao deabaió doib, 7 po maptaó Cuileannán pan deabaiópin. Ag iompóó do Copmac po cuala an pgélpin, 7 ad connaipc pén éoaé a bpátap a láim an loéta po maptb é. Ba oubaé, dobrónaé iapttain Copmac.

Ip in mbliadain pi po maptaó mac bpaonáin, mic Cpíbaill go tpuag ap láp a daingin pén, 7 gép paoil Oiapmaid go maó peppde

---

[1] *A wonderful sign.*—This wonder is entered in the Ann. Clonm. at 902, but in the Ann. Ult. at 910 [911].

[2] *Dunlang.*—Ann. F. M. 906.

[3] *Domhnall.*—Ann. F. M. 906; Ann. Ult. 911. He was the eldest son of Aedh Finnliath, monarch of Ireland, and the ancestor of the family of O'Donnelly.

[4] *Maelmordha.*—Ann. F. M. 905.

[5] *Gaeithin.*—Ann. F. M. 906.

[6] *Buadhach.*—Ann. F. M. 906.

[7] *Dianimh.*—Ann. F. M. 906, where these lines are quoted.

[911.] Kal. A wonderful sign[s], i. e. two suns moving together during one day, i. e. prid. non. Maii. Dunlang[t], son of Cairbre, royal heir of Leinster, died.

Domhnall[u], son of Aedh, King of Ailech, took the [pilgrim's] staff. Maelnordha[x], princeps (i. e. erenach) of Tir-da-glas, died.
Gaeithin[y], son of Ughran, royal heir of Laeighis, died.
Buadhach[z], son of Gossan, royal heir of Ui-Bairrche, died.
Dianinh[a], daughter of Duibhghill, wife of Dunlang, died; unde dicitur:—

Dianinh, shelter of our people, is fettered by the power of the King of the elements.
Alas! that her tall and beautiful person is in a cold house of clay.

The plundering of Osraighe by Cormac, King of the Deisi[b], and many [secular] churches and monastic churches were destroyed by him. The Osraighi killed the brother of Cormac, i. e. Cuilennan. When Cormac was plundering Osraighe, Maelruanaidh, son of Niall, the son of the king who was before him over the Deisi, having a party of the Osraighi with him, pursued Cormac to Cormac's own residence, and the Cuilennan whom we have mentioned before came to oppose them, and gave them battle, and Cuilennan was killed in that battle. On Cormac's return he heard this news, and he saw the clothes of his brother in the hands of those who had slain him, and he was melancholy and sorry in consequence.

In this year the son of Braenan, son of Cearbhall, was piteously slain in the middle of his own fortress, and though Diarmaid[c] thought that

[b] *Cormac, King of the Deisi.*—This entry is not in the published Annals. This Cormac is mentioned by the F. M. at 915, and his death is recorded by them at 917.
[c] *Diarmaid.*—This Diarmaid, King of Ossory, was uncle to the murdered chief-

ᵹeᴘᴘᴅe ᴅó maᴘbaᴅ mic a bᴘácaᴘ, ní amlaıᴅ ᴅo ᴘála ᴅó, uaıᴘ ᴅo
eıᴘᵹᴄcuᴘ Clann Ɗunᵹaıle uıle cᴘıᴅ ᴘın ı ᴄᴄᴀn Ɗıaᴘmaᴅa, ⁊
amaıl na eıᴘᵹᴄᴅ Ceallać aıᴘ, aᴘ amlaıᴅ ᴘo eıᴘᵹe Maolmóᴘᴅa
mac bᴘácaᴘ ᴅó na ᴄᴀn, ⁊ ᴘé cuımneᴄ ın aıncᴘıᴅe ᴅo ᴘıᵹne Ɗıaᴘmaıᴅ ᴘe a a aᴛaıᴘ, ⁊ ᴘé na ᴘᴀóıᴘ ann: ⁊ ᴘo eıᴘᵹe an Maolmóᴘᴅa
ᴘın ᵹo ᴘeoᴄaıᴘ beaᴅa ı ᴄᴄᴀn Ɗıaᴘmaca, ᴘónaıc ᴅá Oᴘᴘaıᵹe ᴅ'Oᴘ-
ᴘaıᵹıb cᴘéᴘ an ᴄoᵹaᴅ ᴘın: ᴘo baoı maᴘbaᴅ móᴘ ᴄcaᴘᴘa. Ɔaınıᵹ
ᴅna mac Cloᴅa mic Ɗuıbᵹıolla, mac ón ınᵹıne Cᴘbaıll mic Ɗun-
laınᵹ, ı n-aıᵹıᴅ Ɗıaᴘınaᴅa, aᴘ ba ᵹoıᴘc leıᴘ mac bᴘácaᴘ a mácaᴘ
⁊ a ᴅala ᴅo maᴘbaᴅ la Ɗıaᴘmaıᴅ. Móᴘ ᴘaoᴘᴄlann ᴘo maᴘbaıc
ᴘaın ᴄaᵹaᴅᴘa, ⁊ móᴘ ceall ᴘó ᴘáᴘaıᵹıc.

Ƙal. Saᴘuᵹhaᴅ Cᴘᴅmacha ᴅo Cᴘnaᴄán mac Ɗuılᵹen, ᴄᴅon,
cımıᴅ [.ı. bᴘaıᵹe] ᴅo bᴘeıc eᴘce, (.ı. aᴘ ın ceıll) ⁊ a báᴅaᵹ Illoᴄ
Cıᴘᴘ. Cᴘnaᴄán ıaᴘ ᴘın ᴅo báᴅaᵹ ᴅo Nıall Ꮡlúnᴅub ın eoᴅem
lacu, ı nᴅíoᵹaıl ᴘáᴘaıᵹᴛe Cᴘᴅmaᴄa.

Maoılbᴘıᵹᴅe ımuᴘᴘo mac Maoılᴅomnaıᵹ, ab Lıᴘ móᴘ moᴘıcuᴘ.

Ƒlann mac Laoıᵹe, ab Coᴘcaıᵹe moᴘıcuᴘ.

Coᴘmac eᴘᴄop Saıᵹᴘe.

Ɔıobᴘaıᴅe ab Imleaᴄa moᴘıcuᴘ.

Maoılbᴘıᵹᴅe mac Ɔoᴘnáın, comaᴘba Ƥháᴅᴘaıcc ⁊ Colum cılle,
ᵹo n-ıoınaᴅ cléıᴘeaᴄ 'Eıᴘeann leıᴘ, ım Mumaın ᴅ'áccuınᵹıᴅ ıonmaıᴘ
aᴘ maıcıb Mumaın ᴅa ᴛabaıᴘc ı ᴘuaᴘlaᵹaᴅ bᴘaıᴅe bᴘᴄcon; ⁊
ᴘuaıᴘᴘıom ᴘaın; ⁊ cuᵹ laıᴘ an mbᴅᴘaıᴅ cᴛᴘuaᵹ ᴘın aᴘ mbáᴅaᴅ a

long,

_d *Cearnachan, son of Duilgen.*—This en-
tain, and is mentioned by the F. M. at the
years 900, 914, 917; but this passage,
which was evidently preserved in some
Ossorian collection of Annals, is nowhere
given by them.

try is given by the F. M. at the year 907,
but in the Ann. Ult. at 911 [912]. The
situation or modern name of Loch Cirr is
now unknown.

_e *Maelbrighde.*—Ann. F. M. 907; Ann.
Ult. 911 [912].

that he would be the better of the killing of his brother's son; it did not turn out so to him, for in consequence of this all the Clann Dunghaile rose up against Diarmaid, and, as if Ceallach would not rise against him, Maelmordha, the son of a brother of his, rose up against him, being mindful of the cruelty which Diarmaid had exercised against his father when he was an old man; and this Maelmordha rose up fiercely and vigorously against Diarmaid, and they divided Osraighe into two parts by that war. There was great slaughter between them. The son of Aedh, son of Duibhghilla (who was the son of the daughter of Cearbhall, son of Dunlaing), came also against Diarmaid, for it was bitter to him that the son of his mother's brother, and his *alumnus*, should have been killed by Diarmaid. Many nobles were killed during this war, and many churches were wasted.

[912.] Kal. The plundering of Ard-Macha by Cearnachan, son of Duilgen[d], i. e. by taking a prisoner out of it [i. e. out of the church], and drowning him in Loch Cirr. Cearnachan was afterwards drowned by Niall Glundubh in the same lake, in revenge of the profanation of Ard-Macha.

Maelbrighde[e], son of Maeldomhnach, Abbot of Lis-mor, died.

Flann, son of Laegh[f], Abbot of Corcach, died.

Cormac[g], Bishop of Saighir [Serkieran], [died].

Tibraide[h], Abbot of Imleach [Emly], died.

Maelbrighde, son of Tornan[i], successor of Patrick and Colum-Cille, with many ecclesiastics, [went] into Munster to solicit gifts from the men of Munster to ransom the prisoners of the Britons, and he obtained them, and he brought with him the miserable prisoners, their

[f] *Flann, son of Laegh.*—Ann. F. M. 907.
[g] *Cormac.*—Ann. F. M. 907.
[h] *Tibraide.*—Ann. F. M. 908.
[i] *Maelbrighde, son of Tornan.*—Something like this is entered by the F. M. at 908, and Ann. Ult. at 912 [913] thus: "Maelbrighte mac Tornain came into Mounster to release pilgrims of the British."

Long, ⁊ aṗ na cċuppiom ı ċċíp, ⁊ aṗ ċċoıṁċċ ṁóıṁ aṗ ıonnṁaṁáıl
Danaṗ ⁊ Loċlann.

ᴋal. Maolınoeṁóc pṗıncepṗ Ḋpoma móṗ moṗıcuṗ.
Tıobpaıce epṗcop Cluana cṁnṁċ moṗıcuṗ.

Caċpaoıneaṁ ṗé Maoılmıċhıṁ mac Flannaṁáın ⁊ ṗc nDonn-
chaṁ hUa Maoılṗeaċloınn poṗ Lopċán mac nDunchaıṁ, ⁊ poṗ
Poṁaṗcaċ mac Tolaıṗṁ, ṁu ı ċċoṗcaıṗ ıle. Laċċnán mac Cṗṗnaıṁ,
ṗí Dúın Naıṗn Laoıṁṗı, moṗıcuṗ. Maolpaṁpaıc mac Flaċṗoe,
ṗí Raċa Doṁnaıṁ, moṗıcuṗ. Ećalṁ, ṗı Saxoın cuaıṗṁṗċ moṗıcuṗ.
Flaıċṁeaṗcaċ mac Ionmaınen ı ṗıṁe Caıṗıl.

Coṁlaċ lánṁóṗ Loċlann [ṁo] ṁaṁaıl aṁ Poṗċ Laıṗṁe, ⁊ ṗoċla
Oṗṗaıṁe .ı. cuaıṗṁṗċ Oṗṗaıṁe, ṁ'ıonṗpaṁ ṁóıṁ; bṗaṁ móṗ ⁊ ıomaṁ
bó, ⁊ eallaıṁ ṁo ṁṗeıċ ṁóıṁ ṁo nuıṁe a longa.

Tanṁaċċuṗ 'ṗan ṁlıaṁaın ṗın ṗlóıṁ móṗa Duṁṁall ⁊ Fıonnṁall
ṁoṗṁıṗı ṁ'ıonṗoıṁċe Saxon aṗ ṗíoṁaṁ Sıċṗuca hUí Iomaıṗ. Ro
ṗuaṁṗaċċuṗ caċ poṗ Saxoın, ⁊ aṗṗṁ ón na ṗo ṗuıṗṁṗċcuṗ Saxoın
aċċ canṁaċċuṗ ṗo ċéṁuaıṗ ṁ'ıonṗoıṁıṁ na bPáṁánac. Ro cuıṗṗṁ
caċ cṗuaıṁ ṗeoċaıṗ eaċċoṗṗa, aṁuṗ ba móṗ bṗıṁ, ⁊ bṗúċ ⁊ coṗ-
naṁ cṗċċaṗnae. Ro coṁaılṁṁ móṗ ṗola ṗaoṗċlann 'ṗan ċaċ ṗa;
ṁıoṗṁ ıṗ ıaṁ Saxoın ṗuṁ buaıṁ ⁊ coṗṁaṗ aṗ maṗṁaṁ oṗṗṁáṗ na
bPaṁánaċ, uaıṗ ṁo ṁaṁ ṁaloṗ ṗí na bPaṁánaċ, ⁊ ṗuṁaṁ aṗ ın ċaċ
é ṁo

ᵏ *Maelmaedhóg.*—His death is entered in the Annals of F. M. at 909.
ˡ *Tibraide.*—Ann. F. M. 909.
ᵐ *Maelmithidh.*—Ann. F. M. 909.
ⁿ *Dun-Nair in Laeighis.*—A place in the Queen's County. This entry is not in the published Annals.
ᵒ *Rath-domhnaigh.*—Now Rathdowney, a small town in the barony of Upper Ossory, Queen's County. It is called Rath-Tamhnaigh.—F. M., A. D. 909.
ᵖ *Ethalbh.*—Æthulf, or Æthelwulf.
ᵠ *Flaithbhertach, son of Inmainen.*—He was Abbot of Inis-Cathaigh, and had been the chief cause of the Battle of Bealach Mughna, in which Cormac Mac Cuillenain was killed. He became King of Munster A. D. 908, and died 944.
ʳ *Lochlanns.*—This entry is given in the Ann. F. M. at 910, but the true year is 913.

their ships having been swamped, and themselves cast ashore, having come to shun the Danes and Lochlanns.

[913.] Kal. Maelmaedhóg[k], princeps [i. e. abbot] of Drum-mor. died.

Tibraide[l], Bishop of Cluain-cidhnach [Clonenagh], died.

A battle was gained by Maelmithidh[m], son of Flannagan, and Donnchadh Ua Maelsechlainn, over Lorcan, son of Donchadh, and Fogartach, son of Tolarg, in which many fell: Lachtnan, son of Cearnach, King of Dun-Nairn in Laeighis[n], died. Maelpatraic, son of Flathrai, King of Rath-domnaigh[o], died. Ethalbh[p], King of the North Saxons, died.

Flaithbhertach, son of Inmainen[q], [was installed] in the kingdom of Caisel.

A very large fleet of Lochlanns[r] settled at Port-Lairgè [Waterford], and plundered the north of Osraighe: they carried off a great number of prisoners, and many cows and small cattle to their ships.

There came in this year great hosts of Black Galls[s] and Fair Galls[t] again into Saxonland, after setting up Sitric, grandson of Imhar, as king. They challenged the Saxons to battle. And the Saxons did not indeed delay, but they came at once to meet the Pagans. A stubborn and fierce battle[u] was fought between them, and great was the vigour, and strength, and emulation on both sides. Much of the blood of nobles was spilled in that battle, but it was the Saxons that gained victory and triumph, after having made great havoc of the

Pagans,

---

[s] *Black Galls.*—Or dark foreigners, i. e. Danes.

[t] *Fair Galls.*—Or fair-haired foreigners, i. e. Norwegians.

[u] *Fierce battle.*—This is perhaps the same battle described in the Saxon Chron. at the year 911, in which Otter the Earl and many other Danish chieftains were slain, but the two narratives do not agree in every particular; nor does the Saxon Chronicle mention Sitric, grandson of Imhar, as the leader of the party.

é go coill baoi coṁpoċpaiḃ ḋóiḃ, ⁊ ba maṗḃ ann ṗin é. Oiccip ono an c-iapla ba moó muipn 'pan caċ pa, ó po ċonnaipc áp a ṁuinn-cipe ꝺo ċup ꝺo na Saxonaiḃ, apeḋ ꝺo piġne, ceiéſḃ po cailliḃ nꝺlúiċ baoi i compoċpaiḃ ꝺo, ⁊ in neoċ po ṁaip ꝺa ṁuinncip leip. Cangaccup ꝺponga ꝺíoṁópa Saxon 'na ḃſġhaiḋ, ⁊ po ġaḃpac mun gcaille maccuapc. Ro iopail imuppo an piogan oppa an ċaill uile no éſpgaꝺ ꝺa cclaiḋṁiḃ, ⁊ ꝺa ccuaxaiḃ: ⁊ apſḃ on ꝺo piġneḋ aṁlaiḋ. Ro cpapgpaḋ an caill ap cúp, ⁊ pa maṗḃaꝺ uile na Pa-gánaig, po baccup pan ccaile. Ra maṗḃaiꝺ cpa aṁlaiḋ pin na Pagánꝺa lapin píogan go po lſċ a clu ap gaċ leiċ.

Oo piġne Eꝺelpiꝺa cpia na gliocap péin pí ́ḋ ppia piopa Alban, ⁊ pe bpeacnuiḃ, giḃé can ciugpaiꝺíp an cinſḃ céꝺna ꝺa hionpoighiḋ, gup po eipxpimippin ꝺo congnam lé. Oamaꝺ ċucapoṁ no ċaopꝺaoip, gup po eipgeḋpi leopum. Céin po ḃap ime pin, po lingpioc pip Alban ⁊ bpſcan po bailiḃ na Loċlonn, pa millpioꝺ, ⁊ pa aipgpioꝺ iaꝺ. Cainig pí Loċlann iapccain, ⁊ pa aipg Spaic cluaiꝺe, .i. pa aip an cíp, aċc ní po cumaing namaiꝺ [ní] ꝺo Spaiċ cluaiꝺe.

˟ *Etheldrida.*—See above, p. 227, note ᴾ, and comp. Lappenberg's History of England (Thorpe's Transl.), vol. ii., p. 92 *sq.* From the manner in which "the Queen" is here mentioned, it would seem that the transactions here recorded must have taken place after the death of Æthelred in 912, or during the illness which incapaci-

Pagans, for the King of the Pagans had contracted a disease, and he was carried from the battle to a neighbouring wood, where he died. But when Otter, the most influential Iarl that was in the battle, saw that his people were slaughtered by the Saxons, he fled to the dense woods which were in his neighbourhood, carrying with him the survivors of his people. Great parties of Saxons followed in pursuit of them, and they encompassed the wood round about. The Queen ordered them to cut all the wood down with their swords and axes. And they did so accordingly. They first cut down the wood, and [afterwards] killed all the Pagans who were in the wood. In this manner did the Queen kill all the Pagans, so that her fame spread abroad in every direction.

Etheldrida[x], through her own wisdom, made a treaty with the men of Alba and the Britons, that whenever the same race should come to attack her, they would rise up to assist her; and that should they come to them, she would assist them. While they were thus joined, the men of Alba and Britain attacked the towns of the Lochlanns, which they destroyed and pillaged. The King of the Lochlanns afterwards arrived, and plundered Srath Cluaide[y], i. e. he plundered the country, but the enemy was not able to take Srath Cluaide.

tated him from taking any part in public affairs.

[y] *Srath Cluaide.*—i. e. Strathclyde, in North Britain.

GENERAL INDEX.

ABHAIN Mor, or Avonmore, 217, n.
Achadh arglais, or Agha, 171.
Achadh mic Earclaidhe, 145.
Adamnan, when a school-boy, story of, 75, seq.; relics of, 55; assumes abbacy of Ia, 89; ransoms captives, 89; comes to Ireland, 93; promulgates "Law of Innocents," 97; his contention with Irgalach, 101; his rule for celebration of Easter, 111; death of, 115.
Adolph, king of the Saxons, 151.
Aedh, son of Ainmire, 8, n., 9.
—— Allan, 12, n., 23, 29, 42, n., 45, 59.
—— king of Ailech, 129.
—— of Carn Tasaigh, 219.
—— son of Cumascach, 155.
—— son of Duibhghilla, 239, 243.
—— son of Dluthach, 95.
—— son of Dubhdabhoirenn, 153.
—— Finnliath, 155, 157.
—— Laigbcan, 42, n., 50, n., 51.
—— son of Maelduin, 99.
—— Menn, 41.
—— Finnliath, son of Niall, 141, 143, 147, 151, 157, 159, 171, 177, 189.
—— Roin, king of Uladh, 59.
—— bishop of Sleibhte, 99.
—— Uairidhnach, 11, 12, n.
—— king of Ui-Leathan, 211.
Aedhagan, son of Finnacht, 177.
Aedhan the leper, 37.
Aedhgen Ua Maithe, 49.
Æthelred, king of the Saxons, 231, n.
Aenghus, king of Fortrenn, 55.
—— son of Faelchu, 55.
—— a sage of Cluain Ferta Molua, 153.
—— the high wise man, 141.
—— son of Bec Boirche, death of, 57.
—— Uladh, death of, 65.
Ailbhe. See Magh Ailbhe.
Aidhne, territory of, 211, n.

Ailech, destruction of, by Finnachta, 71.
Ailech-Frigrinn, 23.
Aileran the wise, death of, 65.
Ailen, the two sons of, 51.
Ailgenan, son of Dunghal, king of Munster, 129, 135.
Ailell Banbhan, abbot of Biror. 153.
—— bishop and abbot of Fore, 195.
—— son of Bodhbhcha, 53.
—— of Clochar, 185.
—— son of Conall Grant, 51.
—— son of Cu-gan-mathair, 103.
—— son of Domhnall, death of, 67.
—— son of Dunghal, 93.
—— son of Dunlang, 195.
—— son of Eoghan, 211.
Aillinn, battle of, 57.
Aindli, wise man of Tir-da-ghlas, 135.
Ainge, river, 118, n.
Aircelltair, or Ailcelltra, battle of, 71, 77.
Airghialla, 34, n.
Airiur-Gaeidhel (or Argyle), 14, n.
Airmeadhach of Craebh, 89.
Airthera, or Orior, 155.
Albain, or Scotland, 40, n.
Albanachs, the, 231.
Albdan, king of Lochlann, 159.
Alle, king of the Saxons, 173.
Almhain, or Allen, hill of, 32, n.; kings slain in battle of, 49–51, 221.
Amlacihh, 223.
—— Conung, 127.
—— son of king of Lochlann, 135, 149, 151, 157, 171, 173, 185, 195.
Anastasius, 21.
Aneslis, or Beal-Borumha, 216, n.
Anglesea, or Mona Conain, 155.
Aodhan Mac Gabrain, 7.
Ara Cliach, 147.
Aradh Tire, 141.

2 K

Arcadians of Cliach, 131.
Ard-Macha, burning of, 69, 185, 243.
—— plundered, 127.
Argyle, ancient name of, 14, n.
Aunites, or Danes, 159.
Attacotts, the word, 237.
Ath-muiceadha, 131.

Badbh, 191.
Baedan, abbot of Cluain-mic-nois, 65.
Baeth-galach, 45.
Baithin, abbot of Beuchair, 67.
Balearic Isles, 163.
Banbhan, scribe of Cill-dara, 89.
Barith the Earl, 173, 197.
Bealach Chonglais, 131.
—— Gabhráin, 189.
—— Lice, battle of, 53.
Bec Boirche, 87.
Beccan, abbot of Cluain-Iraird, 93.
Bece Ua Leathlabair, king of Dal Araidhe, 225.
Bede, date of his work, 56, n.; death of, 65; reference to, 113, 115.
Beg Boirche, slayer of Congall Cennfoda, 71.
Bennchair, deaths of four abbots of, 65.
—— burning of, 69.
Berbha, or the Barrow, 85, 239.
Black men of Erin, 163.
Blathmac, son of Aedh Slaine, 63, 65.
—— son of Maelcobha, 69.
Blue men of Eriu, 163.
Bodhbhchar, son of Diarmaid Ruanaidh, 111.
Boghaine, 48, n.
Boinn, or Boyne, 10, n., 101, n.
Boirinn, battle of, 55.
Boromean tribute, 22, n., 33, 34, n.
Borumha, the tax so called, 76, n.; remission of, 93.
—— book so called, 78, n.
—— Laighen, 82.
Bracn, 225.
Breenan, son of Cearbhally, 241.
Bran, 225.
—— son of Conall Beg, 97, 109.
—— Dubh, 239.
—— king of Leinster, 40.
—— son of Maeluchtraigh, 69.
Breagh plundered by the Lochlanns, 153.
—— Magh, 21, 118, n.
Breasal Breac, ancestor of chiefs of Osraighe, 8, n.
Breifnians, attack on Meath by, 237.
Brenann, 165, 167.
—— of Biror, 6, n., 7.
Brendan, St., 6. n.
Brigit, St., 17, 40, n.
Britain Gaimud, 155.

Bruide, son of Deril, 111.
—— son of Bile, 89, 93.
Bnachail, son of Dunadhach, 195.
Buadhach, son of Gossan, 241.
—— son of Mothla, 239.
Buan of Albaio, 41.

Cadell, son of Roderick, 225, 227.
Caer Ebroic, or York, 159, 171.
Caireog, son of Dunog, 225.
Calatros, battle of, 87.
Caltruim, 65.
Cana, son of Gartnan, 91.
Cantabrian Sea, 159
Carn Lughdhach, 137, 139.
Carrleagh, 14, n.
Carlingford Lough, 120, n.
Casan, scribe of Lusca, 97.
Cathal (son of Aedh), battle of, 60, n., 61.
—— son of Fingaine, king of Munster, 21, 57.
Catharnach, 211, 217.
Cathasach, abbot of Ard-Macha, 143.
—— son of Luirgne, 69.
—— son of Maelduin, 87.
Cathbuaidh, 231.
Carthach, abbot of Tir-da-ghlas, 135.
Ceallach, son of Cearbhall, 207, 211.
—— abbot of Cill-dara and 1, 163.
—— King of Feara-Cualann, 213, 217, 219, 225.
—— son of Guaire, 151.
—— son of Raghallach, 105.
Ceannmaghair, 28, n.
Cearbhall, son of Dunlaing, 129, 131, 135, 139, 141, 143, 147, 153, 155, 157, 177, 189.
—— son of Maelodhra, 95.
—— son of Muirigen, 201, 211, 215, 217, 221, 223, 225.
Cearmait, son of Catharnach, 157.
—— son of Cinaedh, 151.
Cearnachan, son of Duilgen, 243.
Celle, son of Urthuile, Prior of Aghabo, 199.
Ceilechar, brother of Cingégan, 207.
Ceallach, son of Faelchair, 57.
Cele-Christ, 55.
Cele-Dabhaill, 227.
Cenndeilgtin, or Cenndelgtben, battle of, 53, 109.
Cennedigh, son of Gaithin, 157, 159, 165, 170, 173, 189.
Cenn-Etigh, or Kinnitty, 210, n.
Cennfaeladh, son of Colgan, 87.
—— son of Crunmhael, 71, 77.
—— son of Maelbresail, 93.
—— son of Suibhne, 87.
—— king of Ui Conaill, 211.
—— Ua Muichtigherna, King of Caisil, or Munster, 153, 169, 197.

General Index. 251

Cer of Cera, 51.
Cetamun, 57.
Cethernach, son of Nae Ua Ceallaigh, 55.
Chester, 228, n., 233.
Children, mortality of, 89.
Cian, son of Cumascach, 185.
Cianachta, of Meath, or of Bregia, the territory called, 32, n., 116, n., 125, 177.
Cianachta Glinne Gaimhin, 87.
Ciar, daughter of Duibhrea, 87.
Ciarmacan, 199.
Ciarmach Ua Dunadhaigh, king of Ui Conaill Gabhra, 199.
Ciarraighi, or Kerry-men, 167.
Ciarodhar, son of Crunnmhael, 199.
Cicaire, king of Osraighe, 85.
Cill Ausaille, 197.
Cillene Fota, abbot of Ia, 53.
Cill-na-gCaillech destroyed, 239.
—— Nais, 224, n.
—— ruaidh, 53, n.
—— Ua nDaighre, battle of, 177.
Cinnedh, Caech, son of Irgalach, 51, 53, 55, 57, 109.
—— Mac Ailpin, king of the Picts, 151.
—— Cinaeth, son of Conaing, 117, 119.
Cinoide, son of Gaeithin, 153.
Cinel-Cairbre, 50, n.
Cinel-Conaill and Cinel-Eoghain, 30, n., 35.
Cinel-Conaill, sovereignty of Erin separated from, 59.
Claenadh, battle of, 109.
Clane, round hill of, 39, n.
Clereén, king of Ui-Bairche, 213.
Clergy, presence of the, in warlike expeditions, 210, n.
Clonard, ancient name of, 14, n.
Clothna, son of Colgan, 49.
Cluain-Dobhail, 36, n.
—— eidhneach, 11.
—— fearta-Brenainn, 163.
—— Iraird, 14, n.
—— Uamha, or Cloyne, 205.
Cobhthach, abbot of Kildare, 187.
Cobhthach-Cael-mBreagh, 39.
Cochall-Odhar, death of, 57.
Coibhdenach, son of Fincha, 49.
Colga, son of Blathmac, 87.
Colgu, son of Eochaidh, 57.
—— son of Failbhe Flann, 85.
—— son of Domhnall, death of, 65.
Colman Banbain, 53.
—— Beg, 7.
—— son of Fergus, 11.
—— abbot of Benchair, death of, 87.
—— Cas, death of, 65.
—— abbot of Cenn-Etigh, 211, 217, 225.

Colman, son of Dunlang, 163.
—— son of Finnbhar, 105.
—— Ua Altain, 57.
—— Ua Chuasaigh, 61; his sailing to Inis-bofiune, 67; his death, 71.
—— Uamach, 53.
Colum-Cille, his story respecting death of Feradhach, 9; his death, 11; patron of Cinell Conaill, 40, n.; his manner of tonsuring, 21, 113; his relics brought to Ireland, 125, n.; crozier of, 231.
Comauns, plundering of the, 197.
Comhgall of Beanchar, 199.
Comhgan Fota, abbot of Tamlacht, 187.
Compimu, the word, 40, n.
Cunacan, son of Colman, 129.
Conaing, son of Congal, 61, 63.
Conall of Cill Scire, 175.
—— Crau, 49.
—— Men, king of Cinel-Cairbre, 51, 107.
—— son of Domhnall, death of, 65.
—— Gabhra, 107.
—— son of Niall of the Nine Hostages, 30, n.
—— Ultach, 153.
Conchadh, king of the Cruithnigh, 59.
Conchobhar Aired, King of Dal Araidhe, 99.
—— son of Donuchadh, 157.
Condail, the word, 26, n.
Condail of the kings, 44, n.
Congal, 211, 217.
—— Caech, 17, 18, n.
—— Cennfoda, son of Dunchadh, 71.
—— the Senior, king of Ciarraighe, 167.
—— son of Fergus of Fanaid, 26, n., 33.
—— son of Lorchine, 69.
—— son of Maelduin, 93.
Congalach, son of Conain, 49, 95, 97.
Conmael, 36, n.
Connaught plundered by Cearbhall and Duunchadh, 195.
Conneire, or Connor, 66, n.
Connell, Old, 11, n.
Connga, the, 223.
Conula, son of Breasal Breac, race of, 8, n., 9.
Connmach, abbot of Cluain-mic-nois, 177.
Conodhar of the Ui-Toirdealbhaigh, 211, 217.
Coning, son of Godfraidh, 195.
Corann, battle of, 89, 107.
Corban's church, 7.
Corca-Laighde, 8, n., 9; interchange of kings of, with those of Osraighe, 8, n., 9; O'Driscoll, chief of, 8, n.
Corcach, or Cork, 169.
Cormac, son of Cuilenan, 201, 207, 221.
—— king of the Deisi, 211, 213, 217, 241.
—— son of Dunlang, 139.
—— son of Elathach, 165.
—— son of Elothach, 185.

2 K 2

Cormac of Lathrach Brinin, 143.
— son of Mothla, 207, 209.
— son of Maelfothartagh, 69.
— bishop of Saighir, 243.
— Ua Liathain, 175.
Corrbile, 41.
Cosgrach of Tigh Telle, 175.
Crannacht, battle of, 97.
Crimhthann, son of Cellach, 53.
Critan, abbot of Benchair, 67.
Crohane, Co. Tipperary, ancient name of, 134, n.
Cronan Mac Ua Cualna, abbot of Benchair, 93.
— the Dwarf, abbot of Cluain mic nois, 95.
Cruachan Claenta, 39.
Crufait, or Croboy, 125.
Cruachain, in the Eoganacht-Chaisil, or Cruachan Maighe Eamhna, 134, n., 135.
Cruithne, or Cruithnigh, Picts, 59, n., 87.
Cu, names compounded with, 36, n., 37, n.
Cubretan, 36, n., 45.
Cuganmathair, king of Munster, death of, 65.
Cuilennan, brother of Cormac, 241.
Culuin Finn, abbot of Ia, 67.
— Foda, death of, 61.
Cuindles, abbot of Cluain-mic-Nois, 53.
Culoingsi, the son of, 51.
Cumar-na-tri-n-uisce, 139.
Cumascach, son of Ronan, 69.
Cummeni of Mughdhorna, 97.
Cumsudh, abbot of Castlekieran, 187.
— bishop of Cluain-Iraird, 151.
Curui, abbot of Inis Clothrann, 195.
Cuthbertus, bishop, 91.

Dachonna, bishop of Conneire, 53.
Dalach, abbot of Cluain mic Nois, 153.
Dallan, son of Mor, 217.
Danes, the, 131, 133, 173.
— and Lochlanns, the, 117, 159.
— See Lochlanns.
Darerca, St., extract from life of, 9, n.
Deilginis-Cualann, 59.
Deisi, the 169.
Desgabhair, or South Leinster, 219, n.
Desies, the, plundered, 157.
Dianimh, daughter of Duibhghilla, 241.
Diarmaid, 127, 157, 169, n.
— cemetery of, 205.
— son of Aedh Slaine, death of, 65.
— son of Cearbhall, 213.
— abbot of Cluain-Iraird, 17.
— abbot of Ferns, 187.
— Midhe, son of Airmheadhach Caech, 93.
— king of Osraighe, or Ossory, 241, 237.
Dicuill, son of Eochaidh, 69.
Dinertach, abbot of Lothra, 169.

Dinn-Canainn, 39.
Dinnrigh, 38, n.
Disert-Diarmada, or Castledermot, 203.
Dochuma Chonoc, abbot of Gleann-da-locha, 89.
Doer, son of Maeltuile, 71.
Domhnall, son of Aedh, 155, 241.
— Breac, son of Eochaidh Buidhe, 87, 89.
— king of Connaught, death of, 57.
— king of Dun Cearmna, 211, 217, 219.
— grandson of Dunlaing, 157.
— Mac Ailpin, King of the Picts, 153.
Doiriadh, son of Conla, 51.
Dongaluch Ua Aenghusa, 51.
Donnagan, son of Cedfad, 185.
Donnchadh, son of Murchadh, 41, 52, n.
— Ua Fiachrach, 51.
— Ua Maelsechlainn, 245.
Donnbo, 34, n., 38, 47.
Donnsleibhe, son of, 21.
Druim-Coepis, battle of, 69.
— Corcain, battle of, 57.
— eriaidh, or Drumcree, battle of, 237.
— Fornacht, battle of, 55.
Drust, King of Alba, 55.
Duach, King of Osraighe, death of son of, 7.
Dubhaltach Firbisigh, or Mac Firbisigh, 1, 193.
Dubhartach Berrach, 177.
Dubhdabhoirenn, 211, 217, 219.
Dubhdachrioch, son of Dubhdabhoirenn, 51.
Dubhdainbher, King of Ard Cianachta, 91.
Dubhdathuile, abbot of Liath Mochaemhog, 18.
Dubhdibhderg, son of Dunghal, 107.
Dubhghlaise, or Donglas, 85.
Dubhagan, King of Fera-Maighe, 211, 217.
Dubhlach, 217.
Dubhthach, abbot of Cill-achaidh, 195.
— son of Maeltuile, 185.
Dudley Firbisse, 1.
Duibhduin, 69.
Duncannon, 39, n.
Dunbolg, or Donard, 189.
Dun Carman, 218, n., 221.
— Cearmna, 211, n.
— Ceithirn, or Giant's Sconce, 87.
Dunchadh, 225.
Dunchadhs, the two, 105.
Dunchadh, son of Cormac, slain, 57.
— son of Donnghal, 177.
— Muirisge, son of Maeldubh, 89.
— son of Murchadh, 57.
— Ua Ronain, 69.
Dun Dearmhaigh, 219, n.
Dungaile, son of Maeltuile, 69.
Dunghal, King of the Cruithni, or Picts, 87.
Dun-locha, battle of, 87.
Dun-Sobhairce, or Dunseverick, 66, n., 195.

General Index.

Dunlaing, son of Cairbre, 241.
—— son of Muireadhach, 185.
Dun-Neachtain, battle of, 89.

Easter, the celebration of, 111.
Ecbertus, death of, 57.
Eclipse of the sun, 169.
Ederscel, king of Bregia, 53.
Egnechan, son of Dalach, 199.
Eidgin Brit, bishop of Cill-dara, 157.
Eidhen, King of Aidhne, 211, 217.
Eignech, son of Conaing, 49.
Elodhach, son of Flann O'Sgigi, 51.
Emhir's Island, i. e. Ireland, 197.
Eochaidh Iarlaithe, king of Dal-Araidhe, death of, 65.
Eochaidh Leamhna, 107.
Eodhus, son of Dunghal, 185.
Eodus, son of Ailell, slain, 57.
Eoghan, race of, 18.
—— son of Niall of the Nine Hostages, 30, *n.*
Eoganacht Chaisil, 134, *n*, 147, 155.
Erannan, son of Criomhthan, 37.
Escra, a silver drinking vessel, 9, *n.*
Etheldrida, St., daughter of Anna, 91.
Ethelfrid, King of Northumbria, 91.
Ethelfrida, Queen of the Saxons, 227, 247.
Etholo, King of North Saxons, 245.

Faelan, 225.
—— son of Colman, 87.
—— king of Leinster, 55, 69.
—— son of Murchadh, 57.
—— Senchustal, king of Ui-Ceinnsealaigh, 85.
Faelchu, abbot of Ia, 53.
Faelcobhar of Clochar, 103.
Faha, 11, *n.*
Fahan, 20, *n.*
Fail, name of Ireland, 48, *n.*
Failbhe, abbot of Ia, death of, 87.
Falchar, king of Osraighe, 93, 95.
Feara-Cualan, 212, *n.*
Fearchair, son of Maelduin, 97.
Fearna, or Ferns, 239.
Fechin of Tobhar, death of, 65.
Feidhlimidh, son of Maelcothaigh, 103.
Feimhin, battle of, 7.
Feradhach, 211, 217.
—— Finn, death of, 7, 11.
Fera Maighe, 155, 169.
—— Ros, 35, 72, *n.*
Ferdomhnach, abbot of Cluain-mic-Nois, 197.
Ferdoragh, baron of Dungannon, 31, *n.*
Fergal, king of Erin, 40, *n.*
—— Glut, 49.
—— hill of, 41, *n.*
—— Ua Aithechta, 19.

Fergal Ua Tamnaigh, 49.
Ferghal Aidhne, king of Connaught, 97.
—— son of Maelduin, 21, 23, 29, 49, 89.
Fergus, son of Aedan, 93.
—— of Fanaid, 26, *n.*
—— Forcraidh, 107.
Fernmhagh, battle of, 57, 99.
Fersat, battle of, 69.
Ferta Cairech, or Fertach, 155.
Fethghna, comharba of Patrick, 127, 141, 149.
Fiachna, 17.
Fiach Ua Ugfadain, of Deabis, 208, *n.*
Fianamhail, son of Maeltuile, king of Leinster, 87, 95.
—— son of Maenach, 97.
Fiannamhail, son of Oisen, 99, 101.
Fidhgal, son of Fithchellach, 51.
Fidh-Gaible, wood of, 48, *n.*
Fincheallach, abbot of Fearna, 153.
Finech and Rechtin, 239.
Finguine, son of Cu-gan-mathair, 97.
Finian of Cluain-caein, 153.
Finn, 225.
Fionnachta, son of Dunchadh, 23 ; victor in battle of Aircelltair, 71 ; beginning of his reign, *ib.* ; stories told respecting, 71, *seq.* ; battle between him and Bec Boirche, 87; his murder, 95.
Finnglais, 175.
Finnian, festival of, 38, *n.*
Finntan Ua Eachach, 11.
Firbisse, Dudley, 1.
Fithchellach, son of Flann, 93.
Flaithbhertach, abbot of Inis-Cathaigh, 201.
—— son of Iomainen, or Ionmainéu, 205-7, 215, 245.
—— son of Loinsech, 55, 57, 59.
—— son of Niall, 129.
Flaitheamhail, son of Dluthach, 51.
Flaithemh, son of Faelchar, 195.
Flaithir, a poet, 67.
Flanna, daughter of king of Osraighe, 179.
Flann, son of Aedh Odhbha, 51.
—— abbot of Benchair, 55.
—— king of Cianachta, 141, 143,157, 171.
—— son of Conaing, 177.
—— son of Domhnall, 199.
—— king of Erin, 213, 219, 237.
—— Fiona, son of Ossa, 111.
—— son of Irghalach, 51.
—— son of Irthuile, 55.
—— son of Laegh, 243.
—— son of Maelsechlainn. *See* Flann Sionna.
—— Sinna Ua Colla, abbot of Cluain-mic-nois, death of, 59.
—— Sionna, son of Maelsechlainn, 165, 201, 205, 211, 237.

General Index.

Flann, son of Tighernan, 237.
Focbard-Muirtheimhne, 59.
Fogartach, son of Geirtide, 109.
—— son of Niall, 51.
—— son of Tolarg, 245.
—— Ua Cernaigh, 20, *n*., 21, 53.
—— son of Suibhne, 211, 217.
Foichsechan, 95.
Follamhan, son of Oilell, 213.
Forannan, abbot of Ard-Macha, 127.
—— abbot of Cill-dara, 99.
Forbasach, 49.
Forod Geilsheirce, 221.
Fortuatha, 212, *n*.
Foirtrenn, or Pictland, 159, 229.
Fothain, 11, *n*.
Fotharta-Fea, 212, *n*.
—— -tire, 163.
Frighrenn, 217.
Frigrinn, Ailech, 23, *n*.
Frosach, Niall, 21.
Frosts, remarkable, 143.
Furadhran, prior of Cill-achaidh, 199.

Gabhorchenn, 91.
Gabhrán, or Gowran, 137, 191.
Gaditanean Straits, 161.
Gaeidhil, or Scoti, 125.
Gaeithing, son of Ughran, 241.
Gaimide of Lughmhagh, 97.
Gaithin, son of, 177.
Gall Craibhtheach, 43, *n*.
Gall-Gaeidhil, or Dano-Irish, 129, 139, 141, 233.
Gall of Lileach, 57.
Galls of Erin, 135, 157, 159.
—— the Black and the Fair, 245.
Gelshere, daughter of Deirill, 221.
Gerald, Pontifex of Mayo, death of, 59.
Geran, son of Diocosc, 187.
Gilla-na-naemh, or Nehemias, 1, *n*.
Glais Chuilg, 109.
Glaisin, son of Uisin, 199.
Gleann na nGealt, 41, *n*.
Glifit, 131.
Gnathnat, abbess of Cill-dara, 93.
Gnia, abbot of Daimhliag-fianain, 197.
Gnim Cinnsiella, 169.
Goffridh, 195.
Gormflaith, daughter of Flann, 223.
Gormlaith, Queen of Teambra, 153.
Greallach-Dollaidh, 95.
Greenan Ely, 23, *n*.
Gregory the Great, 62, *n*.
Guaire Aidhne, death of, 63.
Guaire, son of Dubhdabhoirenn, 175.
Gwyned, 155.

Haimar, the Lochlaun, 173.
Hingamund, 227.
Iona, chief of the Lochlanns, 145.
Horm, lord of the Danes, 121, 131.
Hugh of Leinster, 42, *n*.
Huidhrine of Maghbile, 95.

Ia, family of, 21.
Iargna, chief of the Lochlanns, 119, 123.
Inbhlech-Phich, or Imleach Fich, battle of, 91, 103.
Imhar, 127, 171. 195.
—— Conung, 229.
Imleach, or Emly, 139.
Immolate, signification of the word, 16, *n*.
Inis-bo-finne, 67, *n*.
—— Breoghain, battle of, 55.
—— an Ghaill, 44, *d*.
—— mac Nesain, or Ireland's Eye, 105.
—— Tarbhna, 139.
Indrechtach, abbot of Hy, 125, 127.
—— son of Dobhailen, abbot of Bangor, 199.
—— son of Tadhg, 51.
—— son of Muiredhach, 53.
Inneirghe, son of Duibhgilla, 213, 219.
Innis-Fail, ancient name of Ireland, 35, *n*.
Innsi Orc, 159.
Irgalach, son of, slain, 57.
Irgalach, son of Conaing, 101, 133, 105.

Jakes, meaning of the word, 12, *n*.
Jewels. *See* Valuables.
Justinian II., 99, *n*.

Killineer, near Drogheda, 183.
Kill-Luaithrinne, 32, *n*.
Kinnaweer, 28, *n*.
Knockfarrell, 41, *n*.

Lachtnan, son of Cearnach, 245.
Lacighis, or Leix, 212, *n*.
Laidhgnen, king of Ui Cinnselaigh, 53.
Lairguen, 153.
Lann, daughter of Dunlaing, 129, 139, 157, 165.
Legionum Castra, 233, *n*.
Leicester, confounded with Chester, 232, *n*.
Leinster devastated by the Ui Neill, 22, *n*.
Leithglinn, or Leighlin, 149.
Leix, the territory called, 165, *n*.
Leo the emperor (i. e. Leo III.), 21 ; died, 55, 56, *n*.
Leoghain (or Ua Eoghain) Fergus, 51.
Letaithech, son of Cucarat, 49.
Lethchaech, 50, *n*.
Leth-Chuinn, 34, *d*.
Liag-Maelain, battle of, 87.
Liamhain, or Dunlavan, 219, *n*.

Lilcach, 43, *n.*
Linn-Duachaill, 120, *n.*
Loch Cend, 143.
—— Cime, 109.
—— Eachach, or Loch Neagh, 99.
—— Feabhail, or Loch Foyle, 157.
—— Gabhair, 71, *n.*
—— Laeigh, 127.
—— Leibhinn, or Lough Leane, 169.
—— Ri, or Ribh, 197.
Lochlanns, or Norwegians, 115, *n.*, 129, 131, 133, 145, 153, 155, 157, 159, 163, 165, 167, 185, 195, 197, 199, 227, 233, 245, 247.
Loichine Menn, abbot of Kildare, 97.
Loingsech, son of Aengus, 33, 97, 105, 107.
—— son of Foillen, 197.
—— victor in battle of Tulach-árd, 69.
Lorcan, king of Feara Cualann, 213, 219.
—— son of Cathal, 157.
—— son of Donchadh, 245.
Luaithrin, the virgin, 32, *n.*
Luan, meaning of the word, 85, *n.*
Lucbrinna, St., 32, *n.*
Luimnech, or Limerick, 147.
Lunatics in Ireland, belief respecting, 41, *n.*
Lusca, oratory of, 143.
Lynch, Rev. John, 1.

Mac Ailerain, of Cill-ruaidh, 53.
—— Andaighe, great oratory of, 185.
—— Concumbri, death of, 57.
—— Conmella, Laidhcenn, 55.
—— Erca, son of Maelduin, 51.
—— Feimhin, 6, *n.*
—— Giallain, 135.
—— Onchon, death of, 57.
—— Radgund, 109.
Madudan, 211, 217.
Maelbrighde, son of Maeldomhnach, 243.
—— son of Tornan, 243.
Maelcaich, son of Scandal, death of, 67.
Maelchallan, son of Ferghal, 213, 219.
Maelciarain, 167, 183, 185.
Maelcobha, 16, *n.*
Maelcron, son of Muireadhach, 139.
Maelduin, son of Aedh, 175.
—— Beg, son of Fergus Conainn, 61.
—— son of Feradach, slain, 57.
—— son of Maelithrigh, 87.
Maelfeichine, 125.
Maelfothartaigh, king of the Airghialls, 97.
—— son of Ronan, 65.
—— son of Suibhne, 69.
Maelguala, king of Munster or Cashel, 137, 141.
Maelmaedhóg, chief of Drum-mor, 245.
Mael-mic-Failbhe, 36, *n.*

Maelmithidh, son of Flannagan, 245.
Maelmona, the son of, 51.
Maelmordha, chief of Tir-da-glas, 241-3.
Maelmuadh, 211, 217.
—— son of Finnachta, king of Airthir-Liffé, 195.
—— son of Donchadh, 171.
Maelmuirtheimhne, son of Maelbrighde, 171.
Maelodhar, abbot of Devenish, 187.
—— O'Tindridh, chief physician of Erin, 153.
Maelpatraic, son of Flathrai, 245.
Mael-petair, abbot of Tir-da-ghlas, 157.
Maelpoil, chief of Sruthair Guaire, 199.
Maelruanaidh, son of Niall, 241.
Maelrubha, son of, 21.
Maelsechlainn, son of Maelruanaigh, 115, 116, 125, 127, 129, 135, 141, 147, 151, 179.
Maeltuile, abbot of Imleach Iobhair, 151.
Maenach, son of Conmach, 157.
—— son of Fingbin, death of, 63.
—— son of Siadhal, 203, 215.
Maenghal, abbot of Bangor, 193.
—— bishop of Kildare, 189.
—— abbot of Fobhar, 149.
Magh Ailbhe, or Ballaghmoon, battle of, 207, 239.
—— Adhair, 217.
—— Breagh, 21, 23.
—— Cuillinn, 109
—— Feimhin, 155.
—— Luirg, 197.
—— Macha, or the Moy, 147.
—— Muirtheimhne, 97.
—— Nairbh, 214, *n.*
—— Raighne, east of, plundered, 239.
—— Leine, 38, *n.*
Mainchine, bishop of Leithghlin, 163.
Mairge, or Slievemarague, 219, *n.*
Maistin, battle of, 55.
Mannan, the Isle of Man, battle of, 7, 7, *n.*
Matodan, king of Uladh, 123, 127, 149.
Manritani, or Moors, 161, 163.
Meath plundered by Aedh, 151.
Menubaireun, abbot of Achadh-bo, 97.
Mencossach, son of Gammach, 51.
Mindroichel, 159.
Mochua of Balla, 95.
Modichu, son of Amairgin, 43.
Molaisse of Leithghlinn, 177.
Moling Luchra, 23, 33, 34, *n.*, 77, *seq.*, 97.
Mona Conain, or Anglesea, 155.
Mughain, lines on battle of, 217.
Mughron, son of Sochlachán, 225.
Muireadhach, son of Cathal, 177.
—— son of Bran, 189.
—— son of Domhnall, 199.
—— son of Indrechtach, 59.

Muircadhach, son of Maelduin, 155.
Muiregan, or Muirigen, son of Diarmaid, king of Naas, 155, 225.
Muirenn, successor of Brighit, 215.
Muirghes, son of Conall, 49.
—— son of Maelduin, 99.
Muirghius, anchorite of Ard-Macba, 153.
Mura Othna, St., 12, n., 15, n., 40, n.
Murchadh, son of Bran, king of Leinster, 21, 23, 41, 45, 49, 55.
Muredbach, the sons of, 51.

Nanny Water, the, 118, n.
Nás, now Naas, 155, 223, 225.
Nehemias Mac Egan, 1.
—— son of Cearnach, 103.
Nia, son of Cormac, 51.
Niall Frosach, 21, n., 23.
—— Glundubh, 223, 243.
—— son of Murghes, 51.
—— of the Nine Hostages, 15, n.
Niallan, bishop of Slaine, 183.
Niar, 141.
Northmen, or Gall-Gaeidhil, 129, 139, 143.
Norwegians, or Lochlanns, 115, n.
Nuada, son of Dubhdunchuire, 51.
Nuada Uirc, king of Gull and Irgull, 49.
Nuadhat, the grandsons of, 51.
Nui, the Danish war-cry, 165, n.

Odhbha, 50, n.
Odolbh Micle, 177.
O'Driscoll, chief of Corca-Laighde, 8, n.
Oeghedchar, bishop of Oendruim, death of, 61.
O'Gaman, battle of, 63.
Oigedhchair, abbot of Coindeire (Connor), 175.
Oilell, son of Feradhach, 49.
Oisle, son of, king of the Lochlanns, 171.
Osraighe, or Ossory, plundered by the Deisi, 241; by the Lochlanns, 155, 245; by Rodolph, 129.
—— Duach, king of. *See* Duach.
—— extent of diocese of, 86, n.
Ossa, king of the Saxons, 69.
Othain Mura, or Othain mor, 11, 20, n.
Otter, Earl of the Danes, 247.
—— son of Iargna, 231.
Owen, race of, 15, n.

Paganism, relapses into, 127.
Pagans and Saxons, battle between, 245.
Patrick, St., invoked by the Danes, 121.
Peter the apostle, tonsure of, 21, 111.
Picts of Dalaradia, 87, n.
Plague, deaths of Blathmac and Diarmaid by, 65.
Pope of Rome, never an Irishman, 62, n.
Port-Lairge, 147.

Port-Manann, 167.
Prediction, Fergbal's, concerning his sons, 23.
R. E., meaning of the letters, 71, n.

Rath-Aedha, or Rahugh, 141.
Ráth-Aedhain, or Fernes, 239.
Rathmor of Magh-line, battle of, 87.
Raghnall, son of Albdan, 159.
Raighne, fair of, 149.
Rechtabhra, son of Cumascach Ua Maine, 51.
Rechtin, 239.
Regner Lodbrok, 124, n.
Riagail of Bennchair, 111.
Robhartach, bishop of Finnglais, 175.
—— of Dearmhach, 197.
Roderick, king of the Britons, 135.
Rodlaibh, the fleet of, 153.
Rodolph, 129.
Roisene, abbot of Corcach, or Cork, 89.
Ronan, king of Leinster, story of his wife, 65.
Ross, diocese of, 8, n.
Rumann, 53.

Saxons, the, 89, 130, n., 155, 173, 235, 245.
Scandinavian nations, ferocity of, 123, n.
Scotland, Albain a name of, 40, n.
Sebhdna, daughter of Corc, 59.
Sechnasach, son of Blathmac, 67, 69.
Segine, bishop of Ard-macha, 91.
Segonan, son of Conang, 153.
Seigine, abbot of Benchar, 63.
Sgama, the word, 169.
Shields, appearance of miraculous, 99.
Showers, miraculous, 21.
Simon Magus, tonsure of, 21, 113.
Sinainn, or Shannon, 76, n.
Sitric, grandson of Imhar, 245.
Slaine, or Slaney, 239.
Slebhte, or Sleaty, 99, 171.
Sliabh-Mairge, or Slievemarague, 149, 205.
Slighe-Asail, 76, n.
Sloighedach Ua Raithnen, 177.
Snánah Aighnech, or Carlingford Lough, 120, n.
Snoring, 24, n.
Sudhomna, bishop of Slaine, 143.
Spain, incursion into, by Scandinavians, 159.
Srath-cluaide, siege of, 193; plundered, 247.
Sruthair, or Shrule, 171.
Star, miraculous, seen, 16, n.
Steersman, Irish word for, 116, n.
Snairleeh, comharba of Finian, 143.
Suairlech, 127.
—— of Inedhnen, 187.
Suibhne, abbot of Ard-Macha, death of, 57.
—— son of Congbalach, 49.
—— abbot of Lis-mor, 143.

Suibhne, son of Maelumha, 89.
—— Menn, 17, 18, n.
Suitheman, son of Arthur, 141.
Sundays, no work performed by Lochlanns on, 185.

Tadhg, son of Aigthide, 51.
—— son of Diarmaid, 157.
—— son of Faelan, 211, 219.
—— son of Failbhe, 97.
—— king of Munster, 32, n.
Tailltin, 20, n.
Tairchealtach Mac na Cearta, 137.
Teamhair, the king of, and Horm, 135.
Teltown, 20, n.
Temhenan, king of Ui-Deaghaidh, 213, 219.
Theodosius III., 21.
Three Plains, plundering of the men of the, 197.
Tiberius Apsimarus, 105.
Tibraide, successor of Ailbhe of Emly, 205, 243.
—— bishop of Cluain-eidhnach, 245.
Tighernach, king of Breagh, 119, 163.
Tigh Telle, 175.
Tipraide Danbhan, abbot of Tir-da-ghlas, 151.
Tir-Chonaill, whence named, 30, n.
Tir-da-ghlas, abbacy of, 157.
Tir-Eoghain, whence named, 30, n.
Tonsure of Peter the apostle, 21, n., 111.
Tonsuring of clerks in Erin, 111.
Tomrar the Earl, 163, 165, 167.
Tomrir Torra, chief of the Lochlanns, 145.
Tribute, Boromean, 22, n.
Tuaim-snamha, king of Osraighe, 85.
—— Tenbath, 38, n.
Tualaith, daughter of Cathal, 57.
Tuath Inbhir, 225.
Tuathal, abbot of Dun Caillen, 163.
—— son of Morgan, death of, 65.
—— Techtmhar, imposes Boruma, 77, n.
—— son of Ugaire, 213.
Tuenoc, son of Fintan, death of, 65.
Tulach-árd, battle of, 69.
Turgesius, 124, n., 169, n.

Ua Aithechta, Fergal, 49.
—— Altain, Colman, 57.

Ua Brachaidhe, Snedhgus Derg, 55.
—— Cluasaigh, Colman, 61.
—— Colla, Flann Sinn, 59.
—— Dainine, Duibhdil, 51.
—— Domhnaill, Focarta, 51.
—— Eoghan (or Leoghain), Fergus, 51.
—— Fiachrach, Donnchadh, 51.
—— Cernaigh, Fogartach, 20, n.
Uallachan, son of Cathal, 239.
Ua Maelcaichs, the two, 51.
—— Maighleine, 43.
—— Maithe, Aidhgen, 49.
—— Tamhnaigh, 49.
Ugaire of Dun Dearmhaigh, 219.
—— son of Oilell, 239.
Ughran, son of Cennedigh, 213, 219.
Ui Aenghusa, 157.
—— Bairche, 212, n.
—— Deaghaidh, 212, n.
—— Drona, 212, n., 239.
—— Felmedha, or Ballaghkeen, 199.
—— Liathain, 211, n.
—— Maceaile, or Innokilly, 199.
—— Muireadhaigh, 213, n.
—— Niallain, 155.
—— Neill, northern, race of the, 15, n.; devastate Leinster, 22, n.
—— Neill, southern, Colman Beg, chief of, 7.
—— Tuirtre, the tribe of the, 68, n.
—— Toirdealbhaigh, the tribe, 212, n.
Uille, 225.
Uladh, plundering of, by Aedh, 129.
Ulbh, 223.
Ultan, son of Dicolla, 87.
—— son of Ernin, 63.
Umhaill, 127.
Urchraithe Ua hOssin, 94.

Valuables, Feradhach's, 9, 10, n.
—— meaning of the word, 9, n.
Vessels, silver drinking, 9.

Wonders, three, in Irish romantic stories, 47, n.

Zain, chief of the Lochlanns, 119, 123.

www.ingramcontent.com/pod-product-compliance
Lightning Source LLC
Chambersburg PA
CBHW032147230426
43672CB00011B/2474